HIGH
KING OF
HEAVEN

HIGH KING OF HEAVEN

THEOLOGICAL AND PRACTICAL PERSPECTIVES
ON THE PERSON AND WORK OF JESUS

JOHN F. MACARTHUR // GENERAL EDITOR

MOODY PUBLISHERS

CHICAGO

THE MASTER'S SEMINARY PRESS

LOS ANGELES

Unless otherwise noted, Scripture quotations in the Preface and chapters 4, 5, 6, 7, 8, 9, 11, 13, 14, 15, 16, 21, and 23 are taken from the New American Standard Bible®, Copyright © 1960, 1962, 1963, 1968, 1971, 1972, 1973, 1975, 1977, 1995 by The Lockman Foundation. Used by permission. (www.Lockman.org)

Unless otherwise noted, Scripture quotations in chapters 1, 2, 3, 10, 12, 18, 19, 20, and 22 are taken from the English Standard Version®, copyright © 2001 by Crossway, a publishing ministry of Good News Publishers. Used by permission. All rights reserved.

Unless otherwise noted, all Scripture quotations in chapter 17 are taken from the Holman Christian Standard Bible®, Copyright © 1999, 2000, 2002, 2003, 2009 by Holman Bible Publishers. Used by permission. HCSB® is a federally registered trademark of Holman Bible Publishers.

Scripture quotations marked KJV are taken from the King James Version.

Scripture quotations marked NIV are taken from the Holy Bible, New International Version®, NIV®. Copyright © 1973, 1978, 1984, 2011 by Biblica, Inc.™ Used by permission of Zondervan. All rights reserved worldwide. www.zondervan.com The "NIV" and "New International Version" are trademarks registered in the United States Patent and Trademark Office by Biblica, Inc.™

Moody Publishers Editor: Kevin P. Emmert
Interior and Cover Design: Erik M. Peterson
Cover photo of crown copyright © 2016 by kovalto1 / iStock (607650022). All rights reserved.

All websites and phone numbers listed herein are accurate at the time of publication but may change in the future or cease to exist. The listing of website references and resources does not imply publisher endorsement of the site's entire contents. Groups and organizations are listed for informational purposes, and listing does not imply publisher endorsement of their activities.

ISBN: 978-0-8024-1809-8

We hope you enjoy this book from Moody Publishers. Our goal is to provide high-quality, thought-provoking books and products that connect truth to your real needs and challenges. For more information on other books and products written and produced from a biblical perspective, go to www.moodypublishers.com or write to:

Moody Publishers
820 N. LaSalle Boulevard
Chicago, IL 60610

1 3 5 7 9 10 8 6 4 2

Printed in the United States of America

CONTENTS

PREFACE

John MacArthur

Several years ago, I was asked to write a book on my favorite passage of Scripture. But picking a favorite text is difficult since whichever verse I'm preaching on is my favorite. When pressed further to the wall to offer a short book on one verse, I chose the verse that most clearly defines sanctification. Election and justification are past. Glorification is future. Between our justification and glorification is the lifelong work of God in us, separating us from sin and increasing our Christlikeness. This is sanctification and it is the present work of God in every believer until we reach glory. The verse that best reveals this work of the Holy Spirit is 2 Corinthians 3:18: "We all with unveiled face, beholding as in a mirror the glory of the Lord, are being transformed into the same image from glory to glory, just as from the Spirit the Lord."

We are not under the shadowy, veiled, fading character of the Mosaic covenant. We live under the new covenant, inaugurated by the death and resurrection of the Lord Jesus Christ. The light has shone, and our veils removed. The mystery of the old covenant is now revealed in Christ. As we gaze into the revelation of the Lord Jesus Christ from Matthew to Revelation, we have a clear vision of the glory of God reflected in His face. Scripture says we are being transformed continuously and incrementally into that glory by the Holy Spirit. That is the heart and soul of what it means to being sanctified. As you look into the majesty of the revelation of Jesus Christ, the fullness of Christ fills your mind and captivates your soul, and the Spirit of God uses the reality of that understanding to shape you into His image. The more you know Christ, the more you reflect Him. So, knowing Christ is critical to our existence as Christians.

Everything about Him is beyond human explanation. Everything about Him is startling and astonishing and shocking and amazing. Everything about Him fills me with wonder. He is the most magnificent, the most beautiful, the noblest, and the most wonderful person that one could ever know *about*, let alone know *personally*. I am forever riveted by every detail about Jesus Christ. That becomes the purpose of all Bible study, the goal of all preaching, and the power of all Christian living.

As I look back at my life and all the years of study and tens of thousands of hours of going through Scripture, I have found that whether I'm writing books or preparing sermons, writing notes for a study Bible or a theology, all of my efforts to understand God's Word do not end with that understanding. My goal has never been to know the facts of the Bible. That's not the end; that's only the means to an end. I want to know Christ. Paul said, "I count all things to be loss in view of the surpassing value of knowing Christ Jesus my Lord" (Phil. 3:8). It is the joy of my life to count everything as loss for the sake of knowing Christ in Scripture. The more I study the Bible, the more glorious Christ is to me. The more I understand Jesus Christ, the fuller my love, obedience, worship, and service are to Him.

The objective of Scripture is to reveal God and the Lord Jesus Christ so that you may be swept away. Such power has the revelation of our Lord that the believer should experience what the hymnwriter called "being lost in wonder, love, and praise."[1]

Sanctification is not about knowing the Bible. Rather, it's about knowing Christ. Lack of understanding about Christ cripples worship, and no amount of music and no amount of mood-inducing theatrics can produce true worship because it rises only out of an overwhelming attraction to Christ.

There is no way that I could ever have pursued the knowledge of Christ the way I have in the ministry were I not committed to biblical exposition. The joy of digging deeply into every text is not for the sake of sermons, but to pursue the knowledge of God through the glorious revelation of Christ. It is really not preaching sermons that attracts me to the ministry. It's about the pursuit of the knowledge and fullness of Christ.

It is my responsibility to open every nook and cranny that I can find and declare every nuance that God has delivered to us about the majesty of His Son so that we can gaze into the glory of God shining in His face and be changed into His image as we are moved from one level of His glory to the next by the Holy Spirit.

It is to this end that this book was put together. Every contributor exalts and extols a unique facet of the diamond that is Christ. I pray that each chapter will cause you to behold the glory of our High King of Heaven, and result in an inevitable transformation into that same image.

---

1. Charles Wesley, "Love Divine, All Loves Excelling" (1747), The *Cyber Hymnal* website, http://www.hymn time.com/tch/htm/l/d/a/ldalexcl.htm.

PART 1

THE PERSON

OF CHRIST

1

THE ETERNAL WORD: GOD THE SON IN ETERNITY PAST

JOHN 1:1–3

Michael Reeves

n the beginning was the Word, and the Word was with God, and the Word was God. He was in the beginning with God. All things were made through him, and without him was not any thing made that was made" (John 1:1–3). It is often the case that familiar sentences are familiar because of how powerful or world-changing they have been. They are familiar because of how defining they are, and so it is here in John 1. These familiar words are revolutionary. They set Christianity gloriously apart from every other belief system.

The Eternal Word

John is simply exegeting Genesis 1. There in the very beginning in Genesis 1, we see how the Spirit of God was hovering over the waters. Why was He doing that? For the same reason He later hovered over the waters of the Jordan at the baptism of Jesus. The Spirit was there to anoint the Word as He went out to do His work. In creation and in salvation, in creation and in new creation, the Spirit anoints the Word, and so God speaks and, on His divine breath, His Word goes out. His Word goes out and light and life and all creation are brought into being.

It's not that in the beginning the Word came into existence as creation came into existence (John 1:3). He is not a creature. No, here is a Word who was with God and who was God. Now, that alone tells us something quite unique, extraordinary, and simply delightful about this God. For it is not simply that here is a God who *happens* to speak (the gods of most religions are said to speak at some point). No, this is a different claim.

It is of the very nature of this God to have a Word to speak. This God cannot be Wordless, for the Word is God. God cannot be without His Word. Here is a God who could not be anything but communicative, expansive, outgoing. Since God cannot be without this Word, here is a God who cannot be reclusive.

For eternity, this Word sounds out, telling us of an uncontainable God, a God of exuberance, of superabundance, an overflowing God, not needy but supremely full and overflowing: a glorious God of grace. Here is a God who loves to give Himself.

It is Genesis 1 that is dominant in John's mind as he wrote these opening verses. "In the beginning"; "the light shines in the darkness" (vv. 1, 5). And that helps us see that John has a Hebrew, scriptural idea of what "word" means. This is not a Hellenistic import on the faith.

But to appreciate a little more deeply what John meant when he wrote of the "Word," it's worth seeing something else from the Old Testament that seems to have been on his mind. Genesis 1 is dominant, to be sure. But in verse 14, John writes that the word "became flesh and dwelt among us, and we have seen his glory." Here, John chooses an unusual verb to express what he means.

More literally, he writes that the Word "tented" or "pitched his tent" among us. And with this mention of glory, it seems clear that John is thinking of the tabernacle, the tent where the Lord would come and be with His people in the wilderness, and where His glory would be seen. As the Israelites saw the bright glory cloud filling the tabernacle, so the Word is where we see the glory of God. It is a surprising glory we see in the One who became flesh and dwelt among us. But in the humility of that One who had no pillow; in His humility, grace, righteousness, gentleness, and faithfulness; in the compassion of the One who went all the way to the cross—we see His glory, a glory unlike the glory of any other.

Now, in the innermost part of the tabernacle, the Holy of Holies, the Lord was described as being enthroned between the cherubim of the mercy seat on the Ark of the Covenant (Lev. 16:2; 1 Sam. 4:4). And inside that gold-plated ark/throne were kept the two tablets on which were written the ten "words" or commandments: the law, *the Word of God*. For the Israelites, it modeled the truth that the Word of God belongs in the presence, in the very throne, of God!

The Word of God, then, is the One who belongs in deepest, most essential closeness with God, and the One who displays the innermost reality of who God is. He is "the radiance of the glory of God and the exact imprint of his nature" (Heb. 1:3). For He Himself is God. He is God's "Amen, the faithful and true witness, the beginning of God's creation" (Rev. 3:14).

This was the subject of what was perhaps the greatest battle that the church fought in the centuries after the New Testament: to uphold the belief that Jesus truly is God, none other than the Lord God of Israel Himself.

That He is, as was enshrined in those stirring words of the Nicene Creed, "God from God, light from light, true God from true God, begotten not made, of one being with the Father." Those doctrinal words are pastoral dynamite. The great Puritan theologian John Owen saw this with great clarity in his wonderful work *Communion with God*.[1] Owen explained in the first third of that book how so many Christians labor under the misapprehension that behind gracious Jesus, the friend of sinners, is some more sinister being, one thinner on compassion, grace, beauty, and goodness—one we would like to know less.

Owen pointed out that since Jesus is this Word, we can be rid of that horrid idea. *There is no God in heaven who is unlike Jesus.* One with His Father, He is the Word, the imprint, the expression, the radiance, the glory of who His Father is. If you've seen Him, you've seen His Father. And that means that through Christ, I know what God is truly like. Through Christ, I see how much this God detests sin. Through Christ, I see that, like the sinful, dying thief, a sinner like me can cry, "Remember me," for I know how He will respond. Though I'm so spiritually lame, leprous, diseased, and dirty, I can call out to Him. For I know just what He is like toward the weak and sick.

Another great Puritan preacher, Stephen Charnock, once wrote,

> Is not God the Father of lights, the supreme truth, the most delectable object. . . . Is he not light without darkness, love without unkindness, goodness without evil, purity without filth, all excellency to please, without a spot to distaste? Are not all other things infinitely short of him, more below him than a cab of dung is below the glory of the sun?[2]

Isn't that the delight in God that we want for ourselves and for every believer? Here was a man besotted with God, a man who, through the gales and storms of life, seemed to carry this core of sunshine with him: his knowledge of God. But where did such gladness come from? Charnock could not have been plainer: true knowledge of the living God is found in and through Christ. But what we see in Christ is so beautiful it can make the sad sing for joy and the dead spring to life:

---

1. John Owen, *Communion with God* (Edinburgh: Banner of Truth, 1991).
2. Stephen Charnock, *The Complete Works of Stephen Charnock*, vol. 4 (Edinburgh: James Nichol, 1865), 91.

Nothing of God looks terrible in Christ to a believer. The sun is risen, shadows are vanished, God walks upon the battlements of love, justice hath left its sting in a Saviour's side, the law is disarmed, weapons out of his hand, his bosom open, his bowels yearn, his heart pants, sweetness and love is in all his carriage. And this is life eternal, to know God believingly in the glories of his mercy and justice in Jesus Christ.[3]

In Jesus Christ, we exchange darkness for light as we think of God. For, unlike all the idols of human religion, He perfectly shows us an unsurpassably desirable God, a righteous and kind God, a God who makes us tremble in awe and rejoice in wonder.

Another great pastoral benefit comes from verse 3: "All things were made through him, and without him was not any thing made that was made." Christ the eternal Word is the one through whom all things were made. But secular thinking in the West has eaten away at this like acid in the church. And it has left many Christians with the sneaking suspicion that while Jesus is a savior, He's not really the Creator of all. So they sing of His love on a Sunday—and *there* they feel it is true—but walking home through the streets, past the people and the places where real life goes on, they don't feel it is *Christ's* world. As if the universe is a neutral place, a secular place. As if Christianity is just something we have smeared on top of real life. And Jesus is reduced to being little more than a comforting nibble of spiritual chocolate, an option alongside other hobbies, an imaginary friend who "saves souls" but not much else.

The Bible knows of no such piffling and laughable little Christ. "All things were made through him, and without him was not any thing made that was made." Christians, therefore, cannot jettison this truth when we walk out into the world. Jesus Christ is the one "from whom are all things" (1 Cor. 8:6). He is the Word, the agent of creation who continues to uphold and sustain the creation He brought into being.

From the tiniest sea urchin to the brightest star, all things bear *His* magnificent stamp. The heavens cannot but declare *His* glory, for they are His craftsmanship, and they continue to hold together only in Him. His character is written into the grain of the universe so intimately that even to think against Christ the Logos you must think against logic and descend into folly—and so it is the fool who says in his heart, "There is no God" (Ps. 14:1). In His world, our faculties work better the more they are harnessed to faith in Him. Then we are able to be more

---

3. Ibid., 163.

logical, more vibrant, more imaginative, and more creative, for we are working with the map of the universe as He made it.

The Eternal Son

But there is another eternal title of Christ that starts creeping into John's prologue.

In the first few verses, John focuses on the title "the Word." But he shifts from this in verse 12. "To all who did receive him, who believed in his name, he gave the right to become *children* of God" (emphasis added). How so? "The Word became flesh and dwelt among us, and we have seen his glory, glory as of the only *Son* from the Father, full of grace and truth" (v. 14; emphasis added). Further, "No one has ever seen God; the only God, who is at the Father's side, he has made him known" (v. 18).

For as well as being God's eternal Word, this One is also God's eternal Son. In those titles, you can feel some of the difference of meaning. "Word" is a title that speaks more of His *oneness* with God, the fact that He *is* God; "Son" brings out the other sweet truth, that He has a real *relationship* with God His Father.

Once again, Christianity has something over every other belief system in the world. It is an infinitely superior truth that no human mind ever dreamed of. John is saying that God is eternally a Father loving His Son. (The Spirit John will teach about later.) Later, in John 17:24, he'll record Jesus saying, "Father . . . you loved me before the foundation of the world." Every other belief system in history has had either fundamental nothingness or fundamental chaos out of which everything has come, or else a god or gods who only want to throw their weight around. Such invented gods want servants or company, and that is their reason to create. But here in John's gospel, we see an entirely different God: an Almighty God who is love.

In his first epistle, John would write that "God *is* love" (4:8; emphasis added), for this God would not be who He is if He did not love. If at any time the Father did not have a Son whom He loved, then He simply would not be a Father. To be who He is, then, He must love. To be the Father *means* to love, to give out life, to beget the Son.

Now the eternal sonship of Christ is such a precious truth to Christians. And why that should be was proven well by Arius in the fourth century when he denied it. As Arius saw it, there once was a time when the Son was not. At some point, in other words, God had created the Son.

But here's how Arius saw God. It was obvious, he thought, that God wouldn't want to dirty His hands with creating a universe. So He created the Son to do that work for Him. First of all, that means that God is not eternally a Father, since

He doesn't eternally have a Son. In fact, He's not really a Father at all. There's the primary comfort of the Lord's Prayer gone up in a puff of philosophy.

Second, for Arius, it's not that the Father truly *loves* the Son; the Son was just His hired workman. And if the Bible ever spoke of the Father's pleasure in the Son, it can only have been because the Son had done a good job. That, presumably, is how to get in with Arius's God. No eternal Son, no Fatherly God, no gospel of grace.

There was also for Arius the problem of the Son's own motivation. Have Philippians 2 in mind, but then imagine that the Son was a creature who had never sat on the heavenly throne at the right hand of God. Now, why would He humble Himself from some exalted, semi-divine, angelic status in heaven? Why would He humble Himself down to the cross? What's His motivation?

His motivation must be that God would exalt Him to a heavenly glory He had never known before. So He's doing it for Himself. But that cannot be with the *eternal* Son. With the eternal Son, God is not using Him as hired help, and He's not using God to get heavenly glory. He's *eternally* been at the Father's side. He is the *eternally* beloved. His motivation was not to get for Himself a glory He had never had, but to *share* with us what He Himself had always enjoyed: sonship! To come to us and bring us in Him back to the exalted position He had always enjoyed with His Father.

And so who He is entirely shapes what it is He offers in the gospel. The person of Christ shapes the work of Christ and the nature of the gospel of Christ entirely. For the eternally beloved Son comes to us to share with us the very love that the Father has always lavished on Him. He comes to share with us and bring us into the life that is His, that we might be brought before the Most High—not just as forgiven sinners, not just as righteous, but as dearly beloved children sharing by the Spirit the Son's own "Abba!" cry. The Father's eternal love for the Son now encompasses us.

In verse 12 we read, "To all who did receive him, who believed in his name, [the Son] gave the right to become children of God." This is a theme that then gets woven throughout the rest of John's gospel. In verse 18, the Son is presented as being eternally "in the bosom of the Father," according to the ESV footnote. He has that closeness and deep intimacy with His Father. Later, in 17:24, Jesus declares that His desire is that believers might be with Him where He is. And that gets modeled for us at the Last Supper in John 13. There, we read, "One of his disciples, whom Jesus loved, was reclining at table at Jesus' side," or more literally, according to the footnote, "in the bosom of Jesus" (John 13:23).

Jesus has eternally been in the bosom of the Father, and John is now in the bosom of Jesus, which is why Jesus can say to the Father in John 17:23, "You . . . have loved them even as you have loved me" (NIV). For the greatest privilege of the gospel—capping off our election, our calling, our forgiveness, our being clothed in righteousness, shaping our sanctification, shaping our glorification—is that the Son shares with us His own sonship, that we might be known as the children of God.

Without the eternal Son, you don't get that gospel! No eternal Son, no sonship. No eternal Son, no eternal Father. If God is not Father, He couldn't give us the right to be His children. If He did not enjoy eternal fellowship with His Son, then one has to wonder if He has any fellowship to share with us, or if He even knows what fellowship looks like. If, for example, the Son was a creature and had not eternally been "in the bosom of the Father," knowing Him and being loved by Him, then what sort of relationship with the Father could He share with us? If the Son Himself had never been close to the Father, how could He bring us close? He could not bring us to that "children of God" relationship.

With no eternal Son, we must see that God would be loveless and that salvation would look entirely different. Distant hirelings we would remain, never to hear the Son's golden words to His Father: "you . . . have loved them even as you have loved me" (NIV). But the gospel of the eternal Son gives us such intimacy and confidence before our Father in heaven. We are beloved children of the Most High!

There is no other God who can do that, to bring us so close, to have us so loved, to give us such an exalted status. No other God could so win our hearts. Only with this God can we say with all sincerity, "Our Father," knowing that we pray, as old John Calvin put it, as if it were through the mouth of Jesus.[4]

The Most High delights to hear us as His very children, and enjoys our prayers as sweet-smelling incense before Him. Only with this God—with the eternal Son—is prayer a delightful privilege.

And, once again, all of this means you've got a salvation that is of grace from first to last. If salvation is not about being adopted into the family of the Father, it's just not so clear that it has to be entirely of grace. We sometimes speak as if our only problem before God is that God is perfect in holiness and we are not. But if our only problem is that we're not good enough, we'll have to give it another go. We'll try to sort ourselves out and do better. But if salvation is to be adopted as children into the Father's family, then our performance is just not going to work, because you simply cannot earn your way into a family.

God's blessing is sonship (v. 12)—becoming a child of God—and so effort can do nothing to get you into the family. Your efforts can only make you a slave,

---

[4] John Calvin, *Institutes of the Christian Religion*, ed. John T. McNeill, trans. Ford Lewis Battles (Philadelphia, PA: Westminster John Knox Press, 1960), 3.20.21.

and no amount of effort can make you a son. All our efforts to win God's salvation by our own strength will only produce slaves—slaves who inherit nothing. But sonship is free!

Five hundred years ago, the neglect of the eternal Son, and how His person and being shapes the gospel, was at the very heart of the problem in the church. The person of Jesus Christ, the Eternal Word and Son—His identity—did not shape and drive the gospel as people heard it. In medieval Roman Catholicism, Christ was only the delivery boy who brought us what we really wanted: "grace."

And, like spiritual Red Bull for the lazy, this "grace" was the thing people really wanted. It was the thing they needed to give them the energy to go out and do the holy things that would earn them heaven. And so the prize for the believer was so often some "thing" other than Christ. The prize was so often heaven, not Christ. Jesus Christ had been reduced to being one little brick in the wall of that system. To be honest, it didn't even have to be Him who'd won grace in the first place. St. Nicholas or St. Barbara or St. Anyone could have done it.

Then, in the Reformation, the world heard a profoundly Christ-centered message: that God does not give us some "thing" called "grace" to energize us so we could earn heaven. No, God gives His Son, His Word who became flesh. And it is from His fullness that we receive grace upon grace. The Eternal Son: *He* is the gift from heaven. Verse 12 says, "to all who did receive *him*... he gave the right to become children of God" (emphasis added). It is in Him we find ourselves clothed with righteousness and justified. In Him, the Son, we are adopted as the children of God. And in Him, we are therefore saved. And because we are in Him, we are kept to the uttermost.

In Reformation thought, Christ is the treasure, Christ is our security. In Reformation thought, Christ is the jewel and the cornerstone of the gospel, giving it its shape and giving us a comfort and a joy that no gospel without Him could match. In Reformation thought, *solus Christus* was the center of the five solas, for it shaped what the Reformers meant when they talked about grace and faith.

Sola Gratia ("grace alone"): when the Reformers talked about salvation by grace alone, they meant not that we're given some "thing" called grace, but that we're given *Christ* by the gracious kindness of God.

Sola Fide ("faith alone"): faith is not some thing we do; it is the empty hand that receives Christ.

Sola Scriptura ("Scripture alone"): Scripture, our supreme authority, our deepest foundation, is about Him.

Soli Deo Gloria ("glory to God alone"): If you would know how to give God alone the glory, you would exalt Jesus Christ. For only through Christ is the living God glorified.

Let us preach Christ: Christ alone, the eternal Word, the eternal Son. For there is no gospel without Him. You can speak of grace, you can speak of faith, you can speak of hope, you can speak of the gospel, you can speak of grace alone. But there is no gospel if you do not preach Christ alone.

This is the center to which we must hold fast. Since we see in Him the radiance of God's glory, what better center is there to pledge ourselves to? In all our preaching, we preach Christ—Christ alone. We preach Him to ourselves, to His people, to the world. We preach His glorious person and His all-sufficient work, and that is what honors the Reformation. That is the beginning of all Reformation. This is what will reform lives and reform the church in our day. For when Christ alone is faithfully preached, the world will see His glory. That is the only light that will drive out and overcome all darkness.

2

SON OF GOD AND SON OF MAN

MATTHEW 26:63–64

Paul Twiss

Romeo, Romeo! wherefore art thou Romeo? Deny thy father and refuse thy name; or, if thou wilt not, be but sworn my love, and I'll no longer be a Capulet.... 'Tis but thy name that is my enemy: thou art thyself, though not a Montague. What's Montague? It is nor hand, nor foot, nor arm, nor face, nor any other part belonging to a man. Oh, be some other name. What's in a name?" Familiar words from Shakespeare's *Romeo and Juliet*, a tale of two star-crossed lovers whose relationship is hindered by virtue of their names. In this short excerpt, Juliet's frustration is evident as she proclaims the supposed trivial nature of a name. She goes on to say, "A rose by any other name would smell as sweet," suggesting, therefore, that neither people nor objects derive their value or their worth by the title by which they're called.

"What's in a name?" she asks, and if we think about it, we may empathize with her confusion. Her logic seems reasonable. Indeed, the whole play revolves around two families that are feuding on the basis of their names. It seems irrational. If it weren't for their names, these two may have enjoyed blissful matrimony. But as we take a step back and consider Shakespeare's point of view, we see that maybe he disagreed.

You see, Shakespeare is ultimately in charge of the script. He is in charge of the narrative, and it is not long after this scene that both lovers' lives end in tragedy. It is as if Juliet is asking, "What value is there in a name?" and Shakespeare replies, "Very much, my dear. You will lose your life on account of it."

As we consider the biblical text and specifically the gospel, we do well to realize that often, specific events, teachings, and interactions are purposefully structured around a name. The trial of Jesus is one example (Matt. 26:57–68). It is significant as it presents a climax to the tension that has been prevalent throughout the gospel story between Christ and the authorities. In this charged situation, we find two of the most Christologically significant titles used for Jesus coming together. Jesus is asked, "Are you the Son of God?" which He affirms, "Yes, you have said that it is so." Then He goes one step further and says, "And I am the Son of Man." In response, the authorities call out for His death (vv. 63–66, paraphrase). Therefore, the question must be asked as to the meaning of these two names and the significance of them coming together. That is what we will think about in this chapter.

The Interconnectedness of the Bible

In order to gain a right understanding of these titles, we must go beyond the borders of this scene. Indeed, we must go beyond the borders of the gospel. It is true that up until this point, "Son of God" and "Son of Man" have occurred many times in the narrative, and it is also true that both have occurred many times in the Old Testament. Thus, we can trace out story lines relating to both the Son of God and the Son of Man that develop through the Old Testament. These story lines imply that by the time we get to the Gospels, we see Jesus drawing from a pre-established body of theology when He uses these two titles. He is tapping into the story lines that exist in the Hebrew Scriptures.

Before considering these two story lines, let me first offer a word on methodology. What we are considering here is what can be referred to as the interconnectedness of Scripture. We have sixty-six books, yet they are interconnected, relating to one another. The way I picture this is to think of those sixty-six individual volumes on a library shelf, and you pull off one book—say, Romans. As you pull Romans off the shelf, what you see is that there is actually a piece of string passing through Romans to the other books of the Bible. In fact, when you look closely, you see many pieces of string passing through one book to all the other books, so much so that it is not possible to pull one book off the shelf alone. To rightly and fully study it, you have to pull all of them off the shelf because the Bible is interconnected.

Why must we rightly consider all of these connections to get to a full understanding of the text? To answer that question, we must think about the Bible's authorship both from a divine and a human perspective. We affirm that God wrote the Scriptures. He is the ultimate author of the Bible. Thus, we expect that there are no theological contradictions. But more than that, as we think about the fact that the Bible tells a story of redemption from Genesis to Revelation, we can consider how the story is told.

As an author communicates a narrative and develops a plot, he does so by way of connections—by way of overlap—from one scene to the next. He employs conceptual and thematic links in order to tell and develop the story. We know this to be true from our everyday experience. When we watch a movie, the director does not feel the need to continually explain every aspect of the plot because he assumes that we are able to make connections. We build a cumulative understanding of characters and themes as the movie progresses. The same is true of the biblical text.

Considering the issue from the human perspective, the Bible is comprised of sixty-six books. It has one ultimate author, God, and many human authors. But how was the Bible written? How did we reach this final product? Picture the community of God's people gathered around the Scriptures. The text is being read out loud day after day. The words, the thoughts, the concepts are slowly working their way into the minds of the audience. Then God raises up another man to add to the canon. As this new author puts pen to parchment, the words, concepts, and ideas of the previous Scriptures are already in his mind. They have already shaped his worldview. Indeed, we can say that to some degree, what he is about to write has already been determined by what came before. More than that, in order to be clear to that audience, the author would intentionally draw on that with which they were familiar—namely, the Scriptures they had already heard.

This is how the inspired text was birthed. The Bible is inherently interconnected. Therefore, it is incumbent upon us to study it in this way. We must always ask how a particular text may be pulling on previous texts. As we think about "Son of God" and "Son of Man," often these two titles are said to refer simply to Jesus' deity and humanity. But if we think about the Bible's interconnectedness, we start to see that those simple definitions do not provide the complete picture.

Jesus as Son of God

Concerning the Son of God story line, we must begin in Genesis 1. Though the narrative is familiar, we must not miss the driving momentum that exists in this chapter toward day six. Day six presents the pinnacle of God's creation as He creates mankind. We see the author's emphasis by virtue of the fact that there is more space given to the sixth day than any other day. We also find the divine plural "let us," which is not found in any other day. And by virtue of the fact that the sixth day is the last creative act, we understand that mankind is the pinnacle of the created order.

We see in verse 26 that God said, "Let us make man in our image, after our like-ness." Now, although Adam is not explicitly referred to as a son of God here, we can infer that this is the language of sonship. He is created in some way to be like the Creator. He imitates God, just as many men and women have sons or daugh-ters that look like them or have similar mannerisms. Then we see in Genesis 5, according to the interconnectedness of Scripture, a repetition of this language: "When God created man, he made him in the likeness of God . . . when Adam had lived 130 years, he fathered a son *in his own likeness, after his image*" (vv. 1, 3; emphasis added). It would seem that the language found back in Genesis 1 is the language of sonship. This is then confirmed for us when we think about the genealogy in Luke 3. Luke traces the lineage of Jesus Christ all the way back to Adam and he finishes the genealogy by saying, "Adam, the son of God" (Luke 3:38). Adam is the very first son of God.

What does it mean to be a son of God? Sonship means privilege. Adam is made in the image and likeness of God. He is unlike anything else in the created order. He receives a unique privilege. But sonship also entails responsibility. In Genesis 1:28, we read that God told them to be fruitful, multiply, fill the earth, subdue it, and have dominion over it. Sons of God have a responsibility as vice regents and representatives of God to subdue the earth and fill it.

Bringing together the privilege and responsibility, we might sum up what it means to be a son of God by saying that he was to mediate God's person to the created order. He is made in the image and likeness of God, and he was to fill the earth and rule over it as a vice regent of God. He was to mediate God to creation.

The son of God story line continues when, in Genesis 3, he fails. One of the beasts of the field usurped man's authority, and Adam sins. He scorns his priv-ilege; he fails in his responsibility. As a result, this crisis initiates a search for another son of God, one who would embrace the privilege and fulfill the respon-sibility, one who would succeed in mediating God to the created order.

The next manifestation of a son of God is in Exodus. It is interesting to note that the Exodus narrative is described in terms of light and darkness, the dividing of waters, and the emergence of dry land. These are linguistic triggers that point us back to a previous event. In accordance with the interconnectedness of Scrip-ture, Genesis 1 already employed these terms to describe the creation event.

There are many observations that could be made regarding this connection, but in terms of sonship we simply note that God's creative work in Genesis gave rise to a son. Thus, as we engage in a close reading of the Exodus narrative and see these terms occurring a second time, we should anticipate a son.

Sure enough, that is exactly what we find. In Exodus 4:22, God says, "Thus says the Lord, Israel is my firstborn son, and I say to you, 'Let my son go that he may serve me.'" Israel is a son of God. Indeed, in accordance with the interconnectedness of Scripture we can infer the theology of sonship from Genesis onto the nation of Israel. They have inherited the privilege and the responsibility. They have the mandate to mediate God to the world. As such, we find in Exodus 1:7 that they were already behaving like a son: "The people of Israel were fruitful and increased greatly; they multiplied and grew exceedingly strong, so that the land was filled with them." That echoes Genesis 1:28.

Now, in the transition from Adam to Israel, there is a significant detail that must not be overlooked. Until this point, sonship has worked out on an individual level. But when you get to Exodus, the son of God becomes a corporate body, a nation. From now on, the mission of the son of God takes on a nationalistic force. From now on, the mediation of God's person to the created order will be achieved not simply by a man to the created order, but by a nation to the nations.

Tragically, just as with Adam, Israel failed in the task. God gave them the law, but they did not obey it. We see in the book of Judges that the people behaved as pagans in the Promised Land. The implication of this was that there was zero international interest in Israel at that time. Nobody wanted anything to do with Israel at the time of the Judges. There was no mediation of God to the nations. So the search continues. The world is in need of another son of God.

We move forward in the story line to 2 Samuel 7 and the Davidic covenant. God answers the issue of Judges—the absence of a king—by raising up a monarch who is beloved of the Lord. He establishes a covenant with him, which becomes the channel through which He accomplishes His purposes in redemptive history. And in the context of that covenant, we find the language of sonship. "I will be to him a father, and he shall be to me a son" (2 Sam. 7:14). Thus, as we move forward in the story line, we shift back from corporate to individual. More specifically, we move from nation to king. This transition doesn't nullify the sonship of Israel, but it simply complements it because a nation needs a king, and a king needs a kingdom. Further, we now have the establishment of a relationship whereby when the individual son of God, the Davidic King, succeeds and mediates the person of God to the nation of Israel, then the corporate son of God, Israel, will succeed and mediate God's presence to the nations. When the king flourishes, the nation will follow. However, David fails. He commits adultery with Bathsheba. He sets the Davidic house into disarray, which in turn sets the nation of Israel into disarray. Because of David's adultery, the nation of Israel takes its first step towards exile.

There are many more passages where sonship theology is in view, but as we go back to Matthew, we understand that it is no small question when Jesus is asked, "Are you the Son of God?" Notice at this point the collocation of terms, "Tell us if you are the Christ, the Son of God." Christ means "Messiah." Messiah means "Anointed." Anointed, in this case, refers to the Davidic King. My paraphrase would be, "Are you the Davidic King, the Son of God?" Jesus says, "Yes." He affirms that He is the Davidic King, the Son of God who has come to reign over them. He affirms that He will mediate the person of God to them, causing Israel to flourish and the nations to turn to Him. This confession has global implications. It is quite some claim for a carpenter from Nazareth.

At this point, we could ask the question, how is it that Jesus can be a son of God who does not fail? How does He succeed where all previous sons failed? The answer to the question is that He is God the Son. He can be the incarnate Son who does not fail because He is the Son Eternal.

So What?

We live in a consumer-driven culture. The appetite for consumerism that we see in society bleeds into the church, such that on a Sunday morning, people want to be told three things to do in their life that coming week. They want some advice to consume; they want "application." While it is by no means wrong to give practical instruction from the Word of God, at the same time, we have a unique opportunity to simply preach the glory of Christ. We have a unique privilege to show people the riches and the profundity of the gospel. And we trust that as we simply set forth this Man in all of His beauty, splendor, and excellences, people's hearts will be led to worship. And as people are led in worship of this Man, we also trust that other more "practical," more "pressing" issues will begin to drop into place. That is to say, we will live wisely when we worship well.

Jesus as Son of Man

Jesus is not content to stop with simply acknowledging that He is the Son of God. He augments the confession. He goes further and essentially says, "I'm not only the Son of God but I am also the Son of Man." This leads us to a second story line in the Bible.

In accordance with the interconnectedness of Scripture, we turn again all the way back to the book of Genesis. Without rehearsing the narrative a second time, we do well to remember that when man was created, he was taken from the earth. There is an intrinsic connection between us and the ground. Thus, when we arrive at Genesis 3, we see that as Adam turned his back on God, he did not simply cause mankind to fall but caused the whole created order to fall. When Adam sinned and fell, he pulled down the cosmos with him. The stars in the sky do not shine today as they once did. The seas, oceans, rivers, the rocks, and mountains do not praise God today as they did once upon a time. The most beautiful scene that we could find on planet Earth is but a faded sepia image of the universe before the fall.

With that in mind we see in Genesis 11 the very first occurrence of the phrase "sons of men" (NASB). We also note in Genesis 11 how the narrative is intentionally crafted in such a way so as to point us back to Genesis 1–3. There are many words that are taken from those first few chapters of Genesis—we read of the heaven (11:4), of all the earth (11:1), of the east (11:2), of building and making (11:3, 4, 5) and naming (11:9), and of the divine plural again (11:7).

Further, we see the theme of filling the earth, though in a negative sense. In Genesis 11, these men basically say, "Let us build a tower to make a name for ourselves—so that we won't be dispersed." These men are refusing to obey the mandate to go and fill.

Thus, if we step back and consider the big picture, we see that Genesis 11 functions as a second fall narrative. Genesis 1–2 give the creation account; chapter 3 records the fall; chapters 4–6 tell of the explosion of sin; chapters 7–10 report the flood, that God starts over and recreates; and then in Genesis 11, we see mankind turning its back on its Creator—again. The Tower of Babel incident brings us right back to square one. It is the fall, take two.

It is important to realize that this is the context for the first use of the phrase "sons of men." The narrator wants us to connect these people with their father, Adam. Indeed, more literally translated, the sons of men are the sons of Adam. They are the offspring of the one who caused all of creation to come tumbling down. What characterizes them is their fallen nature—their sin and transgression. And as you trace this phrase throughout the Old Testament, you find that it always fits this picture. Sometimes the sons of men are portrayed as lost, helpless, weak, and in need of salvation. Other times they are spoken of as rebellious and wicked, those who turn their back on God. In every case, the sons of men are characterized as those who epitomize the fallen nature of humanity and, by implication, the whole universe.[1]

Then we arrive at Ezekiel. His ministry provokes curiosity because God calls Ezekiel "son of man" time and again throughout the book. But when properly considered, we might think this is illogical. Ezekiel the man isn't characterized by wickedness. He seems to be a good guy. He has been training his whole life for the priesthood, and then God raised him up to be a prophet. He seems to be pursuing righteous conduct, and yet somehow God calls him "son of man." How do we relieve this tension? The answer comes by thinking through the nature of

---

[1] Chrys C. Caragounis, *The Son of Man* (Eugene, OR: Wipf & Stock, 2011), 57.

Ezekiel's ministry. Ezekiel was a prophet who more than any other prophet not only spoke the words of God but also acted them out. He not only delivered the oracles of God but also embodied them.

We see in Ezekiel 1–2 that he falls flat on his face as though he were dead, but the Spirit enters him and puts him on his feet. This is a picture of the salvation that Israel will soon receive in chapter 37. In chapter 4, Ezekiel lies on his side for 490 days, and then for 40 days he builds a siege work, sets his face against it, eats the bread of the siege, drinks the water of the siege, cuts his hair and beard, and loses his wife—all of it so as to act out to hard-hearted Israel the judgment that was coming upon them.

Throughout the book, Ezekiel functions like a miniature Israel. Thus, we can say that he assumes an intermediary role. Ezekiel represents the people. He stands before them and identifies with them. God calls him "son of man" not because he is characteristically wicked but because he represents the sons of men. As such, in the son of man story line, Ezekiel indicates an important shift—God's designation for him demonstrates that the term has taken on a representative function.

That then takes us to the culmination and the completion of son of man theology in the Old Testament: the book of Daniel. Daniel presents a schema for salvation from the exile to the end of redemptive history. Daniel 7 is the centerpiece of the book and theological linchpin. Salvation history can be understood by what happens in this chapter. In verse 2, Daniel says, "I saw in my vision by night, and behold, the four winds of heaven was stirring up the great sea." Verse 3 then reads, "Four great beasts came up out of the sea." Now, why did Daniel talk about four earthly, human kings in terms of beasts coming up out of the created order? The answer, in part, is in order to lock our thinking into a creation-type paradigm. We have already read of beasts coming up out of the created order back in Genesis 1. So it is no accident that Daniel describes four earthly human kings in terms of beasts arising from the earth. He wants us to be thinking through a lens of creation, through a lens of Genesis 1–3.

It is with this context established that we work through the logic of the vision. Here we see four arrogant, wicked earthly kings rising up, grasping for power that is not rightly theirs, working against God and ultimately being destroyed (Dan. 7:4–10). Then in verses 13–14 we read, "behold, with the clouds of heaven there came one like a son of man, and he came to the Ancient of Days and was presented before him. And to him was given dominion and glory and a kingdom, that all peoples, nations, and languages should serve him; his dominion is an everlasting dominion, which shall not pass away, and his kingdom one that shall not be destroyed." The question becomes, how does this son of man fit into the larger son of man story line that we have traced out so far? We must pay attention to the details. He is not actually described as a son of man but as one *like* a son of man. That one word in the Aramaic bears much theological weight. He is like a son of man, which means there are some ways in which this Son of Man is similar to the previous sons of men. But he is also dissimilar.[2]

Considering the points of dissimilarity and returning back to the creation metaphor that Daniel has established in verses 2–3, we remember that in Genesis 3, a beast of the field usurped man's authority and triumphed. In Daniel 7, the beasts of the field try and try but they cannot usurp man's authority. In Genesis 3, the beasts win; in Daniel 7, the Son of Man wins. Thus, the first point of dissimilarity is that this Son of Man reverses the fall narrative. He wins and succeeds where the first man failed.

We might ask how this Son of Man succeeds where all others failed. Notice that the Son of Man travels on the clouds of heaven (7:13). In ancient Near Eastern thought, anyone traveling on clouds was understood to be deity. Notice also that in the same verse, this Son of Man comes face-to-face with the Ancient of Days. No one has ever seen God and lived, and yet here is one who stands before Him. Finally, notice that He receives worship and an honor that is normally reserved for God (7:14). This, then, is the second point of dissimilarity: this Son of Man is divine. And that explains how He succeeds in reversing the fall narrative.

What are the results of His success? This question brings us to a point of similarity. The first thing to observe is that He is a man. He is somehow divine, but we see that He is also described as a human being—a son of man. More than that, in accordance with Ezekiel's son of man, this one represents others. We see that most clearly as we look at the second half of chapter 7, which is the explanation of the vision. It is interesting to note that, when you read through the second half of chapter 7, the Son of Man is nowhere mentioned. He is so key to the theology of the vision and to the whole book, and yet He is not mentioned in its explanation. By contrast, we see that the saints of the Most High are in view (Dan. 7:25, 27). They are the ones who receive the kingdom. The reason Daniel can interchange one for the other is because they are so tightly connected. The King reigns over His people and as He succeeds, so they are led in victory. This Son of Man is representing the sons of men.

Furthermore, remembering that the sons of men come from the ground, the Son of Man's ministry has implications for the created order. His success—triumphing

---

[2] I owe this observation and the subsequent discussion to Abner Chou, *I Saw the Lord: A Biblical Theology of Vision* (Eugene, OR: Wipf & Stock, 2013), 142.

over the beast of the field where Adam failed—means not only that the sons of men now succeed but also that the cosmos is redeemed.

Returning then to Jesus' confession at His trial: His double proclamation—that He is the Son of God and the Son of Man—is the Christological climax of the gospel narrative so far. He is basically saying, "In every way that you might conceive, I am the centerpiece of redemptive history. For Israel, yes, and for the whole universe." And understanding the implications of this confession, the authorities cry out for His death.

Son of Man *and* Son of God?

The only question that remains then is: What is the significance of the two terms being brought together? Is there a relationship between Son of Man and Son of God that is in view at the trial scene? In response, we note that this is not the first time the two titles have been paired together. Indeed, when we read the Gospels closely, we see an interplay between the Son of God and Son of Man woven throughout. Often, there are confessions in the gospel narrative that Jesus is the Son of God, the Son of the Most High, the Son of the Blessed One, to which Jesus replies not by teaching them about the Son of God, but by teaching them about the Son of Man. For example, Jesus asks, "Who do you say that I am?" Peter replies, "You are the Christ, the Son of the living God." And in turn Jesus does not say, "Let me tell you about that Son of God." Rather, He essentially says, "The Son of Man has to suffer" (Matt. 16:15–23). The gospel authors have already brought these two titles together in the narrative on several occasions.[3]

The probable significance of their being brought together—at the trial and elsewhere—is that the fulfillment of one is contingent upon the fulfillment of the other. Specifically, the mediation of God to the nations through the Son of God is the means by which the Son of Man's cosmic reconciliation can happen. Or to put it another way, it is because Jesus succeeds as the Son of God that He can also succeed as the Son of Man. Like a domino effect, one precipitates the other.

Conclusion

Do not be content to rehearse a message the profundity of which you have not sorted out. Rather, give yourself to every word of the text and understand that in the names of Christ, in the corners of the narrative, in all of the details, there is a glory and a richness that we can spend eternity delighting in, meditating upon,

---

[3] Seyoon Kim, *The Son of Man as the Son of God* (Grand Rapids: Eerdmans, 1985), 1–5.

and preaching to others. Further, work diligently to communicate the story line of Scripture. We must understand the inherent interconnectedness of every single text. We must do the hard work of seeking out those connections and understanding rightly the meaning that is built into them. We must labor to show people the drama of redemptive history as it has been given to us from Genesis through Revelation, knowing that we showcase God's glory when we show them the bigger picture.

3

THE SON'S RELATIONSHIP WITH THE FATHER

ISAIAH 50

Mark Jones

In examining the topic of the relationship between the Father and the Son, I want to make some observations on several truths about the servant described in Isaiah 50, from the third of the four "Servant Songs."

The first of these songs is in Isaiah 42, where the Father, Yahweh, speaks of a "servant" whom He equips by putting His Spirit upon the servant. Isaiah, I believe, is the Old Testament prophet of the Holy Spirit. Isaiah, therefore, is the companion to Luke's accounts, since Luke emphasizes—more than anyone else—the role of the Holy Spirit in the life of Christ. Moving to the second servant song in Isaiah 49, we find a dialogue between the Father (Yahweh) and the Son (the servant), with the Gentiles and Jews being given to the servant as His reward.

But then you come to chapter 50, and the servant speaks:

> "Where is your mother's certificate of divorce, with which I sent her away? Or which of my creditors is it to whom I have sold you? Behold, for your iniquities you were sold, and for your transgressions your mother was sent away. Why, when I came, was there no man; why, when I called, was there no one to answer? Is my hand shortened, that it cannot redeem? Or have I no power to deliver? Behold, by my rebuke I dry up the sea, I make the rivers a desert; their fish stink for lack of water and die of thirst. I clothe the heavens with blackness

and make sackcloth their covering." The Lord GOD has given me the tongue of those who are taught, that I may know how to sustain with a word him who is weary. Morning by morning he awakens; he awakens my ear to hear as those who are taught. The Lord GOD has opened my ear, and I was not rebellious; I turned not backward. I gave my back to those who strike, and my cheeks to those who pull out the beard; I hid not my face from disgrace and spitting. But the Lord GOD helps me; therefore I have not been disgraced; therefore, I have set my face like a flint, and I know that I shall not be put to shame. He who vindicates me is near. Who will contend with me? Let us stand up together. Who is my adversary? Let him come near to me. Behold, the Lord GOD helps me; who will declare me guilty? Behold, all of them will wear out like a garment; the moth will eat them up. Who among you fears the LORD and obeys the voice of his servant? Let him who walks in darkness and has no light trust in the name of the LORD and rely on his God. Behold, all you who kindle a fire, who equip yourselves with burning torches! Walk by the light of your fire, and by the torches that you have kindled! This you have from my hand: you shall lie down in torment.

Isaiah is the prophet that speaks of his unclean lips (Isa. 6:5). Though he declares himself unclean, is there any other prophet in all of God's Word that rises to the eloquence and beauty of language that Isaiah does? With those lips with which he declared himself unclean, he speaks some of the most majestic words ever spoken. Indeed, perhaps only Job and some of the psalmists come close to him in the Old Testament.

He writes of this mysterious figure as a servant. He writes, of course, of the Lord Jesus Christ. Here we find he has a number of profound truths to tell us about this servant, the Lord Jesus Christ, and His relationship to the Father.

Jesus Was Taught by His Father

The first, in 50:4, is that the servant is taught. "The Lord GOD has given me the tongue of those who are taught." The servant's teaching was astonishing; he caused people to marvel.

People marveled at the gracious words that came from Jesus' lips. At other times in the synagogue, they asked, "Where did this man get these things, and what is this wisdom given to Him . . . ?" (Mark 6:2 NASB). And, "How is it that this man has learning . . . ?" (John 7:15). The answer is right here in Isaiah 50: the Lord God, My Father, has given Me the tongue of those who are taught. That's the answer to their questions. Where did He get His teaching? He got this teaching from His Father who is in heaven.

He will say, "My teaching is not mine, but his who sent me" (John 7:16). He also says, "I have not spoken on my own authority, but the Father who sent me has himself given me a commandment—what to say and what to speak" (John 12:49). Christ Jesus was, morning by morning, taught and instructed by His Father. We don't know exactly how this teaching took place, but one thing is certain: over the course of His life, Jesus devoured the Old Testament continuously so that it became, as it were, part of His DNA. He likely had much of the Old Testament memorized.

Just as kings were to come into office and copy down the Law (Deut. 17:18), so Jesus had the Law written on His heart, memorized in His mind. What is the question most asked by Jesus during the course of His ministry? "Have you not read?" How many times does He have to say that—not to ignorant Gentiles, but to religious Jews? "Have you not read?" What an indictment from the lips of our Savior! "Have you not read?"

For thirty years, Jesus is taught morning by morning so He may be able to teach for three years. Think about that. We reverse it. For thirty years, He was molded, instructed, and trained, so that for three years He could say, "I only speak the words the Father has given to me." That's the submission and obedience of the servant. Can you think of any greater obedience than to simply say, "I only speak the words of my master?" That's precisely what He does.

The servant does speak in Isaiah 50:4 that "The Lord GOD has given me the tongue of those who are taught." Why? As it says, "That I may know how to sustain with a word him who is weary." This is precisely what Moses spoke of in Deuteronomy 18 about the prophet who would come: "I will raise up for them a prophet like you from among their brothers. And I will put my words in his mouth" (Deut. 18:18a). "My words in his mouth"—that is the essence of a prophet who does not speak on his own authority—not Moses, Isaiah, our Lord Jesus Christ, or you or me. "And he shall speak to them all that I command him" (Deut. 18:18b).

James 3:8 says that no man has tamed the tongue, but Jesus did. Why is Jesus given authority? Why is He given dominion? Because, ultimately, He tamed something that nobody could tame: the tongue. Never a word out of place or misspoken. He tamed His tongue because His tongue was tamed by His Father in the power of the Holy Spirit. In one of the earlier Servant Songs, the servant says, "He made my mouth like a sharp sword" (Isa. 49:2). What a description! Not a military conqueror with great armies, but a man who comes and has His tongue tamed by the Father so it could be said to be a "sharp sword." He always knew what to say. He confounded His enemies. He brought peace and healing to those who were broken. He confused people at times on purpose. He spoke in parables. He speaks to the woman at the well, to Nicodemus, His mother, His disciples—and He always knows what to say, and sometimes He knows when He ought to say nothing.

The taming of the tongue includes not only knowing what to say, but also knowing what not to say, which is a great deal harder for some of us than we imagine. If you look at His words, even His words on the cross, are they not a masterpiece of pastoral theology? He's in the greatest agony and yet He's drawing upon the Old Testament in so many of His words. He says, "Father, into your hands I commit my spirit," from Psalm 31:5 (Luke 23:46), and "I thirst," from Psalm 69:21 (John 19:28). It's so natural for Him. It's as though He just opens His mouth and the Old Testament streams out like a river. It's all there because He was taught by His Father in order to speak.

Jesus Was Obedient to His Father

The second truth from Isaiah 50 is that the servant is obedient. "The Lord GOD has opened my ear, and I was not rebellious; I turned not backward. I gave my back to those who strike, and my cheeks to those who pull out the beard; I hid not my face from disgrace and spitting" (vv. 5–6). There's something extremely important here to understand.

Everything Christ did for us and our salvation was done willingly. The emphasis here is: I, I, I did it! "I lay down my life for the sheep" (John 10:15). "No one has taken [my life] away from Me" (John 10:18 NASB). In effect, "I gave them my beard to pull. I gave them my face to strike. I gave them my body to nail to that cross. I did it because if I was not willing, then it was not obedience." The first reference to an ear being opened (as far as I'm aware) is in Exodus 21—a reference to that servant, a slave, who loves his master. When he declares his love for his master, the master takes him to a pole and drives a nail through his ear, which symbolizes obedience, love, and dependence. That is the language used here of the servant. He has opened his ear, and he was not rebellious.

Where did His obedience to the Father lead Him? It led Him to hunger for forty days and nights, to the point where angels had to come and minister to Him (Matt. 4:11). He who is the Son of God, the God-man, needed angels to minister to Him. It led Him to rejection, not only by His disciples, but even by

38

His own family. His brothers thought He was out of His mind (Mark 3:21). The only person who's ever been perfectly sane was declared to be totally insane.

His obedience led Him to be ridiculed: "He has a demon" (John 10:20). The Son of God, filled with the Spirit of holiness, was declared to be possessed by a demon. It led Him to discouragement. He has to ask His disciples in John 6, "Do you want to go away as well?" Was that just a question for rhetorical effect? Of course not. We see the sensitivity of His feelings when He goes to Simon the Pharisee's house and says plainly, "You gave me no water for my feet.... You gave me no kiss" (Luke 7:44–45).

We see in Matthew 4 that His obedience led Him to discouragement and temptation by the devil, who was His wilderness companion, because the Spirit drove Him there. It's most remarkable because there the devil attempts to get the Son of God to cast Himself off a cliff. But soon after, Jesus, filled with the Holy Spirit, preaches, and people marvel at His gracious words. Yet then He speaks to them about Gentile inclusion in God's covenant purposes, and they attempt to do the very thing that Satan did: cast Him off a cliff. That's where His obedience led him. It also led Him to homelessness. "Foxes have holes, and birds of the air have nests, but the Son of Man"—the one who owns the universe, whom heaven and earth cannot contain—"has nowhere to lay his head" (Matt. 8:20).

His obedience led Him to homelessness and betrayal by a disciple whom—I have no doubt—He loved. He loved Judas if for no other reason than that we are commanded to love our enemies. That's where His obedience led Him, but His obedience also led Him to a place called Gethsemane. This is the turning point in many respects, where you see the Son of God coming before the Father, so different from the first Adam in the garden. Adam sins, and what does he do? He hides from the Father. But here, the Son of God comes and says, "Here I am. Here I am."

I agree with Hugh Martin, who states that if Jesus had not petitioned the Father for the cup to pass, we might rightly call into question His sinlessness.[1] If He had not begged the Father three times to "remove this cup," we might question whether He had any real human sense of God's holiness. No one understood God's holiness like the Son of God, and He knows that He is going into the fury of God's holiness. And if He did not shrink back from that, we might question whether this man is an insane fool, or even worse, a masochist.

It was appropriate for Him to say in the garden, "Remove this cup." He had only ever known the smiles and love of His Father. From all eternity and from the time He was born—from His mother's breasts—He had only ever known the love and communion between Him and His Father. He had the prospect of His

---

[1] Hugh Martin, *The Shadow of Calvary* (Edinburgh: Banner of Truth, 2016).

Father turning His face away from Him and the plagues of Egypt where darkness comes over the land and the firstborn dies. How could He not ask, "Remove this cup from me"?

Martin says that to have such impressive views as Jesus had of His Father's wrath and not be filled with earnest longing to escape it would have shown that He did not possess a true human nature with all the sinless sensibilities essential to humanity.[2] But all of those requests were wrapped in the words "your will be done." In other words, "I have not been rebellious. I have not turned backwards. Your will be done." And it led to the cross. We can't afford to be tentative about the fact that Christ has a true human will, and not a divine will only. He's not some phantom going around, offering up prayers that aren't real requests He needs to make, but are only for our sake. He has two wills—one divine, one human—and His human will is brought to the brink of despair. He agonizes and pleads, and all this is proper to true humanity.

To say that Christ has only one will and that God has three wills, with each person of the Trinity having a will, not only is heretical but also raises the problem of how we are justified. Christ's obedience imputed to us by faith alone is real *human* obedience. It is the obedience of the incarnate Son of God—every word He spoke, every thought He thought—that is credited to you and me by faith. It is not a divine will taking care of everything as though He were a phantom. We must hold vigorously to the fact that we cannot, and must not, attribute to the divine will what is proper to human nature: despair and struggle. But it does bring a glory to the incarnation.

Jesus Was Vindicated by the Father

We see a third truth about the servant in Isaiah 50:7–8: his hope. "But the Lord God helps me." What we find, when we read closely, is that Jesus is not the consummate Pelagian. The Father helps Him, equips Him, and pours out His Spirit upon Him. There's no sense in which Jesus says, "Well, I'm going to roll up my sleeves and be obedient, because I'm sinless and I'm able to do so." There's an incredible sense of dependence and hope:

> The Lord God helps me; therefore I have not been disgraced; therefore I have set my face like a flint, and I know that I shall not be put to shame. He who vindicates me is near. Who will contend with me? Let us stand up together. Who is my adversary? Let him come near to me. (vv. 7–8)

---

[2] Ibid., 23.

There's a sort of holy confidence coming right through these words. It's beautiful of the servant. It's almost triumphant, because His confidence is in God, and He knows that He will be vindicated. He knows that He will be glorified and exalted, because He prays this in John 17. Before Jesus is about to be shamed, He prays for His glory because He trusts His Father. He knows that if He's going to receive the mediatorial glory that is His alone as the God-man, He must go through the cross.

Therefore, we can say this much about heaven: it is the eternal vindication of our Savior. Will those who accused Him have anything to say? It's shocking language. It's almost as though Christ is engaging in holy confrontation with His enemies, saying in effect, "Who will stand up against me? I have been obedient. I have not been rebellious. Who is going to stand against me? You will lie down in torment if you do."

What This Means for Us

There are a few points of application to these truths of the servant's teaching and obedience. First, why can't, say, Johnny preach?[3] It's because Johnny sleeps in. Does Johnny wake up to be instructed by His Father morning by morning? Is Johnny a man of the Word? Whatever we may say about why Johnny can't preach, this much I can tell you: theological books are easy to read, but woe to the man who knows his theological books yet is ignorant of the Word of God. That could never be said of Jesus. He was a man of the Word, and that was why He was obedient. You wonder why He was able to be so obedient all of the time? We think, *Well, He was sinless.* That is certainly true. He also possessed the Holy Spirit. But He also had the Word of God dwelling in Him so that in every situation He knew how to respond, saying, "It is written . . ."

That's how He responded when He was *really* tempted with *real* temptations. He was hungry, so Satan didn't say, "Well, you know, let's see if you can go on a diet." He says to Jesus, "Command these stones to become loaves of bread" (Matt. 4:3). That is a real temptation. Yet Jesus responds, "It is written . . ."

Also, notice something else. People say, "God doesn't give you more than you can handle," referencing 1 Corinthians 10:13. It appears to me, however, that He does give you a lot more than *you* can handle. He did so to His own Son, did He not? Those cries from the cross are similar to those used of believers in Romans 8:15: "by which we cry out, 'Abba! Father!'" That is the cry of someone who has been given more than they can handle. Otherwise, we

---

[3] See T. David Gordon, *Why Johnny Can't Preach: The Media Have Shaped the Messengers* (Phillipsburg, NJ: P & R Publishing, 2009).

wouldn't need God. Jesus, as a true human, needed God, just like we do.

Doing God's will leads to heartache, blood, and tears, but it also leads to heaven. Christ has to live by faith, because there were so many times in His ministry where we could forgive Him if He had said, in John 6, for example, "Are you sure, Father? Look at how poorly my church-building has gone. Are you sure I need to continue to say these things?" In Luke 4, after His listeners marvel at the gracious words that come from His lips, Jesus seemingly makes a catastrophic mistake: He keeps on preaching. He had them, but then He zeroes in because He must speak the words the Father has given Him. He zeroes in on their nationalistic pride. God saved Naaman, the Syrian, and the widow of Zerephath, both of whom were not Israelites. God saved those we think don't deserve to be saved. Yet Jesus had to trust His Father's ways were better than the ways of appearance. Is that not our struggle daily?

Hebrews 5:9—it has taken me roughly ten years to come to a point where I'm prepared to tell what I think is the accurate interpretation. Speaking of our Savior, it says, "And being made perfect, he became the source of eternal salvation to all who obey him." Now, how can we say, "And being made perfect"? How can we say of the perfect and glorious one, chief among ten thousand, the radiance of God's glory and the image of the invisible God—that He was "being made perfect"? Because the context is Christ as the High Priest. When was He made perfect? He was made perfect upon His death on the cross and His resurrection life.

Why is this the case? If He had been taken by the Father before the cross, could He have been a merciful High Priest? The answer is no. Why? Because He cannot minister to the person who feels abandoned by God unless He Himself is abandoned by God. How is He going to minister to the person who feels as though Psalm 22 or 88 is their living reality? How is He going to minister to someone who says, "Why have you forsaken me?" You see, once He had been forsaken by the Father—once He had undergone the terrors of the Lord and experienced that separation—then we have a merciful High Priest able to minister to us in every conceivable situation. That is the glory of the Christian faith.

We do not look to a God who doesn't understand. We don't look to a Savior who simply saves by His infinite power. No. We look at someone to whom we can say, "You do understand. In fact, You understand a whole lot better than I'll ever understand. You can minister to me in my time of need because You were once in a time of need." And I'm glad, as painful as it is to say this, that God has given me more than I can handle at times because those are the precious times when I've come to a tipping point in my ministry and simply fallen on my knees. When that happens to you, it's as though you lack strength to even say anything to God except, "Have mercy upon me." You can be sure He will give you mercy, too, because He is a merciful High Priest.

Finally, notice the obituary of the servant, Christ, in Isaiah 50:7–8. After He says in verse 5, "I was not rebellious," He says in 7–8, "The Lord GOD helps me therefore I have not been disgraced. . . . He who vindicates me is near." Sometimes, when someone introduces me from the pulpit, I feel like I am hearing my obituary read. If I could have my wife and children sign my obituary, I would consider myself a blessed man. But even more than that, if these words are the obituary God is able to offer not just to His Son but to all of His servants ministering in churches around the world, we would be blessed.

I like to think that as that stone rolled across the tomb and Christ was placed on that slab, you could see these words by the Father: "He has not been rebellious. I have helped him. I will vindicate him." And His resurrection is His vindication, justified by the Spirit (Rom. 1:4).

Is your ministry perhaps nothing more than a vindication of Jesus Christ? Whatever else it is—and it is many things—your ministry, Lord willing, is nothing but a vindication of the One who was obedient, who turned not backwards, who gave His cheeks to be struck, had His beard pulled out, and cried, "My God, my God, why have you forsaken me?" This is why we are here. This is what we will live for, not only in this life but also in the life to come. The Father's reputation was on the line when it came to the servant. As much as the servant vindicated the Father, the Father vindicated the servant. What will you do with your remaining years in ministry? Will it be your own vindication, or will it be the vindication of the only One who is to be vindicated? That is our joy, our glory, and our boast.

Hallelujah! What a Savior!

4

In December 2016, the evangelical community in North America was once again confronted with the biblical teaching concerning the virgin birth of Jesus Christ. First, Andy Stanley, pastor of North Point Community Church in Alpharetta, Georgia, ignited controversy when he stated on December 3, "Christianity doesn't hinge on the truth or even the stories about the birth of Jesus. It really hinges on the resurrection of Jesus."[1] He acknowledged that one of the challenging truths about Christmas is the unbelievable nature of the stories in the Bible describing Jesus' miraculous conception. Stanley later affirmed his belief in the virgin conception of Jesus in a message on December 17, but still left the door open for other Christians not to affirm the doctrine.

Second, on December 23, *The New York Times* published an interview between columnist Nicholas Kristof and Timothy Keller. In the column, Kristof point blank questioned Keller if one had to believe in the virgin birth of Christ among other things to be a Christian. Keller answered that if one did not believe in the virgin birth, they are outside of the boundary of Christian faith. Concerning the virgin birth, Keller stated, "If it were a legend that could be dismissed, it would damage the fabric of the Christian message."[2] During the past two centu-

---

[1] Andy Stanley, "Who Needs Christmas?" series messages, December 3, 10, and 17, 2016, http://northpoint.org.
[2] Nicholas Kristof, "Am I a Christian, Pastor Timothy Keller?" *The New York Times*, December 23, 2016, http://www.nytimes.com/2016/12/23/opinion/Sunday.

ries, many others have raised the question of whether it is necessary for a Christian to affirm the virgin conception and birth of Jesus. This is the question I wish to pursue in this chapter as we look together at what the Bible teaches.

Important Definitions

Before describing the biblical data, it is important to define a number of terms associated with the discussion of the virgin birth.

Virgin Birth: In the strict sense, this means that Mary was a virgin when she gave birth to Jesus. "But [Joseph] kept her a virgin until she gave birth to a Son; and he called His name Jesus" (Matt. 1:25). Mary had no sexual relationship with Joseph or any other man before Jesus was born. In the broader sense, "virgin birth" is used to refer to all that led up to the birth of Jesus, the announcement to Mary by the angel Gabriel, the conception, and the events of the pregnancy to the birth itself. It is in this broader sense that "virgin birth" is used in this chapter.

Virgin Conception: Mary was a virgin when Jesus was conceived (Luke 1:27, 31), thus making the conception of Jesus a miracle. All of the further events of Mary's pregnancy and the birth itself followed the normal human process. There is no biblical warrant for the belief that Mary had a pain-free pregnancy and birth.

Perpetual Virginity: This is the assertion that Mary was a virgin before, during, and after the birth of Jesus—until she died. However, the Bible clearly states that Jesus had brothers and sisters, most likely children born to Joseph and Mary after the birth of Jesus (Matt. 13:55–56; John 7:3, 5; Acts 1:14). Luke referred to Jesus as Mary's "firstborn son" (2:7), implying that more children were born to Mary. The tradition of the perpetual virginity can be traced only from the late second century onward. The *Protoevangelium of James*, a noncanonical writing, was the first source of this teaching.

Immaculate Conception: This is the teaching that Mary was conceived in her mother's womb without the stain of original sin. In this way, Mary was herself without sin and thus not able to pass on original sin to Jesus as His human parent. Even though this teaching started to develop and become predominate in about the thirteenth century, it did not become official Roman Catholic dogma until 1854. There is no biblical foundation for this teaching.

The Biblical Data

The explicit statements concerning the virgin birth of Jesus are confined to the narratives recorded in the books of Matthew and Luke. In both books, most of the narrative is concentrated on the events leading up to and following the actual birth of Jesus. Even though Matthew begins his record of the birth of Jesus with the heading "Now the birth of Jesus Christ was as follows" (1:18), his only state-ment concerning the actual birth was "she [Mary] gave birth to a Son" (1:25). The bulk of the narrative is devoted to Joseph and his obedience to the Lord in taking Mary as his wife. In Luke's lengthy narrative concerning the events lead-ing up to and following the birth of Jesus (1:5–2:52), the only words referenc-ing the birth itself are: "the days were completed for her to give birth. And she gave birth to her firstborn son" (2:6b–7a). The emphasis in both books is not on describing the actual birth of Jesus itself, as vital as it was to the outworking of God's plan, but on how the events before and after the birth demonstrated how God was actively fulfilling His Word in providing salvation and redemption for His people through the incarnation of His Son through the virgin birth.

Matthew

Matthew was one of the twelve apostles (10:3). As such, he was one who had personally witnessed the public ministry and resurrection of Jesus. Thus, his nar-rative was based on his eyewitness of the later events in Jesus' life and his earwit-ness testimony from Jesus Himself. Matthew's book in the present biblical canon was the first written, probably by AD 50, so there were many other witnesses to the truthfulness of his account still alive.

In the first chapter of Matthew, the Greek term for "virgin" (*parthenos*) is only used once (1:23) and only indirectly refers to Mary. Though some have argued that this Greek term meant no more than "maiden," the vast majority of its us-ages in extrabiblical Greek literature point to its understanding of the woman being described as more than a young girl. It was used to describe a female who was also a virgin, never having a previous sexual union with a man.

Matthew uses the term *virgin* after describing the events surrounding Mary's pregnancy (1:18b–21). In verse 23, Matthew declared that these events were a fulfillment of the prophecy given by the prophet Isaiah over seven hundred years previously. In about 735 BC, the Davidic king of Judah then exercising rule, Ahaz, was fearful because his enemies, the kings of Aram and Israel, were plotting to remove him from the throne and then install their own king (Isa. 7:1–6). However, the Lord instructed Isaiah to tell Ahaz that the plot would not come to pass (7:7–9). To help Ahaz believe Isaiah's words about the security of his rule, the Lord said that Ahaz could ask for a supernatural sign as a guaran-tee of His promise (7:10–11). However, Ahaz refused to ask for a sign (7:12). So the Lord Himself gave the sign that would be His guarantee that the rule of the house of David was secure. That supernatural sign was that a virgin would both conceive and give birth to a son who would be "Immanuel," God is with us (7:13–14). Matthew stated that Mary and Jesus were the fulfillments of that prophecy (1:22–23). Mary was the virgin, and Jesus as "God with us" was the Savior. In applying the promise of Isaiah 7:14 to Jesus, Matthew also implied that Jesus was the Messiah who would fulfill the Lord's covenant promise to David concerning the "forever" rule of a Son of David (2 Sam. 7:12–16). The virgin birth was the means that God had predicted He would use to bring His Messiah into the world.

This explicit statement of virginity in Matthew 1:23 is supported by four implicit statements that further point to the virginity of Mary when she conceived and gave birth to Jesus. First, consider also Matthew 1:16—"Joseph the husband of Mary, by whom Jesus was born"—which records the final link in the genealogy of Jesus that Matthew began with Abraham in 1:2. This genealogy links Joseph to Abraham and, more importantly, to David (note that David's name is recorded first in 1:1). Although Jesus will be legally recognized as the son of Joseph, Matthew clearly indicated the Joseph was not the natural father of Jesus. In Greek, the relative pronoun "whom" matches in gender and number of the noun to which it refers. The relative pronoun is a feminine singular, so Matthew was indicating that Mary was the one "by whom Jesus was born." Further, the verb "was born" in Greek is an aorist indicative passive. In his list of Abraham through Jacob (2–16b), Matthew consistently used the aorist indicative active—that is, X "begat" or "fathered" Y. By changing the verb voice from active to passive, Matthew indicated that even Mary was not the active agent in the birth of Jesus. This allowed Matthew to describe the virgin birth in such a way that God through the Holy Spirit is considered the active agent in the birth of Jesus while Mary is the passive means.

The second implicit statement is 1:18: "When His mother Mary had been betrothed to Joseph, before they came together she was found to be with child by the Holy Spirit." In Jewish custom at the time, there was a one-year betrothal period where the man and woman were considered to be legally married. However, the man's taking of the woman into his home and consummating the marriage did not occur until after the year-long period was completed. It was during this betrothal period that the pregnancy of Mary occurred through the agency of the Holy Spirit. Joseph's plan to divorce her indicated clearly that he was not the human father of Jesus (1:19). This led to an angel of the Lord revealing to Joseph how Mary had become pregnant, the third implicit statement.

In verse 20, we read, "The Child who has been conceived in her is of the Holy Spirit." Joseph was told by the angel exactly how Mary had become pregnant. The child that had been "begotten" in her womb was through the agency of the Holy Spirit [the verb in the Greek is the same as had been used throughout the genealogy—"begat" or "fathered"]. Further, the verb is an aorist participle passive, indicating again that Mary was the passive agent in her pregnancy, which accords with verse 16. In response to the angel's words, Joseph took Mary as his wife (1:24). By so doing, he adopted Jesus as his legal son. Jewish custom asserted that if a man married a woman, any children born to the woman would be considered to be from her husband.

The fourth implicit statement is found in 1:25: "But he did not know her until she gave birth to a Son" (my translation). Isaiah had predicted not only that the Messiah would be conceived by a virgin, but also born to a woman who was still a virgin. By not consummating the marriage until after the birth of Jesus, Joseph made sure that the prophecy was literally fulfilled. In this way, Matthew demonstrated how the Lord had fulfilled His Word. Jesus was the one and only fulfillment of Isaiah 7:14; Mary was the virgin through whom the conception and birth had been accomplished.

Luke

Luke's narrative was written about a decade after Matthew, around AD 58. Luke was a missionary companion of the apostle Paul (Acts 16:10) and he wrote his account of the life of Jesus to a Gentile convert to Christianity named Theophilus (Luke 1:3). He sought to give his reader assurance that the things he had been taught, probably through Paul and his associates, were accurate (1:4). Luke affirmed that he had carefully investigated the matters of which he wrote, so that his narrative was historically accurate (1:3). To deny that Luke's report is true to what happened is to accuse the writer of failing to uphold his claim to accuracy. What Luke recorded about the events surrounding the birth of Jesus is to be accepted as historical fact.

Luke's explicit statement about the virgin birth is found in 1:27: "To a virgin engaged to a man whose name was Joseph, of the descendants of David; and the virgin's name was Mary." Here Luke uses the Greek word for "virgin" (*parthenos*) twice, with the second usage relating directly to Mary. Like Matthew, Luke affirmed that Mary was betrothed to Joseph. The angel Gabriel was sent from God to Nazareth (1:26) to communicate with a virgin during the betrothal period when Mary was clearly still a virgin. Thus, Luke demonstrated with certainty that Mary was a virgin when the angel spoke with her.

Now for the implicit statements. The first is found in 1:31: "You will conceive in your womb and bear a son." Upon hearing the angel's words that she was richly blessed and the Lord was with her (1:28), Mary was perplexed and was pondering for a time what the angel's salutation meant (1:29). Gabriel responded to Mary's perplexity by reasserting her favor with God (1:30). He then predicted that Mary in the near future would conceive and ultimately bear a son to be named Jesus by her (1:31). The angel's words implied that Mary would conceive while still a virgin during the betrothal period before any sexual union with Joseph. Gabriel continued, declaring to Mary that Jesus would fulfill the covenant promises that the Lord had made with David (1:32–33; cf. 2 Sam. 7:11–16). Luke did not explicitly link Gabriel's words with Isaiah 7:14, but the prophecy concerning the virgin-conceived and virgin-born Son as the guarantee of the Lord's faithfulness to the house of David certainly would come to mind to one who knew the Old Testament.

The second implicit statement comes in Luke 1:34: "How can this be, since I am not knowing a man?" (my translation). Mary clearly understood that the angel's words meant that she would conceive in the near future. This was reflected in her response to Gabriel. She did not know how she could possibly conceive since she was then not in a sexual relationship with any man. Mary was confirming her present virgin status.

Next, third, in verse 35, we read, "The Holy Spirit will come upon you, and the power of the Most High will overshadow you; and for that reason the holy Child shall be called the Son of God." In response to Mary's query, the angel affirmed that Mary would not conceive through the agency of a man. Rather, the conception would be the result of the Holy Spirit coming upon her and the power of God the Most High overshadowing her. The incarnation of the Son of God was to be the result of the powerful, sovereign work of God Himself.

Then, fourth, in verse 37, the angel declares, "For nothing will be impossible with God." That Mary would conceive as a virgin was impossible according to mere human ability. However, what was not possible with man was possible with God. God was able to give conception to a virgin in the same way that He had granted conception to a postmenopausal Elizabeth (1:36). As God was able to do the impossible in giving a barren woman conception, so also He was able to do the even greater miracle in giving a virgin conception. Mary declared her submission to the Lord that it might happen to her as the angel had spoken (1:38). Mary was willing to endure the scandal of a woman being pregnant outside of marriage. This implies that Mary knew that she would conceive as a virgin, which was humanly impossible.

The fifth implicit statement of the virgin birth comes in 2:5: "With Mary, who was engaged to him, and was with child." There are numerous reasons why the details recorded in Luke 2:1–4 have been questioned concerning historical accuracy. First, there is no extrabiblical evidence that Caesar Augustus ever called for an empire-wide census (see 2:1). Second, there is uncertainty that Quirinius was a Roman governor in Syria as early as 6 to 2 BC, though he was later (see 2:2). Third, there is no evidence that a first-century BC Jewish male would have to go back to his home town (see 2:3). Fourth, even if Joseph had to return to Bethlehem, he was under no obligation to take Mary with him (see 2:4–5). However, the first two attacks are arguments from silence. Just because there is no extrabiblical evidence at present does not mean Luke was wrong. (Consider that until 1961, there was no extrabiblical evidence that Pilate had been governor of Judea, but now there is!) As to the third argument, twice Luke emphasized that Joseph was of the house of David (1:27; 2:4) and that David's birthplace was Bethlehem. Concerning the fourth argument, maybe Mary was not required to go with Joseph, but rather he took her along so as not to leave her alone in Nazareth to face further scandal when she gave birth to her son. In conclusion, there is no reason to doubt the veracity of Luke's testimony in 2:1–7.

Having established reasons to support Luke's historical accuracy, it is interesting to note that in 2:5 he refers to Mary as betrothed, rather than married, to Joseph. It seems that Luke was implying that not only the conception but also the birth of Jesus took place during the one-year betrothal period when the man and the woman would have no sexual relations. This is a further implication from the text as to the virginity of Mary when Jesus was both conceived and born.

The sixth and final implicit statement of the virgin birth in Luke comes in 3:23, in his introduction to the genealogy of Jesus: "Jesus . . . being, as was supposed, the son of Joseph, the son of Eli" (3:23). Joseph was *thought* to be the father of Jesus, but Jesus was in fact the son of Eli, probably either the father or grandfather of Mary. Thus, Luke, as in his announcement and birth narratives of Jesus, put his emphasis on Mary rather than on Joseph. Fittingly, Luke's genealogy concluded with Adam (3:38) and traced the human line of Jesus through His mother. Joseph was only the *supposed* father of Jesus, but not His human father, since He had been born to a virgin.

Some Doctrinal Deductions[3]

The narratives of Matthew and Luke give clear and convincing evidence of the virgin birth. Even though no other New Testament writer specifically mentions the virgin birth, nothing in the other twenty-five books contradicts the testimony presented by Matthew and Luke. However, it is difficult to move from narrative to theology because a narrative simply states what happened. Narratives describe; they do not prescribe. There is nowhere in the New Testament where there is "theologizing" by apostolic authors on the virgin birth. They theologize about Jesus being fully God and fully man, but not the means by which He became the God-man. However, comparing the gospel narratives with other

---

[3] See also the discussion on the virgin birth of Jesus in John MacArthur & Richard Mayhue, eds., *Biblical Doctrine: A Systematic Summary of Bible Truth* (Wheaton, IL: Crossway, 2016), 261–63.

biblical material does allow us to draw some doctrinal deductions concerning the virgin birth.

First, the virgin birth was the sign given by God to point to Jesus Christ as the fulfillment of the Davidic covenant (see Isa. 7:14; Matt. 1:23; Luke 1:32–33). In both Matthew and Luke, there is a close connection between the birth of Christ and the Lord's covenant promise to David. Matthew's only use of the word *virgin* was in his quotation concerning the fulfillment of Isaiah 7:14 (1:23). This prophecy declared God's determination to fulfill His covenant oath to the house of David through a virgin-conceived and virgin-born Son who would be God in flesh. Thus, the virgin birth was viewed as a divine necessity in the Lord's goal of ultimately providing a Davidic descendant who would reign over both Israel and the nations (Isa. 9:6–7). Without the virgin birth, the Davidic promise would be null and void. But the historical truth of the virgin birth means that the hope that the Lord will one day establish His throne upon the earth through this Davidic seed, Jesus, is still possible and will become a reality when Jesus returns (Matt. 25:31). Therefore, belief in the virgin birth of Christ is vital to the Christian's ultimate eschatological hope.

Luke also demonstrated a close link between the virgin birth and the fulfillment of the Davidic covenant. His two uses of *virgin* were in his narrative explanation of how Gabriel was sent by God to speak to Mary who was betrothed to Joseph who was of the house of David (i.e., he was a descendant of David). The culmination of Gabriel's revelation to Mary was that her virgin-conceived and virgin-born son Jesus was to be the fulfillment of the Davidic covenant (1:32–33). Jesus would be the Son of God as well as a son of David who will receive from the Lord God the throne of David, from which He will reign over the house of Jacob forever. He will be the Davidic ruler whose kingdom will have no end. As in Matthew, Luke affirmed the close connection between the virgin birth and the ultimate fulfillment of the Davidic covenant. Thus, the historical fact of the virgin birth is again shown to be foundational to the Christian's eschatological hope.

Second, the virgin birth was the means chosen by God for the Savior to enter the world (Matt. 1:21, 23; Luke 1:32, 68–75; 2:11). The virgin-born Son was to be named Jesus, for He will save His people from their sins (Matt. 1:21). This goes back to Old Testament prophecy that the one who was going to be Israel's Messiah was also going to be Israel's Redeemer and Savior (Isa. 49:5; 52:13–53:12). The virgin birth was the means chosen by God for the Savior to enter the world. Both Zacharias (Luke 1:68–75) and the angel (Luke 2:11) affirmed that Jesus entered the world to provide salvation for Israel and for all with whom God was well pleased.

The question has been posed: could God have brought the God-man into the world any other way? The answer is that we do not know. What the Bible does state, though, is this was the means chosen by God. He was able to see all of the potentials and possibilities, and this was what best fit His plans. The virgin birth was the means by which the Savior of His people, the Deliverer, and the one who would be their sin bearer would enter into the world.

Third, the virgin birth allowed Jesus to be fathered by God in a similar way that Adam had been fathered by God (Gen. 5:1; Matt. 1:1; Luke 1:35; 3:38), without sin (Gen. 1:27, 31; Luke 1:35). Matthew significantly entitled his gospel, "The book of the generations of Jesus the Christ, the son of David, the son of Abraham" (1:1; my translation). This title echoes Genesis 5:1: "This is the book of the generations of Adam." In fact, the first phrase of Matthew 1:1 was an exact replication of the first phrase of Genesis 5:1, except that the words "Jesus the Christ" replaced "Adam." This parallel shows that there is both a comparison and contrast between Jesus and Adam. Both were uniquely "fathered" by God so that they were called "Son of God" and "son of God," respectively (Jesus in Luke 1:35; Adam in Luke 3:38). Adam and Jesus shared in common what is true of no other human: they both came into being without a male father. Since they were "birthed" by God Himself, they also came into the world without sin. However, there is also a great contrast between the two. Whereas Adam was the first listed in the genealogy of Genesis 5, Jesus was the last listed in the genealogy of Matthew 1. In Genesis 5, all but one (Enoch) in Adam's line died; sin and death passed from Adam to his heirs. In Jesus and by His physical death, there can be salvation from the sin that is the heritage from Adam (Matt. 1:21).

Fourth, the virgin birth resulted in God dwelling in a human body with humanity (Matt. 1:23; John 1:1, 14) and was how a divine being who was preexistent could take to Himself a human nature without the procreation of a new person. According to John 1:14, the Word (who was God; 1:1) became flesh—that is, God became a man. This is known as the incarnation. As the Scripture narrates, this incarnation took place by means of the virgin conception, God the Holy Spirit generating the fetus in the womb of a virgin named Mary. After this conception, the development and birth of Jesus followed the normal gestation and birth process of every other human being. Thus, the preexistent God (John 1:1) was able to enter into the world not only as fully God, but also as fully man. He was one being who was both God and man; this was a result of the virgin birth, the incarnation of God.

Fifth, the virgin birth was a testimony to the power of God to do that which is impossible for man to do (Luke 1:37). The angel Gabriel declared, "For nothing will be impossible with God" (Luke 1:37). This includes giving postmenopausal Elizabeth conception through her husband, Zacharias, and giving Mary conception without a human male through the virgin birth. These miracles were two of the many mighty acts of God that He did throughout history as recorded in Scripture. In a God-created world, the Creator can do that which is impossible for man to do.

Sixth, the virgin birth tests whether a theologian or theology is approaching the Scriptures with merely naturalistic assumptions or is open to the supernatural. That a woman could conceive a child without a male is naturally impossible. Therefore, if a theologian or theology operates on purely naturalistic assumptions, the virgin birth is impossible—as is the bodily resurrection from the dead. However, the Bible-believing Christian has a worldview affirming that the Creator God steps into human history at times to do that which is naturally impossible. If one believes in the supernatural, then one will have no problem accepting the virgin birth. If one also accepts the inerrancy of the Bible, then one will have no problem affirming the virgin birth as fact. One's conclusion concerning the virgin birth demonstrates the foundation of one's theology and whether it embraces supernatural revelation or naturalistic reasoning.

Seventh, the virgin birth ought to be a part of the Christian's confession of faith (1 Tim. 3:16; Heb. 2:14; 1 John 4:1–3). During the past two centuries, there has been great debate over whether the virgin birth actually occurred and an even greater debate over whether it is necessary to affirm belief in the historicity of the virgin birth to be a Christian. The apostolic declaration of the gospel in the book of Acts was based upon the historical reality that Jesus was the Messiah (Christ) who, as a man, had died and been raised from the dead (2:29–36; 3:12–16; 5:27–32; 10:34–43; 13:26–41; 17:2–3, 30–31). This truth of the death and resurrection of Jesus Christ was also affirmed by Paul in his summary of the gospel he had delivered to the Corinthians (1 Cor. 15:3–8). To be sure, the oral gospel proclamation did not include the mention of the virgin birth according to the New Testament canonical record. But the New Testament was not silent concerning the need for Christian believers to affirm that Jesus was truly a man of flesh, which implied that He came into the human race by birth like any other man (cf. Rom. 1:3; Gal. 4:4). First John 4:1–3 makes clear that true Christian believers knew and confessed that "Jesus Christ has come in the flesh . . . from God" (4:2b). To deny this truth was proof that one was not from God. Thus, a confession of belief in the human birth of Jesus was one of the truths that separated true believers from false teachers and their followers (1 Tim. 3:16; Heb. 2:14–18). The confession of the full humanity of Jesus along with His full deity was a necessary component of Christian faith. However, the virgin birth as the means that God used to birth Jesus as fully human was not explicitly a part of the gospel proclamation or the earliest Christian confessions of the first century.

But by the second century, this changed. Among the earliest confessions of the post-apostolic church was the so-called "Apostles' Creed." The creed was referred to by Irenaeus and Tertullian in the latter part of the second century. By that time, the Creed was a part of at least the Western church and confessed by every convert before baptism. The earliest form of the creed included at least the words "born of the Holy Spirit and the virgin Mary," if not the full statement now used: "conceived by the Holy Spirit, born of the virgin Mary."[4] From the second to the twenty-first centuries, the confession concerning the virgin birth has been an integral component of the Christian faith based upon the New Testament evidence. As such, all confessing Christians need to affirm the virgin birth as part of their assurance that they are truly redeemed children of God.

In conclusion, the gospel message orally proclaimed according to the New Testament did not include a reference to the virgin birth of Jesus. Thus, one could respond in faith for salvation without confessing the virgin birth. However, as a believer matured in his faith and learned more of Jesus, it should be assumed that he gave testimony to the truth of the virgin birth. If one believes in the resurrection of Jesus from the dead (a great miracle), there is no logical problem in believing the equally great miracle of the virgin birth of Jesus. The virgin birth of Christ is absolutely necessary to the Christian faith.

---

[4] J. Gresham Machen, *The Virgin Birth of Christ* (New York: Harper & Row, 1930), 3. See 2–43 for a full discussion of the second-century evidence.

5

THE BREAD OF LIFE

JOHN 6

Ligon Duncan

John 6 is a glorious text, overflowing with the glorious theme that Jesus is the sufficient bread of life. The apostle shows us our deepest need of faith in Christ and how we are utterly blind apart from the grace of God, which opens our eyes to the solid joys and lasting treasures found in His Son. John sets forth the absolute necessity of faith in Jesus by displaying Him as the sole source of salvation and life in this sin-sick world.

However, the study and rehearsal of these truths for the sake of speaking them to others is not our greatest need. We must know, believe, remember, and rehearse them first for ourselves, because without the bread of life, we cannot survive. To feed on the Bible in order only to feed others is an occupational hazard of a pastor's calling. We cannot commend one whom we ourselves do not supremely cherish. If a pastor is not satisfied by the bread of life, he will poorly commend the bread of life to those who need Him for life and salvation. For this reason, it is essential for pastors to dwell on the truths of John 6, not just so that we can preach the bread of life to others, but so that we ourselves may feed on Jesus, who is the true bread.

John 6:22–59 is fundamentally about Jesus—who He is, what He came to do, what He accomplished for us, and why we must trust Him. Indeed, the massive crowd at Jesus' bread of life discourse encircled Him because He had just miraculously fed five thousand hungry people. After this event, which is meant to remind us of God's provision of manna for His people in the desert, Jesus comes to His disciples in the dead of night while walking on the water. We find that the crowd, although pursuing Jesus to the other side of the sea, is unspiritual and in desperate need of Jesus to open their eyes to their need of faith. Jesus does just that as He teaches the swelling crowd to put their trust in Him as the bread of life.

By Jesus' own diagnosis, the crowd is not pursuing Him for the right reasons. The misguided crowd compels Jesus to speak to them about three crucial matters:

1. Jesus clarifies the crowd's true need by contrasting perishable bread with the living bread (vv. 22–27).
2. Jesus teaches them how they can obtain the living bread through faith (vv. 28–29).
3. As the one who identifies Himself as the bread of life, Jesus points the crowd to His own glory (vv. 30–51).

Our True Need

After witnessing the miracle of the loaves and fish multiplied into enough food to feed thousands, the crowd is confused about what they really need. They hunger to see another food miracle by alluding to God's provision of manna in the wilderness (vv. 30–31). In response to the crowd's request, Jesus does not give them what they seek and instead questions their desire for further signs. In verse 26, Jesus says, "You seek Me, not because you saw signs, but because you ate of the loaves and were filled." Jesus' ministry to the crowd has not lacked miraculous manifestation. What is lacking is the crowd's reception of those miracles. The crowds are earthly and want their bellies filled again. With concern for their souls, Jesus says, "Do not work for the food which perishes, but for the food which endures to eternal life, which the Son of Man will give to you" (v. 27).

Pastors in particular have much to learn from Jesus' treatment of the crowds. Jesus does not assume that the presence of crowds necessarily means that something good is happening. He does not interpret the presence of the crowd as a stamp of approval for His ministry. He did not come to feed His own ego by using the crowd for Himself. Rather, Jesus came selflessly to find lost sheep and to feed them. When crowds seek Jesus for the wrong reasons, He does not commend Himself but expresses concern for their souls. Jesus "did not come to be served, but to serve, and to give His life a ransom for many" (Mark 10:45). He cared enough about the crowd to lovingly confront them with their real need: true spiritual bread.

The crowd was seeking the bread that perishes while Jesus was offering the bread of eternal life. This problem of the crowd's pursuit of perishable bread continues to the present day. Perishable bread has many manifestations. The health and wealth gospel teaches that God will make you healthy, wealthy, and wise if you have faith—and a certain kind and certain amount of faith—in Him. This is perishable bread. Attending church in order to be seen as a respectable member of society is perishable bread. Many people see Christ and the gospel not as the bread of life itself, but as a token that will help them obtain what they really desire. There are all manner of reasons why people join the crowd. As pastors, our call is not to use them in order to assuage our own insecurities but to show them, with a heart of compassion, their real need for the bread of life.

How to Acquire the Bread

The crowd not only needed to be shown their real need for true bread. They also needed to be taught how to acquire it. This is why they ask, "What must we do, to be doing the works of God?" (John 6:28). Their question is not unlike the rich young ruler's question (Mark 10:17) or the crowd's question during Pentecost after Peter's gospel proclamation (Acts 2:37). Jesus' answer to them—"This is the work of God, that you believe in him whom he has sent" (John 6:29)—emphasizes the divine origin of faith. If the work required to obtain their need of bread is going to be done, Jesus says, then it must come down from above. Jesus is essentially saying that they are not going to work this work because creating faith is the work of God.

Jesus' words are similar to other texts that remind us that the entirety of the Christian life is of grace and divine origin. The apostle Paul rejoices that both sanctification and justification are gracious works of God: "It is God who is working in you, both to will and to work, for the sake of his good pleasure" (Phil. 2:13). If God is at work in sanctification, is He not also at work in justification? Yes, and even in faith! The whole working of salvation is of grace (see Rom. 8:30; Eph. 2:8–9).

As Jesus stresses the utter necessity of faith, He uses two particular descriptions: faith is coming, and faith is eating and drinking. He states, "I am the bread of life; whoever comes to me shall not hunger, and whoever believes in me shall never thirst" (John 6:35). The famous line of the hymn, "Out of my bondage, sorrow and night, Jesus, I come," beautifully captures how we are called to approach Jesus.[1] It's a picture about where we find rest, refuge, and belonging.

My father died in 1992, when I was thirty-one years old. I have never had a home in this world since he departed. I cannot remember how many times I

---

[1] William T. Sleeper, "Jesus, I Come" (1887), *Timeless Truths* website, http://library.timelesstruths.org/music/Jesus_I_Come/.

thought in my first thirty-one years, "If I can just come home to my father, I'll be all right." In the same way, Jesus calls us to come home through faith. Coming to the place of refuge, love, and safety is like a bride coming down the aisle to her bridegroom and saying, "Forsaking all others, I will keep me only to thee, to thee I pledge my troth." In the same way, Jesus beckons the crowd to come to Him through faith.

Charles Simeon's reflection upon faith is noteworthy:

> [Faith] is not a mere assent to the truth of his messiahship, but a humble betrothal in him as the Savior of the world. We must feel our need of him; we must see the suitableness and sufficiency of his salvation. We must actually go to him as the appointed Savior and seek acceptance with God through Him alone. We must renounce every other hope and make him all our salvation and all our desire.[2]

For this reason, the only work needing to be done is the Father's. The crowd is commanded simply to come.

The Bread of Life

After beckoning the crowd to come, Jesus calls the crowd to do the unthinkable: to eat His flesh and drink His blood. "Unless you eat the flesh of the Son of Man and drink his blood, you have no life in you" (6:53). This image is designed to cause maximum offense. Although eating a sacrifice was not unheard of—the Levitical priests, after all, consumed parts of the sacrifice—no one drank sacrificial blood. Blood was forbidden! You could not even eat an animal with the blood remaining in it. To Jewish ears, "You must eat my flesh and drink my blood," is utterly provocative.

What exactly is Jesus referring to by using the imagery of flesh and blood? Flesh and blood are the constituent parts of a covenant sacrifice. Both the body and the blood of the animal were integral in sacrificial offerings. In this passage, Jesus is speaking of Himself as the one true sacrifice to which all other old covenant sacrifices pointed (v. 56). Jesus' call to come and eat and drink is a call to faith and trust in the once-for-all covenant sacrifice, lest we die in our sins.

We are accustomed to eating and drinking metaphors. For example, "I drank in that lecture" or "I devoured that book" are common idioms in our day. But

---

[2] Charles Simeon, *Horae Homileticae: Luke XVII to John XII*, vol. 13 (London: Holdsworth and Ball, 1833), 377.

Jesus is saying something far more significant. He says to the crowd that they need Him more than food. If we do not eat and drink and trust in His life-giving provision and sacrificial death, we will die as starved and thirsty people in the desert wilderness of our sin.

In showing the crowd their need for living bread and how to obtain it through faith, Jesus points to none other than Himself as the bread of life. If the crowd is going to have life, they are going to need to know Jesus' identity as life-giving bread. As such, Jesus declares Himself to be greater than the manna given in the desert. Jesus, the bread of life, *is* life and gives life by His death. The life He gives is our deepest satisfaction, our eternal security, our salvation, and our communion.

Jesus declaring that "I am the bread of life" (v. 35) should remind us of His words about living water to the Samaritan woman at the well. After Jesus describes the water that wells up to eternal life (John 4:14), the Samaritan woman responds by requesting that water so she no longer has to visit the well. The woman does not grasp Jesus' words because she does not realize that Jesus is using water metaphorically to speak of a greater reality. The same confusion takes place with the crowd in John 6. Jesus tells them that "my Father gives you the true bread from heaven" (v. 32). Like the Samaritan woman, the crowd accepts His offer of bread without realizing that His offer is far greater than can be imagined. To clarify His bread analogy, Jesus declares Himself to be the provisional bread of life that God has sent from heaven to satisfy the world. Jesus does not mince words: "I am the bread of life. . . . I am the living bread that came down from heaven (vv. 48, 51). Jesus responds to the crowd's desire for another food miracle by offering Himself as the true and greater manna, the imperishable eternal bread of God. Jesus has reoriented the crowd's desire. The crowd does not so much need Jesus to perform another miracle attesting to who He is as much as they need Jesus Himself, the bread that can be eaten unto eternal life.

The language of satisfaction that Jesus uses with the woman at the well, He also uses with the crowd: "I am the bread of life; whoever comes to me shall not hunger, and whoever believes in me shall never thirst" (v. 35). He says to the Samaritan woman, "Everyone who drinks of this water will be thirsty again, but whoever drinks of the water that I will give him will never be thirsty again" (4:13–14). Jesus is seeking to satisfy an ancient human longing and the root cause of every sin. Jesus, the bread of life, is the answer to our pursuit of satisfaction in something other than God.

The reality of misplaced desires is written large on the first few pages of the Bible. In the Garden of Eden, Satan said to the woman, "God knows that when you eat of [the Tree of the Knowledge of Good and Evil] your eyes will be opened, and you will be like God, knowing good and evil" (Gen. 3:5). Satan's words suggest that God was withholding something from our first parents, and this something would be more satisfying than God and all the benefits that come with right relationship with Him. In other words, Satan suggests that there is greater satisfaction outside of God than in relationship with God. Satan deceives Eve into believing that God is not worth living for and that Satan can provide something better than God Himself. The same is true for us. Every time we sin, we have made the decision to be satisfied in something other than God. Satan has been running the same play for many, many years: If you disobey God, life will be better for you. Seek satisfaction in the creation, not the Creator (see Rom. 1:25).

Jesus also offers security to those in the crowd who will come to Him. He declares that all who come to Him will not hunger or thirst, on the grounds that "All that the Father gives Me will come to Me, and the one who comes to Me I will certainly not cast out." (John 6:37). We are beckoned to come to the one who cannot lose one, "This is the will of Him who sent Me, that of all that He has given Me I lose nothing" (v. 39). The hymn "In Christ Alone" powerfully captures the security that God's people enjoy, exclaiming that neither hell nor man can pluck us from Christ's hand.[3]

The author of Psalm 119 reflects on this same reality. For 175 verses, the psalmist glories in how good the Word of God is as he devotes himself to it. He declares over and again, "Blessed are those whose way is blameless, who walk in the law of the LORD" (Psalm 119:1), identifying himself as one who is near to God. After 175 verses of rapturous reflection, the psalmist suddenly shifts in the concluding, 176th verse. His magnificent reflection on the sufficiency of God and His Word is ended with: "I have gone astray like a lost sheep; seek your servant." Verse after verse, the psalmist finds His security and satisfaction in God and His Word, but suddenly he has found himself needing to be pursued by God again. In the same, we will get to places in life that, if God doesn't come seek us, we will not come home. Like the parable of the lost sheep, the Shepherd will at some point have to leave the ninety-nine sheep to bring the one—who is us—back home (Luke 15:3–7). The Shepherd will not send a telegram with instructions on the best way to get back home. The Good Shepherd Himself will go out and find us, put us on His back, and bring us home with Him. We are secure because Jesus will not lose those whom the Father has given Him (John 6:37–39).

The final outcome of God's securing and satisfying work of His own is salvation, resurrection, and eternal life. "This is the will of my Father," Jesus assures us, "that everyone who beholds the Son and believes in Him will have eternal

---

[3] Keith Getty and Stuart Townend, "In Christ Alone" (2002), Thankyou Music (PRS) (adm. worldwide at CapitolCMGPublishing.com).

life, and I Myself will raise him up on the last day" (v. 40). Jesus says that salvation from eternal death comes through partaking of Him who is the bread of life, "This is the bread which comes down out of heaven, so that one may eat of it and not die" (v. 50). The language of eating and dying contrasts the warning that was given to Adam in the garden: "In the day that you eat from it you will surely die" (Gen. 2:17). Jesus declares that if the crowd will eat of Him, the living bread, they will not die. In other words, Jesus leads the crowd back to the Garden of Eden and calls them not to eat perishable bread, but to eat of Himself and live forever! The apostle Paul reflects on this truth when he says to the Corinthian church, "As often as you eat this bread and drink the cup, you proclaim the Lord's death until He comes" (1 Cor. 11:26). It is Jesus' death that gives life and makes possible our future bodily resurrection unto the full enjoyment of joy and eternal pleasures that await God's people for all eternity (see Ps. 16:11). Because Jesus is the bread of life sent by the Father, we can be satisfied, secure, saved, and commune with our God forever.

The similarities shared between the Samaritan woman's and crowd's interaction with Jesus are striking. The Samaritan woman does not understand what Jesus is talking about when He offers her water that will quench her eternal thirst. Likewise, the crowd does not understand what Jesus is referring to when He offers them bread that never perishes. They both are confused by Jesus' use of metaphor to reach beyond their physical needs to their greatest need. The Samaritan woman wants well water, while Jesus wants for her water that will satisfy her soul so that she may overcome her serial adultery (John 4:13–18). The crowd wants another food miracle to fill their bellies, while Jesus wants them to be satisfied by living bread. Although the stories of the woman at the well (John 4) and Jesus' bread of life discourse spoken to the crowd (John 6) share many parallels, there is one fundamental difference. The Samaritan woman took up the life-giving water and drank deeply unto eternal life. The truth about a coming Messiah is met inside her with a trust in the person of the Messiah when Jesus reveals Himself to her by speaking, "I who speak to you am He" (4:26). Unlike the crowd, the Samaritan woman comes home. She eats and drinks of His flesh and blood. She comes to know the satisfaction, and security, and salvation, and communion that are found only in Jesus, the bread of life. May we all do the same!

6

THE GOOD SHEPHERD

JOHN 10

Steven J. Lawson

In John 10:11–18, we learn much about Jesus Christ, the Good Shepherd. What makes this passage so special is that this is Jesus' own commentary on His death and resurrection. This is Jesus preaching Christ and Him crucified. This is the greatest preacher who ever walked the earth, Jesus Christ, preaching on the greatest subject there is, His own sin-bearing, substitutionary death. Here, Jesus is both the speaker and subject, both teacher and theme, both preacher and proposition.

These verses are not more inspired than other portions of Scripture that focus on the cross, but they are far more personal. Here, Jesus Christ is baring His soul concerning His death and resurrection. Strangely, the congregation that day was the false shepherds of Israel. The timing for this discourse immediately follows Jesus' healing the blind man in chapter 9, and there is no break in the continuity of this address as we move from chapter 9 to 10. Jesus now addresses the false shepherds of Israel by referring to Himself as the true shepherd of the sheep.

In verses 1–10, Jesus sets the context in what John identifies as a "figure of speech" (v. 6), which is an allegory. While we are not to allegorize the Bible when we interpret it, it nevertheless contains allegories, which are like enlarged parables with greater complexity. With a parable, there is one central truth that drives its story. Any interpreter will quickly find himself in trouble whenever he pushes the secondary details of a parable to fit the analogy. But an allegory is different. It is intentionally multifaceted with more details to be interpreted in its various parts. This discourse on the good shepherd is one of those allegories.

The Sheepfold, Thieves, and Robbers

In verses 1–10, we first learn of "the fold of the sheep" (v. 1), representing the nation of Israel. Inside this sheepfold are many different flocks, representing the various factions of the nation of Israel at this time, and it is even full of unregenerate Jews in the dead religion of Judaism. In this culture, a typical shepherd would leave his flock during the night under the care of the doorkeeper. He would retire for a night's rest and then return the next day to call out his own flock.

We also read about thieves and robbers (v. 1), those to whom Jesus is speaking. These are the Pharisees, who have made the temple in Jerusalem to be a robber's den and have stolen glory from God (Matt. 21:13; Luke 19:46). With no concern for the sheep, these thieves and robbers have fleeced the flock and reveal they are not the rightful owners of the sheep. It is these Pharisees that Jesus is addressing and identifying as thieves and robbers.

The Shepherd and His Sheep

By stark contrast, we are introduced to the true shepherd of the sheep (v. 2), who is Jesus Christ Himself. Jesus unmistakably identifies Himself as this shepherd, "the good shepherd" (vv. 11, 14) who gives loving care to the flock of God. The doorkeeper in verse three is subject to various interpretations, which we will refrain from discussing. "The sheep" (v. 3) who are drawn to the shepherd are the elect of God. They are those chosen by God before the foundation of the world. They belong to the Father by His sovereign election and have been entrusted to the care of this good shepherd (v. 29).

One of the main features of the shepherd's "voice" is the effectual call that draws these elect sheep to Him (vv. 3–5). They are the ones who recognize the "voice" of their shepherd and respond by coming to Him. In this large community sheepfold, the sheep of the other flocks hear His audible voice, but do not recognize it as that of their own shepherd. They keep their heads down, nibbling on grass. But when the chosen sheep hear the "voice" of their shepherd, they immediately go to that voice. The shepherd calls them by name because He knows them. They hear the voice of their shepherd, raise their head, and move toward that voice, and thus separate from the other sheep.

The elect sheep hear what the other sheep do not discern, because they are given ears to hear. The Good Shepherd cannot leave them in this apostate sheepfold. He must lead them out of this spiritual graveyard with its stench of death. As they leave, the other shepherds call out to the elect sheep. But a stranger's voice, they will not hear. They will only follow the voice of their shepherd as He leads them out of the city and into the countryside. The sheep have left the apostate sheepfold behind, never to return.

The Door of the Sheep

Once in the countryside, the Good Shepherd builds another sheepfold. He gathers rocks from the field to build a circular wall and leaves an opening in it. At night, He lays in the opening and becomes the door for the sheep (v. 7). Once they all are in the sheepfold, He seals them into its protective walls and keeps out any predators that will try to come against them. In order to attack the sheep, the wild beasts have to go through the Shepherd. He is a heroic Shepherd, full of courage in the face of any danger that would threaten the sheep.

In the morning, the good Shepherd will arise from the opening in the wall and lead them out into green pastures and beside still waters. He gives them abundant life and feeds their soul until they are fully satisfied (v. 10). This good Shepherd leads them into the sheepfold for protection at night and leads them out into the pastures for provision during the day. This routine is repeated day after day. The closest relationship exists between this Shepherd and His sheep. He is responsible for all their needs. If need be, He will even lay down His life to protect them.

Understanding the context, there are three things to note in verses 11–18. At the beginning of verse 11, we find the exclusive claim of Jesus: "I am the good shepherd." Second, we learn about the excellent character of Jesus (vv. 11b–16). Here, Jesus gives three compelling reasons why He is the Good Shepherd. Finally, we read the emphatic choice of Jesus (vv. 17–18). Here, we find the first person singular pronoun "I" mentioned six times, which underscores the determined will of the Shepherd to lay down His life for the sheep.

The Exclusive Claims of Jesus

Jesus begins this latter part of His discourse by making the exclusive claim, "I am the good shepherd" (v. 11). This is the fourth of seven "I am" statements in the gospel of John. These strong assertions form the backbone of this fourth gospel. This particular "I am" statement by Jesus is located in the apex position of these claims. Three "I am" statements lead up to this one, and three lead away from it. Jesus has already said, "I am the bread of life" (6:35), "I am the light of the world" (8:12), and "I am the door of the sheep" (10:9). In the premiere position is "I am the good shepherd." Then leading away from it are "I am the resurrection and the life" (11:25–26), "I am the way, and the truth, and the life" (14:6), and "I am the vine" (15:5).

This fourth "I am" claim is in the center because the cross is in the center of Christianity. This is Jesus' fullest explanation of His substitutionary death and bodily resurrection. The cross is the cardinal doctrine of the Christian faith and occupies the preeminent place in the "I am" claims of the gospel of John. But what exactly does "I am the good shepherd" entail?

Jesus' Deity and Sufficiency

First, this exclusive claim, "I am the good shepherd," is a declaration of His deity. When Jesus said, "I am," He was claiming the divine name by which God revealed Himself at the burning bush as "I AM WHO I AM" (Ex. 3:14). "I am" is from the same Hebrew root meaning "to be" from which the sacred name for God ("Yahweh" or "Jehovah") is derived. This divine name means that God is the self-sufficient, autonomous God who is not dependent upon anyone or anything for His existence. In unmistakable terms, Jesus is taking this holy and sacred name for God upon Himself. By saying "I am," Jesus is claiming to be truly God, fully God. This cornerstone truth is taught throughout the entire Bible as Jesus performed the works that only God can perform, receives worship that only God can receive, possesses attributes that only God can possess, is called names that only God is called, and is equated with God. Those who heard Jesus that day understood that He was making Himself out to be God. John 10:33 makes this clear. By identifying Himself as "I am," Jesus is claiming to be co-equal with God the Father.

Likewise, God identified Himself as the shepherd of His people. David wrote, "The LORD is my shepherd" (Ps. 23:1). The psalmist addressed God as "Shepherd of Israel" (Ps. 80:1). In another psalm, we read that we are the people of God, "the sheep of His pasture" (Ps. 100:3). Throughout the Old Testament, God is identified as the Shepherd of His people (Isa. 40:11). God says, "As a shepherd cares for his herd in the day. . . , so I will care for My sheep" (Ezek. 34:12).

Second, this exclusive claim of "I am" states His sufficiency. A shepherd assumed the total responsibility to meet all the needs of his sheep. This imagery pictures Jesus attending to all the needs of His people. This is precisely what David states: "The Lord is my shepherd, I shall not want" (Ps. 23:1). This means He supplies all of the needs of all His people. Jesus will say to His disciples, "Apart from Me you can do nothing" (John 15:5), and Paul writes, "I can do all things through Him who strengthens me" (Phil. 4:13). To know this Shepherd is to know the One who meets all the needs of His flock. Whether directly or indirectly, whether personally or providentially, He has assumed the care of His own.

Jesus' Uniqueness and Goodness

Next, this exclusive claim of "I am" means that He is the one and only Good Shepherd. He is not merely one of many good shepherds, but is *the* Good Shepherd.

There are no other good shepherds but this one. He is the only Shepherd of His sheep who is leading them into the presence of God. Peter testified, "There is salvation in no one else; for there is no other name under heaven that has been given among men by which we must be saved" (Acts 4:12). There is no other shepherd who can rescue perishing sinners or meet their needs except this Shepherd, the Lord Jesus Christ.

Fourth, this exclusive claim of "I am" is a guarantee of His goodness. When Jesus says, "I am the good shepherd," He is pledging Himself to meet all the needs of His flock. This word "good" (*kalos*) means "noble, excellent, beautiful, choice, ideal, superior." This is the kind of shepherd Jesus is. He is perfect in His person, character, and being. As the Good Shepherd, He always does good to His sheep all their days. David writes, "Goodness and lovingkindness will follow me all the days of my life, and I will dwell in the house of the LORD forever" (Ps. 23:6).

No preacher will ever preach any better than when he proclaims the exclusive claims of this Good Shepherd, Jesus Christ. If the flock is to be fed, the more they must be told of Him. There needs to be less of the preacher and more of Jesus in his preaching. No true preacher wants his congregation to be deprived of hearing about Jesus. Pastors must point their listeners to this Chief Shepherd (1 Peter 5:4). We must do all that we can to hold forth His goodness, glory, and greatness.

The Excellent Character of Jesus

Jesus Christ also testifies to His excellent character. He does more than simply announce that He is the Good Shepherd; He proceeds to give compelling reasons why He is the Good Shepherd. Jesus offers four reasons why He is this Good Shepherd: He dies for His sheep, loves them, gathers them, and unites them.

Jesus Dies for His Sheep

Of first importance, Jesus explains His excellent character by asserting that He dies for His sheep. He says, "The good shepherd lays down His life for the sheep" (v. 11). This figurative language pictures His substitutionary death on behalf of His sheep in order to protect His sheep who are constantly exposed to great danger. When His flock is vulnerable and defenseless, the Good Shepherd delivers them from the danger in which they find themselves by laying down His life unto death.

Jesus stresses the voluntary nature by which He lays down His life for the sheep. When He says, "The good shepherd lays down His life for the sheep," He indicates that His life would not be taken by others, but be given by Him. Jesus will stress this aspect of His death five times in this passage (vv. 11, 15, 17, 18a, 18b). He will say, "I lay it down on My own initiative," and "I have authority to lay it down" (v. 18). To be sure, this means that His blood was not spilt, but was poured out. Further, this indicates that the cross was not a human accident but a divine appointment. He did not say, "I am finished," but "It is finished" (19:30). Jesus chose the time and place to give His life for the sheep.

This statement, "The good shepherd lays down His life for the sheep," also emphasizes the vicarious nature of His death. The little preposition "for" (*huper*) is vitally important. As large doors swinging on small hinges, major theology hinges on this little preposition "for." *Huper* means "for the benefit of, for the sake of, instead of, in the place of." This teaches the substitutionary nature of the death of Jesus Christ. He died in the place of His sheep. Elsewhere, Jesus said, "The Son of Man did not come to be served, but to serve, and to give His life a ransom for many" (Matt. 20:28). The apostle Paul said the same: "[the Lord Jesus Christ] gave Himself for our sins" (Gal. 1:4). Additionally, Christ "gave Himself up for us" (Eph. 5:2).

Moreover, Jesus states how specific His death would be. When He says, "The good shepherd lays down His life for the sheep," He stresses it is for the sheep that He will die. The sheep are those who have been given to Him by the Father before they ever come to Him (v. 29). They are those who recognize His voice and are drawn to it. The sheep are those who are led out of apostate Israel to follow the shepherd. Jesus will lay down His life for His sheep, but not for other sheep who are not His own possession. Nor will He die for the thieves and robbers who are not His sheep. Not every person in the world has been given to Him by the Father (v. 26). But all for whom Jesus dies will never perish. With these words, Jesus is the Expositor of the cross, interpreting His own death and teaching a definite atonement. According to Jesus, He did not die a universal atonement for an anonymous group of unnamed people. Rather, He made a definite atonement for those who have been chosen by the Father in eternity past and given to Him. He died for those sheep whom He calls by name.

When Jesus says, "I lay down My life for the sheep," His words are abundantly clear concerning for whom He died. He repeats the exclusive nature of His atonement: "I lay down My life *for the sheep*" (v. 15; emphasis added). The intent of Jesus in dying upon the cross defines the extent of His death. Answer why He died, and you will know for whom He died. In this discourse, Jesus teaches that He did not come to die for the entire sheepfold. If Jesus died for everyone, then all would be saved. But He came for His sheep, and it is for His sheep that He will die. None of them will ever perish.

This specific extent of the atonement is further taught in an analysis of the unity of the Trinity. Jesus will say, "My Father, who has given them to Me" (v. 29), referring to the sheep who hear His voice and follow Him (v. 27). These are the same sheep to whom He gives eternal life (v. 28). None of these sheep will ever perish or be snatched out of His hand or the hand of the Father (v. 29). Jesus then says, "I and the Father are one" (v. 30). This does not mean that the Father and the Son are one person. Such a statement would be heretical. Instead, this claim means the Father and the Son are one in mission, one in purpose, one in saving intent. Those whom the Father has chosen have been given to the Son, and the Son has received them as the Father's love gift. In turn, the Son has come into this world to be the Good Shepherd who lays down His life exclusively for the very same sheep that the Father chose and entrusted to Him.

A few years ago, I spent some time at London Seminary. It happened to be the week of the annual John Owen lecture series, and I asked some of the pastors who were attending the conference, "What in particular is the focus of the conference?" They explained that the lectures were addressing Owen's teaching on definite atonement. So I asked them to give me the most convincing argument that this great Puritan theologian offered for definite atonement. According to this Puritan divine, they replied that it is the unity of the Trinity. Specifically, it is how the Father, the Son, and the Holy Spirit operate in perfect harmony as one Savior, saving one group of people.

This oneness in purpose is why Jesus commanded that baptism is to be in the name of the Father, the Son, and the Holy Spirit (Matt. 28:19). All three persons of the Godhead work together in perfect unity, each one a Savior, saving one flock of sheep. This cohesive unity necessitates a definite atonement by Jesus to work in oneness with the saving purpose of the Father. Before time, the Father chose His elect, and within time, God the Son laid down His life for those same chosen ones. Day by day, God the Spirit then regenerates them. Otherwise, God the Father would choose to save those who believe. But God the Son would die to save a totally different group, the entire world. However, the Spirit would try to save yet a different group, those who hear the gospel. This incoherent view fractures the unity of the Trinity, resulting in three different missions.

By stark contrast to this view, Jesus says that He lays down His life for those sheep whom the Father gave to Him. Jesus states that He will die for those who are "My own" (v. 14). Elsewhere, Jesus says that He lays down His life for His friends—namely, His disciples (15:13). Paul teaches that Christ purchased the church with His blood (Acts 20:28). The apostle also writes that Jesus died for the elect (Rom. 8:33). He later emphasizes that Christ gave Himself for His bride, the church (Eph. 5:25). The author of Hebrews writes that Jesus tasted death for "His brethren," who are "the children God has given me" by the Father (Heb. 2:9, 13). Each of these passages teaches the particular atonement of the Good Shepherd, Jesus Christ.

At the cross, Jesus did not purchase the entire world and receive, in return, only those who believe in Him. Instead, there was perfect equity at Calvary. There was no injustice or inequity at the cross. Jesus received all whom He purchased. He was not shortchanged or gypped. Jesus was not cheated in His redemption of sinners. He was not stiffed at Golgotha. Jesus will preserve all that He bought— no more, no less. All whom He redeemed at the cross are His eternal possession.

Some push back, pointing to verses teaching that Jesus died for the world. But such interpreters fail to recognize that "world" (*cosmos*) is used ten different ways in the gospel of John. Only one of those ten uses means, literally, everybody. Nine of these ten has a different meaning. It would be a rush to judgment to go into any text in the gospel of John with the preconceived notion that "world" automatically means every person. For example, Jesus prays, "I am not praying for the world but for those whom you have given me" (17:9). Here, He limits His intercession to those given to Him by the Father. Similarly, Jesus' intercession on the cross would be for the same group for whom He intercedes in prayer. And His present intercession at the right hand of the Father is likewise for the same group for whom He interceded in prayer.

In total contrast to the Good Shepherd are the false shepherds of Israel. Jesus addresses them, saying, "He who is a hired hand, and not a shepherd, who is not the owner of the sheep, sees the wolf coming, and leaves the sheep and flees, and the wolf snatches them and scatters them" (v. 12). These other shepherds—"the hired hand"—are the Pharisees, the very ones to whom He is speaking. They are entirely antithetical to Him, the Good Shepherd. These hirelings are the false shepherds of Israel, who, when they see the wolf coming, leave the sheep and thus expose them to great danger. They abandon the sheep in tough times, because they are not the owner of the sheep. When the wolf comes, Jesus explains, "He flees because he is a hired hand and is not concerned about the sheep" (v. 13). These Pharisees are not the true owners of the sheep and have no interest in protecting them at the cost of their life. The Pharisees also do not recognize the voice of Jesus, because they are not one of His sheep. His teaching is an empty noise in their ears. They cannot hear what Jesus is saying because they do not have ears to hear.

Jesus Loves His Sheep

Jesus gives a further reason why He is the Good Shepherd. It is because He loves His sheep. In verse 14, Jesus repeats the exclusive claim that He made earlier: "I am the good shepherd." This reaffirmation distinguishes Him from the false shepherds to whom He was speaking. When He adds, "I know my own," this does not mean that He has an intellectual knowledge of their existence. He does not say, "I know about my own." While it is certainly true that

He knows about them, His statement here has more in view.

When Jesus says "know" (*ginosko*), He means "to know intimately, to love, to choose to love." That Jesus knows His sheep states that He has the most intimate, loving relationship with them. Elsewhere in Scripture, this word is used to represent the physical intimacy between a husband and wife (Matt. 1:25). The Hebrew equivalent (*yadah*) is used in the same way to describe that Adam "knew" his wife intimately, and she conceived and gave birth to a son (Gen. 4:1). In the same way, this indicates how Jesus knows His sheep with a deep, redeeming love.

This knowing is reciprocal: "and My own know Me" (v. 14). The order of this knowing is significant. Jesus first knew His sheep in eternity past, and then His sheep know Him within time. This gives insight into what the word *foreknowledge* means, which has nothing to do with foresight. God has never looked down the proverbial tunnel of time and learned anything. Such is a blasphemous view of God. Instead, foreknowledge means that God previously loved His elect and set His heart upon them. It speaks to His eternal covenant love that is intimate, personal, and sovereign. We know and love Him because He first knew and loved us.

The great English evangelist George Whitefield delighted in preaching on the conversion of Zacchaeus and noted that Jesus saw Zacchaeus in the sycamore tree (Luke 19:5). Whitefield paused and stressed that, of course, He saw him in the sycamore tree. Jesus foreknew him from all eternity past. There was no way He could miss him within time. This is the long-standing love relationship that the Good Shepherd has had with His sheep.[1]

Jesus also states the measure to which He knows His sheep: "even as the Father knows Me and I know the Father; and I lay down My life for the sheep" (v. 15). The closeness of this relationship is indicated in the small preposition "with," used also in the first verse of the gospel of John: "In the beginning was the Word, and the Word was with God." "With" (*pros*) means "face-to-face with." Throughout eternity past, Jesus was face to face before the Father, in closest, loving fellowship with Him. John also records that Jesus was "in the bosom of the Father" (1:18), indicating the close intimacy that has existed between the Father and the Son from all time. This same closeness is the exact same intimacy with which Jesus knows His sheep and His sheep know Him.

Jesus Gathers His Sheep

A third reason why Jesus is the Good Shepherd is that He draws and gathers His lost sheep to Himself. He says, "I have other sheep, which are not of this fold;

---

[1] George Whitefield, "The Conversion of Zacchaeus," *Bible Bulletin Board* website, http://www.biblebb.com/files/whitefield/GW035.htm.

I must bring them also" (v. 16). This allegory began with Jesus calling His sheep out of the spiritual deadness of apostate Israel. When He says that He has "other sheep" that are not of this fold, He refers to Gentile sheep that are outside the fold of Israel. Jesus must also draw them to Himself. This is a worldwide enterprise by which these other sheep will come to Him. They will come from "every tribe and tongue and people and nation" and comprise a number that is "myriads of myriads, and thousands of thousands" (Rev. 5:9, 11).

When Jesus says, "I have other sheep," He makes the claim in the present tense. Though they have not yet come to Him, He already possesses them. This is because the Father chose them in eternity past and gave them to Him. Before time began, He was given them by the Father, and they are presently His possession.

These sheep who are given to Him, Jesus says, must come to Him: "I must bring them also" (v. 16). This is the must of divine necessity. It is the must of divine certainty. It is the must of divine sovereignty, effectual calling, and irresistible drawing. When He says, "I must bring them," He indicates that they will not come on their own. The Bible elsewhere confirms this: "All of us like sheep have gone astray, each of us has turned to his own way" (Isa. 53:6). This teaches the wayward nature of all sheep. These lost sheep must be brought because they would not come otherwise.

This "I must bring them" is inseparably connected with what follows: "they will hear My voice" (v. 16). There is an inseparable connection between "I must" and "they will." These other sheep who must be brought will hear His voice and come to Him. By divine certainty, all the sheep for whom Christ dies will also come to Him. Jesus teaches, "All that the Father gives Me will come to Me" (6:37). The reason the sheep have come to Jesus Christ is not that they are smarter than the other sheep. Nor are they more spiritually sensitive or attuned. It is because Jesus must bring them and they will hear His voice.

The great English preacher Charles Haddon Spurgeon lifted up his voice, declaring this truth of sovereign grace. In one particular sermon, the Prince of Preachers cried out,

> Oh! I love God's "shalls" and "wills." There is nothing comparable to them. Let a man say "shall," what is it good for? "I will," says man, and he never performs; "I shall," says he and he breaks his promise. But it is never so with God's "shalls." If he says, "shall," it shall be; when he says, "will," it will be. Now he has said here, "many shall come." The devil says, "they shall not come. " but "they shall come."

You, yourselves, say, "we won't come." God says, "you shall come."[2]

Spurgeon then announced that despite the resistance of the sheep, they will come. No matter their aversion to the gospel, they will come to faith in Jesus Christ:

> Yes! there are some here who are laughing at salvation, who can scoff at Christ, and mock at the gospel; but I tell you some of you shall come yet. "What!" you say, "can God make me become a Christian?" I tell you yes, for herein rests the power of the gospel. It does not ask your consent; but it gets it. It does not say will you have it, but it makes you willing in the day of God's power.... The gospel wants not your consent, it gets it. It knocks the enmity out of your heart. You say, "I do not want to be saved;" Christ says you shall be. He makes your will turn round, and then you cry, "Lord, save, or I perish." Ah, might heaven exclaim, "I knew I would make you say that," and then he rejoices over you because he has changed your will and made you willing in the day of his power.[3]

Concluding this powerful sermon, Spurgeon trumpeted the inevitable triumph of the sovereign grace of God:

> If Jesus Christ were to stand on this platform to-night, what would many people do with him.... If he were to come and say; "Here I am, I love you, will you be saved by me?" Not one of you would consent if you were left to your own will.... He himself said, "No man can come to me except the Father who sent me draws him." Ah! we want that, and here we have it. They shall come! They shall come!... Christ shall not die for nothing.... Christ shall see his seed.[4]

This truth of divine sovereignty in salvation enables preachers to proclaim the gospel with great confidence. This makes His servants bold in heralding the

---

[2] Charles Spurgeon, "Heaven and Hell," in *Spurgeon: New Park Street Pulpit: 347 Sermons from the Prince of Preachers* (OSNOVA, 2012).
[3] Ibid.
[4] Ibid.

gospel of Jesus Christ, knowing that as they preach, God works powerfully in human hearts. Those who put up the greatest resistance can be brought to faith in Jesus Christ when they are made to hear the voice of their shepherd.

Jesus Unites His Sheep

There is yet another reason why Jesus is the Good Shepherd: He unites His sheep into one flock. With the same certainty, Jesus says, "They will become one flock with one shepherd" (v. 16). Here, He stresses that they will become one flock. They will no longer be scattered abroad in many different flocks. There will not be a separate Baptist flock. Nor will there be an isolated Presbyterian flock or an Independent flock. There will not be a Messianic Jew flock. There will not even be a Reformed flock or an Arminian flock. Nor will there be a distinct Charismatic flock. Instead, there will be "one flock with one shepherd."

When George Whitefield preached, he would sometimes look up into heaven and ask, "Lord, are there any Baptists in heaven?" Whitefield then gave the answer, as if from the throne of God, "There are no Baptists here." He then asked, "Lord, are there any Presbyterians in heaven?" The answer came, "Not a single Presbyterian in heaven." Then, "Are there any Congregationalists? Are there any Methodists? Are there any Independents?" Each time, the answer rolled down from the throne of grace: "No, there are none like that known here in heaven." Whitefield finally asked, "Then, who is in heaven?" Whitefield gave the answer from above: "Only those sheep who have been washed in the blood of the Lamb."[5]

This is the point that Jesus is making. There is only one flock that comprises all His sheep. But tragically, as I hear some Christians talk, when we get to heaven, it is as though we are going to be in different rooms, divided into many separate groups. To the contrary, we will all be as one flock, with one shepherd.

The Emphatic Choice of Jesus

Jesus concludes His explanation of the cross by stressing how intentional will be His death for His sheep. Jesus said, "For this reason the Father loves Me, because I lay down My life so that I may take it again" (v. 17). Here, Jesus states that the Father loves His Son because He obeys His will. God the Father loves obedience and delights in seeing His will performed. The Father loves perfect compliance to His eternal purpose. The Son has not come into this world to do His own will. He did not come to do His own thing. The Father loves the Son because He laid

---

[5] Story adapted from Joseph Belcher, *George Whitefield: A Biography, with Special Reference to His Labors in America* (New York: American Tract Society, 1857), 207.

down His life in full obedience to the direction of the Father.

When Jesus said, "I lay down My life so that I may take it again" (v. 17), He uses figurative language that refers to His death and resurrection. The cross will not be the end but will be followed by the empty tomb. Jesus stresses, "No one has taken it away from Me" (v. 18). This is a strong negative denial that no one will take His life from Him. No Roman ruler can do so. No Jewish leaders, angry mob, or unruly circumstances will take His life. No demon spirits or devil will take His life. They will only be secondary causes under the primary cause of the sovereign will of God. "I lay it down on my own initiative. I have authority to lay it down" (v. 18). "Authority" (*exousia*) means "out of one's own being, out of one's own self." By this statement, Jesus claimed to possess the right to exercise power over His own being.

Even in His incarnation, Jesus retained the supreme authority to exercise His right to lay down His life at the time and place of His own choosing. Jesus possessed uncontested authority to lay down His life, and He had unrivaled authority to take it up again. Jesus gave His life unto death and then raised Himself from the dead. In reality, the resurrection of Jesus Christ was a Trinitarian resurrection in that all three persons of the Godhead were involved in the resurrection of Jesus. Jesus nevertheless raised Himself from the dead, and He came walking out of the tomb a risen, living, victorious Savior who is able to save His sheep.

Jesus concludes this discourse by stating, "This commandment I received from My Father" (v. 18). This commandment refers to His saving mission that He was given by the Father. He was commanded by the Father to leave heaven, be born of a virgin under the Law, and live in perfect obedience to the Father. Jesus came to earth under strict orders from His Father. Before the world began, the Father gave His chosen sheep to His Son to be His future bride. The Father then commanded the Son to enter this world, live a sinless life in order to secure the perfect righteousness that is given to His sheep in the act of justification. Jesus was commanded to give His life for His sheep and then raise Himself from the dead. In response to this command, Jesus obeyed the Father.

A Good Shepherd to Worship and Follow

How can any of the sheep ever come to the Lord's table the same again? Are not our hearts melted down with love for this Good Shepherd? That our names were written upon His heart as He was hanging upon the cross must cause our hearts to explode with affection for Him. Are not our eyes filled with tears? Do not our voices quiver when we take communion? Do not our jaws drop and our knees bend before God every time we take the bread and the cup as we remember His death?

This is the Christ every undershepherd must imitate in their shepherding. They must give themselves to the flock entrusted to them. They must lay down their lives for the good of the sheep. They must know them and call them by name. They must allow themselves to be known by the flock. They must do all that they can to unite the sheep in one flock.

Have you ever taken that decisive step of faith and come all the way to saving faith in this shepherd? You must respond to the voice of the Good Shepherd. You must come to Him by faith and entrust your life to Him. The Bible says, "Whoever will call on the name of the Lord will be saved" (Rom. 10:13). He invites you to come to Him by entering through the narrow gate. The gate is small and the way is narrow that leads to life, and few are those who find it. Take that step of faith and come to the Good Shepherd of His sheep.

7

THE WAY, THE TRUTH, AND THE LIFE

JOHN 14:6

Miguel Nuñez

In John's gospel, we find a lengthy discussion of the events that took place the night before Christ was crucified. Looking at chapters 13 and 14, we will emphasize some of the most remarkable words that Christ uttered on that occasion. At the end of the day before the Passover, Jesus and His disciples went into the upper room to share their last supper together. After gathering together those whom He loved to the end (13:1), Jesus began to unfold to them the suffering that He would face in the following hours. The Master communicated clearly to them not only the ordeal ahead of Him but also how they could still have hope despite His impending departure. They did not understand and they became confused.

As He spoke to them, they posed a number of questions. One of these questions came from Thomas, and Jesus answered him, "I am the way, and the truth, and the life; no one comes to the Father but through Me" (John 14:6). These words uttered by Jesus at one of the most critical moments in His entire life must be among the most hated statements in our pluralistic, relativistic, anti-authority, postmodern, and post-Christian society. In fact, many believers would not even dare to repeat those words in the workplace, for fear of being rejected or being considered narrow-minded and unsophisticated.

That is the milieu in which we live today. In a pluralistic society, people with different cultures and beliefs should be able to enjoy freedom of religion and coexist peacefully. Nevertheless, when we move from such a healthy idea to the conviction that every belief is just as valid as the next, then we can expect a society that has no value for truth and, therefore, no value for Christ. Such is our society. In some ways, this is not new. As Pilate asked the question, "What is truth?" he did not wait for the answer. Instead, he turned around and left the immediate presence of the only person who embodied the truth. Pilate neither had any value for truth nor for Christ, and that was two thousand years ago.

Confusion around the Person of Jesus Today

We live in the middle of what some have called a "soteriological pluralism"—the idea that different religions can lead to God, especially if people are sincere. A U.S. Religious Landscape Survey conducted in 2007 by the Pew Research Center reported that "most Americans who claim a religious affiliation take a non-exclusivist view of salvation, with seven in ten saying that many religions can lead to eternal life while less than one-quarter say theirs is the one, true faith leading to eternal life."[1] The Roman Catholic Church has been moving in that direction ever since the Second Vatican Council (1962–1965) when it stated, "Those who through no fault of their own, do not know the Gospel of Christ or His Church, but who nevertheless seek God with a sincere heart, and, moved by grace, try in their actions to do his will as they know it, through the dictates of their conscience—those too may achieve eternal salvation."[2]

As one can see, rather than reforming itself in the right direction, the Church of Rome continues to distance itself from biblical revelation. Sadly, many evangelical leaders have come to believe and teach this very doctrine. If evangelical Christians arrive at such a conclusion, they must understand that the only way to do so is by disregarding Jesus' teaching altogether. The New Testament teaches, in different ways and passages, the exclusivity of our faith, but many have succumbed to the pressure of our times.

Others consider themselves "particular inclusivists." They call themselves "particular" because they believe that Christ's saving work is essential for one to be saved. And they called themselves "inclusivists" because they understand that those who do not know Christ can be saved through other mediators or religions.[3] Clark Pinnock, for example, affirmed that we cannot negotiate the saving work of Jesus Christ.[4] From this point of view, he would be considered a "par-

---

[1] Pew Research Center Religion and Public Life, "Many Americans Say Other Faiths Can Lead to Eternal Life," December 18, 2008, http://www.pewforum.org/2008/12/18/many-americans-say-other-faiths-can-lead-to-eternal-life/.
[2] Catholic Church, *The Catechism of the Catholic Church* (Libreria Editrice Vaticana, 2000), Article 847.
[3] Ronald H. Nash, *Is Jesus the Only Savior?* (Grand Rapids: Zondervan, 1994), 103–16.
[4] Clark Pinnock, "The Finality of Jesus Christ in a World of Religions," in *Christian Faith and Practice in the Modern World*, eds. Mark Knoll and David F. Wells (Grand Rapids: Eerdmans, 1988).

ticularist." However, Pinnock, along with others, believed that Christ's work on behalf of mankind allows people to be saved through different pathways that lead to God. So, this second belief would make him an inclusivist.[5]

Now, if we merge the two ideas, he would qualify as a "particular inclusivist." In other words, Christ's saving work is what allows others to act as mediators of salvation through different religions or pathways, thus contradicting the apostle Paul's words in 1 Timothy 2:5: "For there is one God, and one mediator also between God and men, the man Christ Jesus."

It's amazing to see how many inclusivists take the exclusive claims of Christ and change their meanings to fit their own ideas. One example of this error can be seen in the teaching of Deepak Chopra, who believes that when Jesus says, "I am the way, the truth, and the life, no one comes to the Father, except through me," it is nothing more than Jesus' attaining "God-consciousness."[6] Jesus was not gaining God-consciousness. If He did, then He must have been a liar, since He affirmed to be God from all eternity.

For many, Jesus is just one great teacher among many. That may be politically correct in our generation. However, it is not biblical—and it is not even logically consistent. Jesus accepted the worship of men, and in different ways affirmed His own divinity. If He was not, He was, then, either a deceiver or a lunatic, but not a great teacher since a good teacher must be a truthful teacher.[7] Salvation requires people to believe not in a Jesus that is superior to others in some respects, but in a Jesus who is equal to no one. "He is something other than all men."[8]

As stated already, many are convinced that all pathways lead to God, and such is only true if we are thinking about the judgment seat of Christ as Paul stated: "We must all appear before the judgment seat of Christ, so that each one may be recompensed for his deeds in the body, according to what he has done, whether good or bad" (2 Cor. 5:10). As such, the Christian, the Hindu, the Buddhist, the moralist, and the rest of humanity will all stand before God one day, but before His judgment seat. In some sense, the question is not whether the path I am following will bring me to God. Rather, the question is: On what basis am I going to stand before Him? For if we do not stand by faith in Christ, our Redeemer, we will not stand at all. We must stand by faith on the finished work of Christ and Christ alone. All paths will bring us to God, but only one will continue to glory with Him. All others will result in eternal damnation.

---

[5] Nash, *Is Jesus the Only Savior?*, 103–106.
[6] Ravi Zacharias, *Why Jesus?: Rediscovering His Truth in an Age of Mass Marketed Spirituality* (New York: Faith Words, 2012), 261.
[7] Josh McDowell, *The New Evidence that Demands a Verdict* (Nashville: Thomas Nelson Publishers, 1999), 158–63.
[8] Rod Rosenbladt, *Christ Alone*, Kindle version (Irvine, CA: NRP Books, an imprint of 1517), 387.

Christ's Teaching about Himself

These words in John 14:6—"I am the way, and the truth, and the life"—are part of a long conversation that took place between Christ and His disciples in the upper room the night before His crucifixion. The hours before our Lord's death were incredibly dark and gloomy. That night, Jesus told His disciples that He was going to leave them. He then made an announcement of His betrayal, followed by an announcement regarding His death. He also stated that one of them was going to deny Him. Additionally, He mentioned to them that the entire group was going to abandon Him soon.

Try to picture yourself in the midst of all those announcements. They really couldn't quite follow the Master as He continued to set the stage of what would transpire in only a few hours. We can only imagine how tense the atmosphere must have been. The disciples were probably emotionally disturbed, perhaps even terrified! And Christ knew it. That is why He began this portion of the conversation with these words: "Do not let your heart be troubled; believe in God, believe also in Me" (John 14:1). In saying this, Jesus was seeking to assure them, but the assurance was in Him and not in their circumstances.

Moments before those words were pronounced, Jesus said to them, "Little children, I am with you a little while longer. You will seek Me; and as I said to the Jews, now I also say to you, 'Where I am going, you cannot come'" (John 13:33). Jesus frequently led people to ask questions that He desired to answer with astonishing revelations, for their benefit. Immediately after these words, a question arose, then another, and another, and finally a fourth. What do we do when we don't understand something? We ask questions, as did they. Peter asked the first question (13:36), then Thomas (14:5), then Philip (14:8), and finally Judas (not Iscariot; 14:22). Peter asked: "Lord, where are You going?" Jesus answered, "Where I go, you cannot follow Me now; but you will follow later" (13:36).

The conversation in the upper room continued to progress as Jesus revealed more important truths in anticipation of His departure: "If I go and prepare a place for you, I will come again and receive you to Myself, that where I am, there you may be also. And you know the way where I am going" (John 14:3–4). Thomas, then, asked a logical question, "Lord, we do not know where You are going, how do we know the way?" One can see how confused they were. Jesus told them first that He was going to a place that they do not know and where they could not follow Him, and then that even though they do not know *where* He is going, they do know the *way*. Thomas asked the question that Jesus was looking to answer: "how do we know the way?" So Jesus answered: "I am the way, and the truth, and the life; no one comes to the Father but through Me."

One step at a time, Christ led the disciples to ask the questions that would result in the answers they needed to know. This time the answer was about Jesus' self-identity. One remarkable feature about Jesus was how frequently He spoke about who He was as opposed to what He was doing. Often, when He did something for someone, He instructed that person not to tell anyone. Yet such was not the case when He revealed who He was to them. He was very open about who He was.

Consider these pronouncements that appear in the Gospel of John:

- I am the bread of life (6:35)
- I am the light of the world (8:12)
- I am the door (10:9)
- I am the good shepherd (10:11)
- I am the resurrection and the life (11: 25–26)
- I am the way and the truth and the life (14:6)
- I am the true vine (15:1)

The text being discussed in this chapter is the sixth "I am" statement of Jesus Christ. Every single "I am" phrase that appears in John's gospel expresses His self-identity. It's been said by more than one author that the gospel of John contains more revelation by Christ about Himself than any other New Testament book or letter. Christ was the object and the subject of the revelation of God, and for that reason, He spoke about Himself all the time.

The Jewish rabbis were unable to do that. They continually talked about the Law of Moses, which they called the Torah. For them, the authority was in the Law, and thus the rabbis debated based on the verdicts of the Torah. For Christ, however, the authority was not in the Torah but in Himself. When Christ came, He dared to say: "You have heard that it was said; but I say to you . . ." Other teachers spoke about what the Torah said. Jesus spoke about who He was: "I am the way, and the truth, and the life." He was the Lord of the Torah and the giver of the Law, which He came to fulfill. The rabbis spoke of the content of the Torah, but Christ spoke of the essence of His being: I am, I am, I am. Again, these "I am" statements were Jesus' self-identity or self- revelation. When the rich, young ruler approached Jesus to ask what he must do to obtain eternal life, Jesus did not say that he should follow the Torah. In fact, this young man told Jesus that he had fulfilled all the commandments of the Torah. But Jesus said to him, "Go and sell all that you have and follow me." He was and is the way.

Eternal life is not found in rituals, books, mantras, prophets, or teachers. Rather, it is found in Him who is the way, the truth, and the life. Jesus did not say, "I tell you the truth." No. One can tell the truth today and lie tomorrow. Jesus said, "I *am* the truth." With that phrase, He defined the essence of His being. He would never lie because truth is what He is. Jesus did not say, "I will show you the way." Rather, He said, "I *am* the way. Therefore, just follow me." He was a person to relate to, not a religious system. He was a person to follow, not a law to obey. He was a teacher to learn from, not a despot that dictates verdicts. Jesus did not say, "I am capable of giving life," though indeed He was able. Rather, He said, "I *am* the life." If He is the life, then anyone not found in Christ is dead.

No one before had ever spoken like Jesus, and no one has since. In fact, no one could ever. Only God can speak the way He did. As James Edwards says, most religions try to encapsulate their main teaching in one single phrase.[9] For Judaism, the key phrase was the Shema: "Hear, O Israel! The LORD is our God, the LORD is one" (Deut. 6:4). For Islam, it is: "There is no God but Allah, and Muhammad is his prophet." The Buddhists speak of the Four Noble Truths. For communists, the key phrase was: "From each according to his ability, and to each according to his need."

It would be impossible to summarize Christ's essence or His teachings in a single sentence, but we could potentially summarize Christ's identity in relation to His mission in one phrase by quoting John 14:6: "I am the way, and the truth, and the life; no one comes to the Father but through Me." This single phrase tells us who He is, what He came for, and how to obtain eternal life. These are Jesus' four Spiritual Laws:

1. I am the way
2. I am the truth
3. I am the life
4. No one comes to the Father but through Me

Having covered Christ's statement broadly, let us now review each phrase separately.

Jesus Is the Way

Before the fall, Adam had access to God, but he eventually sinned and could not find the way back to his Creator. He lost the map, as it were. In the garden, Satan offered the fruit to Adam and Eve, making it the perfect garden temptation. But if you are in a sophisticated society like ours, then the temptation or enticement

---

[9] James R. Edwards, *Is Jesus the Only Savior?* (Grand Rapids: Eerdmans, 2005), 100.

would be more refined or savvy. So, Satan has offered different avenues to man according to the times and cultures:

- Morality
- Philosophy
- Religion
- Your best effort

And under each one of them he has placed a suffix that says, "to God":

- Morality to God
- Philosophy to God
- Different religions to God
- Your best effort to God

Being in such a condition, the only way to return to God would be if a person came from God and, knowing the way, take us there. That is precisely what Jesus did.

First, He said earlier in His ministry, "No one has ascended into heaven, but He who descended from heaven: the Son of Man" (John 3:13). Later, that final night with His disciples, He added, "If I go and prepare a place for you, I will come again and receive you to Myself, that where I am, there you may be also" (14:3). He came and is taking us to where He now reigns.

The psalmist knew that man had lost his way, so he cries out to God, "Teach me Your way, O LORD, And lead me in a level path because of my foes" (Ps. 27:11). If God doesn't show us the way, we will never find it. Yet if He were to show us the way and leave us alone to follow it, we would lose it again. So what did the Father do? He sent His Son, who takes us by the hand until we arrive home. He promised, "I will never desert you, nor will I ever forsake you" (Heb. 13:5).

A path is a way that joins two points. It takes you from one place to another. That is exactly what Jesus is. He is the:

- person who reconciles man to God;
- one who takes man from darkness to light;
- redeemer who takes us from slavery to freedom;
- person who finds an orphan and makes him into an adopted child;
- one who brings you from death to life.

That's why He is called the Way.

The primitive church knew this terminology well. In fact, they were called "the Way" on six different occasions in the book of Acts: 9:2, 19:9, 23; 22:4; 24:14, 22. "The Way" was considered a sect by outsiders and, therefore, worthy to be persecuted. People reject the idea of Christ being the only way because, in our fallen condition, we are born with a desire for being independent and autonomous. Rebellion is natural for us, and the crucifixion of the Son was the solution.

In his commentary on John, James Montgomery Boice speaks on three different ways of how man plans to reach God.[10] The first is the path of nature. Some think they can worship God by contemplating His creation rather than worshiping the Creator. Man would much rather do that. Surely, because creation cannot hold him accountable. The second is the path of morality. Here we find those who believe that a moral life, however they define it, will lead them to God. The problem is that even the most moral person still has fallen short, immensely short, of the glory of God. As it is written: "None is righteous, no, not one; no one understands; no one seeks for God. All have turned aside; together they have become worthless; no one does good, not even one" (Rom. 3:10b–12 ESV).

Many have entered into eternal damnation thinking that they accumulated enough good deeds to get into heaven. The problem is that their good deeds were actually bad deeds. Their best lives now brought them to the worst ending ever. There is only one thing worse than being lost without God and that is being lost all the while thinking that you were saved. This happens to the moralists. The apostle Paul was following this path for a while, and he then found the way. He says in Romans 7 that sin deceived him and that his sin used the commandments of the law to kill him (Rom. 7:11). He was following the commandments, believing all along that he was obeying them perfectly, yet he was falling short of each of them.

The way of religion is the third path. Many are convinced that their participation in church activities or their generosity pave their way to God. Sadly, these people will enter an eternity of condemnation. They were convinced but not converted. Others simply choose another religion such as Hinduism, Buddhism, or Islam. Christ is the way that is always before all people, but because unbelievers live in darkness, they cannot see what is in front of them. The lack of light does not allow them to see the way. The solution to their darkness is God's Word. As the psalmist said, "Your word is a lamp to my feet and a light to my path" (Ps. 119:105). The Truth lights the Way.

---

[10] James Montgomery Boice, *The Gospel of John*, vol. 4 (Grand Rapids: Baker Books, 1999), 1083–1085.

Jesus Is the Truth

Adam fell when he ceased to believe the truth and exchanged it for a lie. It was that simple. This very exchange is the origin of idolatry as revealed in Romans 1:25 ESV: "because they exchanged the truth about God for a lie [and now, the consequence] and worshiped and served the creature rather than the Creator, who is blessed forever! Amen." Man ended up worshiping the creature instead of the Creator because he exchanged the revelation of God for a lie. Every idol of the heart is the result of a lie that the mind has embraced. As a result of this embrace, man has become a slave to his own value system, which he built based on a distorted view of reality. We do not see things the way they are, but the way we are. Since we all are liars (Ps. 116:11), we perceive the truth as a lie and the lie as the truth until we are regenerated. Why? Once again, because we do not see things the way they are, but, rather, the way we are.

Christ is the lens that allows us to see things as they really are. The believers in the Old Testament believed the truth of God, but things were not very clear to them. Many things looked more like shadows of the truth. But Christ, being the culmination of the revelation of God, has revealed the realities behind those shadows. Without the truth, man cannot be saved. This is so true that Jesus summarized His entire mission, His entire purpose for coming, in one single verse: "For this I have been born, and for this I have come into the world, to testify to the truth" (John 18:37). Knowing the truth is paramount because it affects the entire spectrum of human existence. As Vince Vitale put it:

> If all truth is ultimately grounded in the person of God, then every question asked is a question asked about a person, and every answer given is an answer received from a person. Every question about science is a question about how and why God has made and sustains the universe as He has. Every question about morality is a question about the character of God. Every question about politics and economics is a question about what it means to be made in the image of God and granted dominion over the earth. Every truth, no matter the discipline, says something about who God is and what He has done.[11]

We cannot survive without the truth. Christ came not only to speak the truth but also to embody it. As such, we can now follow the Way, and we can now

---

[11] Vince Vitale, "Love the Truth," in *Jesus Among Secular Gods: The Countercultural Claims of Christ,* by Ravi Zacharias and Vince Vitale (New York: Faith Words, 2017), 229–230.

know Him, the Truth. Notice how the psalmist links the themes of the way and the truth: "Teach me Your way, O Lord; I will walk in Your truth" (Ps. 86:11). Why? Because His way is the way of truth, and only the true way can bring man to the true God. For that reason alone, "there is no other name under heaven that has been given among men by which we must be saved" (Acts 4:12).

In the same way that light dissipates the darkness and reveals everything once hidden in the darkness, truth dispels error and reveals what man is really like. Without truth, one cannot have a moral order and a moral world.

On May 10, 1996, a major storm descended upon the Himalayas; by the next day, eight mountain climbers from different expeditions had died trying to climb Mount Everest. Another four climbers died before the climbing season was over that year. Two Japanese climbers (Eisuke Shigekawa and Hiroshi Hanada) were ascending and passed by two of the climbers who were injured, freezing, and in danger. The two Japanese climbers apparently had enough provisions to share with them, but they decided to continue on without lending help. Shigekawa later recounted, "We were too tired to help. Above 8,000 meters is not a place where people can afford morality."[12]

One cannot have morality when one doesn't know the truth. The absence of Christ in the climbers explains why they did not stop to help two dying human beings who bore the image of God. Christ came to infuse our world with truth for the salvation of man. And when He infused truth into the world, He infused morality as well. Knowledge of the truth reveals that which is moral.

The exchange of the truth for a lie created a number of sinful pathways to God. The real spiritual warfare we are engaged in consists of fighting these different belief systems that compete with the single truth of God. We are in a battle for the truth. As a result of the fall, man is lost in darkness and ignorance.

Jesus Is the Life

The truth is Adam's problem was worse than simply that he lost his way to God and could not discern truth from error. He lost not only his ability to return home and the truth, but also his spiritual life. Adam could not keep one simple command: do not eat. As soon as Adam and Eve ate the fruit, they died. They lost communion with God, experienced fear and shame, and lost their purpose in life. Adam's descendants inherited the same impoverished life. For that reason, Jesus came to give us life abundant (John 10:10). Animals have one type of "life." Unbelievers have a better life than animals do. But only those who are

---

[12] Jon Krakauer, *Into Thin Air: A Personal Account of the Mt. Everest Disaster*, reprint edition (New York: Anchor Books, 2009), 302.

born again are truly alive. God's children have a regenerated soul and a body that awaits glorification. We have a better quality of life now and the very best awaiting us. The life that Jesus shares with the Father is the life that He gives to us. Yet unbelievers have a spiritually poor life now and the worst awaiting them.

In the same way that our parents died by eating the forbidden fruit, we come to life by eating of the bread of life. We need the forgiveness of God, certainly, but we also need the life of Christ. We need the cross, but we also need the resurrection because we were dead in sins and transgressions. Apart from Christ, there is no resurrection, and if there is no resurrection, there is neither life nor gospel. And if there is no gospel, there is no hope. It's incredible that Jesus gave us life by dying. His is the only death that gives life. I cannot be born again spiritually without His death. In Jesus' days, the funeral homes did not want Jesus near them. He was not good for business. Every time He showed up, the dead would come back to life. As light dissipates darkness, so His life dissipates death.

The unregenerate man is dead and, therefore, does not seek God. He cannot "because the mind set on the flesh is hostile toward God; for it does not subject itself to the law of God, for it is not even able to do so" (Rom. 8:7). The carnal mind is not interested in the things of God until it becomes alive through the new birth.

Apart from Christ, we may have existence, but we do not have true life. You must have Christ to have true life. Right before the resurrection of Lazarus, Jesus said to Martha, "I am the resurrection and the life; he who believes in Me will live even if he dies, and everyone who lives and believes in Me will never die. Do you believe this?" (John 11:25–26). From God's perspective, we experience life only when we are in intimate relationship with God, enjoying the fullness of His blessings. And this is only possible in Christ Jesus.

Unbelievers are dead in their trespasses and sins (Eph. 2:1). Dead people do not understand God's Word (the Bible) or His purposes for mankind. We come to life by knowing the Truth and following the Way.

Jesus Is the Only Way to God

When Christ said, "No one comes to the Father but through me," He was likely speaking the most offensive words that ever came from His lips. That single statement establishes Christianity as an exclusive faith. There is no other way of salvation. As Martyn Lloyd Jones said, "There is no knowledge of God apart from Him; there is no communication with God apart from Him."[13] Then he added,

---

[13] Martyn Lloyd Jones, *Let Not Your Heart Be Troubled* (Wheaton, IL: Crossway Books, 2009), 115.

"Unless this Christ, the Son of God, is in the central place as the only way to God, there is no gospel."[14]

If there is no gospel, there is no life. This is why Jesus wanted Mary and Martha—and all of us for that matter—to know that He is the resurrection and the life. If these words of Jesus were offensive then, imagine how offensive they must be today. The world hates it when we say that Jesus is the only way to God. Our pluralistic society does not like an exclusive truth, let alone one that is exclusive. I am convinced that we Christians are in the truth. But if we were not, then someone else is, and everyone else is not. Truth is always exclusive.

Some other religions are willing to accept Jesus as one of their many deities or great teachers. Error always has room for the truth, but the truth has no room for error. A person who makes counterfeit bills is willing to receive a real one from someone else, but a bank will not take a counterfeit from anyone. False religious systems can accommodate Christ into their beliefs, but Christianity will never do so with other religious leaders in addition to Jesus. Truth is always exclusive, as is Christianity.

Christ asserted that there is only one entrance into heaven: "Truly, truly, I say to you, he who does not enter by the door into the fold of the sheep, but climbs up some other way, he is a thief and a robber. But he who enters by the door is a shepherd of the sheep" (John 10:1–2). He goes on to define who that exclusive door is: "I am the door; if anyone enters through Me, he will be saved, and will go in and out and find pasture" (10:9). Jesus did not say He was one of many doors. Rather, He said He was *the* door. Jesus could not be more specific in identifying Himself as the only entrance into the kingdom of heaven. In Matthew 7:13–14, we learn more about this door: "Enter through the narrow gate; for the gate is wide and the way is broad that leads to destruction, and there are many who enter through it. For the gate is small and the way is narrow that leads to life, and there are few who find it."

There is only one way, and it is Christ. There is only one truth, and it is the one that He proclaimed: Himself. And there is only one eternal life, and it is the one that He gives.

In a pluralistic society, establishing the way is necessary. In a postmodern generation, affirming Christ as the source of absolute truth is vital. In a collapsing and dying Western culture, to proclaim Christ as the source of life is hope-giving to people. It is the pulling away from Him that brings about the demise of our society.

---

[14] Ibid.

Final Reflection

When Truth became incarnate in the person of Jesus, every religious system was negated, and Judaism was replaced. A new authority was in place. Because of it, no one has spoken as Jesus did. Think of these examples:

Buddha died looking for more enlightenment, which would require truth and light.[15] However, Christ said, "I am the truth," and "I am the light of the world." Buddha was looking for Jesus without knowing it. Jesus was the truth he was looking for.

Muhammad thought of himself as a prophet, but Christ thought of Himself as God. In fact, this is why the Jewish people wanted to kill him (Matt. 26:65; Luke 5:21; John 10:33). He accepted the worship of men yet did not consider equality with God something to be grasped (Phil. 2:6). He made Himself a man, a servant to all (Phil. 2:7–8).

Confucius apparently stated on one occasion, "I never said that I was holy."[16] But Jesus asked, "Which one of you convicts Me of sin?" The answer was no one. Confucius supposedly had a difficult relationship with his wife and died a divorced man.[17] Muhammad had thirteen wives and many concubines,[18] although the Qur'an only allows four.[19] And Buddha abandoned his wife and son when he left to search for enlightenment. But Christ died without sin:

- Pilate could not find any fault in Him. Pilate's wife called Him a righteous man.
- Herod found Him innocent.
- One of the thieves on the cross acknowledged that Jesus had done nothing wrong.
- The centurion at the foot of the cross said, "Surely this man was the Son of God."

Buddha taught for about twenty-five years and Muhammad for about twenty-two years. Confucius taught for about the same period of time. Among the three, they taught for almost seventy-five years. Jesus taught for only three, but no other person in human history has impacted the course of civilization as much as Jesus did in those three years.

---

[15] Erwin W. Lutzer, *Christ among Other gods* (Chicago: Moody Press, 1994), 113.

[16] This quote appears in multiple books and articles, but the original source seems to be unknown.

[17] Jonathan Clements, *Confucius, a Biography*, Kindle version (Albert Bridge Books, 2017), Loc 240 of 2445.

[18] Shamim Aleem, *Prophet Muhammad(s) and His Family: A Sociological Perspective* (Bloomington, IN: AuthorHouse, 2011), 85.

[19] See Holy Quran Chapter 4, Surah Nisaa verse 3.

Jesus was born in a manger in an obscure village, and yet His is the most famous birth in history. God the Father called Him "My Beloved Son." The prophets called Him "Messiah." Isaiah said that the child that will be born would be called "Wonderful Counselor, Mighty God, Everlasting Father, Prince of Peace." His disciples called Him "Master" and eventually "Son of God." Yet He called Himself "Son of Man." John called Him, "The Logos that was from the beginning with the Father." Demons called Him the "Holy One of God." He fulfilled the Law and became our jubilee. He was nailed to a cross where He paid for the sins of God's elect. The cross, an instrument of curse, became an instrument of blessing. Therefore, we called Him "Savior." When He died, hell trembled and He disarmed the rulers and the authorities and the spiritual forces of wickedness in the heavenly places (Col. 2:15). He was buried in a borrowed tomb that was closed with a large stone, and three days later, He left it open and empty. He fulfilled every prophecy about Him, put an end to the law, and then cried out, "It is finished!" And before He ascended into heaven, He gathered His disciples and said, "All authority has been given to Me in heaven and on earth. Go therefore and make disciples of all the nations, baptizing them in the name of the Father and the Son and the Holy Spirit, teaching them to observe all that I commanded you; and lo, I am with you always, even to the end of the age" (Matt. 28:18–20). He has all authority in heaven and on earth. No one goes to the Father but through Him. We either enter heaven through Him or we go to hell without Him, and that is the brutal truth. Therefore, knowing now the fear of the Lord, we must persuade men (2 Cor. 5:11). He is the way back to the garden, to the ultimate garden, the Promised Land, our final home. He is the truth that sets you free from bondage to sin and death. And He is the life in whom we live and move and have our being eternally.

He is the Christ we preach!

8

THE HEAD OF THE CHURCH

COLOSSIANS 1:18

Mark Dever

had the experience of living in England in the 1980s. At the time, there were festivals among evangelical churches trying to show how great it is to follow Jesus. Some held parades, which even included clowns. They were trying to communicate that Christians are great people who have a fun time. And they wanted non-Christians to join the fun. I was never part of one of those festivals, but I appreciated their attempt to witness for the gospel. However, I thought it was strange how they had chosen to witness what it meant to follow Jesus Christ.

There is a reason why when we preach Christ—who He is and what He's done—we inevitably turn to how the truth about Him affects us. Why? Because He is the One who bids us to come and take up our cross and follow Him. While the Christian life is indeed filled with joy, it is nevertheless a hard journey. It is one of cross-bearing, filled with many trials. In this chapter, I want to focus on endurance, continuing strong in the faith. And whom better to learn from than Paul?

When we consider Paul at the end of his life, as he writes about himself in 2 Timothy 4, we want to be like him, don't we? We want to breathe that rarefied air. We want to endure like he did, yet we also realize it's a challenge. We sometimes feel intimidated to call ourselves Christ's followers because we know the truth about our lives. I think whenever we consider how we can endure and be in the presence of God, we of course find ourselves talking about Jesus Christ most importantly, and Colossians 1.

Paul writes in verse 23, "If indeed you continue in the faith firmly established and steadfast, and not moved away from the hope of the gospel that you have heard." We want to not be moved from our hope that's held out in the gospel of Jesus Christ. In order to not be moved, we are wise to consider Paul's teaching here, especially verses 15–20, which discuss our beliefs about Christ, and verses 21–23, which discuss our belief in Christ.

Our Beliefs about Christ

In verses 15–20, Paul outlines our beliefs about Christ. Christ is the answer to the great questions about God, the world, the church, and the plot to humanity's story. In the very center and the answer of every single one of these is Christ. Let's consider four matters that Paul teaches us about Christ in this passage—that Christ shows us God, that Christ is the author of creation, that He is the author of the new creation, the church, and that He is the answer to our really big problem.

The Image of God

Verse 15 states that Christ shows us God. Paul wakes up these Colossian believers from their religious daydreaming by raising a simple issue: what kind of God are you worshiping? He wanted to help the Colossian believers rediscover the One they worshiped. This was important, of course, because unlike all the other people in Colossae, the God they worshiped was invisible.

Most of the people living in Colossae would have been pagans who worshiped at temples with images of their god. They would have learned legends about their god and they could tell you even what their god looked like. But the God that Paul was presenting was the invisible God, and that presented some challenges in understanding who this God was. Maybe you've always thought God could only have one meaning, but if you talk to people in the world today and begin asking them what they think of when you say the word God, you'll find they mean lots of differ things—many of which conflict with the Christian understanding of God. C. S. Lewis said that religious experience can be made to yield almost any sort of god.[1]

People refer to God as a voice, a fantasy, a term of poetry, a mere convention of language, a guarantee, a quality, a substance, a solution, or the epitome of human intelligence or creative force. When people say the word *God*, they mean many different and often divergent things. But the God who Paul is writing about is not simply the God of the earnest monotheists, the Creator and Sovereign of all. No, this God has come close to us.

---

[1] C. S. Lewis, *God in the Dock: Essays on Theology and Ethics*, ed. Walter Hooper (Grand Rapids: Wm. B. Eerdmans Publishing Co., 1970), 149.

One of the most incredible things about this great invisible God that Paul describes here is that this God wants to be known. In John 1, we learn that the Word was in the beginning and that the Word was with God. It is in the very nature of God to desire to communicate and establish relationship. We see this self-revealing quality of God in Colossians 1:15, where we read that He is the image of the invisible God, the firstborn over all creation. Or down to verse 19: "It was the Father's good pleasure for all the fullness to dwell in Him." Looking at verses 13 and 14, we learn that the "He" in verse 15 is the Lord Jesus Christ. Jesus is the visible expression of the invisible God. He shows us what the invisible God is like. Thus, Christ shows us what the content of the Christian faith about God is.

The Author of Creation

Christ is also the author of creation. Paul moves on in verse 15 to write about not only what God is like, but also what creation is like. I think he does this at least in part because it seems like the Colossian Christians had been tempted to wrongly understand the world. They are not so different from you and me. Many of us today have a basically secular idea of reality and then spread a little Jesus on top. Paul explains here how creation is related to Jesus Christ, and he makes five claims to help us understand clearly who Christ is.

First, Christ is eternal, and creation is limited. He says that Christ was before creation (v. 17). Paul denied any talk of an infinite, eternal world, the kind of philosophical materialism that reigns in universities and colleges today. Here Paul declares that Christ is eternal and this world is not. Therefore, by implication, the existence of Christ Himself is more a given than the existence of our world.

Second, Christ created all creation. Christ was the agent of creation. By Him, all things—which Paul mentions twice in verse 16—were created: "By Him all things were created, both in the heavens and on earth, visible and invisible, whether thrones or dominions or rulers or authorities—all things have been created through Him and for Him." There is only one God who's meant to be the sovereign of our lives and over the world He has made.

Paul restates this tersely and powerfully in verse 17: "He is before all things, and in Him all things hold together." The statement that He is "before" all things has a double connotation. Not only is He before all things temporally because He is eternal; He is before all things in terms of status. Christ is primary. He is first. In other words He is Lord. He is sovereign, as Paul indicated in verse 16.

Words and concepts like primary or precedence, even author and authority, are embedded in every culture around the world. The one who creates is the one who rules. Hebrews 7 uses this very idea in describing the majesty of Christ.

Paul reminds the Colossian Christians that God is the one who has created everything. He basically says, "Colossians, whatever being you would consider worshiping other than Christ—invisible heavenly thrones or powers or rulers or authority or earthly people or animals or image—they were all created by Him. Why would you worship what is created rather than the very One who created them?"

Third, Christ is the ruler of creation. He is the beginning, the firstborn, as Paul says (v. 18). That word "firstborn" has different connotations. It can mean firstfruits or the first of something in terms of time. It can also mean having pre-eminence in terms of status and authority, and that is clearly what Paul has in mind here. Christ was not a creature. If you learn nothing else from this volume on Christology, I hope you learn and are sensitized to the fact that Arius—who taught that God the Son was a created being and not the eternal in essence with the Father—was deceived. People are always, by nature, remaking God into their own image. We are especially tempted to do that with the incarnate God, because He has made Himself so like us. He has become truly and fully human. Jehovah's Witnesses are not the only Arians these days. Many of our liberal Protestant friends are devaluing the incarnation. They also are writing off Jesus as something less than He has revealed Himself to be.

According to Paul here, Christ created all things. Here, the term firstborn seems to be saying not that Jesus was in a Mormon sense the first one born to Jehovah, but that Christ exercises the privilege over creation that is His because He created it all. It's His authorial right to rule what He has made. Creation was an act of love, and love is at the center of Christ's creating and recreating activity.

Fourth, Christ sustains creation. "In Him all things hold together" (v. 17). Paul picks up this popular idea from the philosophies and religions of his day that taught that some underlying force existed in the world, and he says that force is in fact God. His status as Creator and Sovereign manifests at this very moment. What we call the laws of nature—gravity and so on—are ultimately God's sovereign act of sustaining. God is the reason that our cosmos doesn't collapse into chaos this very moment. He is the reason you don't literally just come apart at the seams. As it says in Hebrews 1:3, "[He] upholds all things by the word of His power." God sustains all things. Christ sustains all things. There is nothing that is not utterly dependent upon Him every second.

God is not a reality you and I create. We all can be wrong about God, and that fact does not change Him one bit. No, He is who He is, and we know what we do about Him because He has revealed Himself to us. Unlike these gods that Paul opposed, the true God is speaking to us and He is speaking to us through His Word by His Spirit. He is not like you and me. He is not a creation. He is the Creator. He did not originate in your wish-fulfilling revelations. He is the eternal

God who was before the world, and we learn this in part through Jesus Christ when we see who Christ is.

Fifth, Christ is the purpose of creation. "All things have been created through Him and for Him" (v. 16). Paul states that the universe not only was created by Christ, but also that it owes its allegiance to Him. The entire world and all the heavens tell His glory (Ps. 19:1). And we should do all things for His glory. Think of the familiar line from Shakespeare: "all the world's a stage."[2] Many Christians have thought that to be an apt image for what God has planned for our world. John Calvin wrote of this world as the theatre of God's glory. Jonathan Edwards wrote of the display of the Creator to His creation through the progress of the plan of redemption throughout history, all to God's glory.

When learning this, some people might assume God is being prideful in doing everything for His own glory. But I don't think we can use the kind of categories we would with our own children, when we tell one of our kids not to take precedence over everything and boss another around. When we think about God, analogies begin to break down. But think of our solar system. It would be prideful if Mercury, Venus, Mars, or even Earth wanted to be at the center of our solar system. Those bodies don't have the weight to pull it off. But it's not prideful for the sun to be at the center of our solar system because it's meant to be that way.

When we try to put something other than God—whether it's career, family, or ministry—at the center of our lives, it simply doesn't work. They—and ultimately we—weren't made to be at the center. They might be fine as immediate goals, as actions and commitments, through which we please the Lord. We should work hard at these things and discipline ourselves. Similarly, the powers and authorities that Paul mentions in verse 16 weren't necessarily bad in themselves. But if we try to place supernatural or natural objects at the center of our lives, we find that before too long, we've lost God, them, and even ourselves. Only Christ is to have that central place in our lives. He is the final audience to which we and all creation plays, and we should study to find what pleases Him.

The Head of the Church

Having established Christ's relationship to creation, Paul now turns to Christ's role as the author of new creation or as the Head of the church. Paul states, "He is the beginning, the firstborn from the dead, so that He Himself will come to have first place in everything. For it was the Father's good pleasure for all the fullness to dwell in Him, and through Him to reconcile all things to Himself, having made peace through the blood of His cross" (vv. 18–20).

---

[2] William Shakespeare, *As You Like It,* Act II, Scene VII.

All of these pronouns in our passage refer not simply to God the Father, but to God the Son. God has revealed Himself generally in all those ways we have been thinking about so far, but God has revealed Himself especially to us in Jesus. Not only that, Paul teaches that the church is the special focus of God's work of revealing Himself in creation.

We see in verse 18 that the church is created by Christ. Christ is the beginning, the firstborn from among the dead. Even as God created the world through Christ, so God especially began the church through Christ. Even as God called the universe into being from nothingness and made the world out of chaos through Christ, so God has created the church from among the dead through Christ. If we are Christians, we belong to Him twice over—by virtue of having been created by Him in the first place and by having been recreated by Him in Christ.

This passage presupposes the fact that the entire world is enslaved to death and that only in Christ is there freedom and new life. Because of what God has done in Christ, all of your sins can be forgiven. God sent His only Son to live a life of perfect trust and complete holiness and goodness and rightness, the life that all of us should have lived. He died on the cross as a substitutionary sacrifice for all of us who would ever turn from our sins and trust in Him. Turn to Christ, repent of your sins, find the truth of everything that we are reading here. As Jesus said to Nicodemus, "You must be born again."

That's what Jesus Christ has come to do. He has gone into the grave at the cost of His life and has blasted through to life on the other side. I love the old saying: "Born once, die twice. Born twice, die once." Christ resurrected is a sign of what God is going to do in all His church. In that sense, the new creation has begun; the final resurrection began the day Jesus walked out of the grave. He is the firstborn from among the dead. So as Christ was over the old creation, so He's the beginning of the church, the firstborn from among the dead, and the founder of a new humanity. Paul implies that as with the first creation, so this new creation is affected by the agency of Christ.

We see in this passage that the church is ruled by Christ. Christ directs the church. He's the head of the body of the church. Christ is not only the sovereign sustainer of the universe, but He is especially and particularly the sovereign sustainer of the church. He is its Head. He is the one who ultimately gives us life and direction—not any demigod we may try to substitute, whether a pope or president, bishop or presbyter, deacon or an elder, pastor or popular Christian author, convention speaker or Bible study leader. No. Christ is the Head of the church. We look to Him for direction. He shows us how personally involved God is in the church, so much so that what does He call the church here? His body. I don't know whether you are concerned about your local church, but I know you are concerned about your own physical body. Paul uses that image here under the inspiration of the Holy Spirit to show us how concerned Christ is for the church. The church is created and ruled by Christ, sustained by His care, attentive to His judgment. As Paul says, "So that in everything, He may have the supremacy."

The Maker of Peace

The fourth and final piece of the big story about God that Paul sets before the Colossian Christians is that Christ is the answer to our big problem. Look at verse 20: "For it was the Father's good pleasure for all the fullness to dwell in Him, and through Him to reconcile all things to Himself, having made peace through the blood of His cross." Perhaps the strangest truth for many in Paul's day—and in our own—is that this sovereign God became a man. He says in the stupefying phrase, "God was pleased to have all his fullness dwell in Him." I can barely conceive what that must mean. He wasn't saying that God became a man in the sense that a god of Greek mythology would temporarily assume the form of a human and then leave the human world. No. The eternal Son of God, in His fullness, became the man, Jesus Christ. And this God—unlike the faint-hearted mocking Greek gods, who tended to exit when there was a problem—came to the very people that He had created for Himself, but whom the Bible says were at war with Him. And do you see here what He did? He made peace. He brought reconciliation. And He did it through His blood shed on the cross.

The God we see in this text is not only a sovereign Lord, but also an almost unbelievably loving reconciler. In Christ, God has rescued us from the dominion of darkness and brought us into the kingdom of His Son, in whom we have redemption and the forgiveness of sins. Paul's language of reconciliation in verse 20 assumes some kind of estrangement, some kind of enmity, even war going on, between two parties. But between whom?

The sides are clearly laid out in verses 19–20. On one side is God, the totality of whose fullness is in Christ. God who is concerned with all things. On the other side is creation. Because of the position of authority God gave humanity, when we fell, we caused the whole world to be in some ways bent, to be fallen as well. And so we read in another place that creation groans (cf. Rom. 8:22). Colossians 1:20 indicates that, beginning with the church, God is in the process of putting all things back into their appropriate relationships with Him, things on earth and things in heaven.

We might wonder: Really? All things? The Greek word translated "all" here is similar to the English word "all." It can mean every single individual. Yet it could also mean just a whole bunch. So what exactly does Paul mean here? Does it mean that finally, at the end of history, everything, especially every individual that has ever lived, will be saved? Because the word "all" grammatically could mean that. Or does it mean that a whole lot of people will be saved? As the book of Revelation puts it, a numberless multitude from every tribe and language and people and nation. Here's an example where, grammatically, you could sustain either meaning. But we are governed by the analogy of Scripture. We must look at what God has revealed outside of Colossians 1. What we find throughout Scripture is that not everyone will be saved, but that a great multitude will.

But Paul's primary focus here is on those who are found in Christ. Paul is presenting the problem here because he wants to talk about the solution. If we pay careful attention to the text here, we see that we must communicate clearly to our people certain truths. We need to be clear that God is not morally indifferent. He has not decided that by virtue of creation, He is obliged to overlook whatever His mischievous creatures get into. I am shocked and saddened to see how effective Satan is in deceiving so many people into thinking that because God made us and loves us, we can do whatever we want. Just because we are made in the image of God doesn't mean we are good for eternity, because being made in God's image is a gigantic responsibility of representing Him. And there is not one of us who has done that as we should have. We need to be clear in our own understanding from Scripture about what this God is like. In another place, Paul argues that the sentence of death stands as evidence that God's judgment of each person unfailingly hits its mark. God is not morally indifferent to the lives we live. He has a keener sense of justice than our clearest thoughts can imagine. It is clear throughout the Old and the New Testaments that He detests, resists, and condemns sin. And the death of Christ is the clearest picture of how much God hates sin.

But also, God has shown His righteousness in the most extraordinary way by rescuing us despite the cost to Himself. The cross is not presented here as showing how loving Jesus was and how mean and cruel His heavenly Father was. No, it is the righteousness of God that shows itself in saving the ungodly. Paul says in Romans, "For while we were still helpless, at the right time Christ died for the ungodly" (5:6). And two verses later he states, "God demonstrates His own love toward us, in that while we were yet sinners, Christ died for us" (5:8). The Father and the Son work in harmony and in love, and the sacrifice of Christ reveals the love of the Father as fully as the love of the Son. And in Acts 20:28, Luke writes in almost unbelievable words that God bought the church with His own blood. That's the kind of God we worship, a God who has reconciled us, as Colossians 1:20 states.

Notice what Paul was concerned about with the Colossians. He didn't simply recall that they had decided to follow Jesus and that there was no turning back now, as true as that may be. Paul set up this whole grand scheme of redemption before them. He didn't assume their understanding of the gospel. May you never assume that the people who come into your church understand the gospel. Make sure that the songs you sing represent the truth of the gospel clearly. Make sure that those who lead the services understand the gospel and present it clearly. It's not just the non-Christians present who need to hear and understand the gospel. You and I will not endure in Christ if we don't hear the gospel and understand it. We have to hear and embrace the good news. When we know the truth about ourselves and what God has done for us, then we truly have hope. Hold out the gospel and the glory of Christ as the Head of the church every time you gather. In your membership interviews, ask the prospective members to summarize the gospel of Jesus Christ so you, or the other leaders in your church, know they truly understand it. It is our task as under-shepherds to help them understand, as best as we can, the good news that God has given us in Christ.

Our Belief in Christ

In Colossians 1, Paul doesn't talk about just the content of the Christian faith, our beliefs about Christ. He also talks about our belief in Christ. Just as the content of the Christian faith focuses on Christ, so our faith as individual Christians focuses on Christ. Paul was concerned that these Christians do more than simply know various facets of Christology. He didn't want them merely to know something about what God was like or even that God had revealed Himself most fully in Jesus. Certainly, he wanted people to know that. But he also wanted to ensure that the Colossian Christians knew God personally. So Paul turns to talk to them more directly.

Notice how in verses 21–23, Paul switches to the second person "you," to connect the doctrine in verses 15–20 to their personal lives. He basically says, "You, if you keep believing positively and if you continue in your faith . . ." This was Paul's concern for them and should be our concern for ourselves: to be established and firm. Negatively, it means that we not move from the hope held forth in the gospel.

The gospel is the focus of our unity. Clearly, disunity was the danger that prompted Paul's letter to the Colossians. Paul was concerned that they would not continue together in the faith. The Colossians heard this very gospel (v. 23) and they represent every believer's present reconciliation with God, as His Spirit sanctifies, and our future presentation to God when it's all completed. The constant temptation we face in this world is to lose the gospel, which is why Paul exhorts them to such faithfulness.

Paul says the Colossians—and us, no doubt—were once alienated, far off from God, doing evil (v. 21). He spoke specifically of their former evil behavior. He doesn't delineate what these evil actions were. It's not like Romans 1. He doesn't give a list. But remember, Paul had never met these people. This is one of the churches, like the church in Rome, to whom he's writing on the basis of what he's heard. But he knew that their actions were, he says here, evil. How? He says they were formerly enemies in their minds. Paul knew that their evil behavior simply reflected the deeper problem of their evil thoughts. Paul is saying they did the wrong things because they thought the wrong things.

So what does it mean to be hostile in mind? No doubt, there was a hostility toward God. If you look at your own heart and you examine your own struggle with sin, you'll find sin is not merely law-breaking. When we sin, we are reminded that we have a sinful nature and that we were once alienated from God. The effect of sin is always to estrange the creature from the Creator. That's how it had been in their lives. That is the situation the Colossians were in.

In all this, of course, the Colossians represent the past of every single one of us who believes in Christ. There's not one of us who was converted that had not struggled with sin and needed to be forgiven by God's work through Jesus Christ. And we continue to be alienated from God unless we repent and believe that God has reconciled us to Himself by Christ's physical body through death (v. 22). So it was not that the Colossians had been so virtuous that somehow they managed to reverse their own course, but rather that God had actually taken the initiative to bridge the gulf, to break down the wall of separation, to come as the bridegroom coming for the bride. The coming, the seeking—this is what God has done in Christ.

Paul is not focusing here on the whole of Christ's incarnation. He says, "Through death ..." (v. 22). I remember opening a Christian magazine, supposedly evangelical, and finding out that some men I knew and respected were too atonement-centered, at least in the judgment of that writer. I deny it is possible to be too atonement-centered. The gospel writers focused on the cross, and they're not too atonement-centered. That's why we focus on the cross in our Christian worship, because this is our way to God. He is a Holy God, and we are not. He is a God who has made us in His image, and we have rejected Him. Paul focuses on the atonement in Colossians, because it is by Christ's death that He may "present you before Him holy and blameless and beyond reproach" (v. 22). The change Paul wanted to see was complete and had already begun. And this happens not by simply believing the right things about Christ. We must believe *in* Christ!

Not too long ago, I was showing one of our church's interns a treasured picture that hangs on my wall. At my fifteenth anniversary as pastor, the church surprised me. They flew in men from around the country and around the world, men who had gone out from our church who are now in pastoral ministry. The church held a surprise service in the evening, and all of these men just started appearing on stage. It was a wonderful time. That picture is of me and all those men on stage. I was telling the intern the name of every man on that stage and where he is in the world. I was able to go through and say, "This brother's in L.A. This guy is in Romania. This brother is here in D.C. This brother is pastoring in London." I told him about forty or fifty men in the picture. Then we came to one, in the last row, and I had to tell this intern that this one man no longer believes in God.

The way to be steadfast is to be attracted by the center or reason for our existence, Jesus Christ Himself. If you know you are loved and redeemed by Christ—who is the express image of God, the author of creation, the Head of the church, our peacemaker—you will do anything for Him. In verse 15, we learn that Christ is the image of the invisible God, the firstborn over all creation. Paul says in Romans 8 that "God causes all things to work together for good to those who love God, to those who are called according to *His* purpose. For those whom He foreknew, He also predestined *to become* conformed to the image of His Son" (vv. 28–29). He says elsewhere, "Just as we have borne the image of the earthy, we will also bear the image of the heavenly" (1 Cor. 15:49). And in 2 Corinthians 3:18, he writes, "But we all, with unveiled face, beholding as in a mirror the glory of the Lord, are being transformed into the same image from glory to glory, just as from the Lord, the Spirit." We were meant to be conformed to His image, and some day we will be like Him, provided we endure!

I think Martyn Lloyd-Jones is something of a latter-day Paul who teaches us how to finish strong. Nearly forty years ago he went home to be with the Lord. I was reading just a few months ago Ian Murray's collection of Lloyd-Jones's letters. It's fascinating to see how he interacted with things over the 20th century. But I was most moved by the end of the collection. Included are two letters from February 11, 1981, that Murray thinks were probably the last ones Lloyd-Jones dictated. With his health quickly deteriorating, Lloyd-Jones, with a shaky hand, wrote on a scrap of paper for Beth, his wife, and the family on February 24, "Do not pray for healing. Do not hold me back from the glory."

With smiles and gestures, he was able to continue to express himself until the early morning of March 1, when the day broke and all shadows fled away. Then Murray quotes two pieces of the doctor's own preaching as a kind of epitaph, a conclusion to the letters.

This is my final comfort and consolation in this world. My only hope of arriving in glory, lies in the fact that the whole of my salvation is God's work.... This is my final comfort and consolation in this world. It is grace at the beginning, grace at the end. So that when you and I come to lie upon our deathbeds, the one thing that should comfort and help and strengthen us there, is the thing that helped us at the beginning, not what we have been, not what we have done, but the grace of God in Jesus Christ our Lord. The Christian life starts with grace. It must continue with grace. It ends with grace—grace, wondrous grace. By the grace of God, I am what I am, yet not I, but the grace of God which was with me.[3]

Believe and preach the truth about Christ. Lean on Christ until the day breaks and all the shadows flee away. It is only through Christ that we continue in our faith, firmly established and firm, not moved from the hope held out in the gospel. Only through Christ.

---

[3] Martyn Lloyd-Jones, *D Martyn Lloyd-Jones Letters*, ed. Ian Murray (Edinburgh, Scotland: Banner of Truth, 1994), 237.

PART 2

THE WORK

OF CHRIST

9

HE EMPTIED HIMSELF: THE KENOSIS

PHILIPPIANS 2:5–11

Mike Riccardi

The incarnation of the Son of God." For many of us long-time believers, that kind of theological shorthand has become so familiar that we cease to be amazed at the truth it describes. The eternal, preexistent Word—ever with God, ever God Himself—became flesh and tabernacled among sinners (John 1:1–14). It is rightly called the miracle of all miracles. The infinite, eternal, self-existent, self-sufficient, almighty God made Himself nothing by taking on the nature of finite, temporal, dependent, mortal humanity—without shedding His divine nature (Phil. 2:5–8). The immutable God became what He was not, while never ceasing to be what He was. The Irish Reformer James Ussher rightly said that the incarnation is "the highest pitch of God's wisdom, goodness, power, and glory."[1] Pastor and author Mark Jones has written, "The incarnation is God's greatest wonder, one that no creature could ever have imagined. God himself could not perform a more difficult and glorious work. It has justly been called the miracle of all miracles."[2]

There is a peculiar glory to this greatest of God's miracles. Among all the works God has accomplished, the incarnation has a special luster of magnificence. The juxtaposition of the majesty of the infinite God with the humility of finite man, united in one magnificent Person, renders the glory of the incarnation more bril-

---

[1] James Ussher, *Immanuel, or, The Mystery of the Incarnation of the Son of God* (London: Susan Islip for Thomas Downes and George Badger, 1647; reprint, Swansea, 1810), 2.
[2] Mark Jones, *Knowing Christ* (Carlisle, PA: Banner of Truth, 2015), 25.

liant than all the other of God's glorious works. Therefore, we must devote our minds to the study of this wonder. We must peer into this mystery with the hope of enflaming our hearts with the worship that God rightly deserves.

In studying the incarnation, we encounter the doctrine of the kenosis of Christ. That term derives from the Greek verb *kenoō*, which Paul uses in Philippians 2:7 to speak of the humility of Christ in the incarnation. Rather than insisting on His own rights to continue in manifest divine power and authority, the eternal Son of God selflessly surrendered those rights by taking on a human nature in order to accomplish salvation for sinners. The doctrine of the incarnation entails the doctrine of the kenosis, and, therefore, it is worthy of our attention, study, and adoration.

But that is no easy task. The study of the incarnation and the kenosis of Christ confronts us with some of the loftiest ideas able to be conceived by the human mind: the metaphysics of defining a nature and a person, confessing the union of two distinct natures in one person without contradiction, and more. Many Christians deride such study and counsel others not to waste their time on what they view to be overly speculative and philosophical discussions.

However, our praise to Christ is only as deep as our understanding of His glorious person and work is rooted in the truth. The heights of our worship will never exceed the depths of our theology. Therefore, the genuine worshiper of Christ must always be a student of Christ. John Murray wrote of the incarnation and *kenosis*: "It is high and heavenly doctrine and for that reason of little appeal to dull minds and darkened hearts. It is the mystery that angels desire to look into. But it is also the delight of enlightened and humble souls; they love to explore the mysteries which bespeak the glories of their Redeemer."[3] Looking into that mystery begins by asking the question, "What is the kenosis of Christ?" Three observations from Paul's comments in Philippians 2:5–8 provide the answer to that question.

The Glory of the Eternal Son

First, we must apprehend the glory of the Eternal Son. Paul writes, "Have this attitude in yourselves which was also in Christ Jesus, who, although He existed in the form of God" (vv. 5–6a, author's translation). While most translations translate "existing" in the past tense, Paul uses a present participle to express ongoing, continuous action. Before He took on human flesh, the Eternal Son was eternally existing in the form of God.

---

[3] John Murray, "The Mystery of Godliness," in *The Collected Writings of John Murray*, 4 vols. (Carlisle, PA: Banner of Truth, 1982), 3:240.

Now, "form" does not mean that Jesus only seemed to be like God. The Greek term *morphē* does not connote merely the outward appearance of something, as we think of in English. The word is notoriously difficult to translate. One scholar writes, "'Form' is an inadequate rendering of *morphē*, but our language affords no better word."[4] Rather than a single, one-to-one word equivalent, we have to explain what the term means. In the next verse, it describes the genuine humanity that Christ assumed to Himself in the incarnation. Christ took the *morphē doulou*, the form of a slave. He did not merely appear human or merely have the external features of humanity; that is the very docetic heresy the rejection of which the apostle John makes the test of orthodoxy (1 John 4:2–3). Instead, the *morphē doulou* refers to the fact that Christ was fully and truly human—that He possesses a genuine human nature. In the same way, then, the *morphē theou* refers to the fact that Christ was fully and truly God—that He possesses the genuine divine nature.

Yet *morphē* is not just a synonym for *ousia* or *physis*, the other words that refer to one's substance, essence, or nature. *Morphē* is used nowhere else in the New Testament (except in the long ending of Mark, the authenticity of which is disputed), but in the Greek translation of the Old Testament, it is used to speak clearly of one's appearance.[5] Besides this, a cognate form of *morphē* is used to describe Jesus' transfiguration: He was *metemorphōthē*—changed in *morphē* (Matt. 17:2). But Christ's immutable divine essence was not changed at the transfiguration. Rather, the outward expression of the glory of Christ's divine nature had been veiled, and for a moment He was removing the veil and once again letting His glory shine forth.

Taking that all together, we ought to conclude that *morphē* refers to the outward manifestation that corresponds to the inward essence, to the external form that represents what is intrinsic and essential.[6] It is "a form which truly and fully expresses the being which underlies it."[7] In other words, *morphē* is not the essence, but no one can appear or exist in view of others in the form of God, manifesting all the perfections of God, unless that person is in fact God.[8] Christ was existing in the *morphē* of God precisely because in His very essence and His being He *is* God from all eternity.

The context of Philippians 2 makes that clear. In verse 6, Paul says that Christ

---

[4] Marvin R. Vincent, *A Critical and Exegetical Commentary on the Epistles to the Philippians and to Philemon*, International Critical Commentary (Edinburgh: T. & T. Clark, 1902), 57.

[5] Judges 8:18; Job 4:16; Isaiah 44:13; Daniel 3:19, LXX.

[6] Homer A. Kent, Jr., "Philippians," in *The Expositor's Bible Commentary*, vol. 11, ed. Frank E. Gaebelein (Grand Rapids: Zondervan, 1981), 123, 126.

[7] J. H. Moulton and G. Milligan, *Vocabulary of the Greek New Testament* (London: Hodder and Stoughton, 1930), 417.

[8] Charles Hodge, *Systematic Theology*, 3 vols. (Peabody, MA: Hendrickson Publishers, 2013), 2:386.

did not regard equality with God a thing to be grasped (v. 6b). "Equality" is rendered from the Greek word *isos*, from which we get the word *isomers*, which describe chemical compounds that have the same number of the same elements but different structural formulas. They are distinct compounds, but on a chemical level, they are equal to each other, so we call them *isomers*. To switch from chemistry class to geometry, an *isosceles* triangle is a triangle that has two equal sides. Jesus is "*isa theō*," equal to God. When one considers such statements as Isaiah 46:9, in which God says, "For I am God, and there is no other; I am God, and there is no one like Me," the conclusion is inescapable. If (a) no one can be equal to God but God Himself, and (b) Christ is equal to God, then (c) Christ Himself must be fully God. "The form of God" refers to the dignity of the Son's essence, while "equality with God" refers to the dignity of the Son's station, or position.

If *morphē* refers to the outward manifestation of the inner essence and nature, what is the outward manifestation of the inner essence and nature of God? Answer: glory. Throughout the Old Testament, when God's presence is represented as dwelling with His people, there is always a manifestation of that *shekinah* glory—the pillar of cloud, the pillar of fire, the bright light that filled the tabernacle and the temple. Well, the Son is the very radiance of the glory of God (Heb. 1:3), the image of God in whose face the glory of God shines in fullness (2 Cor. 4:4, 6). He is the exalted Lord seated on the throne of heaven, the train of whose robe fills the heavenly temple, of whom the angels declare, "The whole earth is full of His glory" (Isa. 6:1–8; cf. John 12:37–41). Before the world was, the Word that became flesh and dwelt among us was eternally existing in the very nature, essence, and glory of God.

The Humility of the Eternal Son

Having beheld the glory of the eternal Son, we may also observe from this passage the humility of the eternal Son: "although [Christ Jesus] existed in the form of God, [He] did not regard equality with God a thing to be grasped, but emptied Himself, taking the form of a bond-servant, and being made in the likeness of men" (Phil. 2:6–7).

Even though Christ existed eternally in the very nature of God, equal with the Father, ruling creation in majesty and receiving the worship of the saints and angels in heaven, He did not regard that equality as something to be grasped. He did not regard the dignity of His station something to cling to or to take selfish advantage of and use to further His own ends.[9] Rather, He humbly accepted the mission of His incarnation, in which He would renounce the glories of heaven for a time, take on the nature of a human being, and veil the splendor and majesty of His deity behind the form of a slave. Though He had every right to continue in unlimited manifest power and authority, to radiate the very essence and glory of deity, to receive nothing but the most exalted worship of the host of heaven— immune from poverty, pain, and humiliation—He did not selfishly count those blessings to be slavishly held onto, but sacrificed them to become man and accomplish salvation for sinners. He "emptied Himself" (Phil. 2:7).

But of what did Christ empty Himself? Some theologians, who embrace what is called kenotic Christology,[10] have answered, "He emptied Himself of His deity" or "of His 'relative' divine attributes" or "of His divine consciousness" or "of His divine prerogatives." However, these answers fall short of biblical fidelity and theological soundness.

In the first place, Scripture presents Jesus as conscious of His deity,[11] as exercising His divine prerogatives,[12] and as exercising His divine attributes.[13] Further, Jesus could never shed any aspect of His deity, divine attributes, or divine consciousness without ceasing to be truly and fully God.[14] Of what, then, did the divine Son empty Himself? Even asking the question demonstrates a misunderstanding of the language. Though *kenoō* literally means "to empty," everywhere it is used in Scripture it is used in a figurative sense (cf. Rom. 4:14; 1 Cor. 1:17; 9:15; 2 Cor. 9:3). According to New Testament usage, *kenoō* doesn't mean "to pour out," as if Jesus was pouring His deity, attributes, or prerogatives out of Himself. If that was Paul's intent, he would have used *ekcheō*, which he employs

---

[9] Gordon D. Fee, *Paul's Letter to the Philippians*, New International Commentary on the New Testament (Grand Rapids: Eerdmans, 1995), 209.

[10] Kenotic Christology was birthed out of the rationalism that dominated the church in light of the so-called Enlightenment of the nineteenth century. It is nearly impossible to define kenoticism briefly, but it basically teaches that it was impossible for Jesus to be truly and fully human while also remaining truly and fully God. Seizing on Paul's statement that Christ "emptied Himself" (Phil. 2:7), kenoticists conclude that in the incarnation, the Son subtracted, relinquished, or restricted some aspects of His deity in order to become truly human. A recent summary and insightful refutation of kenotic Christology may be found in Stephen Wellum, *God the Son Incarnate: The Doctrine of Christ* (Wheaton, IL: Crossway, 2017), 355–419.

[11] He speaks consciously of His equality with the Father (John 5:17–18) and that He is God Himself (John 10:30, 33). He also appropriates the divine name Yahweh (John 8:58–59; cf. Ex. 3:14).

[12] He gives life to whom He wishes, just as the Father does (John 5:21; cf. 11:25); forgives sins, which only God can do (Luke 5:18–26); teaches with authority on par with the Old Testament Scriptures (Matt. 5:22–44); possesses a unique sovereignty exclusive to God (Matt. 11:27; John 10:17–18); and receives worship (John 20:28; cf. Rev. 19:10).

[13] Such attributes include those to which kenoticists object most: omnipresence (Matt. 28:20), omniscience (Luke 5:22; cf. Mark 2:6; John 1:47–49; 4:18; 2:25; 6:64; 16:30; 21:17), and omnipotence (Matt. 8:26–27; 14:15–21; John 2:1–11; 11:43–44; Col. 1:16–17; Heb. 1:3; cf. John 1:14; 2:11; 10:37–38; 14:10–11).

[14] For a fuller treatment of kenotic theology's failure as a biblically and theologically faithful position, see the forthcoming article: Michael Riccardi, "Veiled in Flesh the Godhead See: A Study of the Kenosis of Christ," *The Master's Seminary Journal* 29, no. 2 (Fall 2018).

elsewhere to speak of pouring something out of something else (e.g., Rom. 5:5; Titus 3:6). But everywhere in Scripture, *kenoō* is used to mean "to make void," "to nullify," "to make of no effect." Paul uses it that way in Romans 4:14, where he says, "For if those who are of the Law are heirs, faith is made void (*kekenōtai*) and the promise is nullified." Yet no one thinks to ask, "Of what has faith been made empty?" The idea is that faith would be nullified—it would come to naught—if righteousness could come by the Law.[15]

Our text, therefore, teaches not that Christ emptied Himself of something, but that He emptied *Himself*. He nullified Himself; He made Himself of no effect. The Son Himself is the object of this emptying. He did not empty the form of God or the divine attributes or His divine prerogatives, but Himself. The King James Version captures this well by translating verse 7 thus: "[He] made himself of no reputation." The NIV's rendering is also helpful: "[He] made himself nothing." Then, the very next phrase explains the manner in which the Son made Himself nothing: "[He] emptied Himself, taking the form of a bond-servant, and being made in the likeness of men." Christ made Himself of no effect by taking on human nature in His incarnation. He nullified Himself not by subtracting from His deity, but by taking on humanity. This is an emptying by addition! John Murray writes,

> It is sometimes thought that, when the Son of God became man and humbled himself, he thereby ceased to be what he was and in some way divested himself of the attributes and prerogatives of deity, that he changed the form of God for the form of man. He became poor, it is said, by emptying himself of divine properties, became poor by subtraction, by divestiture, by depotentiation. The Scripture does not support any such notion. ... Even in his incarnate state, in him dwelt all the fullness of Godhood (Col. 2:9). When the Son of man became poor, it was not by giving up his Godhood nor any of the attributes and prerogatives inseparable from Godhood. When he became man, he did not cease to be rich in his divine being, relations, and possession. He did not become poor by ceasing to be what he was, but he became poor by becoming what he was not. He became poor by addition, not by subtraction.[16]

---

[15] Moises Silva, *Philippians*, Baker Exegetical Commentary on the New Testament (Grand Rapids: Baker Academic, 2005), 105.

[16] John Murray, "The Riches and the Poverty of Jesus Christ," in *The Collected Writings of John Murray*, 4 vols.

Christ remained what He was, even when He became what He was not. He did not exchange His deity for His humanity. Nor did He become a human *person*. As a divine person, He assumed a human *nature*.[17] The divine, second Person of the Trinity, who was eternally existing in the form of God, nullified Himself by taking the form of a slave and being born in the likeness of man. In the majesty of heaven, to look on Him would have been to look on the epitome of all beauty. But being found in appearance as a man (Phil. 2:8), He had "no stately form or majesty that we should look upon Him, nor appearance that we should be attracted to Him. He was despised and forsaken of men . . . and like one from whom men hide their face He was despised, and we did not esteem Him" (Isa. 53:2–3). The rich became poor (cf. 2 Cor. 8:9). The worshiped became the despised. The blessed One became the man of sorrows. The Master became the slave. As John Calvin wrote, "Christ, indeed, could not divest himself of godhead, but he kept it *concealed* for a time, that it might not be seen, under the weakness of the flesh. Hence he laid aside his glory in the view of men, not by lessening it, but by *concealing* it."[18] And Herman Bavinck adds, "He laid aside the divine majesty and glory . . . in which he existed before the incarnation, or rather *concealed* it behind the form of a servant in which he went about on earth."[19]

We ought then to understand that a significant aspect of the kenosis was a *krypsis*—that is, a concealment or a veiling of the glory that is the external manifestation of His nature.[20] Christ fully possessed His divine nature, attributes, and prerogatives, but for the sake of becoming truly human, He did not always fully express the glories of His majesty. And so when He is tempted by Satan in the wilderness to exercise His divine omnipotence to turn the stones into bread or to throw Himself from the top of the temple and manifest His divine glory by being rescued by angels, He refuses (Matt. 4:1–11). When Jesus is betrayed by Gethsemane, He is the divine Son who has twelve legions of angels at His disposal (Matt. 26:53), but refuses to dispatch them to His service. Whenever any exercise of His divine power or any manifestation of His divine glory would have functioned to benefit only Himself, or to ease the limitations of a truly human existence, and would not be for the benefit of those He came to serve in accor-

---

(Carlisle, PA: Banner of Truth, 1982), 3:230–31.

[17] The proper definitions of and distinctions between *person* and *nature* are essential to orthodox Christology. See the discussion in Wellum, *God the Son Incarnate*, 290–93.

[18] John Calvin, *Commentaries on the Epistles of the Paul the Apostle to the Philippians, Colossians, and Thessalonians,* Calvin's Commentaries, trans. and ed. by John Pringle (Grand Rapids: Baker, 2009), 56–57 (emphasis added).

[19] Herman Bavinck, *Reformed Dogmatics*, ed. John Bolt, trans. John Vriend, 4 vols. (Grand Rapids: Baker Academic, 2006), 3:432, (emphasis added).

[20] See Wellum, *God the Son Incarnate*, 370.

dance with His messianic mission, He refused to exercise those prerogatives.

However, there certainly were times when He did exercise His divine power and did manifest His unique divine glory, such as when He turned water into wine, rebuked the waves, read minds, and raised the dead. In these instances, it was essential to His ministry for the Son to display His divine glory. When the mission He received from His Father required Him to suffer hunger in the midst of His temptation, in order that the obedience imputed to His people would be the obedience of a man, Jesus willingly refused to insist upon His right to be free from hunger (Matt. 4:3–4). But when that same divine mission required Him to display His glory in order to prove His divinity and work faith in the hearts of the elect, Jesus turned water into wine (John 2:11).

Such was the humility of the eternal Son. He eternally existed in the perfect blessedness of heavenly communion with the Father and the Holy Spirit. From the foundation of creation, He enjoyed the unfettered worship of the hosts of heaven. Even if His divine mission sent Him to be born into the lap of luxury rather than in the humble stable, for the eternal Son of God to experience just a single pang of hunger would have been an infinite condescension. Free from all weakness, infirmity, decay, and sorrow, the eternal Son contemplated the riches of His pre-incarnate glory, and humbly chose to become poor (cf. 2 Cor. 8:9)— to veil His glory by taking on human nature and the weakness of human flesh in order that He might live and die as the slave of all.

The Humility of the Incarnate Christ

And yet the Son's humility did not stop at taking on a human nature. We go on to observe the humility of the incarnate Christ: "Being found in appearance as a man, He humbled Himself by becoming obedient to the point of death, even death on a cross" (Phil. 2:8).

The divine Son became not just a man, but an obedient man. From all eternity, the Son was equal to the Father in glory, majesty, and authority. In His incarnation, however, He began to relate to the Father in terms of authority and submission (e.g., John 5:30; 6:38). The Master had become the slave. The Lord who rightfully issues commands subjected Himself to obeying commands.

And that is not all. He was not only obedient, but obedient to the point of death. The Author of Life humbly submitted to death. The One without sin humbly submitted to sin's curse. The One who has life within Himself (John 1:4; 5:26)—who gives life to whomever He wishes (John 5:21)—humbly released His grip on His own human life in submission to the Father and in love for those whom His Father had given Him. Here is humility shining like the sun in its full strength. We rightly sing, "Amazing love! How can it be, that Thou, my God, shouldst die for me?"

And yet there are greater depths to plumb before the humiliation of the Son of God reaches rock bottom. He was not just man, not just obedient, and not just obedient unto death. The holy Son of God, the Lord of glory, "humbled Himself by becoming obedient to the point of death, even death on a cross." The horrors of the cross scarcely need describing. One commentator said, "The cross displayed the lowest depths of human depravity and cruelty. It exhibited the most brutal form of sadistic torture and execution ever invented by malicious human minds."[21] In crucifixion, metal spikes were driven through the victim's wrists and feet, and he was left to hang naked and exposed, sometimes for days. Because the body would be pulled down by gravity, the weight of a victim's own body would press against his lungs, and the hyperextension of the lungs and chest muscles made it difficult to breathe. Victims would gasp for air by pulling themselves up, but when they would do that, the wounds in their wrists and feet would tear at the stakes that pierced them, and the flesh of their backs—usually torn open from flogging—would grate against the jagged wood. Eventually, when he could no longer summon the strength to pull himself up to breathe, the victim of a crucifixion would die from suffocation under the weight of his own body. This was the most sadistically cruel, excruciatingly painful, and loathsomely degrading death that a man could die. And on Golgotha two thousand years ago, the Son of God died this death. God on a cross.

Even at that point, though, His mission was not complete. The shame and pain of the cross was not the lowest depth to which the Son of God submitted Himself. Deuteronomy 21:23 taught that anyone hanged on a tree is accursed of God, and Paul quotes this verse in Galatians 3:13: "For it is written, 'Cursed is everyone who hangs on a tree.'" Worse than the pain, torture, and shame brought by crucifixion was the divine curse. This is rock bottom. This is the Highest of the high gone to the lowest of the low. Here is the eternal Son cursed by God the Father. He never deserved to know His Father's wrath, but only ever His delight and approbation. Yet on Calvary, He was cut off from the apple of His eye, the joy of His heart. What bewilderment must the Son of God had experienced when for the first time in all of eternity He felt His Father's displeasure. What it must have been to utter that harrowing cry: "My God, My God, why have You forsaken Me?"

This was the purpose for the kenosis. Man had sinned against God, and so *man*

---

[21] Walter Hansen, *The Letter to the Philippians*, Pillar New Testament Commentary (Grand Rapids: Eerdmans, 2009), 157.

was required to make atonement for sin, but was absolutely powerless to do so. Only God can atone for sin, and yet only man's sacrifice would be accepted on behalf of man. So in the marvelous wisdom of God, God became man to reconcile man to God:

> Therefore, since the children share in flesh and blood, He
> Himself likewise also partook of the same, that through death
> He might render powerless him who had the power of death,
> that is, the devil, and might free those who through fear of
> death were subject to slavery all their lives. . . . Therefore,
> He had to be made like His brethren in all things, so that He
> might become a merciful and faithful high priest in things
> pertaining to God, to make propitiation for the sins of the
> people. (Heb. 2:14–15, 17)

Lessons from the Kenosis

What are we to take away from our study of the kenosis of Christ? First, we must trust in this divine-human Mediator who became man in order to bear man's curse. The incarnation and the kenosis of Christ mean nothing to you if you are not a beneficiary of the salvation for which He became incarnate. Your first order of business is to admit your sin before an infinitely holy God, confess your own inability to satisfy the demands of His righteousness, look outside of yourself to this glorious Savior who has accomplished all that is necessary for salvation, and trust in Him to avail with God on your behalf.

Second, have this attitude in yourselves which was also in Christ Jesus (Phil. 2:5). It is interesting to note that Paul's primary point for writing Philippians 2:5–11 is not to discourse on the fine points of high Christology. Those theological truths are there in the text, and they are glorious! But Paul employs them as an illustration and example of the humility in which the church must walk. You are to "do nothing from selfishness or empty conceit, but with humility of mind regard one another as more important than yourselves; do not merely look out for your own personal interests, but also for the interests of others" (Phil. 2:3–4). If Christ could come from the glories of heaven itself, all the way down to the abject degradation of the cross, surely we, mere creatures of the dust who have been saved by that humility-driven gospel, can surrender our rights for the sake of maintaining the unity of the Spirit in the bond of peace (cf. Eph. 4:3). In the midst of a conflict with a brother or sister in Christ—or with a spouse or family member—though we might be right, and though we might be entitled to deference and respect and recognition, we can think on the only One who ever had a right to assert His rights and refused, and regard one another as more important than ourselves, giving preference to one another in honor (cf. Rom 12:10) for the sake of unity. The kenosis is a call to imitate the humility of Christ.

Third, apprehend the inextricable link between the loftiest of theology and the most practical elements of Christian living. The most mundane, applicable matters of Christianity—such as personal humility and corporate unity (Phil. 2:3–4)—are wedded to the deepest and most difficult doctrines for the mind to conceive (Phil. 2:5–8). So many professing Christians say things like, "I don't want to hear about doctrinal debates and theological controversies. I want practical teaching. I want a Christianity that shows me how to live right where I am." In the light of Philippians 2, however, such thinking is pure foolishness. There is no such dichotomy between theology and practice! Theology is the very soil out of which practice grows. Christian living is inescapably rooted in theology. John Murray said it well: "The most transcendent of mysteries of our holy faith are the fountain springs of the most common and practical Christian duties. The streams of Christian liberality are fed from the ocean of the mysteries of God. If we evacuate thought and interest and faith of the mystery of godliness we lose not only the fountain of faith but we dry up the streams of practical grace."[22]

Finally, the kenosis teaches us to worship our triune God. Worship the God whose mind is so vast, whose wisdom is so unsearchable, that the truths we struggle and strain so mightily to understand do not make God break an intellectual sweat. They are elementary to Him, and yet wonderful for us. We ought to express our worship to God as Charnock did when he wrote,

> What a wonder that two natures infinitely distant should be more intimately united than anything in the world … that the same person should have both a glory and a grief; an infinite joy in the Deity, and an inexpressible sorrow in the humanity; that a God upon a throne should be an infant in a cradle; the thundering Creator be a weeping babe and a suffering man; [the incarnation astonishes] men upon earth, and angels in heaven.[23]

May it never cease to astonish us. May it be a cause of perpetual worship of God the Son incarnate, through the Holy Spirit, to the glory of God the Father.

---

[22] Murray, "The Riches and the Poverty of Jesus Christ," 3:235.
[23] Stephen Charnock, *The Existence and Attributes of God* in *The Works of Stephen Charnock*, 5 vols. (Edinburgh: Banner of Truth, 2010), 2:150.

10

IN OUR PLACE: THE ATONEMENT

2 CORINTHIANS 5:21

Matthew Barrett

One of the marks of outstanding theological thinking is the ability to demonstrate how each doctrine of the faith is linked together. Christian doctrine is like a web in which each silk, doctrinal strand is connected to another. If you break one silk strand, you put the entire web at risk. More positively, by themselves, each strand is unimpressive, but together they all form a cohesive web, and its detail, integration, and beauty take our breath away.

In 2 Corinthians 5:21, Paul weaves two strands together—substitution and imputation—which prove to be at the very core of our doctrinal web. "For our sake he made him to be sin who knew no sin, so that in him we might become the righteousness of God." "True," says D. A. Carson, "the text does not explicitly *say* that God imputes our sins to Christ, but as long as we perceive that Jesus dies in our place, and bears our curse, and was made 'sin' for us, it is extraordinarily difficult to avoid the notion of the imputation of our sins to him."[1]

Similarly, Thomas Schreiner adds, "Saying that Jesus was made to be sin either means that Jesus was counted as a sinner, even though he was sinless, or it means that Jesus became a sacrifice of sin for our sake." Either way, says Schreiner, "the sin of human beings was placed on Jesus so that as a substitute for sinners, he

---

[1] D. A. Carson, "The Vindication of Imputation: On Fields of Discourse and Semantic Fields," in *Justification: What's at Stake in the Current Debates*, eds. Mark Husbands and Daniel J. Treier (Downers Grove, IL: InterVarsity, 2004), 69.

took on himself the penalty we deserved. This is the great exchange, for Jesus took on himself human sin, and believers receive the righteousness of God in and through Jesus Christ."[2]

Imputation assumes a sacrificial, penal quality, as becomes clear in Paul's other epistles, for the substitute's intention is to act vicariously on behalf of *the ungodly* whose only recompense is divine wrath (see Rom. 1–2; Eph. 2:1–3). So closely does the substitute represent the sinner that Paul can say Christ was made sin. When 2 Corinthians 5:21 is coupled with Paul's understanding of propitiation in his other letters (e.g., Rom. 3:25), we begin to see what theologians have identified as the very heart of the cross: penal substitutionary atonement (PSA).[3]

Yet Paul, in the very same breath, explains the purpose and outcome of such substitution: For our sake Christ was made to be sin "so that in him we might become the righteousness of God." Here is the atonement in its full dogmatic beauty, one silk strand of the doctrinal web (substitution) inseparably linked to another (imputation).

Theologians going back to the early church (e.g., the epistle to Diognetus) have read passages like 2 Corinthians 5:21 as articulations of the "great exchange."[4] As our substitute, Christ became sin, taking sin's penalty in full, and in exchange we have received His perfect righteousness. For Paul, the substitutionary nature of the atonement is irreversibly tied to the imputation of Christ's righteousness in the justification of the ungodly. It is precisely because a sinless substitute has been made sin that the ungodly are considered righteous by God.[5] "Becoming God's righteousness," says Brian Vickers, "is not an attribute but a declaration that God counts individuals as having a right standing before Him, because He sees them with respect to their union with Christ their representative rather than

---

[2] Thomas Schreiner, *Faith Alone: The Doctrine of Justification,* ed. Matthew Barrett (Grand Rapids: Zondervan, 2015), 187. For a "sacrifice" understanding that does not preclude imputation, see Brian Vickers, *Jesus' Blood and Righteousness: Paul's Theology of Imputation* (Wheaton, IL: Crossway, 2006), chapter 5.

[3] J. I. Packer, "What Did the Cross Achieve?: The Logic of Penal Substitution," in *Tyndale Bulletin* 25 (1974): 25, states, "The notion which the phrase 'penal substitution' expresses is that Jesus Christ our Lord, moved by a love that was determined to do everything necessary to save us, endured and exhausted the destructive divine judgment for which we were otherwise inescapably destined, and so won us forgiveness, adoption and glory."

[4] See Schreiner, *Faith Alone,* 29.

[5] We must be careful not to misunderstand Paul's use of the word *become.* N. T. Wright, observes Schreiner, has "several objections to interpreting this passage [2 Cor. 5:21] in support of imputation. For instance, how could this text refer to the imputation of Christ's righteousness since Paul speaks of the righteousness of God? I don't find this question persuasive, for even though Paul does speak of the righteousness of God, such righteousness is ours in and through Jesus Christ. The righteousness of God is 'in Him.' Hence, God's righteousness, which is given to us as believers, becomes ours through union with Christ." And again: "Wright thinks the verb 'become' (*genōmetha*) can't be equative, that the verb carries the notion of 'becoming.' He doubts that imputation can be intended if we *become* the righteousness of God. But the verb 'become' (*ginomai*) is flexible in Paul and can easily be taken as equative (cf. Rom. 11:6; 12:6; 1 Cor. 3:18; 4:16). And even if the verb means 'become,' it doesn't rule out imputation, for believers become something they weren't before ('righteous!') by virtue of union with Christ. They receive right standing with God as a gift" (Ibid., 187).

as part of the old age of sin and death."[6] For Paul, the imputation of our sin to Christ is for the purpose of securing atonement, which is in part the basis for God's justification of the unrighteous.[7]

Yet in the twenty-first century, Paul's words to the Corinthians stand in stark contrast to much of contemporary theology. To Reformed evangelicals, passages like 2 Corinthians 5:21 may be basic to the gospel itself, but the vast array of literature on atonement and justification reveals that we can no longer take Paul's foundational statements for granted. In fact, the situation has become incredibly complex.

In years past we might have assumed that a denial of PSA could be countered by an appeal to specific biblical texts. While that, no doubt, remains absolutely essential, it is becoming increasingly apparent that denials of PSA are due in large part to one's modification of other doctrinal strands, such as original sin, divine justice, the hypostatic union, and union with Christ.[8] Strands in the web have been removed.

Therefore, we need not pay attention merely to Paul's theology in 2 Corinthians 5:21 but also to his methodology. We too must recognize that the nucleus of the gospel web only hangs majestically in mid-air because it is supported by numerous other silk, doctrinal strands. In other words, the task before us is dogmatics, perhaps in a way that the apostle Paul never could have imagined. Like a tapestry in which each doctrinal thread is connected to the next, we will weave in and out of several doctrinal threads, demonstrating how each contributes to the fabric of atonement theology.[9]

We will explore the contours of several doctrinal domains to determine their

---

[6] Vickers, *Jesus' Blood and Righteousness*, 188.

[7] Vickers helpfully qualifies, however, that Paul's language in 2 Cor. 5:21 is not saying the exact same thing as Rom. 4 and 5. "Here the emphasis is not primarily on the appropriation of righteousness (faith), or the foundation for righteousness (Christ's obedience), but on the means by which it is possible for God to count people as righteous, i.e., Christ's sacrificial death on the cross" (Ibid., 188–189).

[8] E.g., see chapters by Gregory A. Boyd, Joel B. Green, and Bruce R. Reichenbach in *The Nature of the Atonement: Four Views* (Downers Grove, IL: IVP Academic, 2006); Joel B. Green and Mark D. Baker, *Recovering the Scandal of the Cross: Atonement in New Testament and Contemporary Contexts* (Downers Grove: IVP Academic, 2000).

[9] Or we could state our purpose as a question: What should one's theological web look like if one is to properly reach the same conclusions that the biblical authors do in texts like 2 Corinthians 5:21? And should one misstep in one doctrinal domain, how might that harm that which is most central to the gospel itself? It should be clear that I am after a dogmatic rationale for PSA since I am convinced that what we need is a doctrine of PSA that is not based just on a few proof texts but one wrapped within a larger theological framework. My approach is not novel. In his essay, "What Did the Cross Achieve?" (42–43), Packer has a helpful summary in which he spells out the logic of PSA. He gives us 9 building blocks, each one building off the others: 1. "God . . . 'condones nothing', but judges all sin as it deserves: which Scripture affirms, and my conscience confirms, to be right. 2. My sins merit ultimate penal suffering and rejection from God's presence (conscience also confirms this), and nothing I do can blot them out. 3. The penalty due to me for my sins, whatever it was, was paid for me by Jesus Christ, the Son of God, in his death on the cross. 4. Because this is so, I through faith in him am made 'the righteousness of God in him', *i.e.*, I am justified; pardon, acceptance and sonship become mine. 5. Christ's death for me is my sole ground of hope before God. 'If he fulfilled not justice, I must; if he underwent not wrath, I must to eternity.' [Packer quoting John Owen's *Works*, 10.284]. 6. My faith in Christ is God's own gift to me, given in virtue of Christ's death for me: *i.e.*, the cross procured it. 7. Christ's death for me guarantees my preservation to glory. 8. Christ's death for me is the measure and pledge of the love of the Father and the Son to me. 9. Christ's death for me calls and constrains me to trust, to worship, to love and to serve."

relation to the atonement: (1) original sin, imputation, and union with Christ, (2) the divine perfections, specifically divine justice and simplicity, and (3) the Trinity.

The Judicial Nature of Original Sin, Imputation, and Union with Christ

In his recent systematic theology, *The Christian Faith*, Michael Horton makes a profound observation:

> If the problem of sin were merely negative actions, behaviors, or social systems, a moral example or a demonstration of God's opposition to such actions would perhaps suffice. If the problem were simply disease, disappointment, and suffering, it might make some difference to know that God cares and heals, and even that he has made eternal life possible. However, the condition of sin and its penalties is first of all judicial. Christ's death saves because it resolves the serious crisis between God and human beings in the cosmic courtroom.[10]

This connection between original sin and atonement becomes conspicuous when we consider theories on the transmission of original sin. Fourth-century Pelagianism immediately comes to mind, though of course it was not limited to the monk Pelagius but was revived in the nineteenth-century by Albert Barnes (1798–1870), in the twentieth-century by biblical scholar C. K. Barrett (1917–2011), and by theologians such as Emil Brunner (1889–1966) and Rudolph Bultmann (1884–1976).[11]

According to Pelagianism, we do not inherit Adam's guilt or corrupt nature. Rather, mankind merely mimics the bad examples he witnesses. The tragedy of Adam in Genesis 3 is not that all mankind is condemned as a result of Adam's representation, but that Adam was a terrible role model. The imitation view is especially apparent in how Pelagius interprets Romans 5:12: "The statement that all have sinned in Adam was not uttered on account of a sin contracted by reason of their origin through being born, but on account of the imitation of Adam's sin."[12] Nevertheless, mankind is capable of resisting this habit to sin; actually, he

---

[10] Michael Horton, *The Christian Faith: A Systematic Theology for Pilgrims on the Way* (Grand Rapids: Zondervan, 2011), 516.

[11] Two contemporary Catholics who hold a type of Pelagianism include Daryl Domning and Monika Hellwig, whose views are dependent upon their denial of Adam's historicity. For example, see Domning's 2006 book in the Ashgate Science and Religion series, titled *Original Selfishness: Original Sin and Evil in the Light of Evolution* (New York, NY: Routledge, 2016).

[12] Quoted by Augustine, *Nature and Grace*, in *Answer to the Pelagians I*, trans. Roland J. Teske, ed. John E. Rotelle, I/23 of *The Works of Augustine* (New York: New City Press, 1997), 10.

is capable of not sinning at all since he has not inherited Adam's sinful disposition or inclined necessarily to sin.

What is the purpose, then, of sending Christ into the world? According to Pelagius, the Father sent His Son to bring a better Law than the Law of Moses. Justification, for Pelagius, is still by means of God's Law, as it was in the Old Testament, but now, with the coming of Christ, one is justified by obeying Christ's commands. Where does the cross fit into this equation? While mankind took a wrong turn by following the example of Adam, it can be reversed if Christ's exemplary godliness is followed.[13]

If one removes the doctrine of original sin, then a sin-bearing substitute who removes guilt and pays its price is unnecessary and irrelevant. Sin is no longer a judicial problem, and by consequence the cross is no longer a satisfaction of divine justice, nor the basis upon which a righteous status can be imputed to the account of the one who trusts in Christ. Turning original sin into imitation rather than imputation has little ability to explain why the New Testament counters the effects of original sin with a mediator who acts as the head of a new covenant in order to redeem God's covenant people by means of a propitiatory sacrifice. Misunderstanding man's plight inevitably misconstrues the forensic nature of the cross.

The situation differs entirely, however, when the cross is interpreted in light of a conception of original sin that operates by corresponding theological categories. Space precludes an evaluation of the debates between realism, mediate imputation, and immediate imputation.[14] Nevertheless, for the sake of the argument, consider the ways immediate imputation safeguards PSA.

The immediate view can be found in Protestant scholastic literature, and has been taught by both Reformed and Baptist theologians since the sixteenth century.[15]

---

[13] For more on Pelagius, see my *Salvation by Grace: The Case for Effectual Calling and Regeneration* (Phillipsburg, NJ: P&R, 2013), chapter 2.

[14] However, see my forthcoming *40 Questions About Salvation* (Grand Rapids: Kregel, 2018).

[15] For example, consult Francis Turretin's (1623–1697) *Institutes of Elenctic Theology*, 3 vols., ed. James T. Dennison Jr., trans. George Musgrave Giger (Phillipsburg, NJ: P&R Publishing, 1992–1997), 1:591–685. Also notable are The Westminster Confession of Faith (1647), the Savoy Declaration (1658), and the Second London Confession (1689). The position is also present in the thought of Old Princetonian theologians like Charles Hodge (1797–1878), as well as Dutch Reformed theologians like Herman Bavinck (1854–1921). See Charles Hodge, *Systematic Theology* (Grand Rapids: Eerdmans, 1986), 2:130–279; Herman Bavinck, *Reformed Dogmatics,* ed. John Bolt, trans. John Vriend (Grand Rapids: Baker Academic, 2006), 3:25–125. In the early twentieth century, Reformed theologians in America, such as J. Gresham Machen (1881–1937), John Murray (1898–1975), and Louis Berkhof (d. 1957), provided notable treatments of the view. John Murray's commentary on Romans and his book *The Imputation of Adam's Sin* are formidable defenses. E.g., John Murray, "The Imputation of Adam's Sin," in K. Scott Oliphint, ed., *Justified in Christ: God's Plan for Us in Justification* (Fearn, Ross-shire: Mentor, 2001), 205–284. Berkhof's articulation of the immediate view is summarized in his well-known *Systematic Theology* (Edinburgh: The Banner of Truth, 2003), 219–226.

Basic to the immediate view is the concept of federal headship. When Adam sinned, he represented his progeny and his guilt was imputed directly to all covenant children. Since his guilt is credited to mankind, each person is born into a state of pollution. Turning to Paul's argument in Romans 5:12–21, advocates of immediate imputation contest that Adam's guilt is not mediated through corruption (mediate imputation), nor is solidarity with Adam solely or primarily based on a realist conception of a common human nature. Instead, Adam's guilt is imputed *directly*, and, logically speaking, mankind receives his corrupt nature as a result. Because Adam is not only mankind's physical (natural) head, but its federal representative, his status and, by consequence, his nature are reckoned to his children.

Immediate imputation possesses the theological tools necessary to make sense of Paul's forensic conception of the atonement and his Adam/second Adam covenant typology in Romans 5 as well as 1 Corinthians 15:22.[16] Justification stems from Christ's one act of righteousness, which counters the condemnation that originates from Adam's one act of disobedience (see Rom. 5:18–19).[17] "We are constituted sinners in Adam," says Turretin, "in the *same way* in which we are constituted righteous in Christ."[18] Such a constitution entirely depends, therefore, upon who we are in union with—namely, Adam or Christ.

The second Adam is like the first Adam in that He acts as our representative, our covenant head. In doing so, the second Adam takes upon Himself the guilt imputed from the first Adam. Yet such headship is only possible if this new covenant head acts as substitute. Notice, since it is guilt that the second Adam bears, the cross must have a penal nature to it as well, not merely a substitutionary nature. As those who are *in Adam*, we inherit his guilt, which is the source of our condemnation, judgment, and punishment. The remedy can only be found in a Mediator who is condemned in our place, pierced for our transgressions, and crushed for our iniquities (Isa. 53:5). Our union with Adam must be countered by our union with Christ, a union that involves a double imputation: our guilt imputed to Him upon the cross and His perfect obedience and righteousness imputed to us upon faith.

We are far better equipped to draw biblical conclusions concerning the atonement when we have in place an equally biblical, and equally consistent, paradigm of original sin.

---

[16] I cannot go into depth here, but for a defense of immediate imputation, see my forthcoming *40 Questions About Salvation* (Grand Rapids: Kregel, 2018), chapters 2 and 3.

[17] See Thomas R. Schreiner, "Original Sin and Original Death: Romans 5:12-19," in *Adam, the Fall, and Original Sin: Theological, Biblical, and Scientific Perspectives*, ed. Hans Madueme and Michael Reeves (Grand Rapids: Baker, 2014), 271–88.

[18] Turretin, *Institutes*, 1:618 (emphasis added).

Atonement, Justification, and the Divine Perfections

Whether or not we reach the conclusion Paul does in 2 Corinthians 5:21 is dependent upon whether we have in place not only a biblical notion of original sin, but also a proper understanding of the divine perfections.

Divine Justice and Divine Justification

One of the major reasons critics of PSA react negatively to the doctrine is they have not considered exactly why Christ would need to be made sin in the first place. To them, substitution seems unnecessary and irrelevant because they cannot fathom a God who would stand against sin and demand a penalty.

Not unrelated to our discussion of original sin, immediate imputation assumes that guilt and corruption directly oppose the holiness and justice of God. If God does nothing in response to Adam's fall, then one is warranted to ask whether this God actually is a just deity to begin with. Justice cannot turn a blind eye to wickedness and injustice. Nor can it ignore violation of the Law. Neither will a just God relax His Law. Any court system assumes this much, otherwise its credibility is questioned. Why would one assume that the God who *is* justice Himself, who defines and determines the very meaning of justice, and who exemplifies justice be any different?

The reason penal substitution seems so offensive is that we have a deeper allergy—that is, an allergy to the very concept of retributive justice itself. Yet retributive justice stems from the very character of God. As the God who is unwavering in holiness, immutable in righteousness, He must—at least if He is to remain holy—punish those who transgress His holy Law. It's not merely that this God must punish wickedness; this God must burn hot in anger against wickedness because it represents everything He is not and threatens a full assault upon everything He is.

This last emphasis has been missed by advocates of the governmental theory of the atonement. Its father, the seventeenth-century theologian Hugo Grotius (1583–1645), rightly understood God to be the supreme governor of the universe. Yet Grotius believed that God is the type of governor who can stand above the Law, which led Him to conclude that this God might relax His Law in order to solve the sin problem. As long as the Law was retained, even if it be a relaxed version, God's holiness is still exemplified, moral order is still preserved, and our relationship to God as governor is left intact. It is for our "common good" that there be a "conservation and example of order" in our world, Grotius concluded.[19]

---

[19] *Defense of the Catholic Faith on the Satisfaction of Christ, against F. Socinus*, 3; quoted in H. D. McDonald, *Atonement of the Death of Christ: In Faith, Revelation, and History* (Grand Rapids: Baker, 1985), 204.

Why, then, does Christ experience punishment at the cross? At the cross, the relaxed version of the Law is met, sin is exposed, and we learn to hold God's Law in honor. Calvary's fundamental purpose, for Grotius, is not satisfaction; after all, Christ is only satisfying a relaxed version of the Law. Instead, its primary purpose is to preserve God's identity as moral governor.

Ironically, the governmental view does not take divine government and justice seriously enough. Violation of God's Law is not merely legal but is most fundamentally antithetical to God's own moral integrity. To relax the Law and reduce the cross to a lesson in moral order is to depersonalize sin and treat the moral integrity of God mechanically, as if the breach of His justice needs merely public restitution rather than personal propitiation. "The cross," says Horton, "not only *demonstrates* God's justice (as if it took the cruel death of the Son of God to offer us merely an object lesson) but *fulfills* God's justice."[20]

God is not merely *irritated* that those made in His image have disrupted the balance of the world's moral order. Sinners stand condemned in the hands of an angry God. "The bow of God's wrath is bent," Jonathan Edwards observes, "and the arrow made ready on the string, and Justice bends the arrow at your heart, and strains the bow, and it is nothing but the mere pleasure of God, and that of an angry God, without any promise or obligation at all, that keeps the arrow one moment from being made drunk with your blood."[21]

At the same time, it is critical to abandon caricatures that picture God as a drunk, abusive husband who erupts for no reason. That is an unrighteous, arbitrary anger that results in brutality. God's anger, on the other hand, is a righteous indignation, a holy wrath, against His enemies—those who have joined the kingdom of darkness.

The display of God's retributive justice pervades the biblical story line: It is the flood engulfing the wicked, whose hearts were filled with evil continually. It is the fire and sulfur falling upon Sodom and Gomorrah because they persistently perverted the beauty of sexuality as God intended. It is the Egyptians drowning in the Red Sea because they insisted, after numerous opportunities to desist, upon enslaving God's covenant people. It is Israel being dragged into exile by Assyria and Babylon because they traded the one true God for idols they made in the image of creation. It is Jesus overturning tables in the temple because He is outraged at the sacrilegious indifference to His Father's holy space for worship. It is Jesus outraged at the Pharisees, condemning them to eternal punishment

---

[20] Horton, *The Christian Faith*, 515.
[21] Jonathan Edwards, "Sinners in the Hands of an Angry God," in vol. 22, *Sermons and Discourses, 1739-1742*, ed. Harry S. Stout (WJE Online), http://edwards.yale.edu/e?path=aHR0cDovL2Vkd2FyZHMueWFsZS-5lZHUvY2dpLWJpbi9uZXdwaGlsby9YXZpZZ2F0ZS5wbD93amVVvLjlx.

because they have used the name of God to mask their hypocrisy.

These are not random acts of divine madness, as if God has lost control of His anger, an assumption that violates divine impassibility. Such a reading divorces retributive justice from the biblical story line, failing to see that there is an enemy marching against the kingdom of God, and that Adam's children have joined rank, holding their fists in the air, shouting a rebel's cry. Man has inherited Adam's guilt and corruption, and he acts upon that polluted nature the first chance he has. He is not coerced but gladly indulges, only furthering his condemnation.

For this reason, retributive justice is deserved. The solution is not that such justice be sidelined, but met. The reason Christ is such good news to sinners is that His substitution is for the very purpose of satisfying such justice. Unless the incarnate Son, the head of the new covenant, drinks the cup of wrath by means of spilling His blood of the new covenant (Luke 22:20), man will forever and always be the recipient of the justice he deserves.

Notice, however, that PSA not only addresses the justice humanity deserves, but also preserves the sanctity of divine justice. Isn't this Paul's reason for rejoicing in Romans 3:26? It is only because God put Christ forward as a "propitiation" (Rom. 3:25) that God could justify the ungodly without forfeiting His own identity as the "just" one.

Because retributive justice is satisfied by a propitiatory sacrifice, a corner is turned, one in which divine righteousness no longer is active but passive, to borrow Martin Luther's categories.[22] In other words, propitiation is the very ground upon which justification is based. It is because Christ took upon Himself the righteousness *of* God that the righteousness *from* God can be reckoned to the account of those united to Christ.[23] To return to Pauline language, "now the righteousness of God has been manifested apart from the law . . . the righteousness of God through faith in Jesus Christ for all who believe" (3:21a, 22). It is through the "redemption that is in Christ Jesus, whom God put forward as a propitiation by his blood" (3:24–25) that we are "justified by his grace as a gift" (3:24).

Retributive justice is assumed in 2 Corinthians 5 as well. It is unsurprising that Paul, in verse 18, introduces the concept of "reconciliation." Through Christ,

---

[22] The "afflicted conscience," Luther advised, "has no remedy against despair and eternal death except to take hold of the promise of grace offered in Christ, that is, this righteousness of faith, this passive or Christian righteousness." Rather than trusting in one's own righteousness through the Law (what Luther labelled "active righteousness"), one should instead look to "passive righteousness," that is, the righteousness of Jesus. "Thus I put myself beyond all active righteousness, all righteousness of my own or of the divine Law, and I embrace only that passive righteousness which is the righteousness of grace, mercy, and the forgiveness of sins." The righteousness of Christ, says Luther, is not a righteousness we "perform but receive;" it is not one we "have but accept, when God the Father grants it to us through Jesus Christ." *Luther's Works,* ed. Jaroslav Pelikan (St. Louis and Philadelphia: Concordia, 1963), 26:5–6.

[23] Horton uses these categories: *of* vs. *from.* See *The Christian Faith,* 620–647.

God "reconciled us to himself and gave us the ministry of reconciliation" (5:18). Could this reconciliation to God through Christ have anything to do with our legal standing? Verse 19 answers in the affirmative: "in Christ God was reconciling the world to himself, *not counting their trespasses against them*" (emphasis added). Reconciliation is only possible as an outcome if man's trespasses are not counted against him (non-imputation) but are instead counted to Christ (imputation). That explains why Paul says at the start of verse 21, "For our sake he made him to be sin who knew no sin." On that basis alone, we become the "righteousness of God" (5:21b).[24]

Divine Simplicity

Divine justice is not the only doctrinal strand woven into the PSA web; divine simplicity is as well, perhaps in a way evangelicals have not been attuned to noticing.

In the literature against PSA, it is striking how often critics elevate divine love in order to set it against divine justice.[25] Fault lies in a common caricature: the angry Father punishes His loving Son. Notice, however, how mercy and love, as opposed to wrath and justice, become the controlling hermeneutical perfections. Yet they are not just given priority, they are perceived to be *antithetical* to a God who expresses anger and wrath.

Many Christians today find this argument incredibly persuasive. Nevertheless, if evangelicals would respect classical theism, they would instinctively see through such a maneuver because it betrays divine simplicity.

Though denied by some (Arminian) Remonstrants and Socinians in the sixteenth and seventeenth centuries, simplicity is an old doctrine, articulated and defended by Patristic, Medieval, and Reformation thinkers.[26] Augustine would write in *On the Trinity*, "The nature of God is simple and immutable and undisturbed, nor is he himself one thing and what he is and has another thing."[27] In order to counter those arguing that the Trinity results in "three things" rather than three persons united in one essence, Anselm likewise appealed to simplicity.

---

[24] Note how Colossians 1:20–21 likewise connects atonement (the "blood of the cross") to reconciliation as the solution to our alienation and hostility.

[25] See the many critics in Steve Jeffery, Michael Ovey, and Andrew Sach, *Pierced for Our Transgressions: Rediscovering the Glory of Penal Substitution* (Wheaton, IL: Crossway, 2007).

[26] Only in the modern era has a doctrine like simplicity (as well as other classical attributes like impassibility, immutability, eternity, and omnipresence) been denied. See my forthcoming book where I put forward the significance of attributes like simplicity: Matthew Barrett, *A Pathway into the Heart of God* (Grand Rapids: Baker Books, 2019).

[27] Augustine, *The Trinity*, ed. John E. Rotelle, trans. Edmund Hill (Brooklyn, NY: New City, 1991), VII: 10. Also see idem, *City of God*, trans. Marcus Dods (New York: Random House, 1950), XI: 10. Turretin, *Institutes*, 1:194, builds off of Augustine to make his own case for simplicity.

God's substance is a "simple substance," and cannot be "composed of parts." God cannot be a "composite" being, for a "composite thing of necessity can be actually or conceptually divided into parts."[28] Aquinas makes a similar point:

> God is not composed of extended parts (since he is not a body), nor of form and matter, nor does he differ from his own nature, nor his nature from his existence. Nor can we distinguish in him genus and difference, nor substance and accidents. It is therefore clear that God is in no way composite. Rather, he is entirely simple.[29]

In affirming with Augustine, Anselm, and Aquinas that God *is* His attributes, we preserve the unity of God's perfections.[30] Applied to our discussion, simplicity means the wrath displayed at the cross is a *holy* wrath. Simplicity guards us from the caricature that would turn the Father's wrath into a capricious, whimsical tantrum. The type of anger God expresses is one consistent with His whole being, which means this anger may burn hot but does so as a justified, righteous anger. Leon Morris puts it this way:

> If we think of an uncontrollable outburst of passion, then we have a pagan conception, completely inapplicable to the God of the Old Testament. But if we think rather of a wrath which is the reverse side of a holy love, a flame which sears but purifies, then we have a conception which is valuable not only for an understanding of the ancient Scriptures, but also for any right conception of the nature of God.[31]

Can the same be said of divine love? While it might seem counterintuitive to say God's wrath is a loving wrath, it nevertheless is consistent with Scripture. Scripture never divorces propitiation from the loving intention of the Father to save His elect. The very reason His wrath is poured out on His Son is that God so loved the world (John 3:16), not despite His love for the world.

---

[28] Anselm of Canterbury, *On the Incarnation of the Word*, in *The Major Works* (Oxford: Oxford University Press, 1998), 244.
[29] Aquinas, *Summa Theologiae, Questions on God*, Cambridge Texts in the History of Philosophy, ed. Brian Davies and Brian Leftow (Cambridge: Cambridge University Press, 2006), 40.
[30] For recent treatments of divine simplicity, see Katharin Rogers, *Perfect Being Theology* (Edinburgh: Edinburgh University Press, 2000), 24–39; James E. Dolezal, *God without Parts: Divine Simplicity and the Metaphysics of God's Absoluteness* (Eugene, OR: Pickwick, 2011); Steven J. Duby, *Divine Simplicity: A Dogmatic Account*, vol. 30, T&T Clark Studies in Systematic Theology, ed. John Webster, Ian A. McFarland, Ivor Davidson (London and New York: Bloomsbury T&T Clark, 2016).
[31] Leon Morris, *Apostolic Preaching of the Cross* (Grand Rapids: Eerdmans, 1965), 159.

Can we reverse the order and say God's love is a wrathful love? That might give the wrong impression, as if God's love is not actually loving in the end. But we can say something related: God's love is a *jealous* love. How many times in the Old Testament does God discipline His people, and even judge them, because He, as their bridegroom, is jealous not only for His own name but also for the covenant faithfulness of His bride (Ex. 34:14; Deut. 4:24)?[32] Far from a "careless sentimentality indifferent to the moral integrity of the loved ones," says Leon Morris, God's love is a "purifying fire."[33]

Within this same doctrinal domain, it is necessary to say that God's love is a *righteous* love. A righteous love brings us back to divine justice. While the cross exhibits the greatest love of all—the Father giving His own Son over to death—this love should not be reduced to mere will power. God will not, by merely a declaration of His will, simply forgive sin without exacting its due punishment. That type of love would violate His justice and smack of an absolute, voluntaristic power that is unpredictable, unreliable, and potentially unethical. The necessity of the atonement assumes that the love of the Father in sending His Son to the cross is a righteous, holy love.[34]

Such logic can be taken a step further to argue that PSA, contrary to popular belief, actually makes more sense out of divine love, due to its commitment to divine simplicity, than other theories of the atonement. Texts like John 3:16–17, John 15:13, Romans 5:8, and especially 1 John 4:8–10 not only pair propitiation with the love of God, but also ground PSA in the love of God. It is only because the Father loved us so much that He sent His Son to bear our punishment. The love referred to in these verses is not restricted to the Son but is applied to the Father as well. Not only did Jesus substitute Himself out of love for God's people, but the Father's love moved Him to give up His beloved Son. "God did not demand first satisfaction and then love," Horton observes, "but was moved by his love to send his Son to make satisfaction."[35]

Additionally, the Father's love is equaled by the Son's love.[36] He is no passive victim on the cross, coerced into an abusive reception of His Father's wrath. Jesus says in John 10:15 and 18 that He lays down His own life of His own accord, a deliberate act that stems from His voluntary covenant with the Father in eternity, what theologians have labeled the *pactum salutis* ("the covenant of redemption").[37] The

---

[32] For a treatment of divine jealousy, see Erik Thoennes, *Godly Jealousy: A Theology of Intolerant Love* (Fearn, Ross-shire: Christian Focus, 2005).

[33] Morris, *Apostolic Preaching of the Cross*, 158.

[34] Assumed in what I've just said is yet another strand of simplicity: God's power is not that of the voluntarist, but His power must be consistent with His righteousness and love, or His righteous love.

[35] Horton, *The Christian Faith*, 511.

[36] Ibid., 514.

[37] See J. V. Fesko, *The Trinity and the Covenant of Redemption* (Fearn, Ross-shire: Mentor, 2016).

Father appoints His Son, and the Son willfully embraces His mission.

PSA, more than any other theory, highlights the horror of the cross: not just the physical torment but also the affliction of divine wrath. Nevertheless, such horror only accentuates the love of our triune God. It shows just how far God would stoop in order to redeem His people. "If the true measure of love," says J. I. Packer, "is how low it stoops to help, and how much in its humility it is ready to do and bear, then it may fairly be claimed that the penal substitutionary model embodies a richer witness to divine love than any other model of atonement, for it sees the Son at his Father's will going lower than any other view ventures to suggest." Christ not merely endured crucifixion, but PSA, says Packer, "adds to all this a further dimension of truly unimaginable distress. . . . This is the dimension indicated by Denney—'that in that dark hour He had to realize to the full the divine reaction against sin in the race.'"[38]

Packer criticizes McLeod Campbell, who claimed, much in line with Socinus before him, that the Reformed view "reduced God's love to an arbitrary decision which does not reveal his character." By contrast, PSA stems from within the character of God. Far from arbitrary, the motive behind the cross is not only the satisfaction of our deserved retribution but the salvific benevolence that defines all three persons of the Godhead. With simplicity in view, we can conclude that the cross is the ultimate demonstration of righteous love. The cross is Psalm 85:10 in action: "Steadfast love and faithfulness meet; righteousness and peace kiss each other."[39]

Atonement, Wrath, Love, and Inseparable Operations in the Trinity

So far, we've seen why it is illegitimate, in light of divine simplicity, to set in opposition divine perfections like love and righteousness. Those who do so do not merely risk placing divine *perfections* at odds with one another, but divine *persons* as well. Caricatures of PSA tend to situate the Father and Son against one another, victimizing the Son to an angry Father. If true, PSA is guilty of turning the atonement into a mechanism by which the Godhead is divided. How do we avoid this distortion?

On this point, we are wise to learn from the Fathers and Reformers who claimed that the external works of the Trinity are undivided (*opera ad extra trinitatis indivisa*

---

[38] Packer, "What Did the Cross Achieve?," 40.

[39] Ovey's conclusion is spot on: "We cannot speak of God's love as though it were a 'part' of God, separate from his holiness. Rather, all God's attributes are in harmony with each other: his holiness is a loving holiness, a merciful holiness; his justice is a truthful justice, a holy justice, and so on. Within this framework, none of God's attributes should be regarded as more 'central' or 'essential' than any of the others" (*Pierced for Our Transgressions*, 138).

sunt), often labeled the doctrine of inseparable operations. According to Augustine, the Father, Son, and Spirit "are indivisible" and so they "work indivisibly."[40] Just as the three persons are indivisible in essence and will, so they are indivisible in their redemptive purpose and activity.[41] Richard Muller explains, "Since the Godhead is one in essence, one in knowledge, and one in will, it would be impossible in any work *ad extra* (q.v.) for one of the divine persons to will and to do one thing and another of the divine persons to will and do another."[42] Since the three persons equally share one nature and one will, so too is the economic work of the Trinity in salvation history a reflection of that one, undivided essence.[43]

Does that mean, then, that there is no distinction in how each person acts at any particular moment in salvation history? Have we slipped into the territory of a functional Modalism? Not at all. Though the three persons are indivisible in essence and will, and therefore indivisible in their salvific work, nevertheless, they are distinct persons, with one or more persons of the Godhead being manifested in the fulfilment of that one, indivisible work at any point in redemptive history. "The incarnation and work of mediation," for example, "terminate on the Son, even though they are willed and effected by Father, Son, and Spirit," Muller concludes.[44]

How is this relevant to the atonement? Caricatures of PSA can exist only within an atonement paradigm where the doctrine of inseparable operations is absent. Unlike the caricature, it is inconceivable that the persons of the Trinity be set against one another, as if an angry Father is pitted against His victimized Son. Nor is it the case that one trinitarian person acts independently or in contradiction to another.

Rather, the three persons are united in their redemptive work leading up to the cross. Apart from this unity and indivisibility, atonement would be impossible

---

[40] Augustine, *The Trinity: De Trinitate*, in *The Works of Saint Augustine*, ed. John E. Rotelle, trans. Edmund Hill (New York: New City, 1991), 70. Elsewhere Augustine states, "Therefore, as there is an equality and inseparability of the persons, not only of the Father and the Son, but also of the Holy Spirit, so also the works are inseparable." *Tractates on the Gospel of John 11-27*, The Fathers of the Church, trans. John W. Rettig (Washington, DC: The Catholic University of America Press, 1988), 166. Also see Augustine, *Sermons: III (51-94) on the New Testament*, The Works of Saint Augustine, ed. Jon E. Rotelle, trans. Edmund Hill (New York: New City, 1991), 50–52.

[41] Inseparable operations is grounded in the way the members of the Trinity mutually indwell one another (i.e., perichoresis; see John 14:10; Ovey, *Pierced for Our Transgressions*, 130).

[42] Richard A. Muller, *Dictionary of Latin and Greek Theological Terms: Drawn Principally from Protestant Scholastic Theology* (Grand Rapids: Baker Books, 1985), 213.

[43] Wellum writes, "Because the nature is where the *capacity of willing* is located, we can say that the three persons *act* as distinct persons according to their eternal-immanent relations, in and through the *capacities* of the divine nature, which includes the same will" (Stephen J. Wellum, *God the Son Incarnate: The Doctrine of Christ*, ed. John S. Feinberg [Wheaton, IL: Crossway, 2016], 402).

[44] Ibid. And we should also qualify, since it is the Son alone who becomes incarnate, that while there is one will in the Godhead tied to the one divine nature, nevertheless, there are two wills in the undivided person of Christ, each will tied to its corresponding nature; a divine will and a human will.

at Golgotha.[45] Nor would certainty be attainable; after all, what assurance could the Son have that His Father would justify His atonement by vindicating Him from the grave if there is no unity in purpose?[46] On the other hand, inseparable operations means that when any particular member of the Trinity acts in salvation history, He does so in a way that is consistent with the one will of the triune Godhead. Regardless of whether a particular person of the Godhead is on the receiving end or on the distributing end, no disunity can be smuggled into the external works of the Trinity.

In *Pierced for Our Transgressions*, Mike Ovey explains that this Trinitarian structure means that one person of the Trinity can be the subject of an action, while another is the object, and that there not be (as critics assume) a division within the Trinity.[47] Consider the many ways Scripture speaks in this manner:

- Father (subject) and Son (object)
  - Father loves Son (John 3:35; 5:20; 17:23)
  - Father sends Son (John 6:39)
  - Father gives Son to redeem world (John 3:16; Rom. 8:32)
  - Father raises Son from the grave (Gal. 1:1; Eph. 1:20; Acts 2:24; Rom. 6:4; 1 Cor. 6:14)
  - Father exalts Son (Phil. 2:9)
  - Father glorifies Son (John 17:1, 22, 24)

- Son (subject) and Father (object)
  - Son loves/obeys Father (John 14:31)
  - Son glorifies Father (John 17:1)

- Father and Son (subjects) and Spirit (object)
  - Father and Son send Spirit (John 3:34; 14:16, 26; 15:26; 16:7; Acts 1:4)

- Spirit (subject) and Son (object)
  - Spirit sends Son into desert (Mark 1:12)
  - Spirit glorifies Son (John 16:14)[48]

Such scriptural warrant demonstrates that the persons of the Trinity can act as subject and/or object in any one redemptive act. Why would the cross be an exception?

---

[45] Ovey, *Pierced for Our Transgressions*, 130.
[46] Ibid.
[47] Ibid.
[48] I have summarized Ovey's longer discussion (ibid., 131).

Such an insight was obscured by C. H. Dodd, who significantly revised a biblical definition of divine wrath, which does not "describe the attitude of God to man," but "an inevitable process of cause and effect in the moral universe."[49] He then exchanged propitiation for expiation (as exemplified in the New English Bible [1961]; see its translation of *hilastērion* in 1 John 2:2; 4:10; Rom. 3:25), and concluded that the Son cannot be the subject who propitiates His Father nor the object who absorbs divine wrath. Though Dodd's exegesis has been substantially critiqued by Leon Morris and Roger Nicole,[50] many today, such as Paul Fiddes, Joel Green, Mark Baker, and Tom Smail, perpetuate Dodd's aversion to propitiation and have added a theological element, arguing that a subject-object distinction would create a breach in the Trinity.[51]

Yet none of these contemporary authors pay sufficient attention to how the doctrine of "inseparable operations" preserves the cohesiveness of the atonement. At the cross, the Son acts as subject, propitiating His Father, the object. Yet we might also acknowledge that the Father acts as subject, pouring down His wrath upon His own Son, the object. Yet this object-subject interplay is the very fulfilment of the one, undivided will of the triune Godhead. The incarnate Son voluntarily submits Himself to the preordained purpose of the Father, as evident in Jesus' Gethsemane prayer, and the Father in turn approves the work of the propitiation that His Son accomplishes, most visibly manifested when He raises Him from the dead, thereby vindicating His Son and justifying His work of atonement (Rom. 4:25).

What should one make of the Son's cry of dereliction? After all, He does quote from Psalm 22 to express how God has forsaken Him. In response, His cry should not be interpreted as the moment the Trinity ontologically dissolved or ruptured. Instead, His cry should be interpreted in redemptive, covenantal, and forensic categories. Here is where the doctrine of original sin is strategically necessary. The Son is forsaken by the Father but only in the sense that He, our second Adam, our federal head, has taken upon Himself our guilt and with it our forsakenness as covenant-breakers. He does not deserve this punishment (as Paul says in 2 Cor. 5:21, He "knew no sin"), but He was "made . . . sin . . . so that in him we might become the righteousness of God" (2 Cor. 5:21). Or to use the language of Galatians, "Christ redeemed us from the curse of the Law, having become a curse for us" (3:13 NASB).

In such a representational sense, Christ is cursed and forsaken by the Father,

---

[49] C. H. Dodd, *The Epistle of Paul to the Romans* (London: Hodder & Stoughton, 1932), 23.
[50] See Morris, *The Apostolic Preaching of the Cross*; Roger Nicole, "C. H. Dodd and the Doctrine of Propitiation," *Westminster Theological Journal* 17 (1955): 117–157.
[51] This point is made by Ovey in *Pierced for Our Transgressions*, 131.

receiving the due punishment of a sin-bearer. Yet even here, in His forsakenness, the Trinity is in another sense immutably indivisible and omnipotently undivided because the Son has accomplished the very mission He was appointed to accomplish *by the Father.* As counterintuitive as it may seem, in this dark moment of forsakenness, the triune God displays His unbreakable Triunity.

Conclusion

Certainly, other doctrinal strands in the web of atonement could be explored.[52] The doctrinal web has many silk, theological strands, each connecting to another. Whether they properly connect to one another will in large part determine what kind of atonement theology one subscribes to in the end.

The ramifications for pastoral ministry are profound as well. As important as it is to exegete individual passages of Scripture in preparation for Sunday's sermon, that is just the beginning. Much more is needed. Pastors must think theologically. The pastor must be a theologian. Only then will one behold the atonement in all its dogmatic glory. Only then will the sheep see the atonement in all its systematic beauty.

---

[52] See my unabridged address at The Shepherds' Conference where I explore various Christologies and their influence upon the atonement: https://www.gracechurch.org/sermons/12959?AspxAutoDetectCookieSupport=1.

11

UP FROM THE GRAVE: THE RESURRECTION

I CORINTHIANS 15:1–20

Tom Pennington

Take a comparative religion course, and you will discover that most world religions are based on philosophical propositions. Only four are based primarily on their founders: Judaism, Buddhism, Islam, and Christianity. And all four of those founders died. Abraham died around 2000 BC and was buried in Hebron. Buddha died in the fifth or sixth century BC—tradition says at the age of eighty, and his body was cremated. Muhammad died June 8, AD 632. His body is buried in Medina, Saudi Arabia, and millions visit his grave every year on their pilgrimage to Mecca. Jesus died in the year AD 30 or 33 and was buried in a borrowed grave just outside Jerusalem. They *all* died.

But Christianity is unique in that it alone boasts an empty tomb. Only the Christian faith claims its founder was raised permanently, eternally from the dead. The reason we preach Christ is that we preach Christ *risen from the dead*!

The greatest minds in the history of the church have understood the vital importance of this issue. Martin Luther wrote, "The greatest importance attaches to this article of the faith. For were there no resurrection, we should have neither comfort nor hope, and all that Christ has done would be in vain."[1] John Calvin wrote, "The resurrection of Christ is the most important article of our faith;" "the chief point of the gospel," and "the main article of religion."[2] Later, B. B. Warfield

---

[1] Martin Luther, *What Luther Says*, compiled by Ewald M. Plass (Saint Louis, MO: Concordia, 1959), 181.
[2] John Calvin, *Calvin's Wisdom: An Anthology Arranged Alphabetically*, compiled by Graham Miller (Edinburgh, Scotland: Banner of Truth Trust, 1992), 300.

wrote, "Christ Himself deliberately staked His whole claim upon His resurrection. When asked for a sign, He pointed to this sign as His single and sufficient credential."[3]

No article of our faith is more essential, and no passage of Scripture more clearly articulates its importance to the Christian faith than 1 Corinthians 15. Paul wrote this chapter to respond to what he had heard was being taught in Corinth. In 15:12, Paul says, "How do some among you say that there is no resurrection of the dead?" Where did that idea come from? It certainly didn't come from Paul.

The Corinthian believers were primarily Greek. Many in their culture believed in the immortality of the soul. Plato, for example, assumed that the human soul is immortal, but he also taught that the body is a prison and that death releases the immortal soul from its prison. The Greeks found the idea of the resurrection of the body ludicrous. Why would you want to retain your prison forever? That's why when the Athenians heard Paul speak of the resurrection of the dead, some began to sneer (Acts 17:32).

Tragically, as often happens with the church, secular thinking—in this case, Hellenistic dualism—found its way into the church. Paul heard there were some in the Corinthian church who denied that the bodies of believers would be raised. They were apparently teaching that once the believer dies, he exists forever as a spirit. That's the false teaching Paul is correcting in 1 Corinthians 15.

The first section of this chapter is merely Paul's introduction of the issue he wants to address. In verses 1–11, he reminds us that the resurrection of Jesus is a central tenet of the gospel. "Now I make known to you, brethren, the gospel which I preached to you, which also you received, in which also you stand, by which also you are saved, if you hold fast the word which I preached to you, unless you believed in vain" (vv. 1–2). This was the gospel that he and the apostles had preached and that the Corinthians had believed. And it's the gospel they must continue to believe in order to be saved.

Paul then summarizes his gospel: "For I delivered to you as of first importance what I also received" (v. 3). Paul had delivered this very gospel message to them during the eighteen months he ministered to them, as recorded in Acts 18. And Paul states that he didn't invent his message. He says, "I received it." In Galatians, Paul tells us how and where he received it: "For I would have you know, brethren, that the gospel which was preached by me is not according to man, for I neither received it from man, nor was I taught it, but I received it through a revelation of Jesus Christ" (Gal. 1:11–12). Paul wants us to understand that the

---

[3] B. B. Warfield, cited in Josh McDowell, *The New Evidence That Demands a Verdict* (Nashville: Thomas Nelson, Inc., 1999), 208.

gospel he is about to summarize is not his gospel. It's the gospel that was directly taught to him by Jesus Christ Himself!

And this message is of first importance. It is primary, central, and indispensable. Paul calls this central message of the Christian faith the *euangelion*, "the good news" (v. 1). Then, in verses 3–11, he summarizes it. It's even possible that this passage is a fragment of an early confession of the church; many church historians believe that to be true.

> For I delivered to you as of first importance what I also received, that Christ died for our sins according to the Scriptures, and that He was buried, and that He was raised on the third day according to the Scriptures, and that He appeared to Cephas, then to the twelve. After that He appeared to more than five hundred brethren at one time, most of whom remain until now, but some have fallen asleep; then he appeared to James, then to all the apostles, and last of all, as to one untimely born, He appeared to me also. For I am the least of the apostles, and not fit to be called an apostle, because I persecuted the church of God. But by the grace of God I am what I am, and His grace toward me did not prove vain; but I labored even more than all of them, yet not I, but the grace of God with me. Whether then it was I or they, so we preach and so you believed. (vv. 3–11)

In these verses, Paul reduces the gospel—the core message of the Christian faith that he preached, which our Lord Himself gave to him—to four basic propositions. The structure of the passage is clear. In each case, he introduces the gospel propositions given to him by Christ and he delivered to the Corinthians, with the common Greek subordinating conjunction "that" (*hoti*). He says, "I delivered" these truths to you: "*that* Christ died for our sins according to the Scriptures" (v. 3), "*that* He was buried" (v. 4), "*that* He was raised on the third day according to the Scriptures" (v. 4), and "*that* He appeared" (vv. 5–8; emphasis added).

All four of those propositions stand at the core of the gospel and are about our Lord Jesus Christ. The heart of the gospel is captured in these four events from Jesus' life.

The Four Propositions of the Gospel in Detail

His Substitutionary Death

First, we see here that "Christ died for our sins according to the Scriptures" (v. 3). The Greek word translated "for" here is a general word meaning "on behalf of or for the benefit of." The death of Jesus accomplished some benefit with regard to the sins of those who believe. The key question—and this debate about the nature of the atonement continues in our day, sadly—is what is the nature of the relationship between Jesus' death and sin? In Mark 10:45, our Lord explained clearly that the relationship between His death and our sin was *substitution*. He came to "give His life a ransom *for* many" (emphasis added). In Mark 10:45, the Greek word translated "for" is *anti*, meaning "instead of" or "in the place of." Christ died for our sins, therefore, in the sense that He died *in the place of* those whose sins had merited death.

Because of His holiness and justice, God cannot allow a single sin to go unpunished. But in the marvelous transaction of justification, the Father, driven by His love and grace, credited to Christ the guilt for every sin of every person who would ever believe. Every wicked thought that has ever crossed your mind, every foul attitude you have ever displayed, every ungodly word you have ever spoken, every sinful act you have ever committed, God knew them all, and they all demanded punishment. But in His grace, the Father credited every one of those sins to Jesus Christ, and then He poured out on His own Son the divine justice that every one of those sins deserved.

Romans 3:25 says that God the Father publicly displayed His Son at the cross as the propitiation—the satisfaction of His just wrath against our sins. Second Corinthians 5:21 says that God made Christ "who knew no sin to be sin on our behalf." First Peter 2:24 says, "He Himself bore our sins in His body on the cross." This is what our Lord has done for us.

The idea of the Messiah dying as a substitute for sinners wasn't something Paul invented. He says in verse 3 that it was according to the Hebrew scriptures. In fact, it goes all the way back to Genesis 3:15. There God told the serpent that a unique human male would come into the world and ultimately deal with sin. In Genesis 12:3, God told Abraham that through his descendants, all the nations of the earth would be spiritually blessed even though they deserve to be cursed. Genesis 22:17–18 got more specific. It speaks of Abraham's seed in a general sense, his physical descendants, but then the Lord says, "Your seed shall possess the gate of their [literally, the Hebrew text says "his") enemies." There, God is not talking about Abraham's seed in a collective sense. Instead, He is talking about one Descendant. And that Seed will possess the gates of His enemies! By that one descendant of Abraham's, God would spiritually bless people from all the nations who deserve only His wrath.

Through His work, the Messiah would enable God to spiritually bless sinners who deserve only wrath. But exactly how that would be accomplished did not become clear until about seven hundred years before our Lord was born. It came through the prophet Isaiah in the familiar words of Isaiah 53: "But he was pierced through for our transgressions, He was crushed for our iniquities; the chastening for our well-being fell upon Him, and by His scourging we are healed. All of us like sheep have gone astray, each of us has turned to his own way" (vv. 5–6). Literally, Isaiah says that Yahweh caused the guilt of us all to strike the Messiah. It fell on Him. Isaiah goes on to say, "He was cut off out of the land of the living for the transgression of my people, to whom the stroke was due" (v. 8). Verse 10 then explains the reason for the death of the suffering servant: "He would render Himself as a guilt offering." And verse 11 adds, "My Servant, will justify the many, as He will bear their iniquities." Clearly, the Messiah would die in the place of sinners as their substitute. Christ died for our sins according to the Scriptures.

His Burial

In 1 Corinthians 15:4, Paul adds a second core proposition of his gospel: I delivered to you "that He was buried." All four Gospels refer to the burial of Jesus Christ. They describe how His body was taken down from the cross on Friday afternoon before sunset and how two men, Nicodemus and Joseph of Arimathea (wealthy, influential members of the Jewish High Council who had secretly become His followers), prepared His body for burial.

They quickly wrapped it in strips of cloth with seventy-five pounds of aromatic spices between the layers and then hurriedly placed His body in a new tomb nearby, a cave dug out of the soft, native limestone. It was the tomb of Joseph of Arimathea likely located in what is today the Church of the Holy Sepulcher. Once Joseph and Nicodemus placed His body in the tomb, they sealed the tomb with a large circular stone. The Gospels tell us at least four of Jesus' female followers witnessed the burial. Paul preached the gospel he received from Christ, and that included the fact that our Lord was buried—His dead corpse was placed in the grave.

Why is this a crucial part of the gospel? Because it was evidence of Jesus' death. The Roman soldier had guaranteed Jesus' death with the point of his spear. The centurion had then certified His death to Pilate. Jesus' burial was simply further evidence that He was, in fact, dead. But Jesus' burial is also evidence of His resurrection. One of the primary pieces of evidence that convinced the disciples of the resurrection was the empty tomb. And their certainty of the empty tomb was based on the eyewitness testimony of His burial and the exact location of His grave. There were the testimonies of two members of the Jewish Sanhedrin, the testimony of at least four women, and the testimony of the Roman guard placed there to guard it. Jesus died for our sins according to the Scriptures *and* He was buried.

His Triumphal Resurrection

The third great proposition of the gospel Paul preached is that "He was raised on the third day according to the Scriptures" (v. 4). All four Gospels reach their crescendo in the resurrection. And if you examine the sermons of the early church, you quickly discover that the resurrection is at the heart of them all. The Christian faith and the salvation it promises stand or fall with the resurrection of Jesus Christ.

Literally, Paul says, "He has been raised"—the perfect tense describing a past event with continuing results into the present. Jesus has been raised. He is *still* alive. He has the power of an indestructible life! The Father miraculously restored physical life to the body of Jesus. But Jesus wasn't raised like those whom He Himself had raised. When the Father raised Jesus, He gave Him a new, glorified body. Paul describes it in Philippians 3:21 as "the body of His glory." It was and is a real physical body with flesh and bones. It can be touched. It can eat and drink. And it is a body no longer subject to human weakness, illness, and death.

Again, the Messiah's resurrection is not a new idea. Paul says it happened "according to the Scriptures" (1 Cor. 15:4). The Old Testament text most often cited by the apostles in the book of Acts is Psalm 16:10: "You will not abandon my soul to Sheol; nor will You allow Your Holy One to undergo decay." In his sermon at Pentecost, Peter explains that David prophesied that the Messiah would indeed die, but that His body would never experience decay. Without embalming, decay begins within several days, so the fact that Jesus was raised on the third day—really within about thirty-six hours—was very important to the fulfillment of this prophecy. Another key Old Testament passage that implies the resurrection is Isaiah 53:10: "The Lord was pleased to crush Him, putting Him to grief; if He would render Himself as a guilt offering." To be a guilt offering, the Messiah had to die. But the next phrase says that although He would die as a guilt offering, "He will see His offspring, He will prolong His days, and the good pleasure of the LORD will prosper in His hand." Isaiah 53:12 adds that after the Servant's death, "I will allot Him a portion with the great, and He will divide the booty with the strong; because He poured out Himself to death." Jesus was raised on the third day according to Scripture.

His Glorious Resurrection

The fourth proposition of Paul's gospel in 1 Corinthians 15 is that Christ appeared after His resurrection to many eyewitnesses (vv. 5–11). Here is another part of that core gospel message Paul delivered that had been given to him by Christ: "And that He appeared" (v. 5).

God chose to establish the historical reality of the resurrection through as many as fourteen different post-resurrection appearances. Jesus appeared to a total of more than five hundred different people at different times in at least ten different locations. He appeared to individuals, He appeared to groups of disciples, and He appeared to a large crowd of five hundred. He appeared to men and women. He appeared in public and in private, at different times of the day, in Jerusalem and in Galilee. In verses 5–8, Paul records six of the fourteen or so post-resurrection appearances of Christ. Paul's point is that the good news we have come to embrace is not a blind leap of faith. It's based on the record of the Old Testament Scripture. It rests on the written record of Jesus' hand-picked proxies, the apostles, who passed down that record in the New Testament. It relies on the eyewitness testimony of more than five hundred believers who saw the resurrected Christ.

There are the four foundational propositions at the heart of the gospel, the core of the message we preach. Paul concludes this first section in verse 11: "Whether then *it was* I or they [the other apostles], so we preach and so you believed."

Consequences of Denying the Resurrection

All of that was Paul's introduction. In verses 12 to 19, he finally comes to his chief concern. He wanted to show the Corinthians the contradiction in their thinking. It was illogical for them to reject the future physical resurrection of believers while still claiming to believe in the gospel that has the physical resurrection of Jesus as one of its core propositions.

"Now if Christ is preached, that He has been raised from the dead, how do some among you say that there is no resurrection of the dead? But if there is no resurrection of the dead, not even Christ has been raised" (v. 12). Paul essentially says, "If you deny the resurrection of believers, then logically, no one has ever been raised from the dead. That means Christ has not been raised." And the results of denying the resurrection of Jesus Christ are absolutely catastrophic.

In verses 14 to 19, Paul catalogs the frightening consequences of their position in order to prove the centrality of our Lord's resurrection. If Christ has not been raised, all is lost. If this keystone is removed, Christianity collapses in a heap of rubble. It is fit only for history's trash bin of dead, worthless religions. If Jesus' body still lies buried in a remote grave in Israel, the consequences are beyond calculation and even imagination. Specifically, Paul points out five tragic consequences if Christ has not been raised.

No Legitimate Gospel

The first consequence is that there is no legitimate gospel. Verse 14 says, "If Christ has not been raised, then our preaching is vain." The Greek word translated "preaching" here is *kerugma*. It refers not to the act of preaching, but rather to the content Paul officially proclaimed on behalf of his Lord. He has just explained that content to us in verses 1–11. He basically says, "If Christ has not been raised, then that gospel is vain." The word for "vain" means "empty, without substance, void of spiritual value." Either the tomb is empty, or the gospel is empty. If Christ has not been raised, the gospel is a worthless message and the entire superstructure of Christianity collapses.

One of the most devastating disasters in American history was the Johnstown Flood. After several days of rain, on May 31, 1889, the South Fork Dam experienced a catastrophic failure. It was fourteen miles upstream of the town of Johnstown, Pennsylvania. When the dam broke, twenty million tons of water were released, flowing at a rate equal to the Mississippi River. Several minutes later, a wall of water and debris thirty-five to forty feet high traveling at forty miles an hour hit downtown Johnstown. Four square miles of the downtown were destroyed and 2,200 people died. Ninety-nine entire families were wiped out.

Why did the dam fail? Historian David McCullough, in his book on this catastrophe, explains: "In the case of the South Fork dam, the men in charge of rebuilding it, those who were supposed to be experts in such matters, had not been expert—either in their understanding of what they did or, equally important, in their understanding of the possible consequences of what they did."[4] As a result, the structural integrity of the dam was flawed.

The superstructure of our faith has the resurrection of Christ as its center. It's what supports the gospel and the Christian faith. If it isn't true, the entire structure collapses just like the South Fork Dam, destroying all those who have put their trust in it. If Christ's body has not been raised and remains to this day in an obscure Jewish grave, the good news Paul and the other apostles preached is an ancient fiction that deserves to be forgotten. There is no legitimate gospel, and we have no message to preach.

---

[4] David McCullough, *The Johnstown Flood* (New York: Simon & Schuster, 1968), 262.

No Reasonable Faith

That brings us to a second tragic consequence: if Christ has not been raised, there is no reasonable faith. Paul told the Corinthians, "If Christ has not been raised, then our preaching is vain, your faith also is vain" (v. 14). It's empty, without reality. You may believe, but your faith is worthless, completely void of all spiritual value.

Christ's substitutionary death and His resurrection stand or fall together. Either both are historical events that are true as the apostles described them and our faith is reasonable, or both are fabrications and our faith is unreasonable. Contrary to postmodernism, reality is not whatever you want it to be.

Perhaps you read the news article about those poor children in Mexico whose cancer was treated with fake chemotherapy. A government official reported, "We have results from a laboratory that pointed out that the chemotherapy that was given to the children was not really a drug but an inert compound. It was practically distilled water."[5] That is truly tragic. Those families believed those drugs were real and were helping their children. Sadly, several children died. That is a tragic illustration of the fact that no amount of faith helps if the object of your faith is flawed.

Our faith is in a risen Lord, and if He's still dead, our faith is worthless. Our confidence in the gospel is completely unreasonable. If Christ has not been raised, there is no legitimate gospel and no reasonable faith.

No Reliable Revelation

Thirdly, there is no reliable revelation. In verse 15, Paul writes, "Moreover, we are even found to be false witnesses of God, because we testified against God that He raised Christ, whom he did not raise, if in fact the dead are not raised." There is a picturesque word choice by the apostle Paul in this verse. The verb "are found" is often used of discovering the true nature of someone's character.

If some of the Corinthians were right and the dead aren't raised, then Christ has not been raised. That means all who have taught that there is a resurrection have been found out to be false witnesses of God. Paul says, "Not only is our testimony false," but "we have borne witness against God." It's a serious crime to claim to speak for God when God hasn't spoken and didn't send you.

In Jeremiah 23, for example, God says, "I did not send these prophets, but they ran. I did not speak to them, but they prophesied. But if they had stood in My

---

[5] Andrew V. Pestano, "Mexico probing 'brutal sin' alleging cancer kids given water, not chemo," *UPI* website (January 20, 2017), https://www.upi.com/Top_News/World-News/2017/01/20/Mexico-probing-brutal-sin-alleging-cancer-kids-given-water-not-chemo/5181484920103/.

council, then they would have announced My words to My people" (vv. 21–22). Jeremiah goes on to pronounce God's judgment on those self-appointed prophets with their man-made messages.

Paul is saying that if Christ hasn't been raised, then all who have taught that God raises the dead are just like those worthless prophets in Jeremiah's day. They are liars, false prophets, and not to be trusted. They are even under the judgment of God.

Whom does that include? It includes the eyewitnesses of verses 5–7. It includes Paul himself, because in verse 8, he says, "He appeared to me." It includes all the apostles, as verse 5 says, "Jesus appeared to Cephas, then to the twelve," and in verse 7, "to James, then to all the apostles." According to verse 11, the apostles not only witnessed the resurrection but preached it. All the apostles, then, are false prophets if Christ is not risen. Everything they taught—the entire New Testament—is false teaching.

Paul's indictment goes even further than that. It even goes back and captures the Old Testament, because in verse 4 he said Christ "was raised on the third day according to the Scriptures." That means the Old Testament can't be trusted. Paul's indictment even falls on Jesus Christ Himself. How? Because this gospel Paul preached had the resurrection at its core—and Paul received it from Jesus Christ. Our Lord, early in His ministry, said, "Destroy this temple, and in three days I will raise it up" (John 2:19). At least three other times in His ministry, Jesus clearly prophesied His resurrection. So if there was no resurrection, then even Christ cannot be trusted. The Bible is of no more value, is no more reliable than the writings of Confucius, Muhammad, or Joseph Smith. There is no trustworthy message from God, no reliable revelation.

No Real Forgiveness

A fourth tragic consequence of no resurrection is that there is no real forgiveness available to us. "For if the dead are not raised, not even Christ has been raised; and if Christ has not been raised, your faith is worthless; you are still in your sins" (vv. 16–17). Paul reminds his readers of the flow of his argument: "If dead people aren't raised, then Christ hasn't been raised. If that's true, then your faith is worthless." The word *worthless* speaks of that which produces no results and is useless.

Paul explains specifically in what way our faith is useless: It doesn't produce real forgiveness of our sins. Paul says, "You are still in your sins." In other words, the death of Christ accomplished nothing in regard to your sin. The New Testament often connects forgiveness and justification. That's an amazing package, both the forgiveness of our sins and the crediting of righteousness to us through the righteousness of Jesus Christ. And it often connects justification with the resurrection.

For example, Romans 4:25 says, "He was delivered over because of our transgressions, and was raised because of our justification." Jesus' resurrection was necessary to secure our justification. But Paul cannot mean that Christ secured our justification *only* through His resurrection, because a few verses later, in 5:9, he says that we were "justified by his blood."

So if Jesus' death secured our justification, how is the resurrection also related to justification? Primarily, the resurrection proved that the Father had accepted Jesus' sacrifice for sin, thus securing our justification. If the Father had not raised Christ from the dead, it would have been a public statement that Jesus was not who He claimed to be, and, therefore, was in no position to accomplish our redemption. "If Christ has not been raised . . . you are still in your sins" (v. 17).

Martin Lloyd-Jones writes, "The Resurrection is the proclamation of the fact that God is fully and completely satisfied with the work that his Son did upon the cross. . . . In raising him up God was proclaiming that his Son had completed the work, that full expiation has been made, that he is propitiated and completely satisfied!"[6] The resurrection proved that the Father had accepted the sacrifice of the Son, thus securing our justification.

Every US dollar bears the official seal of the Department of the Treasury. That seal has been on every piece of US currency ever issued. The US government began printing money in 1862 when Greenback currency was issued to finance the Civil War. At first, five clerks in the attic of the main Treasury Building had one simple job: to attach the official Treasury seal to each of the bills printed. The seal showed that the money was real and would be accepted for legal tender.

In the same way, the resurrection was God's official seal of approval on Jesus' sacrifice. It was God's way of saying He had accepted the death of Christ as a full payment for the debt we owed. On Friday at three o'clock in the afternoon, our Lord ended His ordeal by crying out with a loud voice, "It is finished." But heaven waited to see if the Father agreed. Sometime before sunrise on Sunday morning, the Father basically said "It is finished" by raising Jesus our Lord from the dead!

Charles Spurgeon wrote,

> The blood of Jesus Christ is blood that has been accepted.
> Christ died—he was buried; but neither heaven nor earth
> could tell whether God had accepted the ransom. There was

---

[6] Martyn Lloyd-Jones, *Romans, An Exposition of Chapters 3:20-4:25—Atonement and Justification* (Edinburgh, Scotland: Banner of Truth Trust, 1998), 244.

wanted [needed] God's seal upon the great Magna Charta of man's salvation, and that seal was put . . . in that hour when God summoned the angel, and bade him descend from heaven and roll away the stone. . . . And when Christ came out, rising from the dead in the glory of his Father's power, then was the seal put upon the great charts of our redemption. The blood was accepted, and sin was forgiven. And now, soul, it is not possible for God to reject you, if you come this day to him, pleading the blood of Christ. God cannot—and here we speak with reverence too—the everlasting God cannot reject a sinner who pleads the blood of Christ: for if he did so, it were to deny himself. . . . *he never can revoke that divine acceptance of the resurrection*; and if you go to God, my hearer, pleading simply and only the blood of him that did hang upon the tree, God must un-God himself before he can reject you, or reject that blood.[7]

The Father put His own seal on the death of Jesus Christ by raising Him from the dead! But if the Father did not raise Christ, it means He rejected the sacrifice, and we still bear the guilt of our sins. There is no real forgiveness.

No Eternal Life

A fifth and final consequence of no resurrection is that there is no eternal life. Paul writes, "Then those also who have fallen asleep in Christ have perished" (v. 18). The word *then* implies this is the inevitable consequence of what Paul just said. If we are still in our sins, then the same must be true of those who have fallen asleep in Christ. If some of the Corinthians were right that there is no resurrection, then those who died believing in Christ died still in their sins. And they "have perished." *Perish* is Paul's word to describe the condition of those who die forever separated from God. First Corinthians 1:18 says, "The word of the cross is foolishness to those who are perishing." Second Corinthians 4:3 says, "Our gospel . . . is veiled to those who are perishing." Second Thessalonians 2:10 defines those who perish as those who did not love the truth so as to be saved. Scripture emphatically rejects the idea of annihilation. In Matthew 25:46, our Lord Himself makes it clear that those who die without Him will exist as long as those who have eternal life: "These will go away into

---

[7] Charles Spurgeon, "The Blood," in *Spurgeon: New Park Street Pulpit: 347 Sermons from the Prince of Preachers* (OSNOVA, 2012). Emphasis added.

eternal punishment, but the righteous into eternal life."

Paul does not mean that those who died believing in Christ have ceased to exist—they will continue to live forever. But if Christ has not been raised, they are lost for good, forever separated from God in the eternal suffering of hell. For them, there is no eternal life, only eternal punishment.

Paul summarizes the tragic consequences if Christ has not been raised in the sobering words of verse 19: "If we have hoped in Christ in this life only, we are of all men most to be pitied." Why? Because it means that the gospel we believe has no substance, faith in Christ is worthless, and God's word is a lie. We still live under the penalty of sin, and all who died trusting in Christ are irretrievably lost. And at death, we, too, will forever be separated from God. That's why we are of all men most deserving of pity.

Then comes verse 20: "But now Christ has been raised from the dead." The word *now* is not chronological but logical. For the purpose of argument, Paul has assumed for one long, dark moment that Christ had not been raised. But with the word *now*, he brings us back to reality.

I don't usually remember my nightmares, for which I'm grateful. But periodically, I have one I do recall. And it's always the same. I show up at a venue where a large group of people have gathered, clearly for worship. It's about five minutes before the service begins, and I suddenly discover that I'm supposed to preach. What makes this a nightmare is that I'm totally unprepared. As the congregation is singing the last song expecting me to get up and share the Word of God, I am rifling through my Bible trying to find a message I can preach. Perhaps you have had even more unsettling nightmares. When you wake up from a nightmare and realize it's not true, that it didn't really happen, there is a huge sense of relief that sweeps across your soul.

That's what should happen to us when we get to verse 20: "But now Christ has been raised." Welcome back to reality! Because Christ has been raised from the dead, all those terrible consequences are not true. In fact, exactly the opposite is true. The gospel is a legitimate message of grace and hope. Our faith is reasonable; our confidence in the gospel is thoroughly justified. All those who have taught Christ's resurrection are trustworthy witnesses, and therefore, the Scripture is God's reliable revelation. Christ's death accomplished genuine and permanent forgiveness. "My sin—oh the bliss of this glorious thought—my sin, not in part but the whole, is nailed to the cross and I bear it no more!"[8] All believers who have died are in the presence of Christ. And someday those believers

---

[8] Horatio G. Spafford, "It Is Well with My Soul" (1873), *Timeless Truths* website, http://Library.timelesstruths.org/music/It_Is_Well_with_My_Soul/.

will experience the resurrection of their bodies just as our Lord Himself did. As Paul explains in the rest of this wonderful chapter, we can have great confidence in all those realities because of the resurrection of Jesus Christ.

Walking in Light of the Resurrection

Likely, you already believe in the resurrection. But how should we respond to what this passage teaches? I encourage you to examine *Biblical Doctrine*, where you'll find a list of about twenty results of the resurrection.[9] But let me explore just a few implications of Christ's resurrection for those who preach God's Word and shepherd God's people.

Remind yourself and your people that the gospel always includes the resurrection. In verse 4, Paul says the resurrection was one of the key tenets of the gospel he and the other apostles preached. Romans 10 states that to be a Christian, you must believe in the resurrection of Jesus Christ from the dead. Charles Hodge explains that passage this way: "As the resurrection of Christ was the great decisive evidence of the divinity of his mission, and the validity of all his claims, to believe that he rose from the dead, is to believe he was the Son of God, the propitiation for our sins, the Redeemer and the Lord of men; that he was all he claimed to be, had accomplished all he purposed to effect."[10] There is no salvation for the one who does not believe all that Jesus claimed and taught as authenticated by the resurrection. Determine to always include the resurrection in the gospel that you preach.

Remind yourself and your people that the resurrection proves Jesus' claims. He claimed to be the Son of God and had the audacity to stake the validity of that claim on His resurrection. In John 2:18, the Jews said to Jesus, "What sign do You show us as your authority for doing these things?" He answered them, "Destroy this temple, and in three days I will raise it up" (v. 19). It was Jesus' claim to be the Son of God that caused the Jewish leaders to condemn Him to death. In Mark 14:61–64, the high priest Caiaphas questioned Jesus, saying to Him, "'Are you the Christ [the Messiah] the Son of the Blessed One?' And Jesus said, 'I am; and you shall see the Son of Man sitting at the right hand of Power, and coming with the clouds of heaven.' Tearing his clothes, the high priest said, 'What further need do we have of witnesses? You have heard the blasphemy; how does it seem to you?' And they all condemned Him to be deserving of death." They would

---

[9] John MacArthur and Richard Mayhue, eds., *Biblical Doctrine: A Systematic Summary of Bible Truth* (Wheaton, IL: Crossway, 2017).

[10] Charles Hodge, *A Commentary on Romans* (East Peoria: Banner of Truth Trust, 2009), 129.

have been right if there were no resurrection. But Jesus' resurrection proved that His claim to be the Son of God was not blasphemy—it was absolutely true!

That's why Peter on the day of Pentecost could say, in light of the resurrection and the ascension, "Let all the house of Israel know for certain that God has made Him both Lord and Christ—this Jesus whom you crucified" (Acts 2:36). Romans 1:4 adds, "[He] was declared the Son of God with power by the resurrection from the dead, according to the Spirit of holiness, Jesus Christ our Lord." The resurrection proved Jesus' claims.

Remind yourself and your people that the resurrection secures and guarantees all the blessings Jesus purchased in His death. Romans 5:10 says, "If while we were enemies we were reconciled to God through the death of His Son, much more, having been reconciled, we shall be saved by His life." Literally, the Greek text says, "We shall be saved in His life." It's our connection to Jesus Christ, our union with the resurrected Christ, that guarantees all the blessings He secured will become ours. Romans 8:34 says, "Who is the one who condemns? Christ Jesus is He who died, yes, rather who was raised, who is at the right hand of God." What is He doing there? "Interceding for us." Hebrews 7:25 says, "He is able also to save forever those who draw near to God through Him, since He always lives to make intercession for them." What He secured for us in His death is guaranteed to us by His life.

Remind yourself and your people that all who will die in Christ will be raised from the dead. I have often had the experience of standing over a casket with those in my church family who are looking down at the body of someone they loved. When you do something similar, tell your people that, for the Christian, death is not final. Remind them that we preach Christ risen and that our risen Lord has defeated death; He has removed its sting. And He has the keys of—the authority over—death and the grave.

Remind them that we don't have to fear death. Rather, we can face it with joy and confidence. Later in 1 Corinthians 15, Paul says, "O death, where is your victory? O death, where is your sting?" (v. 55)? I don't recommend this, but as a boy growing up in southern Alabama, I remember on occasion searching through the clover for bees. I waited until an unsuspecting bee had landed on a piece of clover, and then I stepped on it gently—not enough to crush it, but just to stun it. Then, I picked it up by its wings, pushed its stinger into the tip of my belt, and the stinger would lodge in the leather. Then, I could play with the bee without the fear of being stung. That is exactly what Christ has done with death. He removed its sting—by taking the stinger Himself!

Tell unbelievers that the resurrection means Jesus will be their judge. How should those who have never repented and embraced Jesus Christ as Lord and Savior respond to the fact that Jesus has been raised? Paul makes it clear in his message in Acts 17. He says, "God is now declaring to men that all people everywhere should repent, because He has fixed a day in which He will judge the world in righteousness through a Man whom He has appointed, having furnished proof to all men by raising Him from the dead" (vv. 30–31). There is only one simple application of the resurrection for the sinner: repent. In the resurrection, God gave them all the proof they need to validate that command. But if they refuse, some day they will stand before Jesus Christ as their judge. In Romans 2, Paul calls that day "a day of wrath." It will be a day when there is nothing but wrath. Warn sinners that the resurrection means they must either repent or face the full fury of the Lamb.

Finally, remind yourself and your people that the resurrection drives us to a life of faithful ministry. At the end of 1 Corinthians 15, Paul gives one implication of the truth of Jesus' resurrection and our future resurrection: "Therefore, my beloved brethren, be steadfast, immovable, always abounding in the work of the Lord, knowing that your toil is not in vain in the Lord" (v. 58). Be steadfast in your conviction of the truth of the gospel. Christ died for our sins, was buried, and was raised again. Be immovable in your confidence that, just as He was raised, we who believe in Him will be raised. Be always abounding in the work of the Lord. Be committed to a life of obedience and service because you know your labor in the Lord is not in vain.

We preach Christ *risen from the dead*!

12

HIGH ABOVE THE HEAVENS: THE ASCENSION

EPHESIANS 1:15–23

H.B. Charles Jr.

It was forty days after the resurrection of the Lord Jesus Christ, yet the disciples remained clueless about the magnitude of what had taken place and what it meant for the future. "Lord, will you at this time restore the kingdom to Israel?" they asked (Acts 1:6). They were preoccupied with the occupying powers of Rome and the political fortunes of Israel, rather than with the spiritual needs the finished work of Christ met. They were still looking in the wrong direction. Jesus answered, "It is not for you to know times or seasons that the Father has fixed by his own authority. But you will receive power when the Holy Spirit has come upon you, and you will be my witnesses in Jerusalem and in all Judea and Samaria, and to the end of the earth" (vv. 7–8).

This was Jesus' final instruction to His disciples, before His ascension to the right hand of the Father in heaven. Then the conversation ended abruptly. The Lord's Uber showed up. Jesus was snatched away on a cloud, and then He was out of their sight. As Christ ascended into heaven before their eyes, angels announced, "Men of Galilee, why do you stand looking into heaven? This Jesus, who was taken up from you into heaven, will come in the same way as you saw him go into heaven" (v. 11) After this glorious event, we get only glimpses of the exalted Christ, as the disciples spread the good news of the risen Savior to the ends of the earth.

As Stephen was stoned to death, he looked into the heavens and saw the glory of God and Jesus standing at His right hand (7:54–60). As Saul of Tarsus traveled

153

the Damascus Road to find and arrest the followers of Christ, heaven's stadium lights blinded him and knocked him off his beast. And a voice asked him, "Saul, Saul, why are you persecuting me?" (9:4). When Saul asked the voice to identify Himself, the Lord replied, "I am Jesus, whom you are persecuting" (9:5).

Outside of these snapshots of the risen, glorified, and exalted Christ, the focus of Luke's writing in Acts is on the earthly ministry of the church. Empowered by God the Holy Spirit, the disciples turned the world upside-down with the gospel of Christ. It is not until Ephesians 1 that we get a direct follow-up on the events that took place in Acts 1. Ephesians 1:15–23 records Paul's intercessory prayer for the saints at Ephesus. In this prayer, the ascension of Christ is assumed as Paul focuses on the resurrection, exaltation, and enthronement of Christ. But it is here that we see the meaning, significance, and benefits of Christ's ascension.

After Paul's opening salutations (1:1–2), this first chapter of Ephesians records the Hymn of Grace, a song of praise to the sovereign grace of the triune God who alone saves sinners (vv. 3–14). In verse 3, Paul exults, "Blessed be the God and Father of our Lord Jesus Christ, who has blessed us in Christ with every spiritual blessing in the heavenly places." After this call to worship, Paul sings praise to God the Father, God the Son, and God the Holy Spirit, who graciously saves sinners by the finished work of Christ at the cross. Then Paul's praise to God overflows into prayer for the saints in 1:15–23. This is the first of two prayer reports in this letter. Ephesians 1:15–23 is a prayer for spiritual enlightenment, a prayer to know God better, and 3:14–21 is a prayer for spiritual empowerment, a prayer for strength.

This first prayer, for divine illumination, begins with the occasion of the prayer in verses 15–16: "For this reason, because I have heard of your faith in the Lord Jesus and your love toward all the saints, I do not cease to give thanks for you, remembering you in my prayers." The news Paul received about the church at Ephesus convinced him that they were true believers, authentic converts to Christ who had saving faith in Him. They also had genuine love for one another, as brothers and sisters in Christ. This moves Paul's heart to continuously give thanks to God for these saints and to remember them in his prayers.

In verses 17–18, we find the main petition of this prayer for the saints: "that the God of our Lord Jesus Christ, the Father of glory, may give you the Spirit of wisdom and of revelation in the knowledge of him, having the eyes of your hearts enlightened, that you may know what is the hope to which he has called you, what are the riches of his glorious inheritance in the saints." This lofty language represents a simple prayer request. Paul prays for spiritual enlightenment, that they may know God better and know what God has done for us in Christ. He prays that the eyes of their hearts would be opened and enlightened, so they may know the great blessings God has granted by the bloody cross and empty tomb of Jesus. Of course, this letter was not written *to* us. But it was written *for* us. And we need this prayer just as much as the original recipients did. We need to know God better, to understand more fully the truth, work, and power of God's amazing grace. This is what the people we serve in the church need the most. For that matter, this is what we, as servant-leaders, need the most!

In verses 18–19, Paul states the intended results of this big petition: "that you may know what is the hope to which he has called you, what are the riches of his glorious inheritance in the saints, and what is the immeasurable greatness of his power toward us who believe, according to the working of his great might." Three spiritual benefits result from the divine answer to this great prayer Paul offered on the behalf of the saints. Each is worthy of its own extended study. But in this chapter, I want to focus on the third spiritual benefit, found in verse 19: "the immeasurable greatness of his power toward us who believe, according to the working of his great might."

Paul prayed that the saints would personally experience the immeasurable great power of God in their lives. The omnipotent power of almighty God defies description. In fact, there are four different Greek words used in verses 19–20 to describe the power of God. The power of God is so great that it is beyond our comprehension. But this immeasurably great power of God that is beyond our understanding is at work on our behalf. Paul presents it as the immeasurable greatness of His power toward us who believe. The immeasurably great power of God is at work on behalf of those who believed in His Son, the Lord Jesus Christ.

D. A. Carson comments, "Paul cannot be satisfied with a brand of Christianity that is orthodox but dead, rich in the theory of justification but powerless when it comes to transforming people's lives."[1] Neither should we. The people we minister to need to know the truth of God's sovereign grace. They also need to experience the power of God's sovereign grace. May that be true of us as well. Our people need to know the truth of the sovereign grace of God. They also need to experience the power of the sovereign grace of God. This in no way is meant to diminish the priority of preaching Christ (see Col. 1:28). However, it reminds us that our pastoral call requires devotion to prayer and the ministry of the Word.

On one occasion, a young pastor asked me which is more important: prayer or the ministry of the Word. I answered, if you are on an airplane that is 30,000

---

[1] D. A. Carson, *A Call to Spiritual Reformation: Priorities from Paul and His Prayers* (Grand Rapids: Baker, 1992), 117.

feet in the sky, which is more important, the left wing or the right wing? If either wing malfunctions, you are going down. Similarly, Warren Wiersbe wrote, "So, like two wings carrying a bird in flight or two oars propelling a boat through the water, the Word of God and prayer keep us balanced and moving ahead."[2]

Yes, Paul prays that the saints will know God better and have a greater understanding of the sovereign grace of God that has saved us by the redeeming blood of the Lord Jesus Christ. But his concern is not to merely know God in Christ for the sake of knowledge. It is that we might experience the life-transforming power of God that Paul describes as "far more abundantly than all that we ask or think, according to the power at work within us" (3:20). By the Lord Jesus Christ, the power of God is at work on our behalf so that we might resist temptation, overcome sin, live obediently, love selflessly, serve faithfully, witness boldly, and even suffer joyfully. You may not feel it. Yet the power of God in Christ is presently and perpetually at work on your behalf. John Phillips wrote: "It is as gentle as the forming of a dew drop, as imperceptible as the growth of a tree, and as lasting as the throne of God."[3] So don't worry if you don't feel strong. This is how God works to keep us in a posture of dependence. The weaker you feel, the more you lean on God. You may not feel it, but God will give you strength as it is needed.

How do we know this immeasurably great power is at work on our behalf? Verse 20 says God's power toward us who believe is the power "that he worked in Christ." We cannot experience God's power by focusing on ourselves, our circumstances, or the world around us. Hebrews 12:2 says we finished the race of faith by "looking to Jesus, the founder and perfecter of our faith, who for the joy that was set before him endured the cross, despising the shame, and is seated at the right hand of the throne of God." We are prone to skip from the crucifixion and resurrection of Jesus right to Pentecost, overlooking the ascension. We tend to treat the ascension as an afterthought, if we think of it at all. But in Ephesians 1:20–23, the ascended Christ is presented as the ultimate proof of the power of God at work in us, through us, and among us. Verses 20–23 highlight four ways God's power was on display in the ascended Christ.

God Raised Jesus Christ from the Dead

There are many biblical truths that distinguish Christianity from other religions. One of the most significant and glaring distinctions is the resurrection of Jesus. Christians believe Jesus rose from the dead after He was crucified and buried.

---

[2] Warren W. and David W. Wiersbe, *10 Power Principles for Christian Service* (Grand Rapids: Baker Books, 2010), 83.
[3] John Phillips, *Exploring Ephesians and Philippians* 2nd ed. (Grand Rapids: Kregel Academic & Professional, 2002), 102.

And after His resurrection, Jesus was seen by many witnesses. This is the epicenter of historical Christianity. Christianity is the only religion whose adherents go to the burial site of its leader only to confirm that His body is not there. The most hostile and hard-hearted unbeliever cannot refute these facts: the tomb is empty, and the body of Jesus is missing. Various theories and competing philosophies attempt to explain—or explain away—these facts. But there is no better explanation than the biblical one: Jesus lives! There are no skeletons in God's closet. Jesus is alive today.

Christianity stands on the historical fact of the resurrection of Jesus. It also stands on the dynamic power of His resurrection. In Ephesians 1:19, Paul prays that believers would know the immeasurably great power of God that is at work on our behalf. The measure of God's power at work on our behalf is beyond our understanding. But this immeasurable power of God was put on display in Christ. Verse 20 states the first way God's power was displayed in Christ: "that he worked in Christ when he raised him from the dead."

I grew up in a church tradition where the preacher had not done his job if he did not get to the cross. No matter what text he was preaching, he better tell the story of Calvary. But the preacher had better not leave Jesus on the cross. The church waited to hear that Jesus died one Friday, was buried in Joseph's new tomb, and he rose from the dead early Sunday morning. Indeed, Jesus got up from the dead on the third day. But that is not how the Bible describes it. The New Testament consistently speaks of the resurrection in passive terms, as Paul does here. Jesus did not just get up. God raised Him! God raised Him to prove that Jesus is the only begotten Son of God. God raised Him to declare His approval of the atoning and substitutionary death of Jesus on the cross. God raised Him to accomplish and complete the exaltation of Jesus Christ as Lord of all.

Ephesians 1:19–20 tells us that God also raised Jesus from the dead to prove to us who believe that He has the power to change our lives. The crucifixion of Jesus was the love of God on display. But the resurrection of Jesus was the power of Jesus on display. Paul called the saints at Rome to live sanctified lives by explaining the meaning of baptism: "Do you not know that all of us who have been baptized into Christ Jesus were baptized into his death? We were buried therefore with him by baptism into death, in order that, just as Christ was raised from the dead by the glory of the Father, we too might walk in newness of life" (Rom. 6:3–4). The glorious power of God that raised Jesus from the dead empowers us to walk in the newness of life.

Later in Romans, Paul writes: "If the Spirit of him who raised Jesus from the dead dwells in you, he who raised Christ Jesus from the dead will also give life to your mortal bodies through his Spirit who dwells in you" (8:11). This is the stress test of God's power toward believers. If it does not require more power than what it took for God to raise Jesus from the dead, you have a guarantee that God can handle it. In 1 Corinthians 15:58, Paul tells us how to live, trust, and serve God in light of the resurrection of Christ: "Therefore, my beloved brothers, be steadfast, immovable, always abounding in the work of the Lord, knowing that in the Lord your labor is not in vain."

God Seated Jesus Christ at His Right Hand

Verse 20 says believers have access to the power of God "that he worked in Christ when he raised him from the dead and seated him at his right hand in the heavenly places." The power of God that raised Christ up also sat Christ down. The immeasurable greatness of God's power toward believers is seen in where God seated Christ: "at his right hand in the heavenly places." Hebrews 1:3 says: "After making purification for sins, he sat down at the right hand of the Majesty on high."

The Lord Jesus Christ is seated at the right hand of God in the heavenly places. He is not standing at God's right hand as a servant or kneeling at God's right hand as a slave. He is sitting at God's right hand as a Son. The right hand of God is a biblical idiom for divine strength, favor, and majesty. This is where Christ is seated, enthroned in coequal sovereignty with almighty God. In John 17:5, Jesus prayed: "And now, Father, glorify me in your own presence with the glory that I had with you before the world existed." God the Father answered this prayer by raising Jesus from among the dead and seating Him at His right hand. In verse 21, Paul further describes the enthronement of Christ by its relationship to creation. It is "far above all rule and authority and power and dominion, and above every name that is named, not only in this age but also in the one to come." This verse gives two facts about the sovereign authority of the exalted Christ.

First, the authority of Christ is universal. Verse 21 says the sovereign authority of Christ is "far above all rule and authority and power and dominion." These four terms describe the invisible realm of spirit beings. Ephesians 6:12 says: "For we do not wrestle against flesh and blood, but against the rulers, against the authorities, against the cosmic powers over this present darkness, against the spiritual forces of evil in the heavenly places." The spirit-beings listed in Ephesians 1:21 most likely refer to Satan and his army of fallen angels. But we need not try to sort out the distinction between these terms. The key term is the word "all." God seated Christ "far above *all* rule and authority and power and dominion, and above every name that is named" (emphasis added). In case He failed to mention some spiritual being or force, Paul declares that if you can name it, Christ has authority over it.

We need not be afraid of, cannot be bound by, and will not be defeated by

Satan and his evil forces. Christ is seated far above all of the powers of this present darkness. There is no place where the Lord Jesus Christ does not reign. I did not learn this first by studying theology. I learned this as a little boy in the children's choir at church, where I was taught to sing, "He's got the whole world in his hands! He's got the little bitty baby in his hands! He got you and me, brother, in his hands!" The authority of Christ is universal. He alone reigns over every name that can be named!

Second, the authority of Christ is unending. Verse 21 says the authority of Christ is "far above all rule and authority and power and dominion, and above every name that is named, *not only in this age but also in the one to come*" (emphasis added). The authority of Christ is both universal and unending. It is over all things at all times. Wherever you are and whenever it is, Christ is in charge there and then. No matter the age, era, period, season, or time, the sovereign authority of Christ never changes. Hebrews 13:8 says, "Jesus Christ is the same yesterday and today and forever." The sovereign authority of Christ is unending. Isaac Watts wrote, "Jesus shall reign, wherever the sun does his successive journeys run. His kingdom spread from shore to shore, till moon shall wax and wane no more."[4]

The authority of Christ is universal and unending. This is because the power of God has raised Him and seated Him at His right hand. Elsewhere in Ephesians, Paul writes,

> But God, being rich in mercy, because of the great love with
> which he loved us, even when we were dead in our trespasses,
> made us alive together with Christ—by grace you have been
> saved—and raised us up with him and seated us with him
> in the heavenly places in Christ Jesus, so that in the coming
> ages he might show the immeasurable riches of his grace in
> kindness toward us in Christ Jesus. (2:4–7).

If you are in Christ by faith, what God has done for Christ, He has also done for you. You were dead in trespasses and sins. But God has raised you up with Christ. You were without God and without hope in the world. But God has seated you with Christ in heavenly places This is one of the loftiest claims the New Testament makes about the redeemed. We have been seated with Christ, meaning that, in Christ, we have spiritual authority, transcendent perspective, and eternal security.

---

[4] Isaac Watts, "Jesus Shall Reign Were'er the Sun" (1719), https://hymnary.org/text/Jesus_shall_reign_whereer_the_sun.

God Placed All Things under the Feet of Jesus

Verse 22 says, "And he put all things under his feet." At first glance, this statement seems to be a restatement of verse 20. But there is a different point made here. Verse 20 is a statement about Christ. God has seated Him at His right hand. Verse 22 is a statement about creation. God has placed everything that exists in the created world under the feet of Christ. In Great Britain, Queen Elizabeth II sits on the throne, but the prime minister runs the government. The queen's authority is only ceremonial. That is not the case with the Lord Jesus Christ. God has seated Christ at His right hand and placed everything in creation under the direct authority of Jesus Christ. Psalm 2:7–9 says, "I will tell of the decree: The LORD said to me, 'You are my Son; today I have begotten you. Ask of me, and I will make the nations your heritage, and the ends of the earth your possession. You shall break them with a rod of iron and dash them in pieces like a potter's vessel.'"

Christ reigns and rules over everything in creation. Philippians 2:9–11 says: "Therefore God has highly exalted him and bestowed on him the name that is above every name, so that at the name of Jesus every knee should bow, in heaven and on earth and under the earth, and every tongue confess that Jesus Christ is Lord, to the glory of God the Father." This passage does not mean that every person will be saved. Sinners who do not repent of their sin and trust the blood and righteousness of Christ for salvation will die in their sins and suffer eternal punishment in hell. But there will be universal submission to the Lordship of Christ.

This is the sovereign authority, exhaustive Lordship, and unimpeachable reign of the Lord Jesus Christ. Even in hell, every knee shall bow and every tongue shall confess that Jesus is Lord. Further, 1 Corinthians 15:25–28 says,

> For he must reign until he has put all his enemies under his feet. The last enemy to be destroyed is death. For God has put all things in subjection under his feet. But when it says, "all things are put in subjection," it is plain that he is excepted who put all things in subjection under him. When all things are subjected to him, then the Son himself will also be subjected to him who put all things in subjection under him, that God may be all in all.

God Gave Jesus Christ as Head of All Things to the Church

Verses 22–23 say, "And he put all things under his feet and gave him as head over all things to the church, which is his body, the fullness of him who fills all in all." The Lord Jesus Christ is the head of the church. Jesus declared, "On this rock I will build my church, and the gates of hell shall not prevail against it" (Matt.

16:18). He did not say, "I will build your church," or, "You will build my church." The church belongs to Christ, and He is building it. Colossians 1:18 says, "And he is the head of the body, the church. He is the beginning, the firstborn from the dead, that in everything he might be preeminent." Indeed, Christ is the supreme and sovereign head of the church. But Paul's language here seems to make a loftier claim. Verse 22 says that God has made Christ the "head over all things." The Lord Jesus Christ is the sovereign ruler over all things. And God "gave him as head over all things to the church."

Did you get that? My head rules over my body. But it does not control what happens to me, around me, or beyond me. If Jesus only is the head of the church, He only has the right to say what happens in the church. God made Christ the head of all things to the church. This is the intimate union between the resurrected, ascended, and enthroned Christ and His redeemed people. One Bible commentator noted: "One of the strange paradoxes among Christians is people who seem to be fascinated by Jesus Christ but who at the same time reject the church. Either they know nothing about the real Christ, or they know nothing about the real church, or both."[5]

Many people have had bad experiences with the church. But you cannot embrace Christ and reject the church. Christ is the head. The church is His body. Christ is the bridegroom. The church is His bride. Christ is the Shepherd. The church is His sheep. Ephesians 1–3 teaches a high view of the church. But there is no more lofty statement about the church than Ephesians 3:21: "to him be glory in the church and in Christ Jesus throughout all generations, forever and forever." All of the doxologies in the New Testament are addressed to the church. This is the only doxology that includes the church. There are those who claim the church gets in the way of God's glory. But Paul declares the church is essential to the glory of God. You cannot have a high view of Christ and a low view of the church at the same time. God has put all things under Christ's feet and gave Him as head over all things to the church.

Verse 23 says the church is "his body, the fullness of him who fills all in all." This statement is a remarkable affirmation of the intimate union of Christ and His church. The church is the body of Christ. The church is not a dead organization. It is a living organism. As Christ's body, the church is "the fullness of him who fills all in all." This is a difficult phrase to interpret, and it is much debated. I agree with John Calvin, who comments, "This is the highest honor of the church that until He is united to us, the Son of God reckons Himself in some measure incomplete."[6]

---

[5] Tom Julien, *Inherited Wealth: Studies in Ephesians* (Winona Lake, IN: BHM Books, 1987), 29.
[6] Quoted from John MacArthur, *Ephesians* (John MacArthur New Testament Commentary) (Chicago: Moody Publishers, 1986), 49.

This is Christ's love for us! This is our union to the Lord Jesus Christ! This is the empowering grace God has given to us in Christ! Christ is so intimately bound to the church that the communion of the saints somehow makes Him complete. This does not mean the presence, power, and purpose of Christ is contingent upon the whims of the church. Verse 23 says the church is "the fullness of him who fills all in all." The church is the fullness of Christ. But Christ fills all in all. Let us serve, preach, witness, suffer, and minister with our eyes firmly fixed on this exalted Christ. May we do so trusting that the power of God in Christ is at work on our behalf that we may live out the message of the gospel to the glory of God.

An author once reflected on his youth, when he lived in a boarding house. A retired music teacher also lived there. Over time, the young author and the old musician struck up a friendship. Every morning, they played out the same routine. The young man would burst through the old man's door and ask, "Hey, old man! What's the news today?" The old man would take out his tuning fork and strike it against his wheel chair. Then he would joyfully announce, "Young man, the good news today is that the note you just heard is Middle C. It was middle C yesterday. It is Middle C today. And a thousand years from now, it will still be Middle C. The tenor upstairs sings off note. And the piano across the hall is flat. But this is Middle C." So it is with the Lord Jesus Christ, yesterday, today, and forever. The exalted Christ is always our hope, strength, and joy!

13

THE RETURN OF THE KING: THE SECOND COMING

2 THESSALONIANS 1:5–10

Michael Vlach

The second coming of Jesus is a major New Testament theme. It is explicitly explained in Zechariah 14, Matthew 24–25, Mark 13, Luke 21, Acts 1, Revelation 19, among other passages. The return of Jesus is also important to Paul's argument in 2 Thessalonians 1:5–10, which is the focus of this chapter. The return of Jesus is a major reason for the believer's hope, yet it will also be an awful time of judgment for those who refuse Jesus as Savior and oppose God's people. The second coming must be taken seriously. It reminds us that the world will not continue as it is forever. Jesus is coming again to remove wickedness and to establish His kingdom of righteousness.

The church has traditionally recognized the importance of Jesus' second coming. For example, The Apostles' Creed states:

> the third day he [Jesus] rose from the dead;
> he ascended into heaven,
> and sitteth at the right hand of God the Father Almighty;
> from thence he shall come to judge the quick and the dead.

Properly Grasping First and Second Coming Fulfillment

Understanding the significance of both the first and second comings of Jesus is important for understanding the Bible's story line. Emphasizing one and not the other can lead to error. Those who emphasize the first coming of Jesus apart from the second coming can tend toward an over-realized eschatology that sees too much fulfillment of eschatological hope in this age. Paul addressed this error in 2 Timothy 2:18, where he referred to "men who have gone astray from the truth saying that the resurrection has already taken place, and they upset the faith of some." Apparently, some were saying the resurrection had taken place already, but Paul said they were in grave error. The resurrection awaits the return of Jesus. Also, in 2 Thessalonians 2, Paul noted that some had fallen for the false belief that the Day of the Lord had already arrived. He pleaded: "that you not be quickly shaken from your composure or be disturbed either by a spirit or a message or a letter as if from us, to the effect that the day of the Lord has come. Let no one in any way deceive you" (vv. 2–3a). Paul had to explain to the Thessalonians that the Day of the Lord had not come yet for two reasons: (1) the apostasy has not occurred yet, and (2) the man of lawlessness had not yet been revealed (vv. 3b–4). It was important to Paul that the Thessalonians properly understand why they were not in the Day of the Lord.

On the other hand, it is possible to appreciate Jesus' second coming but not give enough attention to what He accomplished with His first coming. For example, some people deny that believers today experience the new covenant. But Paul says that Christians today are "servants of a new covenant" (2 Cor. 3:6).

So understanding both comings of Jesus is important. The first century AD brought us the arrival of Jesus in fulfillment of Old Testament prophecy. Jesus is the Last Adam, the Suffering Servant, and Messiah. With His first coming, Jesus purchased salvation for His people with His death. He also has brought new covenant salvation to both Jews and Gentiles who believe in Him. He has also poured out His Holy Spirit upon His people. Concerning the first coming of Jesus, Peter declared, "But the things which God announced beforehand by the mouth of all the prophets, that His Christ would suffer, He has thus fulfilled" (Acts 3:18). As this verse indicates, Old Testament passages that predicted Jesus' suffering have been fulfilled.

Yet the first coming of Jesus is not all there is concerning Jesus' work. There are also many prophecies that still await fulfillment with the second coming of Jesus. Events such as vengeance on the wicked, relief and reward for the righteous, bodily resurrection, the transformation of nature, the coming of Antichrist, and the salvation/restoration of Israel are still unfulfilled. Speaking of future events near the end of His first earthly ministry, Jesus stated: "all things which are written *will be* fulfilled" (Luke 21:22; emphasis added).

That some prophecies have been fulfilled while others still await fulfillment makes good sense. If there are two comings of Jesus it seems natural to understand that certain prophecies were fulfilled with His first coming, while others await Jesus' second coming. A good example of this paradigm is seen in Revelation 5:9–10. According to verse 9, we are told that Jesus was "slain" and that He "purchased" with His blood men from every tribe, tongue, people and nation. That truth was fulfilled with Jesus' first coming and His sacrificial death. Yet verse 10 then says that these people who Jesus purchased "will reign upon the earth." This reign of the saints is a future event and is explained with the events of Revelation 19 and 20, which describe Jesus' second coming and millennial kingdom upon the earth.

2 Thessalonians 1

Second Thessalonians 1 is a strategic second-coming passage. With the first four verses of this chapter, Paul, along with Silvanus and Timothy, greeted the Thessalonians and extended grace and peace to them in the names of God the Father and Jesus Christ. Paul says the church there was a cause for praising God. The faith of the Thessalonians was greatly enlarged. Their love for each other was growing. And they exhibited perseverance and faith in the midst of persecutions and afflictions. So this church was doing well. But the mention of "persecutions" and "afflictions" reveals that some people were hostile toward the Thessalonians because their faith in Jesus. We are not told specifically in 2 Thessalonians 1 what these persecutions and afflictions were. But Acts 17:5–8 states that some Jews from the marketplace formed a mob and set the city in an uproar, even attacking the house of Jason. They dragged Jason and some brethren before the city authorities. So Acts 17 shows that the Thessalonians faced real persecution, and Paul reaffirms that truth in 2 Thessalonians 1:4.

2 Thessalonians 1:3–5

In 2 Thessalonians 1, Paul describes what the return of Jesus will mean for both Christians and non-believers. The second coming of Jesus will change everything! Along with Jesus' cross, His return in glory will be the most dramatic event in history. With it a climactic reversal of circumstances will occur. Those who persecute and afflict God's people will themselves be afflicted by God. And those who are afflicted for the sake of Jesus in this age will eventually find relief. For most of human history, the wicked have prospered (see Psalm 73) and the people of God are often persecuted. But there is coming a time when this situation will be reversed.

In the preface to his 2 Thessalonians commentary, Martin Luther writes that in chapter 1, "[God] comforts them with the eternal reward that will come to their faith and their patience in afflictions of every kind and with the punishment that will come to their persecutors in eternal pain."[1] As the church is persecuted, Paul announces that a day is coming when that will change. The wicked will be judged, and the righteous will be rewarded and given relief.

This brings us to 2 Thessalonians 1:5, which states, "This is a plain indication of God's righteous judgment so that you will be considered worthy of the kingdom of God, for which indeed you are suffering." Here, Paul connects the faith, love, and perseverance of the Thessalonians that he mentioned in verses 3–4 with the persecution they are now facing. He says there is "a righteous judgment" on behalf of the Thessalonians. Even though we will soon see what God's righteous judgment will mean for the enemies of God, there is also a righteous judgment already in favor of the Thessalonians. As those who are in union with Jesus, God has decided in their favor. And their enduring faith is evidence that God's righteous judgment has been passed in favor of them.

The Thessalonians were behaving like those who had been declared righteous and are now in a right relationship with God. Their practice of persevering matches their righteous position in Jesus. When a Christian is faithful under persecution, it is evidence of God's decision on their behalf. Edmond Hiebert says, "That they were enabled to endure was evidence to themselves that a new life had been imparted to them."[2] So God's sustaining presence indicates that He will not allow unjust sufferings to go unrewarded.

Paul also says the Thessalonians "will be considered worthy of the kingdom of God" for which they are now suffering. The kingdom Paul is referring to is a future kingdom that will arrive with the second coming of Jesus. The believing Thessalonians are not currently in the kingdom of God. If they were, they would not experience persecutions and afflictions from the hands of unbelievers. But their suffering now reveals that they are worthy to enter it when it comes with Jesus' return to earth. In 2 Timothy 2:12, Paul says, "If we endure, we will also reign with Him." This present age calls for faithful endurance so that in the future age we will reign with Jesus (see Rev. 2:26–27; 3:21). The church is called to be faithful. And enduring faith in suffering reveals that a person has received God's righteous judgment in their favor.

The Thessalonians (and all Christians) will persevere and be considered worthy of God's kingdom, but this worthiness is not based on meritorious works. Nor is it based on the inherent value of the Thessalonians themselves. Rather, it is because of God who is at work in them, the God who has extended His grace to them.

As 2 Thessalonians 1 continues, Paul will also describe how God's righteous

---

[1] Martin Luther, "Preface to the Second Epistle of Saint Paul to the Thessalonians," *Tyndale House* website, https://www.stepbible.org/?q=version=Luther|reference=2Th.

[2] D. Edmond Hibert, *1 and 2 Thessalonians* (Chicago: Moody Press, 1992), 307.

judgment will impact unbelievers. But before looking further, it will be helpful to know that there has been a righteous judgment passed in favor of the Thessalonians. This is evinced by their perseverance in the midst of trials.

2 Thessalonians 1:6–7

Starting with 2 Thessalonians 1:6, Paul discusses how God will deal with the wicked. Before looking at this verse, though, let's look at three phases of God's interactions with unbelievers in judgment: punishment, ruin, and banishment. All three appear in chapter 1 and they are reaffirmed in the book of Revelation. First, there is punishment, which involves what God does to people who do not obey Him. God takes vengeance upon the wicked. He repays them according to their deeds. This is retribution. And what they deserve is not good. Concerning the lake of fire, Revelation 14:11a states, "The smoke of their torment goes up forever and ever; they have no rest day and night."

Second, there is also the concept of ruin or destruction, which is what hell means for the sinner. It means destruction, loss, and waste. At the judgment there is total loss for the unbeliever.

Third, there is banishment. Sinners are not allowed into God's kingdom or on the new earth. The King (God) does not allow the wicked to participate in the glories and blessings of His kingdom. Thus, the wicked not only face punishment and destruction but are denied access to the beauties and glories of God's kingdom. Concerning banishment from the coming New Jerusalem, Revelation 22:14–15 declares: "Blessed are those who wash their robes, so that they may have the right to the tree of life, and may enter by the gates into the city. Outside are the dogs and the sorcerers and the immoral persons and the murderers and the idolaters, and everyone who loves and practices lying." In sum, God acts as a judge who punishes unrepentant sinners, a warrior who destroys His enemies, and a king who banishes the wicked from His kingdom.

Looking at 2 Thessalonians 1:6–7, we find what the coming of Jesus will mean for unbelievers: "For after all it is only just for God to repay with affliction those who afflict you, and to give relief to you who are afflicted and to us as well when the Lord Jesus will be revealed from heaven with His mighty angels in flaming fire." Paul notes that what God will do is "just." It is right and appropriate. This involves repaying with affliction those who afflict the Thessalonians. In other words, there will be retribution for those who harm God's people. The term *thlipsin* used here means "oppression," "affliction," "tribulation," "distress." The term *antapodounai*, translated as "repay," means to recompense or to give what is due or deserving. So God will repay those who afflict His people. This is a divine irony. Those who afflict the Thessalonians in the present will themselves be afflicted by God in the future. God keeps track of all the wrongs done to His people. And a day is coming when He will afflict those who afflict Christians.

This idea is also found in Romans 12:19, where Paul states, "Never take your own revenge, beloved, but leave room for the wrath of God, for it is written, 'Vengeance is Mine, I will repay,' says the Lord." Christians are not to seek vengeance on those who harm them because vengeance belongs to God alone. And a similar truth is found in Hebrews 10:30: "For we know Him who said, 'Vengeance is Mine, I will repay.' And again, 'The Lord will judge His people.'" Again, vengeance on the wicked is not the church's job. We are not to be involved with inquisitions or any physical retribution.

With the parable of the wheat and the tares (Matt. 13:24–30, 36–43), Jesus reveals that the judgment of the wicked is His responsibility at the end of the age when He uses "His angels" to remove the ungodly from His kingdom. Justice will occur. Christians should expect persecution from the wicked and comfort themselves, knowing confidently that God will not permit the wrongs against His people to continue unpunished and unavenged.

Affliction for God's enemies is part of the second coming. Yet God will also bring "relief" to Christians who have been afflicted. This term for "relief" (*anesin*) means "rest" or "ease." Persecution and affliction will give way to rest and relief. This does not mean that Christians will never again do any work or retire to some heavenly sofa. Multiple passages indicate that Christians will be involved with activity after Jesus returns (see Luke 19:11–27; Rev. 20:4; 22:5). But the second coming means Christians will find relief and rest from oppressors and the difficult circumstances associated with a fallen world.

In 2 Corinthians 7:5, we see the concepts of rest and affliction contrasted: "For even when we came into Macedonia our flesh had no rest, but we were afflicted on every side." Because Paul was afflicted, he was not able to experience any rest or relief.

The idea of affliction first and then relief is also seen in Jesus' message to the seven churches of Asia Minor (Rev. 2–3). These churches often were facing persecution, but each message Jesus gave to the churches promised coming blessings for overcoming and enduring. Revelation 2:26–27 and 3:21 specifically promise ruling positions for those Christians who overcome difficult circumstances and persecutions.

Relief for Christians comes with the second coming of Jesus. Certainly those who die in Jesus before He returns experience some relief from the toils of this world as they enjoy the presence of Jesus in heaven. But the relief that Paul speaks of in 2 Thessalonians 1:7 is connected with the return of Jesus.

An example of this truth is found in Revelation 6:9–11, which describes people who were killed for their testimony for Jesus on the earth. While their dead bodies remain on earth, their souls appear in heaven. Yet as they arrive in heaven, they do not view heaven as their final destination. Nor do they forget what is taking place on earth. They cry out with a loud voice, "How long, O Lord, holy and true, will You refrain from judging and avenging our blood on those who dwell on the earth?" (Rev. 6:10). These saints seek vengeance from the Lord on the people who killed them. Yet in verse 11, they are told to wait a while longer. So these saints in heaven are to wait for a future day when relief and vengeance will occur. This takes place as a result of the second coming of Jesus described in Revelation 19. And according to Revelation 20:4, those who were martyred for the cause of Jesus come to life and reign with Jesus for a thousand years. At that time, the enemies of Jesus will be destroyed and Jesus' saints will rule with Him. This is the fulfillment of Revelation 5:10, which says, "You have made them to be a kingdom . . . and they will reign upon the earth."

The end of 2 Thessalonians 1:7 gives more detail regarding the time that this relief will come to Christians like the Thessalonians: "When the Lord Jesus will be revealed from heaven with his mighty angels in flaming fire" (v. 7b). The term for "revealed" (*apokalypsis*) means "unveiling" or "uncovering." Presently, Jesus is hidden from physical sight. He is currently at the right hand of the Father in heaven with all authority as He shares the throne of deity with the Father (see Ps. 110:1; Heb. 10:12). He is largely hidden from the world in this age. But in a moment He will be revealed, made manifest in glory. Jesus will transition from being hidden from human sight to being revealed. A foretaste of Jesus' manifestation in glory was given to some of the apostles on the Mount of Transfiguration in Matthew 17, where we are told: "Six days later Jesus took with Him Peter and James and John his brother, and led them up on a high mountain by themselves. And He was transfigured before them; and His face shone like the sun, and His garments became as white as light" (Matt. 17:1–2).

The second coming of Jesus is going to be the most dramatic event in human history. With His first coming, Jesus came with gentleness. He came as the Suffering Servant and as the Lamb of God who takes away sin. He allowed Himself to be mistreated and killed on our behalf (see Isa. 53). While Jesus will always remain these things, with His return He will come as a fierce warrior king who conquers and destroys His enemies. Second Thessalonians 2:8 says Jesus will destroy the man of lawlessness (i.e., the Antichrist). Describing Jesus' return, Revelation 19:15 declares, "From His mouth comes a sharp sword, so that with it He may strike down the nations, and He will rule them with a rod of iron; and He treads the wine press of the fierce wrath of God, the Almighty."

Matthew 25:31–46 reveals that Jesus will come in glory with His angels, which involves a removing of the wicked so they will not enter His kingdom. Jesus is coming again with His mighty angels in flaming fire. "But when the Son of Man comes in His glory, and all the angels with Him, then He will sit on His glorious throne" (Matt. 25:31). It is when Jesus comes in glory with His angels that He will sit on His glorious Davidic throne (see Luke 1:32–33). All the nations will be gathered before Him, and He will separate the righteous from the wicked as a shepherd separates the sheep from the goats (Matt. 25:32).

Like Matthew 25 and Revelation 19, 2 Thessalonians 1 is a violent passage. It talks about Christ as a warrior king coming back to establish His kingdom and to deal with His enemies. This is also seen in Psalm 110:5–7, which involves the return of Jesus the Messiah:

> The Lord is at Your right hand;
> He will shatter kings in the day of His wrath.
> He will judge among the nations,
> He will fill them with corpses,
> He will shatter the chief men over a broad country.
> He will drink from the brook by the wayside;
> Therefore He will lift up His head.

Second Thessalonians 1:8 then states: "dealing out retribution to those who do not know God and to those who do not obey the gospel of our Lord Jesus." Again, there is retribution for the wicked. Retribution here means vengeance, full punishment, or justice. This is punishment for crimes committed. This retribution applies to those who do not know God and to those who do not obey the gospel of our Lord Jesus Christ. Some say the first reference to those who do not know God refers to Gentiles. And some say those who do not obey the gospel of our Lord Jesus Christ are Jews. Others say it's just a parallelism where both are describing what it is like to be an unbeliever. Either way, this retribution is coming to the wicked who have rejected the truth.

In 1:9, Paul continues: "These will pay the penalty of eternal destruction, away from the presence of the Lord and from the glory of His power." This verse tells of both destruction and banishment for the unbeliever. First, the mention of "eternal destruction" indicates ruin that lasts forever. There is no annihilation here in which the wicked cease to exist forever. No. This is an eternal conscious destruction. The state of being in total ruin and loss will last forever.

Next, the words "away from the presence of the Lord" indicates banishment from the presence of the Lord. The best thing that could ever happen to a person is to be in God's presence. But for these people they are banished forever from the positive display of His presence. If the best thing ever is living in the presence of God, the worst thing is being banished from His presence with no chance of that being reversed. But that is what will happen to the wicked. The story does not end well for everyone. Only those who trust in Jesus will see God and experience His presence.

Concerning the coming judgment day, Jesus said, "Depart from Me, you who practice lawlessness" (Matt. 7:23). On the judgment day, some will claim to know Jesus and appeal to their religious activity, but they have to depart from Him because they never knew Him. Their lives were characterized by lawlessness. In Matthew 25:41–46, Jesus said, "'Depart from me, accursed ones, into the eternal fire which has been prepared for the devil and his angels.' . . . These will go away into eternal punishment, but the righteous into eternal life."

Coming to 2 Thessalonians 1:10, we read, "When He comes to be glorified in His saints on that day, and to be marveled at among all who have believed—for our testimony to you was believed." On that day, Jesus is coming to be glorified in His saints and to be marveled at by all who have believed. This could mean that Jesus will be glorified *by* His saints on the day of His return. It is also possible that Jesus will be glorified *in* His saints. What Jesus has done for them is openly displayed *in them* who are now in glorified bodies. His glory will be manifested in them. Second Timothy 4:8 says, "In the future there is laid up for me the crown of righteousness, which the Lord, the righteous judge, will award to me on that day; and not only to me, but also to all who have loved His appearing."

That longing for Jesus' appearing should be in the heart of the believer. We should love and eagerly anticipate the second coming of Jesus. If someone does not long for Jesus' return, then a problem in their life might exist. Believers are those who love Jesus' appearing. If being a Christian is all about a relationship with Jesus, then why would we not desire His full manifestation and His glory upon earth?

Paul also says, "To be marveled at among all who have believed" (v. 10). The word for "marvel" (*thaumazo*) means "to be amazed" or "astonished." You might wonder what the coming of Christ is going to be like. There is no way to predict that, but it is going to be far beyond anything you can imagine. We are going to be amazed. We are going to be astonished.

Conclusion

Second Thessalonians 1 affirms that we live in a moral universe with objective right and wrong. It also affirms the necessity of reward and punishment. There is real good and there is real evil. And all this relates to the God of the Bible, who alone is the standard for goodness. Those who know Jesus will find relief from the persecutions, afflictions, and trials of this age when He returns. Yet those who remain in unbelief will suffer punishment, destruction, and banishment from His kingdom. May we encourage those who do not know Jesus to repent and believe. May we encourage those who do know Him to find the hope that this chapter offers. Jesus is coming again. When He does, it will change everything!

PART 3

THE WORD

OF CHRIST

14

NO OTHER GOSPEL: THE TRUE GOSPEL OF CHRIST

GALATIANS 1:6–7

Phil Johnson

Galatians 1:6–10 contains some of the most sharply worded confrontational language in the whole New Testament. It defies all the popular postmodern notions about diversity, tolerance, and open-minded collegiality. Perhaps that's why nowadays this passage is often glossed over or gingerly set aside. But it's a serious mistake to treat these verses so lightly. This is Paul's opening salvo in the most polemical of all his epistles. It sets the tone for the whole letter. And it has profound practical implications for the church at the start of the twenty-first century—this doctrinally loose era of broad, blithe ecumenism.

In short, Paul emphatically says Christians are not to seek fellowship or receive the teaching of anyone who corrupts the simplicity of the gospel. In fact, he pronounces a curse on teachers of alternative gospels: "Even if we, or an angel from heaven, should preach to you a gospel contrary to what we have preached to you, he is to be accursed!" (v. 8).

Background to the Letter

The apostle was writing to a group of churches he knew well. Paul's first missionary journey (Acts 13–14) took him extensively throughout Galatia. He began his church-planting work by preaching at Iconium, Lystra, Derbe, and Pisidian Antioch—all the main municipalities of Galatia. He then went back through those same cities again on his second and third missionary journeys.

Obviously, he had a close personal attachment to those churches and a true fondness for the people there. These were congregations he founded early in his ministry, and they were filled with people who heard the gospel first from Paul himself. He was their spiritual father. So those opening verses of the epistle are understandably full of paternal passion.

But the mood isn't exactly warm and friendly. The epistle's opening contains a scathing tone that sets this letter apart from Paul's other letters. Paul writes with the voice of an indignant parent scolding his children: "I am amazed that you are so quickly deserting Him who called you by the grace of Christ, for a different gospel; which is really not another; only there are some who are disturbing you and want to distort the gospel of Christ" (vv. 6–7).

Paul was confronting an error that was being spread across Galatia by false teachers who insisted Gentiles must first convert to Judaism in order to become Christians. God would never justify uncircumcised Gentiles, they said. They weren't doing any evangelism or church planting of their own; they merely leeched off the apostles' labors. They were typical wolves in sheep's clothing, and they seemed to stalk Paul relentlessly wherever he planted churches.

Acts 15 describes their brand of false doctrine, and there we learn that the leading men behind this heresy were Pharisees who had professed faith in Christ. Acts 15:5 refers to them as "some of the sect of the Pharisees who had believed."

Paul was of course a born-and-bred Pharisee who had once hated Christians and Gentiles alike. He had been suddenly, dramatically converted and given a commission from Christ to take the gospel to the Gentiles. The churches he planted were filled with people converted out of pagan cultures. But when he would move from one region to start a church in another place, these false teachers would come along behind him and tell Gentile church members that if they wanted to be *real* Christians, they had to submit to a list of Old Testament ceremonial and dietary ordinances, starting with circumcision. Acts 15:1 says they were "teaching the brethren, 'Unless you are circumcised according to the custom of Moses, you cannot be saved.'" They said the simple message of salvation by grace alone through faith alone was insufficient to get Gentiles into the kingdom. "It is necessary to circumcise them and to direct them to observe the Law of Moses," they insisted (v. 5).

That was the gist of their error, and it flatly contradicted what Paul had preached to the Galatians. The apostle always stressed that faith is the sole instrument of justification. "To the one who does not work, but believes in Him who justifies the ungodly, his faith is credited as righteousness" (Rom. 4:5). *No good work*—including circumcision—is a prerequisite for justification.

Paul was very specific about this. In Romans 4:9–11, he went back to Genesis and traced the chronology from Genesis 15–17, showing that Abraham was declared righteous several years before he was circumcised. "He received the sign of circumcision, a seal of the righteousness of the faith which he had while uncircumcised" (v. 11).

But these false teachers were essentially telling the Gentiles, "No. Paul is giving you only part of the gospel message. Faith is important, but the works demanded by the law are also required to be justified." They had dragged their Pharisaical legalism into the church. They were forerunners of the Hebrew Roots cults that are gaining popularity today, insisting that true Christianity must be thoroughly Jewish. They are therefore usually referred to as "Judaizers." In the English Standard Version, they are called "the circumcision party" (Acts 11:2; Gal. 2:12; Titus 1:10). And sometimes Paul called them worse names than that. In Philippians 3:2, one of Paul's later epistles, he calls them "dogs . . . evil workers . . . the false circumcision." He uses a Greek word that means "those who mutilate the flesh."

Paul's Rebuke of False Teachers

Paul says the version of the gospel these Judaizers were teaching was in fact no gospel at all. The Greek text in Galatians 1:6–7 uses two distinct adjectives that are close synonyms: "a *different* gospel; which is really not *another*." The word translated "different" is *heteros*, meaning "another of a different kind." The word translated "another" is *allos*, signifying "another of the same kind." So he's saying they are flirting with a whole different kind of gospel, and it's no legitimate alternative to the true gospel. Paul's point is that the expression "another gospel" is a complete misnomer. *There is no other gospel.* That's the theme of this passage.

Paul makes that point with supreme vigor, using the most severe language he can righteously summon. He punctuates it with a double curse: "But even if we, or an angel from heaven, should preach to you a gospel contrary to what we have preached to you, he is to be accursed! As we have said before, so I say again now, if any man is preaching to you a gospel contrary to what you received, he is to be accursed!" (vv. 8–9). The exclamation points in the NASB appropriately convey what an emphatic anathema Paul gives. (If Paul were living today and posting this double curse on Twitter, he would probably put it in all caps.)

It is the strongest language Paul uses anywhere. And it comes at the start of an epistle that is filled with strong words. In Galatians 5:12, for example, the apostle suggests that if circumcision can make a person righteous, these false teachers should take their pernicious doctrine to its logical conclusion and cut off their manhood completely.

That's harsh! But those two verses in chapter 1 are harsher still, because Paul is saying the Judaizers deserve eternal damnation.

Don't pass over those maledictions without considering what *we* ought to learn from them. There's no legitimate way to soften what Paul is saying here. This is inspired Scripture, so we can't brush it aside as an accidental overstatement. Those curses are as God-breathed as any other text of Scripture, and they are meant to show us what a profound evil it is to "exceed what is written" (1 Corinthians 4:6) by trying to redesign the gospel to suit our own tastes and prejudices.

If the false teachers in Galatia were former Pharisees like those in Acts 15, they may have once been colleagues of Paul—men whom he knew personally. They supposedly professed faith in Christ, but Paul does not try to make nice with them. He doesn't show them any kind of artificial academic deference. He doesn't feign polite congeniality. He doesn't invite them to an amiable dialogue. He doesn't even challenge them to a debate.

He also doesn't write to them privately before criticizing them publicly. He simply brushes them off as utter heretics, and he instructs the Galatians to have nothing to do with them. He says we're not to accept anyone who comes along promoting a different gospel *no matter who they are*—even angels or apostles. That, of course, is a pure hypothetical, used to make the point as emphatically as possible. No real angel and no real apostle would ever purposely promote a different gospel. But if they do, Paul says, *let them be damned.*

Paul is using a level of polemical vilification that today's guardians of evangelical etiquette might try to tell us is totally out of place in any discussion of religious belief or biblical doctrine. You're not supposed to say such things. But here we see that it's not always right to be warm and welcoming. There are times when a curse is more appropriate than a blessing.

Of course, it's not a good thing to be so fluent in imprecatory language that damning your adversaries becomes second nature. It's a good idea to avoid those self-appointed wardens of righteous precision who never do anything *but* curse and condemn others. It's not a badge of honor to be a full-time contrarian. If you are immediately inclined to call down fire from heaven on everyone with whom you have any kind of disagreement, you are not demonstrating a godly trait.

Jesus said, "Love your enemies, do good to those who hate you, bless those who curse you, pray for those who mistreat you" (Luke 6:27–28). Paul said, "When we are reviled, we bless; when we are persecuted, we endure; when we are slandered, we try to conciliate" (1 Cor. 4:12–13). First Peter 3:9 says, "[Do not return] evil for evil or insult for insult, but [give] a blessing instead." If you simply *must* be contrary, that's one of the best ways to do it: "Bless those who persecute you; bless and do not curse" (Rom. 12:14).

That's what we are to do when we are the target of an adversary's personal attacks. But that wasn't the case here in Galatians. The problem wasn't some personal affront or indignity to Paul's ego. *The gospel* was under attack. This was a blatant assault against the kingdom of heaven, so such a harsh response was fitting.

When Paul says, "You are so quickly deserting Him who called you by the grace of Christ" (v. 6), he isn't speaking about himself. The phrase "Him who called you" is a reference to God. God is the One who calls and draws believers through the gospel. "*God . . . called us with a holy calling*" (2 Tim. 1:8–9; emphasis added). "[Those] whom He predestined, He also called" (Rom. 8:30). And in Galatians 5:7–8, Paul tells the Galatians, "You were running well; who hindered you from obeying the truth? This persuasion did not come from *Him who calls you*" (emphasis added). God is the one who calls us into the grace of Christ. By flirting with this alternative gospel, the Galatians had gone to the very brink of turning away from God—"deserting Him . . . for a different gospel" (1:6).

So these preachers of a false gospel weren't merely thorns of annoyance in Paul's flesh; they were turning people against the truth of Christ and, therefore, posed a serious threat to the churches of Galatia. That's why Paul called them damnable heretics.

In other words, Paul is defending the message, not the messenger.

But these false teachers were not openly hostile to Christ. They pretended to be preachers of the gospel while systematically attacking the principle of divine grace that is the essential nucleus of gospel truth. They were teaching that the gospel is a message about what sinners must do for God, rather than simply declaring what Christ has done for sinners. It would have been positively sinful to bless the purveyors of such an upside-down message. It would be a sin even to *ignore* the danger they posed. (That's what Peter tried to do in Galatians 2, and Paul rebuked him publicly for it.)

In Titus 1:10–11, Paul mentions these same false teachers. There he calls them "those of the circumcision" and he says they "must be silenced." That would not be a politically correct sentiment in these postmodern times, but it is the only appropriate answer to gospel-corrupting false teachers.

Incidentally, the apostle John, who has been nicknamed "the apostle of love," said something similar. He said we're not to receive people amicably who have an agenda to undermine or attack the essential teachings of Christ. In 2 John 9–11, he said, "Anyone who goes too far and does not abide in the teaching of Christ, does not have God. . . . If anyone comes to you and does not bring this teaching, do not receive him into your house, and do not give him a greeting; for the one who gives him a greeting participates in his evil deeds."

Both apostles are saying that the gospel is simple and specific, and that anyone who tries to tweak it, twist it, or tamper with it is committing a damnable sin. Protestants, I fear, have forgotten how forcefully the apostles stressed that truth.

Worse than that, lots of so-called Protestants seem to have forgotten that there is only one actual gospel. Five-hundred years into the Protestant Reformation, ecumenical relations with Rome have never been more popular among Protestants. But Rome has not budged one inch on the gospel since Luther's time. The Roman Catholic Church still peddles indulgences and still categorically rejects the principle of *sola fide*—the doctrine of justification by faith alone.

Protestants are the ones who have changed their stance on the gospel since the 1500s, and not for the better. If you doubt that, turn on almost any of the large, global religious television networks and spend a few hours watching the various charlatans and religious quacks who traffic in false gospels. They promise divine favor and earthly prosperity in return for money. They are selling their own brand of materialistic indulgences.

There are hundreds more religious hucksters today than there were in Johann Tetzel's time—and most of them are nominally evangelical. The word *evangelical* supposedly means "gospel oriented," but what the televangelists are preaching is the very definition of "a different gospel"—which, as Paul says, is no gospel at all. We desperately need a generation of men with the spirit of Luther and Calvin—true biblical scholars who are not reluctant to wage a vigorous polemical war against false gospels.

It seems to be the prevailing attitude today that if you engage in a verbal bare-knuckle fight against error the way Paul does here, you automatically sacrifice your scholarly credibility. That's an emasculated view of scholarship. The best scholars throughout church history have always been vigorous polemicists.

The evangelical movement right now is overrun with false gospels. There has never been a time when the church was more in need of clear, intelligent, uncompromising voices willing to speak candidly and defend the one true gospel the way Paul does here.

Paul's Rebuke of the Galatians

Consider the context of Galatians 1. Verse 6 is the first verse of the epistle's main body. Verses 1–5 are a greeting and benediction. That was the standard form for a letter like this in the first century, and it's typical for the apostle Paul to follow this pattern. The first word in every one of the Pauline epistles is the apostle's name, "Paul," and sometimes that will be followed by the names of fellow laborers who are traveling or working with him. Then you have the address, naming the person or group of people he is writing to. And then he normally says something encouraging or complimentary to the church or person he is writing to.

Even when he writes to Corinth—that totally dysfunctional congregation with a laundry list of serious problems—he has some words of praise. Think about how disorganized and confused that church was. They had divided into warring factions. People were filing lawsuits against one another. They were neglecting proper discipline, abusing their spiritual gifts, and getting drunk at the Lord's table. They were doctrinally confused on several levels—struggling even with the basic concept of bodily resurrection. And ultimately, the Corinthians would be susceptible to heretics who tried to entice them to rebel against Paul's authority.

But despite the many serious problems Paul needed to deal with in Corinth, barely four verses into that first epistle, he says, "I thank my God always concerning you for the grace of God which was given you in Christ Jesus, that in everything you were enriched in Him, in all speech and all knowledge, even as the testimony concerning Christ was confirmed in you, so that you are not lacking in any gift" (1 Cor. 1:4–7).

That was Paul's normal practice. He liked to start with a word of praise or encouragement. In the very first verse of Ephesians, he commends that church for their faithfulness. Even when he needed to deliver a rebuke or some correction, he would always try to start with some gracious words about the people he was writing to. Every one of his epistles follows that pattern—except Galatians.

There's not a single word of approval or commendation from start to finish in Galatians—not even a hint of gratitude or joy. His greeting is followed immediately by a scolding; and instead of a blessing, he pronounces a curse.

That's what makes our text electric. Rather than the normal polite formalities, Paul jumps straight to the point, and it is a passionate rebuke: "I am amazed that you are so quickly deserting Him who called you . . . for a different gospel" (1:6). And the rest of the epistle is just that candid. It's an urgent, heavily didactic reprimand, and Paul delivers it without mincing words.

In 3:1, he calls the Galatians "foolish," and suggests that some evil agent has put them under a spell. In 4:11, he says, "I fear for you, that perhaps I have labored over you in vain." Nine verses later, he says, "I am perplexed about you." He is never merely insulting, but throughout this epistle, he maintains that stern tone of voice. He never says anything that would soften or blunt the force of what he has to say. He is deeply and seriously troubled by their flirtation with a different gospel—and from start to finish, you can hear that passion in his words.

One other notable characteristic of Paul's epistles is that his opening words nearly always contain a statement of some core gospel truth—or a summary of the gospel itself. And, of course, he does that here, because it's desperately needed. Verses 3–5 contain this simple, concise statement of the true gospel: "The Lord

Jesus Christ . . . gave Himself for our sins so that He might rescue us from this present evil age, according to the will of our God and Father, to whom be the glory forevermore." Anyone familiar with Paul's teaching can immediately see how pregnant with meaning those few words are. It comprises the principle of substitutionary atonement—Christ "gave Himself *for our sins*" (emphasis added).

The point of our Lord's death was not to provide us with earthly and material prosperity; not merely to break down the walls of national boundaries and ethnic prejudice; not to redeem earthly art and culture; not to send a message about social justice; not to point us on a journey toward spiritual self-realization; and certainly not to give a pattern of self-sacrifice so that we can atone for our own sins. He "gave Himself" to make a full and final atonement for sin and thereby "rescue us from this present evil age."

In 2 Corinthians 4:5, Paul says, "We do not preach ourselves but Christ Jesus as Lord." By making the message about circumcision, these false teachers were preaching themselves, not Christ. The gospel is not about you and me and what we must do. It's about what Christ has done already. Paul's message was narrowly and carefully focused on that. He told the Corinthians, "We preach Christ crucified" (1 Cor. 1:23). "I determined to know nothing among you except Jesus Christ, and Him crucified" (2:2). Specifically, Paul proclaimed the good news of Galatians 1:4, that "Christ . . . gave Himself for our sins so that He might rescue us from this present evil age." That's the one true gospel in a single statement, and anyone who comes with a more sophisticated-sounding narrative is to be rejected. We're not supposed to engage them in friendly dialogue so that everyone can consider their point of view.

It's intriguing, and significant, that such serious heresy crept into the church so early in the apostolic era. Even Paul was astonished that the Galatians were so quickly deserting the truth. Some people have the notion that the primitive church was totally pure, and whatever was taught in the early church should automatically be given total credence. But Scripture itself says everything anyone teaches must be examined alongside the Scriptures to see if these things are so— even if the teacher is an angel or an apostle. That's what discernment demands.

Sadly, the church in practically every generation has failed to take the stance Paul takes here. That failure explains why the visible church always needs reforming. There have always been professing Christians who join the church and identify with the people of God, but their faith is superficial. They don't really care for the gospel message, but they think with a little tinkering we can reimagine the gospel and remove the offense of the cross. As if we could fix the message so that Christ wouldn't be a stone of stumbling and a rock of offense in the eyes of a hostile world.

There is something innate in the heart of fallen humanity that makes all sinners wish for a different kind of gospel, and Scripture recognizes this. "The word of the cross is foolishness to those who are perishing" (1 Cor. 1:18). We're called to preach "Christ crucified, to Jews a stumbling block and to Gentiles foolishness" (v. 23). The carnal mind wants something less offensive, more refined, more dignified, or more ritualistic.

A well-known musician who professes to be a believer recently posted a series of messages on Twitter, saying he finds the idea of blood atonement primitive and embarrassing. He declared that the Christian teaching "that God needed to be appeased with blood is not beautiful. It's horrific." He speculated that perhaps the real message of the cross is that "the blood sacrifice idea [is] unnecessary [, and we should] stop trying to get to God with violence." He wants to tone the gospel down, clean it up, get rid of what's disagreeable, and inject it with more noble-sounding religious principles.

That's exactly what the circumcision party was trying to do.

R. C. Sproul tells the story of how he was lecturing on the atonement once, and someone in the audience yelled out, "That's primitive and obscene!"

Sproul answered, "You are exactly right. I particularly like your choice of words, *primitive* and *obscene*. . . . What kind of a God would reveal his love and redemption in terms so technical, and concepts so profound that only an elite corps of professional scholars could understand them? God does speak in primitive terms because he is addressing himself to primitives."

Then Sproul said, "If *primitive* is an appropriate word to describe the content of Scripture, *obscene* is even more so. . . . What is more obscene than the cross? Here we have obscenity on a cosmic scale. On the cross Christ takes upon himself human obscenities in order to redeem them."[1]

Paul said the same thing *without flinching* in 2 Corinthians 5:21: "[God] made [Christ] who knew no sin to be sin on our behalf, so that we might become the righteousness of God in Him." The accumulated guilt of every evil, obscene, or wicked deed ever committed by all the multitudes whom God will ultimately save was imputed to Christ. Spurgeon says this about that text:

> What a grim picture that is, to conceive of sin gathered up
> into one mass—murder, lust and [rape], adultery, and all
> manner of crime, all piled together in one hideous heap. We
> ourselves, brethren, impure though we are, could not bear
> this; how much less could God with his pure and holy eyes

---

[1] R. C. Sproul, *Knowing Scripture* (Downers Grove, IL: InterVarsity Press, 2009), 18–19.

bear with that mass of sin, and yet there it is, and God looked
upon Christ as if he were that mass of sin.[2]

There's no way to understand the cross properly without seeing it as offensive. That means we simply cannot faithfully preach the gospel and avoid offending people. Paul's curse applies to anyone who tries.

I don't believe the typical gospel-corrupting heretic deliberately sets out to commit a damnable sin. It's probably pretty rare—almost unheard of—that someone joins the church with a premeditated plan to become a heretic. I think most false teachers are deceived before they become deceivers. They "think more highly of [themselves] than [they] ought to think" (Rom. 12:3). They assume they can determine what's true or false by reason alone—or worse, by their feelings—even though Proverbs 28:26 says, "He who trusts in his own heart is a fool." And they actually believe they are doing a good thing by trying to fix whatever they find distasteful about the message of the cross.

The visible church today is full of people who are guilty of the sin Paul curses here. They claim they have discovered a "new perspective," have "refreshed" the gospel for the millennial generation, or have invented some postmodern alternative to a message because they think blood atonement is too primitive or too offensive. They may think their motives are pure. They might have the same motives that probably drove the circumcision party to do what they did—namely, trying to make the message more acceptable or more appealing to their audience. But don't miss the point of this text: Paul curses every effort to do that.

To be totally candid, there is a tendency in all of us to think we might be clever enough to be winsome and influential, so we can figure out some ingenious way to minimize the offense of the cross without corrupting the gospel. Most if not all of us have entertained thoughts like that. It's a desire we need to recognize as sinful, and we must mortify it. Paul was emphatic about that: "Just as we have been approved by God to be entrusted with the gospel, so we speak, not as pleasing men, but God" (1 Thess. 2:4). The way to do that, he told Timothy, is not to revise and embellish, but to "guard what has been entrusted to you, avoiding worldly and empty chatter and the opposing arguments of what is falsely called 'knowledge'— which some have professed and thus gone astray from the faith" (1 Tim. 6:20–21).

We have all seen the drift of pragmatic, seeker-sensitive ministry philosophies for four decades, and by now, it ought to be clear that we should beware whenever someone blithely insists that radical contextualization poses little or

---

[2] Charles Spurgeon, "Christ—Our Substitute," in *The New Park Street Pulpit,* 6 vols. (London: Passmore & Alabaster, 1860), 6:194.

no danger—that it's possible to be cool, culturally engaged, wildly popular, and doctrinally sound all at once. People who have that philosophy always end up twisting or eviscerating the gospel, even if they insist they would never do that. If our main aim is to be stylish in the eyes of worldly people and win them through our own charm or popularity, we have already compromised the gospel. In other words, those who think gaining the world's esteem is the key to evangelism are guilty of preaching themselves rather than Christ Jesus as Lord.

The gospel is deliberately unsophisticated. That is God's design. The gospel lands a death-blow to human pride. Try to spice it up or tone it down and you will inevitably corrupt it. In fact, according to 2 Corinthians 11:3, one of the main strategies of Satan is to draw us away "from the simplicity that is in Christ" (KJV).

There are three common desires that subtly draw people away from the faithful proclamation of unvarnished gospel truth—and Paul alludes to all of them here.

A Desire for New Teaching

The first is an itch for something new. This is a malignant tendency that has afflicted the American evangelical movement for at least 250 years. It's the reason today's evangelicals move from one fad to another with such breathtaking speed and ease.

The people we minister to—and even some pastors—are far too easily corrupted from the simplicity that is in Christ. There is an incredible amount of pressure within the church today coming from people who insist that we cannot effectively reach our generation unless we follow the styles of popular culture. It's why so many pastors are exegeting movies rather than preaching the Word.

But whatever is currently in fashion will soon go out of fashion. Not only has it become virtually impossible to stay up to speed with changing styles; we also know from experience that today's fads will be the brunt of tomorrow's jokes.

For decades, American evangelicals have blindly run after a seemingly endless parade of shallow fads. At one point, everyone was reading fictional stories about territorial warfare with demons—*This Present Darkness* and all its sequels. Then we saw the *Left Behind* craze. That started to die out as soon as everyone was reading *The Prayer of Jabez*. That gave way to "Forty Days of Purpose," followed by Mel Gibson's movie, followed by the Emerging Church Movement, followed by hipster religion.

Today, we look back with contempt on almost everything that became wildly popular and then fell out of fashion. No one who has any kind of influence is excited about *The Prayer of Jabez* anymore. We make jokes about *Wild at Heart.* Running after every new evangelical craze doesn't make you more relevant; it guarantees that eventually you will be irrelevant.

In 1887, Spurgeon's friend and fellow pastor Robert Schindler wrote the first of two articles titled "The Down Grade." In it, he said, "In theology . . . that which is true is not new, and that which is new is not true."[3] That's exactly right. If you accept the principle of *sola Scriptura*—that Scripture alone contains everything necessary for God's glory, man's salvation, faith, and life, and that nothing is to be added to what Scripture says—then you must acknowledge the truth of that little aphorism: "Anything new is not true, and whatever is true is not new."

That's Paul's whole point about the gospel.

Notice his words again: "I am amazed that you are *so quickly* deserting Him who called you" (emphasis added). And then just before he gives the curse a second time, he says, "As we have said before, so I say again now." He isn't reminding them that he said this just one verse previously. He wouldn't need to say anything *that* obvious. He is reminding them that while he was with them in person, he had already warned them not to listen if anyone came teaching any different message.

But the speed with which the Galatians turned away from Paul's clear, simple gospel in search of something new was breathtaking. Again, this is a common tendency. It requires firm determination to remain steadfast and unmovable. Someone not deeply anchored in the truth of God's Word will always risk being "tossed here and there by waves and carried about by every wind of doctrine, by the trickery of men, by craftiness in deceitful scheming" (Eph. 4:14). That's what was happening to the Galatians. Something new had caught their fancy, and lacking firm anchorage, they were easily swayed by the sheer novelty of it.

That same tendency is what you see on a global scale, driving *all* culture today—in the church, too. Like the people of Athens in Acts 17:21, people "spend their time in nothing other than telling or hearing something new." The Internet feeds us nonstop lists of what's currently trending, and that stokes this lust for novelty.

The unchanging gospel is the antidote. There is only one true gospel, and it can't be improved. If someone tells you we need to craft a new, more relevant message to reach the next generation, "he is to be accursed!"

The Christian blogosphere right now is full of people who self-identify as evangelicals but have no firm commitment to the truth that Christ "gave Himself for our sins so that He might rescue us from this present evil age." They are enthralled instead with proclaiming everything from social justice to cultural engagement—as if the goal of the gospel were to immerse us in the values, the jargon, and the entertainment of this present evil age rather than to deliver us *from* it.

---

[3] Robert Schindler, "The Down Grade," *The Sword and the Trowel* (March 1887): 126.

Some people would rather talk about almost anything instead of the great themes of the gospel. Remember, Jesus said, "When [the Holy Spirit] comes, [He] will convict the world concerning sin and righteousness and judgment" (John 16:8). But in countless evangelical pulpits today, those topics are deliberately omitted in the name of "relevance."

That is the inevitable result when church leaders allow an itch for something new to influence their message or their ministry philosophy. This is, I think, the besetting sin of the twenty-first century evangelical movement.

The Desire to Change the Gospel

A second fleshly lust that causes preachers to veer off-message is the urge to modify. "There are some who are disturbing you and want to *distort* the gospel of Christ" (Gal. 1:7; emphasis added). Paul makes it clear that these false teachers had a bad motive, born out of an evil desire. They had a premeditated plan to warp and wrench the gospel out of shape.

I don't think he necessarily means to suggest that these guys were self-consciously in league with Satan, seeking to be sinister and knowingly conspiring to do evil out of sheer hatred for Christ. They most likely didn't think of themselves as enemies of Christ. In their self-deceived and spiritually darkened minds, they probably believed they were improving the gospel, making it more harmonious with Moses' Law; removing a serious stigma from the Gentile converts; fixing what they saw as a glaring deficiency in Paul's teaching.

Their problem was not that they had an itch for something new. That love of novelty may have been what made the Galatians so susceptible to false doctrine. But the circumcision party had a different agenda. They wanted to preserve elements of the old covenant that had been brought to an end. And so they had this urge to modify the gospel, perhaps to devise a message that would be more acceptable to their own priests and scholars. They wanted something more sophisticated than the simple message of salvation by grace alone through faith alone in Christ alone. They wanted their religion to be more polished, more ornate, more congenial to human pride.

This urge to modify is the bane of many in academia. Nowadays, if a seminary student writes a dissertation on any of the central doctrines of the gospel, he will very likely be encouraged—or even formally required—to concoct a novel point of view or make an argument no one has ever proposed before against some magisterial principle. In much of the academic world, it seems the prevailing philosophy is "If it's not new, it's of no value."

So, ostensibly, evangelical scholars constantly spin out new perspectives and other modified doctrines. Even the most basic, long-established principles of trinitarianism now get recklessly revamped and reimagined with a fair amount of frequency. That's the fruit of the postmodern idea. Nothing is deemed certain; nothing is settled; nothing is really authoritative. Anything and everything nowadays can be reimagined and refashioned, tweaked and twisted. Even supposedly conservative and evangelical scholars sometimes seem infected with a relentless urge to modify their own confessions of faith.

Dangerous as it was, the circumcision party was not *that* foolhardy. The truth is the modification they made to Paul's gospel seems rather insignificant by today's standards. They didn't question the authority of Scripture or deny the imputation of Christ's righteousness. They didn't directly attack the concept of substitutionary atonement. What they proposed boiled down to a slight change in the *ordo salutis.* They thought it necessary for some kind of good work to precede justification.

Paul taught that good works flow from saving faith, not vice versa. So a sinner is fully justified at the first moment of faith. Then obedience follows as the inevitable fruit of authentic faith. The apostle stressed repeatedly that *faith alone* is the instrument by which sinners lay hold of justification. Again, that's what he expressly says in Romans 4:5: "To the one who does not work, but believes . . . his faith is credited as righteousness." So justification comes first; then works.

The circumcision party said no, a minimal expression of obedience—that first act of compliance with the ceremonial law—is a necessary prerequisite for justification. Obedience first, then justification.

Both sides agreed that faith without works is dead. Both sides believed faith and obedience will always accompany genuine salvation. But they disagreed about the order.

By the standards in vogue today, that may sound like a difference too small to worry about. Here's what J. Gresham Machen said about it:

> About *many* things the Judaizers were in perfect agreement
> with Paul. The Judaizers believed that Jesus was the Messiah
> . . . they believed that Jesus had really risen from the dead.
> They believed . . . that faith in Christ was necessary to salva-
> tion. . . . From the modern point of view the difference [be-
> tween them and Paul] would have seemed to be very slight. . . .
> Surely Paul ought to have made common cause with teachers
> who were so nearly in agreement with him; surely he ought to
> have applied to them the great principle of Christian unity.[4]

---

[4] J. Gresham Machen, *Christianity and Liberalism* (Grand Rapids: Eerdmans, 2009 ed.), 20–21.

However, Machen says, "Paul did nothing of the kind; and only because he . . . did nothing of the kind does the Christian church exist today."[5]

What seemed like such a small point of disagreement was in fact a wholesale attack on the central point of the gospel. The circumcision party made justification hinge on a work performed by the sinner, and that seemingly small refinement destroyed the whole gospel message.

That happens every time someone decides the gospel is not sophisticated enough, scholarly enough, or rigorous enough. When people start to tweak the gospel they almost always inject some kind of work into the formula. Perhaps it's something as insignificant as walking down an aisle, saying a formulaic prayer, being baptized, or following some other simple ceremonial requirement. But to make *any* kind of human work instrumental in justification is to destroy the doctrine completely.

Genuine saving faith is the natural expression of God's regenerating work. *He* is the One who opens spiritually blind eyes, grants repentance, and awakens faith. Regeneration, faith, and repentance are all wrought by God's grace. These are not human works. As Paul says in Ephesians 2:8–9, "By grace you have been saved through faith; and that [i.e., every facet of salvation, is] not of yourselves, it is the gift of God; not as a result of works, so that no one may boast." That is the central tenet of gospel truth, and the Judaizers' tiny little modification totally nullified it, because they eliminated the fundamental truth that no element of salvation is a human work.

When it comes to the gospel, the urge to modify is damnably sinful.

A Craving for Human Approval

A third sinful attitude that commonly results in a corrupted gospel is a craving for the applause of men. "For am I now seeking the favor of men, or of God? Or am I striving to please men? If I were still trying to please men, I would not be a bond-servant of Christ" (Gal. 1:10). Paul could have pleased a lot of people if he had simply acquiesced to the circumcision party—or even ignored their error the way Peter at first seemed prone to do.

A quest for human approval was quite clearly the dominant motive of the circumcision party in the first place. They no doubt thought of their work as a shrewd public-relations campaign. They were trying to remove something that the elite rulers of Judaism found offensive about the gospel.

Paul himself more or less acknowledges that. He says in Galatians 5:11 that by preaching circumcision, he himself could avoid persecution and abolish

---

[5] Ibid., 21.

"the stumbling block of the cross." The circumcision party had probably convinced themselves they were doing Christ a favor by making the message more appealing. What they were really doing was seeking honor from men rather than from God. And Paul says in verse 10 that you cannot do that and think you are serving Christ.

Paul knew very well what it was like to crave the admiration and applause of men, because that was the dominant goal of his life before he was converted on the road to Damascus. He persecuted the church at the behest of the Sanhedrin because it gave him status with Judaism's most powerful ruling body.

According to Jesus, this was the central error of Pharisaism: "They do all their deeds to be noticed by men" (Matt. 23:5). Multitudes in Israel rejected Christ and remained in unbelief for the same reason. "They loved the approval of men rather than the approval of God" (John 12:43). There is no greater impediment to genuine faith. Jesus said, "How can you believe, when you receive glory from one another and you do not seek the glory that is from the one and only God?" (John 5:44). Elsewhere, He said, "That which is highly esteemed among men is detestable in the sight of God" (Luke 16:15).

A sinful craving for the applause of men can produce a harsh and showy brand of legalism, like that of the Pharisees, but not always. In the modern academic world, it makes people tend to stifle their convictions and over-nuance every point of truth, so in the end, all truth lies hidden under a mountain of stammering qualifications and vague uncertainties. But you cannot faithfully proclaim the gospel if you mince words. You won't be clear and definitive if you are terrified of getting a negative reaction. And you are not preaching the true gospel at all if you have modified the message in a way that seeks the appreciation and approval of your listeners.

Note Paul's philosophy. He acknowledged that "Jews ask for signs and Greeks search for wisdom" (1 Cor. 1:22). If he had a ministry philosophy resembling the strategy of practically every church-growth guru in business today, the way ahead would be clear. He certainly had the ability to produce all "the signs of a true apostle . . . signs and wonders and miracles" (2 Cor. 12:12). Further, he was the most highly educated of all the apostles, able to hold his own with the Greek philosophers at the Areopagus. He could have contextualized the gospel in the language of Greek wisdom, with all the trappings of philosophical sophistication. Instead, he said, "We preach Christ crucified, to Jews a stumbling block and to Gentiles foolishness" (1 Cor. 1:23). Rather than catering to the Jewish demand for a sign, he gave them a stumbling block. Refusing to answer the Greeks' demand for erudition and wisdom, he preached a message he knew was foolish to them.

Paul did not have some perverse agenda to frustrate his listeners. He went on to explain that this message and that strategy were *God's* choice, "so that no man may boast before God" (v. 29). The gospel doesn't cater to human pride, and when we are tempted to tone it down or dress it up, we must remember that. There is only one gospel, and it is too easy to nullify it or modify it or otherwise embellish it in order to fulfill some fleshly, self-aggrandizing desire. We need to guard carefully against all those tendencies, as Paul did.

The earthly cost of faithful ministry may seem high, but the glory of heaven makes it more than worthwhile.

15

CHRIST AND THE COMPLETION OF THE CANON

JOHN 14–16

Brad Klassen

An important consideration related to the person and work of Christ is His relationship as the Word of God incarnate to the Bible as the Word of God inscripturated. This relationship is easily discernable with respect to the Old Testament because Jesus spoke directly about its inspiration and authority. John Wenham summarized this well: "To Christ the Old Testament was true, authoritative, inspired. To Him the God of the Old Testament was the living God and the teaching of the Old Testament was the teaching of the living God. To Him, what Scripture said, God said."[1]

Jesus' relationship to the New Testament, on the other hand, cannot be discerned in the same manner. Since its books were written after His earthly ministry, Jesus could not cite it or refer to its particular composition. Consequently, while only radical skeptics argue that Jesus had a low view of the Old Testament, many who claim to be less radical question whether Jesus even anticipated the writing of the New Testament, much less authorized it. In fact, for many scholars today, the New Testament as an authoritative canon on par with the Old Testament has little to do with Jesus. James Barr articulated this position well when he stated, "The idea of a Christian faith governed by Christian written holy scriptures was not an essential part of the foundation plan of Christianity." He continued, "Jesus in his teaching is nowhere portrayed as commanding or even

---

[1] John Wenham, *Christ and the Bible*, 3rd ed. (Eugene, OR: Wipf & Stock, 2009), 34.

sanctioning the production of a written Gospel, still less a written New Testament. He never even casually told his disciples to write anything down."[2] The entire concept of a New Testament canon is argued to have originated in the third-century church rather than in Christ, and that Christ's church existed just fine for its first three hundred years without an authoritative collection of Christian writings.[3]

This low view of the New Testament canon raises a fundamental question: *Did Jesus ever authorize, or even anticipate, a series of writings that would be gathered into a collection known as the New Testament, to serve together with the Old Testament as the church's ultimate authority on matters of faith and practice?*

Certainly, if one requires that an affirmative answer necessitates explicit commands by Jesus to certain authors to write certain kinds of books, then no affirmative answer is possible. But such an expectation is simplistic. Explicit evidence is not the only way to arrive at justifiable confidence that Jesus anticipated and even authorized the writings that comprise our New Testament. Rather, there is an assortment of *implicit* testimony demonstrating that the concept of a New Testament canon is not a convenient third-century ecclesiastical invention, but flows naturally and necessarily out of Jesus' own life and teachings. This testimony will be observed in three particular aspects of Jesus' ministry: (1) Jesus prepared *apostles* to proclaim His Word to the world; (2) Jesus promised the *Holy Spirit* to guide the apostles into all truth; and (3) Jesus prayed that *the church* would be sanctified by the witness of these apostles.

Three caveats must be noted at the outset. First, the study of "canon" is admittedly broad. A work of this nature cannot deal with all the questions commonly associated with the topic, such as the canon's extent or the historical process involved in the church's recognition of these books.[4]

The focus here will be limited exclusively to the question, *Did Jesus ever authorize, or even anticipate, the writing of new, authoritative Scripture by His first-century followers?*

The second caveat relates to the understanding of the term *canon* itself. A definition of *canon* will here only be stated and assumed.[5] The term will not be

---

[2] James Barr, *Holy Scripture: Canon, Authority and Criticism* (Philadelphia: Westminster, 1983), 12.

[3] Christian Smith, *The Bible Made Impossible: Why Biblicism Is Not a Truly Evangelical Reading of Scripture* (Grand Rapids: Brazos, 2012), 120.

[4] For helpful treatments on these issues, see the works of Michael J. Kruger, *Canon Revisited: Establishing the Origins and Authority of the New Testament Books* (Wheaton, IL: Crossway, 2012); and *The Question of Canon: Challenging the Status Quo in the New Testament Debate* (Downers Grove, IL: InterVarsity Press, 2013).

[5] The word *canon* (κανών) was used simply to refer to "a straight rod." Used in a figurative sense, the term referred to "a means to determine the quality of something" or a "set of directions or formulation for an activity" (see κανών in *A Greek-English Lexicon of the New Testament and other Early Christian Literature*, 3rd edition, eds. Walter Bauer and Frederick William Danker [Chicago: University of Chicago Press, 2001], 507; hereafter abbreviated BDAG). Over time it came to be used as an "official list."

understood according to the "extrinsic model," which contends that the third- or fourth-century church conveyed its own authority to the twenty-seven books that make up the New Testament. According to this definition, *canon* simply refers to the list of books that received their authority from the early church.

The term *canon* will also not be understood here according to the "function model," which teaches that the authority of the New Testament books arose gradually as churches began to use certain ones and disregard others as their standard for faith and practice. This approach sees the canon as the result of a pragmatic process, with the most universally respected and utilized books adopted as authoritative and placed into a set collection.

Instead, the term *canon* will be used according to the "qualitative model," which views the New Testament books as canonical by virtue of their *nature*. As soon as a book of the New Testament came into being through divine inspiration (2 Tim. 3:16), it already was intrinsically authoritative and therefore "canonical"—even before the early church became aware of its existence.[6] As B. B. Warfield wrote,

> The Canon of the New Testament was completed when the last authoritative book was given to any church by the apostles, and that was when John wrote the Apocalypse, about A.D. 98. . . . We must not mistake the historical evidences of the slow circulation and authentication of these books over the widely-extended church, for evidence of slowness of "canonization" of books by the authority of the taste of the church itself.[7]

Or as Michael Kruger succinctly stated, "Books do not *become* canonical—they are canonical because they are books God has given as a permanent guide for his church."[8]

The church's role with respect to the canon was therefore one of *recognizing* the books that inherently possessed the qualities of divine revelation.[9]

The third caveat relates to the approach to the text of the New Testament itself. While critical scholars tend not to take the biblical text at face value, and

---

[6] Simon J. Kistemaker, "The Canon of the New Testament," *Journal of the Evangelical Theological Society* 20, no. 1 (Winter 1977), 13.

[7] B. B. Warfield, "The Latest Phase in Historical Rationalism," *Presbyterian Quarterly* 9 (1895), 208, 210.

[8] Kruger, *The Question of Canon*, 40 (emphasis original).

[9] F. F. Bruce, *The Books and the Parchments* (Old Tappen, NJ: Revell, 1963), 112–13; R. L. Harris, *Inspiration and Canonicity of the Bible* (reprint; Eugene, OR: Wipf and Stock, 2008), 116–17; Bruce M. Metzger, *The Canon of the New Testament: Its Origin, Development, and Significance* (New York: Clarendon Press, 1997), 282–88.

while some evangelicals are even willing to approach the question of the New Testament's historical reliability from the perspective of the skeptic, we will presuppose here that the text of the New Testament is historically accurate and inerrant in all it intends to communicate. The words and works of Jesus as described by the Gospel writers will be taken as historical fact and not as later embellishments. And when taken as such, the texts of the Gospels sufficiently prove that Jesus did indeed authenticate the composition of the New Testament canon.

Jesus Prepared Apostles to Declare His Word to the World

Any discussion of the composition of the New Testament canon must begin with Jesus' training of the Twelve.[10] The logic of His preparation of the apostles is sometimes missed because it is so obvious, or because it is assumed that Jesus' three years of earthly ministry were focused solely on His personal preparation for the atonement. But why was it necessary to bring a band of men everywhere He went for three years if His focus was just on the cross?

A fundamental purpose for these three years of ministry was to prepare a small group of chosen men to be firsthand witnesses of His words and works. Considering His greater goal of global evangelization, this focus on just twelve men was astonishingly narrow. Certainly, Luke records that Jesus did have a large group of at least seventy followers whom He could send to advance His agenda (Luke 10:1–24). But out of this larger group, Jesus chose and specifically "named" only twelve of them as "apostles" or authorized messengers (6:13).[11]

Mark records that Jesus selected these twelve men for two reasons. First, they had to "be with Him" (Mark 3:14a)—not because Jesus was lonely or needed menial servants, but because the disciples had to see and hear everything Jesus did and said. Their identity had to become so intertwined with His that when they spoke they would be recognized as those who had "been with Jesus" (Acts 4:13). The time they spent with Him would establish them as authoritative firsthand witnesses. Second, Jesus selected this special group of men in order to "send them out to preach" and "have authority" (Mark 3:14–15). Such preaching was not subjective personal interpretation. The verb Mark uses to describe this preaching—κηρύσσειν—implies the proclamation of a herald who authoritatively conveys to the public a message entrusted to him by his superior. In other words, the apostles were chosen to speak as Jesus' mouthpiece. One writer

---

[10] Wenham, *Christ and the Bible*, 114–16.

[11] As J. B. Lightfoot, *Epistle to the Galatians* (New York: Macmillan, 1865), 89, states, "The 'apostle' is not only the messenger but the delegate of the person who sends him. He is entrusted with a mission, has powers conferred upon him." See also J. Norval Geldenhuys, *Supreme Authority: The Authority of the Lord, His Apostles and the New Testament* (reprint; Eugene, OR: Wipf and Stock, 2007), 53–54.

describes it this way: "In the act of the κηρύσσειν the event becomes reality for the listener. It is therefore of essential importance that the herald brings the right announcement. He is not allowed to give his own opinion, but may only pass on a message he himself has received from the one who sends him."[12]

In addition to his selection of apostles, the logic of Jesus' training of the Twelve also includes the impartation of His words to them through dedicated instruction. If His apostles were to proclaim faithfully Jesus' teachings in His authority, they had to be direct recipients of that teaching from His own mouth.

Thus, for three years, Jesus was in the truest sense of the term the apostles' *teacher* (John 13:13). In fact, most of Jesus' earthly ministry was focused narrowly on the disciples' instruction. Though He did minister to the public, His practice was always to gather His disciples in private to explain everything to them carefully (e.g., Mark 4:34). Day after day, the one who was "greater than Solomon" (Matt. 12:42) and the embodiment of "truth" itself (John 14:6) methodically imparted His words to them and prepared them for their own ministry of proclamation. As A. B. Bruce states,

> From the time of their being chosen, indeed, the twelve entered on a regular apprenticeship for the great office of apostleship, in the course of which they were to learn, in the privacy of an intimate daily fellowship with their Master, what they should be, do, believe, and teach, as His witnesses and ambassadors to the world. Henceforth the training of these men was to be a constant and prominent part of Christ's personal work. He was to make it His business to tell them in darkness what they should afterwards speak in the daylight, and to whisper in their ear what in after years they should preach upon the housetops.[13]

The logic of Jesus' preparation of apostles reaches its crescendo in His commissioning them to fulfill responsibilities in His stead. Initially, Jesus did this through temporary preaching assignments among the people of Israel (e.g., Matt. 10:5–7), and with such assignments came delegated authority. As with the Old Testament prophets whose words were to be treated as the very words of God, the words of the apostles were to be received as the very words of Jesus: "And if anyone will not receive you or listen to your words, shake off the dust from your feet when you

---

[12] Klass Runia, "What Is Preaching According to the New Testament?" in *Tyndale Bulletin* 29 (1978), 8.
[13] Alexander Balmain Bruce, *Training of the Twelve*, 4th rev. ed. (New York: A. C. Armstrong & Son, 1889), 30.

leave that house or town. Truly, I say to you, it will be more bearable on the day of judgment for the land of Sodom and Gomorrah than for that town" (10:14–15 ESV). The unbroken chain of verbal authority extended from the apostles all the way back to the very One who had sent Jesus: "Whoever receives you receives me, and whoever receives me receives him who sent me" (10:40 ESV; cf. John 13:20).

Jesus' final commission to the apostles is particularly important (see Matt. 28:18–20; Mark 16:15; Luke 24:44–49; John 20:21; Acts 1:8). Luke records that just prior to His ascension, Jesus said,

> "These are my words that I spoke to you while I was still with you, that everything written about me in the Law of Moses and the Prophets and the Psalms must be fulfilled." Then he opened their minds to understand the Scriptures, and said to them, "Thus it is written, that the Christ should suffer and on the third day rise from the dead, and that repentance for the forgiveness of sins should be proclaimed in his name to all nations, beginning from Jerusalem. You are witnesses of these things. (Luke 24:44–48 ESV)

Jesus here weaves three sources of truth together into one uniform stream of divine revelation: (1) the words of *Jesus* ("These are my words that I spoke to you," v. 44a ESV); (2) the words of *the Old Testament* ("everything written about me," vv. 44b–46 ESV); and (3) the words of the eyewitness *apostles* ("that repentance for the forgiveness of sins should be proclaimed in his name," and "you are witnesses of these things," vv. 47–48 ESV). Moreover, as Matthew records, Jesus explicitly stated that "all that I commanded" was needed to make disciples from "all the nations," and this would be the standard until "the end of the age" (Matt. 28:19–20). Clearly, without the faithful preservation of Jesus' words, there could be no global mission.

Ultimately, while Jesus' selection, instruction, and commission of apostles is not direct evidence of His anticipation and authorization of the writing of the New Testament scriptures, it does provide a necessary prerequisite to it. Jesus' next two actions develop it further.

Jesus Promised the Holy Spirit to Guide His Apostles into All Truth

In considering Jesus' relationship to the New Testament canon, we must also take into account His promise that the Holy Spirit would guide His apostles "into all the truth" (John 16:13). As Bernard Ramm once wrote, "Here in this ministry of the Spirit is the ultimate credibility of the New Testament; here is the sufficient and necessary cause for the writing of the New Testament; here is the authority of the divine Scriptures traced to their executor; and here is the real ground of our own inward certainty of the Christian faith."[14]

In His Olivet Discourse, Jesus declared that His words possessed everlasting perpetuity: "Heaven and earth will pass away, but My words will not pass away" (Matt. 24:35; cf. Mark 13:31; Luke 21:33). While the statement relates directly to His prophecies concerning the "the end of the age" (Matt. 24:3), the principle is nonetheless clear: the details Jesus taught would not be lost as time passed. Even the permanence of the most immutable objects known to man—heaven and earth—could not compare with the permanence of His words.

There was, however, something that did possess the same kind of perpetuity as the words of Jesus: the Old Testament Scriptures. In His Sermon on the Mount, Jesus affirmed with similar language that "until heaven and earth pass away, not the smallest letter or stroke shall pass from the Law until all is accomplished" (Matt. 5:18; cf. Luke 16:17). Emphasizing the same truth, He also declared that "the Scripture cannot be broken" (John 10:35). Such statements reiterated the teaching of the Old Testament itself. Isaiah stated that "the word of our God stands forever" (Isa. 40:8); David declared that the Law "endur[es] forever" (Ps. 19:9); and the writer of Psalm 119 exclaimed, "Forever, O LORD, Your word is settled in heaven" (v. 89). Without question, the Old Testament was to be taken as a permanent record of God's Word. Jesus claimed that same permanence and authority for His own words.

But just *how* would Jesus' words remain as permanent as the Old Testament Scriptures? Indeed, Jesus had prepared apostles to propagate His teaching to the world, but no record exists that they ever recorded anything during His earthly ministry. Moreover, some who had not been part of this select group would later claim to record these words of Jesus (Luke 1:1–4). How could Jesus make such a claim with such boldness?

The answer is found in Jesus' promise of the Holy Spirit. To those tasked with bearing witness to His life and teachings, Jesus promised a Helper who would ensure their witness would be accurate and enduring. Jesus began to make this promise early in His preparation of the Twelve. Before sending them on one temporary assignment, Jesus stated,

> Behold, I send you out as sheep in the midst of wolves; so
> be shrewd as serpents and innocent as doves. But beware of

---

[14] Bernard Ramm, *The Witness of the Spirit: An Essay on the Contemporary Relevance of the Internal Witness of the Holy Spirit* (Grand Rapids: Eerdmans, 1960), 57–58.

men, for they will hand you over to *the* courts and scourge you in their synagogues; and you will even be brought before governors and kings for My sake, as a testimony to them and to the Gentiles. But when they hand you over, do not worry about how or what you are to say; for it will be given you in that hour what you are to say. For it is not you who speak, but *it is* the Spirit of your Father who speaks in you." (Matt. 10:16–20; cf. Mark 13:11; Luke 12:12)

In the same way that God had told Moses, "Now then go, and I, even I, will be with your mouth, and teach you what you are to say" (Ex. 4:12), Jesus promised that "the Spirit of your Father" would give the apostles their words as they made their defense before the world.

The Upper Room Discourse provides Jesus' most detailed teaching concerning this Helper's ministry. First, Jesus taught that His own departure would signal the coming of this Helper. In the first of five important statements on the ministry of the Holy Spirit (John 14:16–17, 26; 15:26; 16:7–11, 12–15), Jesus states, "I will ask the Father, and He will give you another Helper, that He may be with you forever; *that is* the Spirit of truth, whom the world cannot receive, because it does not see Him or know Him, *but* you know Him because He abides with you and will be in you" (14:16–17).

Jesus' identification of the Holy Spirit as "another Helper" is significant in answering the question posed above. In simple terms, "Helper" (παράκλητος; cf. 14:26; 15:26; 16:7) referred to "a helping presence"[15] or "one who is called alongside to provide aid."[16] In extrabiblical Greek, the term was used to refer to the person called alongside a defendant as an *advocate* or *intercessor*.[17] This was an appropriate term, especially in light of Jesus' earlier promise to the apostles (Matt. 10:16–20), for it described succinctly what the Holy Spirit would do when the apostles would be called upon to testify before Jews and Gentiles.

Jesus further identified this Helper as "the Spirit of truth" (14:17; cf. 15:26; 16:13). Jesus Himself was described as "full of truth" (1:14); He asserted that He spoke "truth" as opposed to falsehood (8:45–46); and claimed to be the embodiment of "truth" itself (14:6). Now, the "Spirit of truth"—this *other* Helper—would be given to the disciples to abide within them (14:17). He would be their

---

[15] Andreas J. Köstenberger, *John*, Baker Exegetical Commentary on the New Testament (Grand Rapids: Baker Academic, 2004), 436, n. 70.

[16] Murray J. Harris, *John*, Exegetical Guide to the Greek New Testament (Nashville, TN: Broadman & Holman Academic, 2015), 260.

[17] BDAG, παράκλητος, 766.

new agent of truth, just as Christ had been in the past.

The purpose for the sending of the Spirit of truth is identified more explicitly in Jesus' second statement concerning this Helper: "These things I have spoken to you while abiding with you. But the Helper, the Holy Spirit, whom the Father will send in My name, He will teach you all things, and bring to your remembrance all that I said to you" (14:25–26). Here, a twofold function is described—that of *teaching* and *reminding*.

First, the Spirit's ministry would involve *teaching*—the impartation of divine knowledge. There had been many truths that the disciples had not yet been ready to receive, but were essential to their commission to preach Christ to the world. As Jesus stated near the end of His discourse,

> I have many more things to say to you, but you cannot bear
> *them* now. But when He, the Spirit of truth, comes, He will
> guide you into all the truth; for He will not speak on His own
> initiative, but whatever He hears, He will speak; and He will
> disclose to you what is to come. He will glorify Me, for He
> will take of Mine and will disclose *it* to you. All things that the
> Father has are Mine; therefore I said that He takes of Mine
> and will disclose *it* to you. (John 16:12–15)

In other words, in light of His imminent departure, Jesus promised the help of the Spirit to "guide" or "assist in acquiring"[18] what He identified as "all the truth" (16:13a), particularly as it related to "what is to come" (16:13b). Certainly, this new revelation would not be qualitatively different from the revelation Jesus already had given. As Jesus went on to state, the Spirit "takes of Mine and will disclose *it* to you" (v. 15). There would be perfect continuity between what Christ already taught in person and what the Spirit would further reveal to these apostolic witnesses. As the Logos of God (John 1:1), Christ would continue His role in heaven as the great revealer of divine truth from the Father, just as He had done historically on earth.

Second, the Spirit's ministry would involve *reminding*—the recalling to mind what Christ had said and done throughout His earthly ministry. Important here is the concept of "testimony." Throughout the Upper Room Discourse, Jesus alluded to the nature of the commission tasked to His disciples. For example, He stated, "When the Helper comes, whom I will send to you from the Father, *that is* the Spirit of truth who proceeds from the Father, He will testify about Me, and you

---

[18] BDAG, ὁδηγέω, 690.

will testify also, because you have been with Me from the beginning" (15:26–27).

The apostles had been selected to bear witness to the earthly ministry of Jesus Christ. But because their time with Christ was all spent prior to the fulfillment of His work, many details of His teaching remained difficult to understand (12:16) and some were even forgotten (2:22). Yet central to their mission was their accurate proclamation of Jesus' words. How would they remember and understand, especially since their time with Jesus would soon be over?

Furthermore, Jesus spelled out the manner by which love to Him would be shown after His departure: "If anyone loves Me, he will keep My word; and My Father will love him, and We will come to him and make Our abode with him. He who does not love Me does not keep My words; and the word which you hear is not Mine, but the Father's who sent Me" (14:23–24). If there was to be a full expression of love for Christ through obedience, nothing less than the totality of Christ's teaching would be needed. Such a standard would be impossible if the witnesses who were entrusted with the words of Christ could not remember what He taught.

Yet Jesus would not leave His apostles helpless. It would be a primary component of the Helper's ministry to "bring to remembrance" all Jesus' teachings (14:26). He would not permit the apostles to remember incorrectly or partially that content of knowledge that was so integral to their love for Christ and their witness to the world.

Ultimately, it was Jesus' own assertions concerning the necessity of His words for faith, love, obedience, and witness that established the need for a canon. Moreover, Jesus' promise of the Spirit of truth ensured that the apostles' recollection, understanding, and communication of His words would meet the necessary criteria to serve as this canon. This canon would first form orally in what came to be called "apostolic teaching" (e.g., Acts 2:42). But with the recognition that their testimony concerning Christ needed to be preserved and spread to "all creation" (Mark 16:15), and that the Holy Spirit had been promised as the guarantor of the accuracy of this testimony, it would be inexplicable for them to believe that their words—unlike the words of the prophets of old who by the power of the same Spirit (cf. 2 Peter 1:19–21) gave testimony concerning Christ (cf. 1 Peter 1:10–12)—did not need to be recorded.

The full impact of Jesus' teaching on the Spirit as it relates to the composition of the canon is often lost due to the tendency of contemporary readers to insert themselves as the direct recipients of Jesus' promises. While portions of the discourse do apply to all believers, promises like that of John 14:26 ("He will teach you all things, and bring to your remembrance all that I said to you") are limited in application. As Sinclair Ferguson writes,

The significance of these words is also commonly short-circuited as though they had immediate application to contemporary Christians. But in fact, they constituted a specific promise to the apostles which found its fulfillment in their writing of the New Testament Scriptures. The Gospels contain what they were reminded that Jesus had said and taught; in the letters we find the further illumination they received through the Holy Spirit.[19]

Jesus Prayed that the Church Would Be Sanctified by the Apostolic Witness

When considering Jesus' relationship to the composition of the New Testament, we must further take into account His intercessory prayer in the garden of Gethsemane. This petition, recorded in John 17, contains the longest recorded communication of the Son of God to the Father and poignantly summarizes Jesus' entire earthly ministry.

The content of Jesus' prayer focuses on three objects: (1) Jesus Himself (vv. 1–5); (2) Jesus' apostles (vv. 6–19); and (3) the future church (vv. 20–26). As Jesus begins to pray for His apostles, the specific men given by the Father to be special witnesses of Jesus' ministry (v. 6), He identifies the centrality of verbal testimony to the success of His mission:

> I have manifested Your name to the men whom You gave Me out of the world; they were Yours and You gave them to Me, and they have kept Your word. Now they have come to know that everything You have given Me is from You; for the words which You gave Me I have given to them; and they received *them* and truly understood that I came forth from You, and they believed that You sent Me. (vv. 6–8)

Jesus' ultimate mission was to reveal the Father ("for this [reason] I have been born," 18:37). He speaks so confidently in His prayer of His success in this mission that He uses the perfective tense: "the words which You gave [perfect] me I have given [perfect] to them" (17:8), and "I have given [perfect] them Your word" (v. 14). At the heart of this mission was a collective content of knowledge ("word," v. 14) made up of specific propositions ("words," v. 8).

However, despite Jesus' success, the overall mission was not yet complete.

---

[19] Sinclair B. Ferguson, *The Holy Spirit*, Contours of Christian Theology (Downers Grove, IL: InterVarsity Press, 1996), 70.

Now it was the responsibility of the apostles to communicate this message. The climax of Jesus' intercession for His apostles, therefore, focuses on the means by which the Father would keep them faithful and consecrated to the task at hand: "Sanctify them in the truth; Your word is truth. As You sent Me into the world, I also have sent them into the world. For their sakes I sanctify Myself, that they themselves also may be sanctified in truth" (vv. 17–19). While by logical extension the designation "*Your* word" (v. 17) could be understood as referring to all the words that proceeded from the mouth of God (which would include the Old Testament), the context of Jesus' prayer—particularly verses 8 and 14—requires that this "word" of the Father be taken as a direct reference to the words that Christ Himself had made known to the apostles.[20] In other words, as Jesus looked ahead to the teaching mission of the apostles, He recognized that the great means to set them apart and keep them faithful would be the very words He had received from the Father and had revealed to them. They would not only need to convey these words; they would also need to be sanctified by them.

Then, as Jesus transitions to pray for the global church (vv. 20–26), He recognizes the central role the "word" would play in the salvation and sanctification of sinners: "I do not ask on behalf of these alone, but for those also who believe in Me through their word; that they may all be one; even as You, Father, *are* in Me and I in You, that they also may be in Us, so that the world may believe that You sent Me" (vv. 20–21)—the word of the apostles. The great means by which others would come to know Jesus Christ salvifically and be spiritually united with Him is now identified as "*their* word" (v. 20). Having been set apart by the words that Christ gave them from the Father, the apostles were to convey these same words to the world. His word became theirs, and their faithful proclamation would lead to the salvation of the lost and their incorporation into the spiritual body of Christ.

The association Jesus makes in His prayer between the *source* of the words (the Father), the *revealer* of the words (the Son), and the *messengers* of the word (the apostles), cannot be ignored. He seamlessly moves between describing divine revelation as "your word" (of the Father) and "their word" (of the apostles), with Jesus Himself serving as the effectual link. In the divine wisdom of God, all three components would be essential to the ultimate success of the revelation of God to the world. As F. F. Bruce commented, "The very message which they are to proclaim in his name will exercise its sanctifying effect on them: that message is the continuation of his message, just as their mission in the world is the ex-

---

[20] C. K. Barrett, *The Gospel According to St. John*, 2nd ed. (Philadelphia: Westminster, 1978), 510; Köstenberger, *John*, 492; Harris, *John*, 290.

tension of his mission."[21] Thus, in a very real sense, the composition of the New Testament as an authoritative and enduring testimony to the world can be seen as part of the Father's answer to the Son's prayer. The ultimate mission could not be achieved without the words of the Father revealed in Christ, nor without the words of Christ conveyed faithfully by His apostles. The first half of the equation was complete; the second half remained unfinished. Jesus prays for its success, and in the providence of God, the apostles begin to take up the pen and write for all the world to read.

Consequently, it can only be argued out of extreme prejudice that "during the first and most of the second century, it would have been impossible to foresee that such a collection would emerge" and that "nothing dictated that there should be a NT at all."[22] Jesus' special preparation of a group of apostles, His promise of the Holy Spirit to guide these apostles in their proclamation of His teaching, and His prayer that the Father would use the apostles' word for the salvation and sanctification of the church all provide the logical framework for affirming the New Testament as anticipated and authorized by Jesus. As Michael Kruger stated,

> The apostles were mouthpieces of Christ and were given the task of delivering and preserving this redemptive message—which was originally delivered orally but eventually was embodied in a more permanent, written form. The New Testament books were considered authoritative not because the church declared them to be so, or even because they were written directly by an apostle, but because they were understood to bear the essential apostolic deposit.[23]

Several decades earlier, John Wenham similarly asserted,

> We seem justified in saying: To Christ his own teaching and the teaching of his Spirit-taught apostles was true, authoritative, inspired. To him, what he and they said under the direction of the Spirit, God said. To him, the God of the New Testament was the living God, and in principle the teaching of the New Testament was the teaching of the living God.[24]

---

[21] F. F. Bruce, *The Gospel and Epistles of John* (Grand Rapids: Eerdmans, 1983), 334.
[22] Harry Y. Gamble, *The New Testament Canon: Its Making and Meaning* (Philadelphia: Fortress Press, 1985), 12.
[23] Kruger, *Canon Revisited*, 193–94.
[24] Wenham, *Christ and the Bible*, 127.

And several decades before him, Geldenhuys wrote,

> The fact *as such* that Jesus possesses supreme divine authority
> is . . . of the greatest significance for the study of the making
> of the New Testament. For it gives us the assurance that the
> Lord of all authority would have seen to it that, through the
> working of his power, an adequate and completely reliable
> account of and an authentic proclamation concerning the sig-
> nificance of His life and work were written and preserved for
> the ages to come. Because the revelation of God in Christ was
> complete and *ephapax*, "einmalig" (once for all), it follows
> logically that the Lord to whom all authority in heaven and
> on earth is given would have regulated the history of the Early
> Church in such a way that the canon of the New Testament
> would be genuine and all sufficient.[25]

Much earlier, less than one century after the last canonical New Testament book
was completed, Irenaeus wrote the following in *Against Heresies* (c. AD 180):

> We have learned from none others the plan of our salvation,
> than from those through whom the Gospel has come down
> to us, which they did at one time proclaim in public, and, *at a
> later period, by the will of God, handed down to us in the Scrip-
> tures*, to be the ground and pillar of our faith. For it is unlaw-
> ful to assert that they preached before they possessed "perfect
> knowledge," as some do even venture to say, boasting them-
> selves as improvers of the apostles. For, after our Lord rose
> from the dead, [the apostles] were invested with power from
> on high when the Holy Spirit came down [upon them], were
> filled from all [His gifts], and had perfect knowledge: they
> departed to the ends of the earth, preaching the glad tidings
> of the good things [sent] from God to us, and proclaiming
> the peace of heaven to men, who indeed do all equally and
> individually possess the Gospel of God.[26]

---

[25] Geldenhuys, *Supreme Authority*, 29.
[26] Irenaeus, *Against Heresies*, in Ante-Nicene Fathers, vol. 1, ed. Alexander Roberts, James Donaldson, and A. Cleveland Coxe; trans. Alexander Roberts and William Rambaut (Buffalo, NY: Christian Literature Publishing Co., 1885), III.1 (emphasis added). Revised and edited for *New Advent* by Kevin Knight, http://www.newadvent.org/fathers/0103301.htm.

Did the New Testament Writers Believe Jesus Authorized Their Writing?

Paul of Tarsus, the most prolific writer in the New Testament, was not one of the original Twelve. His writings provide an excellent test case for determining whether a New Testament writer recognized that he wrote the word of God with the full authority of Jesus Christ. If there were New Testament writers who had no inkling of the canonical nature of their writings, one would expect Paul to be among them. Yet this is not what the testimony demonstrates:

- Paul included himself among the "witnesses" personally commissioned by Jesus Christ to testify concerning his life and teachings (Acts 22:14–15; 23:11; 26:16–18; 1 Cor. 15:3–11).
- Paul identified himself as an "apostle" appointed by God, who had an authority equal to the Twelve to command obedience from the church universally (Rom. 1:1–6; 1 Cor. 1:1, 17; 9:1–2; 15:8–10; 2 Cor. 1:1; 12:11–12; Gal. 1:1; 2:7–10; Eph. 1:1; 3:8–10; Col. 1:1; 1 Thess. 2:6; 1 Tim. 1:1; 2:7; 2 Tim. 1:1; Titus 1:1–3).
- Paul claimed to speak the word of God (2 Cor. 2:17; 4:2; 1 Thess. 2:13) and not his own message (2 Cor. 4:5).
- Paul viewed himself as a messenger of the very words of Christ (1 Cor. 11:23–25; 15:3; Gal. 1:12).
- Paul believed that the church was built upon his words and the words of other New Testament apostles and prophets (1 Cor. 3:10; Eph. 2:19–20).
- Paul claimed that the Holy Spirit was the agent of direct revelation through him (1 Cor. 2:1–4, 12–13; Eph. 3:1–5).
- Paul asserted that his written words were no less authoritative than his preaching (2 Cor. 10:11; 2 Thess. 2:15).
- Paul placed his written words on the same level of authority as the historical teachings of Jesus Christ (cf. 1 Cor. 7:10, 12, 25).
- Paul placed his teachings ("these things," 1 Tim. 4:11, 15–16; 5:7; 6:2b; 2 Tim. 2:2; Titus 2:15) on the same level of authority as "Scripture" (cf. 1 Tim. 4:11, 13).
- Paul stated that what he wrote was part of the authoritative standard—or canon—for the church, and that to reject his words was to place oneself outside the church (Rom. 16:25–26; 1 Cor. 7:17; 14:37–38; 2 Cor. 13:10; Gal. 1:9; 2 Thess. 3:6, 14).
- Paul claimed authority over all the churches (1 Cor. 4:17; 7:17; 11:16).
- Paul commanded the public reading of his letters during the church's worship services (Col. 4:16; 1 Thess. 5:27), consciously placing his writings on the same level as the Old Testament Scriptures, which were also to be read publicly (1 Tim. 4:13).

- Paul, recognizing his unique status as an apostle, was careful to emphasize to his readers that the words in his letters were his own (1 Cor. 16:21; Gal. 6:11; Col. 4:18; 2 Thess. 3:17; Philem. 19). He also warned his readers against accepting letters written by others falsely claiming to be the apostle (2 Thess. 2:1–2).
- Paul recognized the canonical status of Luke's Gospel, even before it had been broadly recognized by the church (cf. 1 Tim. 5:18; Deut. 25:4; Luke 10:7; Paul wrote 1 Timothy c. AD 62–64; Luke's Gospel dates to c. AD 60–61).
- The apostle Peter recognized Paul's writings as "Scripture" (2 Peter 3:15–16).

All told, there are more evidences of Paul's awareness of the canonical nature of his writings than there are in many books of the Old Testament—books which Jesus recognized as true, authoritative, and inspired. John Piper summarizes this well: "Paul claims that in fulfillment of Jesus' promise to send his Spirit to guide the apostles into truth (John 14:25–26; 16:12–13), he was inspired by the Spirit to write truth that was essentially on par with the inspired and authoritative Old Testament Scriptures."[27]

Ultimately, while there are fascinating questions related to the New Testament canon that merit exploration, the effort to distance the canon from Jesus Christ is none other than an effort to undermine its authority and establish a different one (ecclesiastical tradition, subjectivism in the form of rationalism or mysticism, or one's religious community). To separate the New Testament canon from Christ calls into question the very nature of His mission. Yet it is the witness of the apostles themselves as contained in the New Testament, together with the witness of God's Spirit in us, that lead us today to see the perfect harmony between the Word of God inscripturated in the New Testament and the Word of God incarnated in the person of Jesus Christ.

---

[27] John Piper, *A Peculiar Glory: How the Christian Scriptures Reveal Their Complete Truthfulness* (Wheaton, IL: Crossway, 2016), 123.

16

SEEING CHRIST IN THE OLD TESTAMENT

LUKE 24:25–27

Abner Chou

Five hundred years ago, the Reformers declared *solus Christus*, Christ alone. That was the heartbeat of the Reformation. And even half a millennia later, *solus Christus* still stands strong. This should not surprise us. The doctrine of Christ alone cannot be contained to five hundred years. It is eternal truth. Throughout the past, the prophets (Gen. 3:15; Ps. 110:1; Mic. 5:2; Zech. 14:4) and apostles (Gal. 6:14; Heb. 1:1–4; 1 Peter 1:13; 1 John 5:13) proclaimed Him. In the end, every knee will bow before Him (Phil. 2:10–11). All things are from Him, through Him, and to Him (Col. 1:16). Christ alone is an all-consuming and enduring reality.

For this reason, we are all about Christ. After all, we are Christians, and Scripture tells us that this title should not be taken lightly. In Acts 11:26, the townspeople of Antioch named the believers of the city "Christians" because of their preaching and teaching. The title "Christian" did not arise because believers called themselves that but because they gained the reputation of those who followed Christ. This reminds us we have to earn the right to be called a Christian. Like those before us, we must proclaim Christ clearly and boldly.

Such a charge demands that we declare Christ *fully*. We cannot exalt Him merely from the New Testament; we must also exalt Him from the Old Testament. After all, the Lord Himself declares that Moses and the prophets speak of Him (Luke 24:27). Even more, the apostles repeatedly use the Old Testament to explain Christ (Acts 2:33–35; Heb. 1:1–14; cf. Ps. 2:8; 110:1). The

Old Testament is foundational to our understanding of Christ, and so it is critical in the task of magnifying Him.

Additionally, such a charge demands that we declare Christ *faithfully*. Scripture calls us to rightly handle God's Word (2 Tim. 2:15) and not twist what has been written (2 Peter 3:16). People sometimes believe that we need to read Christ into every verse of the Old Testament.[1] However, we do not obey Christ when we misinterpret His Word. We need to honor Christ not only by declaring Him but also in the way we handle Scripture.

Jesus perfectly models this task of preaching Christ fully and faithfully. Throughout His life, our Lord expounds the Old Testament. In doing so, we can observe that Jesus is a master interpreter of Scripture. Even when He was twelve years old, He amazed people with His insight into the Old Testament (Luke 2:41–51). His contemporaries acknowledged that He spoke well from the Scriptures (Luke 20:39). Jesus was an interpreter of Scripture *par excellence*. In fact, our Lord's hermeneutic is the very hermeneutic of Scripture. Jesus, as the final prophet, reads the Old Testament in harmony with the prophets (1 Sam. 15:22; Hos. 6:6; Matt. 9:13; Heb. 1:1–4) and His reading of the Old Testament is the way the apostles read Scripture (Matt. 21:42; Rom. 9:33; Eph. 2:20; 1 Peter 2:4). Thus, Christ's hermeneutic is the hermeneutic of both the Old and New Testaments. He knows exactly how the Scripture works. So when it comes to studying our Bible, there is no better person to learn from than Christ.

And that is precisely what we want to do in this chapter. My goal is for us to sit at the feet of our Lord and learn from Him how to read the Old Testament. He will show us the depths of the Old Testament and that exalting Him never comes at the expense of misreading His Word. In the end, our goal is to honor Christ from beginning to end, to have a hermeneutic that comes from Him to proclaim Him in a way that honors Him. That way, we will truly be all about Christ alone and live up to the name "Christian."

The Way Jesus Read His Bible

So how did Jesus read His Bible? As a master interpreter, what insights does He have about the Old Testament? Luke 24:25–27 provides a way to sum up His hermeneutic:

---

[1] See Bryan Chapell, *Christ-Centered Preaching: Redeeming the Expository Sermon* (Grand Rapids: Baker Books, 1994), 279; Sidney Greidanus, *Preaching Christ from the Old Testament: A Contemporary Hermeneutical Model* (Grand Rapids: William B. Eerdmans, 1999), 203–5; David Murray, "David Murray on Christ-Centered Hermeneutics," in *Christ-Centered Preaching and Teaching*, ed. Ed Stetzer (Nashville: Lifeway, 2013), 9; Graeme Goldsworthy, *Preaching the Whole Bible as Christian Scripture: The Application of Biblical Theology to Expository Preaching* (Grand Rapids: Eerdmans Publishing, 2000), 15–21. For a critique on this view, see Abner Chou, "A Hermeneutical Evaluation of the Christocentric Hermeneutic," *Master's Seminary Journal* 27 (2016): 113–39.

And He said to them, "O foolish men and slow of heart to believe in all that the prophets have spoken! Was it not necessary for the Christ to suffer these things and to enter into His glory?" Then beginning with Moses and with all the prophets, He explained to them the things concerning Himself in all the Scriptures.

At this point, we should clarify what Jesus did *not* do. Some read these verses and assume that Jesus read Himself into every verse of the Old Testament. However, that is not what the text says. Luke states that Jesus talked about "the things concerning Himself" in all the Old Testament. In other words, our Lord presented the relevant texts about Himself found throughout the entire Old Testament. Jesus does not engage in creative interpretation here.

In actuality, Luke 24 shows us that our Lord had a traditional hermeneutic. Our goal here is to show, from this text and others, how Jesus read the Old Testament literally, grammatically, and historically. Even more, we want to see how He used that approach in its full complexity.

With that in mind, the first lesson we can observe from Luke 24 is that our Lord read the Old Testament in light of the prophets' intent and sophistication. He interprets the Old Testament literally in that sense. In Luke 24, Jesus describes the Old Testament as what "the prophets have spoken." With that, Christ affirms that what the prophets meant is the meaning of the Old Testament. That is precisely why He rebukes His disciples for not understanding the Scriptures. If Jesus believed the Old Testament required a different or deeper meaning, then He could not have condemned His disciples. They could not have known better. However, Jesus' point is that the disciples should have known better based upon what the prophets originally said. Jesus does not believe the Old Testament needs any fuller meaning. In fact, our Lord states that the problem is not that the Old Testament is deficient in its meaning but rather that the disciples needed a new heart since they were foolish and slow to believe (Luke 24:25).[2] Thus, Jesus believes that the meaning of the Old Testament is the prophet's intent alone. He really did have a literal hermeneutic.

This is because Jesus believed the prophets knew what they were talking about. He repeatedly declares how the prophets spoke of Him (John 5:39) and how the Old Testament anticipates Him (Luke 24:44). He declared that David spoke of the Messiah and even was aware of His divinity (Matt. 22:41–46). He preached that Isaiah predicted the Lord's power and compassion (Luke 4:17–19). Jesus understood that the Old Testament writers had a complex messianic

---

[2] D. A. Carson, *Collected Writings on Scripture* (Wheaton, IL: Crossway Books, 2010), 283.

theology. Even more, Christ knew that the prophets' theology included far more than messianic theology. He understood they spoke profoundly to various matters of life and godliness. Jesus used the Old Testament to discuss issues such as God's wrath (Gen. 19:1–24; Matt. 10:15), marriage (Gen. 2:24; Matt. 19:5–6), adultery (Ex. 20:14; Matt. 5:27; 19:9), divorce (Deut. 24:1–4; Matt. 19:7–8), and eschatology (Dan. 11:31; Matt. 24:15). Jesus did not read Himself into any of these texts. Rather, He appealed to what the prophets say because He believes they speak knowledgeably and powerfully. All of this shows that Jesus read the Old Testament literally. He did not reinterpret a text but knows how to bring forth what God originally said in all its depth and authority. That is part of what makes Him a masterful interpreter of Scripture.

Second, Luke 24 also teaches us that Jesus upheld authorial intent to the most precise degree. His hermeneutic in this way is grammatical, focusing on the very language and details of the text. In Luke 24:25, Jesus reminded His disciples about "*all* that the prophets have spoken" (emphasis added). With the word "all," our Lord emphasized the totality of the Old Testament in breadth and depth. Jesus certainly showed such precision. He used the word "gods" from Psalm 82:6 to defend His deity (John 10:34). He upheld the tense of a phrase to support the resurrection (Matt. 22:32). He alluded to Isaiah 53 with the phrase "the many" (Mark 10:45). Repeatedly, Jesus showed that He read the Old Testament with a view to individual words and syntax. That is a grammatical hermeneutic.

However, what makes Jesus a masterful interpreter is that His eye to detail provides remarkable insight into the way the prophets weave the Old Testament together to produce theology. We already mentioned that Jesus affirmed the prophets were sophisticated in their own right. This fleshes out that idea. Jesus was aware of how the prophets used certain details to connect back with and expound upon past writings. Christ, in fact, follows that very rationale. The prophets talk about Israel as the vine (Isa. 5:1–3; Jer. 2:21; Hos. 10:1), and Jesus completes that metaphor (John 15:1–9). The prophets talk about various kingdoms as a great tree (Dan. 4:11–16; Ezek. 17:23), and Jesus discusses that imagery (Matt. 13:31–32). The prophets use Leviticus 18:5 to confront Israel about its disobedience (Neh. 9:29; Ezek. 18:9), and Jesus does the same (Luke 10:28). Jesus knew the details of Scripture and how they interconnect. Such a grammatical approach makes Christ exceptionally insightful.

Finally, Luke 24 states that our Lord also had a historical hermeneutic. He read Scripture in a way that affirmed its historicity. In Luke 24:26, our Lord speaks of how the Old Testament establishes the need for "Christ to suffer these things and to enter into His glory." He believes the Old Testament speaks of real events that will happen in history. Such historicity does not merely apply to prophecies concerning His ministry. He also asserts the reality of Adam (Matt. 19:4–5), Isaiah (Matt. 15:7), the Ninevites (Luke 11:30), the queen of Sheba (Luke 11:31), Elijah and Elisha (Luke 4:25–27), Solomon (Luke 11:31), David (Mark 2:25), Abiathar (Mark 2:26), Jonah (Matt. 12:39–41), as well as Abraham, Isaac, and Jacob (Matt. 22:32). Jesus' reading of Scripture is immersed in history.

For that reason, Jesus' reading of Scripture is also immersed in redemptive history or God's plan. Our Lord is aware that history is not random but part of God's sovereign work. Consistently, He looks at the Old Testament as it moves to the New. He speaks of how "the prophets and the Law prophesied until John" (Matt. 11:13). He talks of how the past unbelieving generations of the Old climax in the current generation (Matt. 23:35; Luke 11:51). This accords with how the Old Testament prophets themselves viewed history as all part of God's plan that moves to the culmination of time (Neh. 9:1–38; Ps. 68:1–35). Jesus views history not merely as facts of the past but as the advancing plan of God.

Thus, Luke 24 shows us that Jesus read His Bible in a literal-grammatical-historical fashion. His whole ministry actually attested to this reality. Within this, Jesus knew how these principles played out to their proper end. He abided in the history of Scripture, grasping that it encompassed God's plan as it moved from Old Testament to the New. He affirmed the details of Scripture, understanding how the details weave Scripture together to produce theology. All of this led to His embrace of authorial intent, because He knew how sophisticated the prophets were. He just had to bring forth the full force of the Old Testament. That is what made Him so profound. That is precisely why those who heard Him were so captivated by His teaching (John 7:46) and could never refute Him (Mark 12:34). Jesus never needed to reinterpret the Old Testament. He simply unleashed all the prophets had packaged together.

Our Lord had masterful insight into the nature of the Old Testament. He really understood "all that the prophets have spoken" (Luke 24:25). Jesus' insights show that the Old Testament is not just a bunch of random stories, mere history, or confusing poems and prophecies. It contains profound theology set forth by the prophets to advance toward the New Testament; it is theology that intentionally anticipates Christ in various ways.

Hence, we do not need to devise our own ways of seeing Christ in the Old Testament. Rather, our Lord shows us that the Old Testament already shows Him to us. We just need to read the prophets carefully like our Lord did.

In light of Christ's hermeneutic and insights, we can see four major ways the Old Testament itself magnifies Christ.

The Old Testament Prophesies about Christ

First, our Lord reminds us that the Old Testament prophesies about Him. As just discussed, Jesus read the Old Testament "literally" in the sense that He upheld the prophets' intent. That is because Jesus believed the prophets knew what they were talking about. He believed the Old Testament writers spoke of Him (John 5:39) and had a messianic theology. Accordingly, the Old Testament itself intentionally predicts Christ.

This occurs from the beginning to the end of the Old Testament. Genesis 3:15 declares that a Seed will come forth from the woman and that He will crush Satan's head. Later in Genesis, Jacob proclaims that Judah will possess the royal scepter and that this offspring will be the climax of such dominion. In fact, His reign will restore creation (Gen. 49:10–12). In Numbers, Balaam reaffirms these prophesies. He states that a scepter will arise and crush the head of God's enemies (Num. 24:17). Later, David declares that this Seed will be both priest and king just like Melchizedek (Ps. 110:1–4). He also proclaims that this king will suffer (Ps. 22:1) under God's curse to secure the promises made to both Abraham (Ps. 22:23–29) and David (Ps. 89:1–52). Isaiah builds upon this with the realities of the Suffering Servant (Isa. 52:13–53:12). Daniel does as well by describing the glories of one like the Son of Man (Dan. 7:9–13) who is also cut off for His people (Dan. 9:26). Zechariah also states that this one, who is pierced for His people, will restore His people both spiritually (Zech. 12:10; 13:1) and nationally (Zech. 14:1–10). Malachi, the last book of the Old Testament, concludes with an exhortation to watch out for the messenger who prepares the way for this King (Mal. 3:1–2). These are just a sampling of the messianic prophesies within the Old Testament (see also Isa. 7:14; 42:1–4; 61:1–3; Hos. 3:5; Mic. 5:2; Zech. 6:9–15; 9:9).[3] All this shows that the Old Testament is filled with direct predictions about the Messiah. We can learn much about Christ from prophecy.

However, how do we know if a text is a messianic prophecy? Oftentimes, a prophet will connect his new prediction to an older messianic text to indicate who they are speaking about. For instance, in Psalms 72 and 110, the psalmists discuss how the king will crush the head of his enemies (110:6) and how they will be like a serpent at his feet (Ps. 72:9). This language alludes back to Genesis 3:15, and by this, the psalmist indicates that these psalms also discuss Christ.[4] Likewise, certain psalms (2:8; 22:27; 72:8) and prophecies (Isa. 52:10; Mic. 5:4) use the key phrase "ends of the earth," which exclusively discusses

---

[3] See Walter C. Kaiser, *The Messiah in the Old Testament* (Grand Rapids: Zondervan Publishing, 1995).
[4] See James Hamilton, "The Skull Crushing Seed of the Woman: Inner-Biblical Interpretation of Genesis 3:15," in *Southern Baptist Journal of Theology* 10 (2006): 30–54.

the Messiah's ultimate dominion. In fact, the New Testament even retains this logic. We are to be Christ's witnesses from Jerusalem to "the ends of the earth" (Acts 1:8). Because the phrase is consistently about the Messiah (in both the Old and New Testaments), the prophets use it to show they speak of Him. So we can discern when the prophets give a messianic prophecy. This is because the prophets left indicators of what they intended. They knew what they were doing, and we just need to read them carefully.

Along that line, we need to remember that the prophets wrote prophecy not only to predict Christ but also with a theological purpose. The context of these prophesies brings out his theology. In context, Micah's prophecy about Jesus' birthplace in Bethlehem shows that Christ will be the new David (Mic. 5:2) who will raise up the fallen Davidic line (Mic. 1:4–5). In context, Zechariah's prophecy that the Messiah will return on the Mount of Olives and split it in two (Zech. 14:4) shows how He will turn a place of defeat (cf. 2 Sam. 15:30) into the place of His definitive victory (Zech. 14:4–5). In context, Psalm 22 does not merely predict the Messiah's death but shows the powerful ramifications it has on God's plan and history. The Messiah's death and resurrection will cause Israel to repent (vv. 23–25), the nations to come to God (vv. 27–28), and the dead to live (vv. 26, 29). Indeed, Psalm 22 is not merely a prediction of Christ's death but a theology of our Lord's sacrifice. By looking at prophecies in context, we see that they do not merely serve an apologetic purpose but also provide a rich theology about the Messiah.

Thus, if we are busy trying to find Christ everywhere, we may end up not seeing the full depth of the texts that genuinely speak of Him. The Old Testament is filled with messianic prophecy and so it is filled with profound truths about Christ. We need to do that justice. By reading the Old Testament in context, we can ensure we have the full and deep content the prophets give to us via their prophecies about Christ.

The Old Testament Shows that Christ Participates in God's Plan

The second way the Old Testament magnifies Christ is by showing how He participates in God's plan. Jesus believed the prophets had knowledge of the Messiah and knew what they were doing. So, in addition to prophecy, the prophets often recorded tensions that indicate the work of the second person of the Trinity. Such tensions are discerned through a literal-grammatical-historical hermeneutic, the very approach Christ took.

For instance, Genesis 19:24 states that Yahweh rained down fire from Yahweh in heaven. How can there be two Yahwehs, one in heaven and one on earth? This tension implies that the second person of the Trinity, God the Son, was involved in the demise of Sodom and Gomorrah. Likewise, in Genesis 32:24–30, the Angel of the Lord seems to be distinct from the Lord (for God sends Him) but yet is God Himself. After all, He speaks as God (32:29–30) and renames Jacob to Israel (32:28), an act that God distinctively does (Gen. 1:5). With that, the Son appears to be involved in bestowing the name "Israel." In Exodus 14, the text states that Yahweh looked down from heaven through the pillar of cloud (Ex. 14:24). The context already establishes the pillar of cloud as Yahweh Himself (Ex. 13:21). How can Yahweh look through Yahweh? This too indicates God the Son is guiding Israel in the pillar of cloud.[5] This even occurs in the Conquest. The captain of the Lord's angels appears before Joshua. He is sent from God (Josh. 5:14) and so is distinct from Him, yet He Himself is God, for He receives worship (Josh. 5:15) and is the same One who appeared to Moses in the burning bush (Ex. 3:5). The second person of the Trinity guides the Conquest. The same tension occurs for the Angel of the Lord in the period of the Judges (Judg. 3:13–21) and even the period of the Kings (2 Kings 19:35). The Son orchestrates the birth of Samson and the deliverance of Hezekiah from his enemies.

These examples illustrate the danger of misreading the Old Testament. In trying to find Christ where He is not, we might miss where He is genuinely found. With events like Sodom and Gomorrah, the naming of Israel, the Exodus, and the Conquest, our Lord plays a role in some of the most important events of history. He drives God's plan forward. Thus, a misguided reading of the Old Testament may inadvertently minimize how critical Christ is. It may end up making Him less central. Instead, by having a literal-grammatical-historical hermeneutic, we can pick out the tensions that indicate how Christ participates in and is indeed pivotal to God's plan. We can highlight how the Old Testament demonstrates Christ has always been the hero throughout all of redemptive history.

The Old Testament Prepares for Christ on a Micro Level

Third, Jesus reminds us that the Old Testament provides a theology that relates to Him. As we observed, Jesus had a grammatical hermeneutic that observed how the prophets wove details together to form theology. Those truths not only shape our minds and lives but also, at times, amplify Christ's person and work.

A good way to see this is to walk through different parts of the Gospels and observe how the Old Testament highlights the substance of Jesus' ministry. Again,

---

[5] See Jeffrey. H. Tigay, *Deuteronomy*, JPS Torah Commentary (Philadelphia: Jewish Publication Society, 1996), 57. Tigay notes that Jewish rabbis had difficulty reconciling these tensions as also seen in Deut. 4:37 where Yahweh states He personally brought Israel out from Egypt, yet the Angel of Yahweh is said to have done that. See also James A. Borland, *Christ in the Old Testament* (Chicago: Moody, 1978).

in these instances, the Old Testament does not predict that these events will happen. They are not prophecies per se but rather give us truths that have ramifications on our Lord's life.

This begins right at the birth of Christ. We remember that Herod attempted to kill the male infants, but that God delivered Christ from this massacre (Matt. 2:13–15). The Old Testament brings out the significance of this event. The rescue parallels God's rescue of Moses from Pharaoh and shows that Jesus is the new Moses who will lead Israel in a new Exodus (Matt. 2:15; Hos. 11:1). This event is a divine declaration that Jesus is indeed the true ruler and deliverer of His people (Matt. 1:1).

Old Testament theology shapes the way we see not only Christ's birth but also His ministry. For instance, it helps us see the significance of the places Jesus goes. Jesus comes into Jerusalem and heals all the lame and the blind (Matt. 21:14). This is not random. In the Old Testament, David first conquered Jerusalem and declared that the lame and blind would never enter his town (2 Sam. 5:8). Jesus completes this by entering Jerusalem and healing all the blind and lame. He has a truly triumphal entry.

Likewise, the Old Testament also helps us see the significance of our Lord's teaching. Jesus declares He is the true vine (John 15:1–4). Earlier, the prophets speak of Israel as a decrepit vine unable to produce fruit (Isa. 5:2; Jer. 2:21). Jesus' teaching is epic in light of the Old Testament. Jesus declares, for the first time, that Israel would be able to be fruitful for the Lord. This is because He is everything Israel is not so that they can be everything they should be in Him.

In addition, the Old Testament helps us see the significance of our Lord's activities. Jesus falls asleep on the boat going to the region of the Gentiles (Luke 8:23). This contrasts Jonah who also fell asleep on a boat as he fled from going to the Gentiles (Jonah 1:5). The Old Testament brings out the intentionality of Jesus' actions. He purposefully fulfills God's mission to the nations where Jonah failed. Old Testament theology demonstrates that every aspect of our Lord's life matters.

And Old Testament theology certainly anchors and expounds the theology of Christ's death. Allusions to the Psalms (Ps. 22:1; cf. Matt. 27:46), the suffering servant (Isa. 53:9–11; cf. Mark 10:45), and darkness (Zeph. 1:15; cf. Matt. 27:45) demonstrate that our Lord's death was fundamentally a penal substitutionary atonement. Jesus died to satisfy God's wrath against sin. At the same time, certain psalms (22, 69) also show that Jesus suffered as Israel's King. He was not a victim but the One who bore God's curse as the true ruler of His people. His death, in fact, reversed what Adam had done. In Luke, Jesus says to thief on the cross, "Today you shall be with Me in Paradise" (Luke 23:43). The word

"Paradise" in Greek actually is used to translate "Eden" in the Greek translation of the Old Testament (*Septuagint*, Gen. 2:8). Our Lord's death will return us ultimately to an Edenic state. The theology of the Old Testament grounds and informs us of the nature and immense ramifications of our Lord's death.

The same is true of His resurrection. The fact that Jesus was raised on the third day corresponds with Hosea's promise that God would revive Israel on the third day (Hos. 6:2). In fact, Hosea's later declaration of "O death! where is your sting" (Hos. 13:14) becomes part of Paul's theology of the resurrection. Jesus' resurrection on the third day is not random. God designed it to evince that Israel, too, will be raised just as He was. Even more, Jesus' resurrection on the first day of the week (Sunday) is equally significant. The emphasis of the very "first day" in all the Gospels (Matt. 28:1; Mark. 16:2; Luke. 24:1; John. 20:1) alludes to Genesis 1 and the first day of creation. Jesus' resurrection brings forth a new creation; He will make all things new. Along that line, the fact that Jesus is mistaken for a gardener (John 20:15) is also no accident. Just as Adam was a gardener, so Jesus is the new Adam who rules over this creation. The Old Testament shows that every detail of Christ's resurrection is vital and profound.

The Old Testament shapes the entire life of Christ from His birth to His resurrection.[6] This shows the danger of reading the Old Testament out of context. When we do that, we fail to know the breadth and depth of its theology and, as a result, we cannot see the full significance of Christ's person and work in the New Testament. Thus, by trying to read Christ into places He is not, we ironically diminish His glory. This should drive us to study the Old Testament all the more carefully. By reading the Old Testament grammatically, we can see how the prophets link Scripture together. That not only gives us truths profitable for life and godliness but also sets up an immense theological breadth and depth that prepares us to see the full complexity of our Lord's life.

The Old Testament Prepares for Christ on the Macro Level

Finally, our Lord had a historical hermeneutic, one that was immersed in history and His story. Jesus knew the Old Testament was part of God's plan that moved to the New Testament. The prophets themselves write with a view to this bigger picture. Thus, even though a passage may not speak of Christ directly, it participates in the larger context of a book that is part of God's plan that ultimately connects with Christ. Understanding the Old Testament properly allows us to see the full weight of that plan that climaxes in the Savior.

---

[6] See G. K. Beale, *A New Testament Biblical Theology: The Unfolding of the Old Testament in the New* (Grand Rapids: Baker, 2011), 1–6, 29–248.

The best way to see this is to take a step back and show how each book of the Old Testament links with the bigger picture. That way we can begin to form connections on a macro level that lead to Christ.

In Genesis, God begins His creation and His plan to crush the serpent's head (Gen. 3:15). The story in Genesis moves forward to this end. Exodus continues that as God delivers His people to be a nation that proclaims Him (Ex. 19:6) and exhibit His grace (Ex. 34:6–8). At the same time, Leviticus shows that Israel will also explain God's holiness and the way the unholy can become holy. Numbers moves God's agenda about His Seed forward as He judges and preserves Israel in the wilderness. As they near the nations, God again proclaims through Balaam about the One who will crush His foes (Num. 24:16–17). Deuteronomy explains how Israel is to understand and explain God's law: it is about love for Him (Deut. 6:4). Further, God elaborates on His plan—how there is a need for a new covenant (Deut. 30:6) and a prophet like Moses (Deut. 18:18). At the end of the Pentateuch, God's plan moves to the Seed, a second Moses.

The historical books reveal that history moves toward this Seed. God conquers the land in Joshua, and now the need for a leader arises as evidenced in Judges (Judg. 17:6). Ruth shows that God continues the line of the Seed in the line of Boaz and David (Ruth 4:22). Accordingly, in 1 and 2 Samuel, God raises up this royal line and gives David precious promises of the Davidic covenant (2 Sam. 7:1–14). Both David and Solomon show the power of this covenant; it really has the potential to make all things right (1 Kings 4–5). However, 2 Samuel and 1 and 2 Kings demonstrate that no man can fulfill this covenant and actualize God's promise. Likewise, 1 and 2 Chronicles show that though God desires the best relationship with His people, Israel is rebellious and the king cannot mediate this relationship. Consequently, Israel ends up under God's judgment in exile. However, God is still working out His plan. In Esther, God protects His people and even allows them to have victory over their enemies. Mordecai is even described in the splendor of Solomon (Est. 6:14; 10:3; 1 Kings 1:42; 2:33) because God's plan still moves to a true King who will fulfill it all. Nevertheless, God returns His people back to the land, but this does not mark the completion of God's promise. On one hand, Ezra and Nehemiah show that God continues His work in reestablishing the temple and Jerusalem. On the other hand, that work cannot be done. The temple is small (Ezra 3:12), Jerusalem is feeble (Neh. 4:1–23; 11:1), the people are still wicked (Ezra 10:1–44), and still no king sits on the throne of David. With that, the historical books of the Old Testament show God's plan is not finished; it deliberately moves to the New Testament.

Wisdom literature also reveals God's plan and anticipates Christ. Job, the first book written of all Scripture, introduces the Bible by asking big questions of

God's rightness in a world gone wrong. Job sets up for the entire story line of Scripture and Christ by establishing the need for God's Word (Job 28:1–28) and the gospel (Job 7:21; 9:33; 14:14). Psalms not only contains prophecies about Christ but also intentionally prepares us to worship the coming King of kings (72:1–20; 98:1–9). Proverbs explains royal court wisdom that the Messiah will fulfill as the ultimate King. Even more, it helps us know how to live wisely to honor Him. Ecclesiastes renews our minds in what is valuable in this life and thus prepares us to value the work of Christ. Song of Songs deals with true love, purity, and marriage that honors Christ. Equally, although it does not speak directly of Him, it participates in a larger biblical theme of love, which Christ exhibits for the church (see Eph. 5:22–33). On the macro level, wisdom literature cultivates a people who know how to value, understand, and honor their King in every way of life.

In addition to historical and wisdom literature, the prophets themselves participate in redemptive history. In fact, they not only know about the big picture, but by revelation, they form God's big picture plan. Isaiah discusses God's plan of salvation and how the Suffering Servant will deal with sin (52:13–53:12) and establish God's kingdom (11:1–9). Jeremiah shows that God's plan to break down and rebuild nations (1:10) revolves around the true prophet, priest, and king, the Branch (23:5). Lamentations discusses exile and grief, and how the true Davidic king will bear such suffering in the end (3:1, 19; cf. Ps. 69:21). Ezekiel discusses God's relationship with Israel and how God's glory will fill the earth because of the work of the Good Shepherd (34:1–31). Daniel discusses the breadth of God's plan and shows that in the end, the only true ruler is the Son of Man (7:9–14).

The Minor Prophets also detail parts of the big picture that connect with Christ. Hosea discusses God's love and how that will drive a new Exodus, Moses, and David (1:11; 3:5; 11:1–11). Joel shows God's power in the Day of the Lord, which brings out both God's judgment and the restoration of His people. This includes blessings brought about only by Christ (2:23–29; cf. Acts 2:1–21). Amos reiterates this by showing that God is fair in both His treatment of Israel and also raising up the Davidic dynasty to fulfill His promises to His people (9:11–15). Obadiah talks about the Day the Lord against Edom and all nations, which forms the context of Christ's eschatological work (15–20; cf. 1 Thess. 5:2–9). Jonah talks about God's care for the Gentiles, which also informs God's plan for their inclusion in Christ (cf. Luke 8:23; Acts 10:5–23). Micah deals with God's supremacy in that He forgives sins and raises up the true leader of Israel, a new David born in Bethlehem (5:2; 7:7–20). Nahum shows Nineveh's destruction as a sign that God's big-picture plan stated in Isaiah will come true (1:15).

Habakkuk deals with how the faithful will have faith in God, who will come to champion His Messiah (3:1–15). Zephaniah shows the ramifications of Christ's eschatological work by discussing how God will ultimately refine His people and sing for joy over them. Haggai does so as well by talking about how Israel should be faithful because God will restore them in festivity in the end. Zechariah proclaims that Yahweh remembers His promises, which include the big picture of God's plan and its central figure, the Messiah (6:9–15; 9:9; 12:10). At the very end of Old Testament canon and history, Malachi looks forward to "my messenger" (the name Malachi) who will prepare the way for the Messiah, showing that the big-picture plan laid out by the prophets is indeed moving to Christ.

We have covered how every book of the Old Testament connects with Christ. Rather than forcing Christ into every verse, we can take a step back and see how a book as a whole contributes to God's plan.[7] That provides us the full context of our Lord's person and work as well as how we should live for Him. This reminds us what we can lose if we do not study the Old Testament properly. If we flatten out the meaning of the Old Testament, we will fail to see the full weight of God's plan and how climactic our Lord is. Jesus did not merely accomplish a simple agenda of God but one that encompasses history, nations, individuals, promises, covenants, and the entire cosmos. So by understanding the Old Testament rightly, we not only benefit from its theology but, in turn, see the fullness which Christ alone fulfills. Knowing the Old Testament with a proper hermeneutic demonstrates that Christ is the epic hero.

Conclusion

We preach Christ. In a world that proclaims so many other heroes and solutions, we declare the only One worthy and the only One who is able (Rev. 5:9). This is what the prophets and apostles did. This is what the Reformers recovered. Now, we must join with those who came before us. That is our mission—and even our identity. We are Christians and we are all about Him.

We preach Christ faithfully. We do not make up our own method to interpret Scripture but surrender to the one that our Lord ordained, the very approach of the prophets and apostles, and thus very method of Scripture itself. We thereby understand what the author intends, in the details of what he has said, and immersed in history and God's plan. That hermeneutic is sufficient to help us see the profound theology of the Old Testament that both shapes our lives to

---

[7] See James M. Hamilton, *God's Glory in Salvation Through Judgment* (Wheaton, IL: Crossway, 2010); Walter Kaiser, *The Promise-Plan of God: A Biblical Theology of the Old and New Testaments* (Grand Rapids: Zondervan, 2008); Paul R. House, "Examining the Narratives of Old Testament Narrative: An Exploration in Biblical Theology," in *Westminster Theological Journal* 67 (2005): 229–45.

magnify Christ and displays the totality of His glory. Hence, we do not need to read Christ into every text. Rather, we honor Christ by interpreting the way He has ordained.

We preach Christ fully. We do not preach Him only from the New Testament but also from the Old. We behold the theology of Christ from Old Testament prophecy. We declare how critical He is in God's plan as He drives redemptive history forward from the Old to the New. We expound the complexities of His life brought out by Old Testament theology. We exalt His climactic role as the One who fulfills the total plan of God unveiled throughout all Scripture. We do not simplify Him but present His total glory as the Scripture intentionally unveils.

We preach Christ. May we be those who give Him the fullest glory by proclaiming Him, and in a way that honors His Word. That is truly a Christ-centered hermeneutic.

17

CHRIST, THE CULMINATION OF THE OLD TESTAMENT

LUKE 24:27, 44

Michael Grisanti

Some events in life show up abruptly and without warning. Other things have been carefully planned and have climaxed or reached a crescendo at the right moment. The birth of Christ represents the divinely intended climax of numerous Old Testament passages. This coming of Jesus, in accordance with the revealed plan of our great God, helps us better appreciate various truths.

First, our great and awesome God, as revealed in the Scriptures, brings His plan to pass *just like He promised He would*. He is a God who does what He promises. Second, we will see how the Old Testament weaves a tapestry or builds a structure that finds its amazing culmination in the birth, life, and ministry of Jesus. Although we cannot cover all of this here, it is essential to know that Christ plays a central role in the message of the Bible as well as in the consummation of God's plans for His created universe. *God the Father rules through His Son, Jesus Christ, over the earth and all its inhabitants, including the restoration of a redeemed nation of Israel to the land of promise.* Third, this essay points out the importance of connecting what we understand about Jesus in the New Testament by taking at face value, rather than reinterpreting, what the Old Testament promised in paving the way for Jesus' coming.

A Brief Overview of the Interpretive Controversy

Various scholars have written books relating to this question: "Is the Bible a messianic book?" One could ask even more narrowly: "Is the Old Testament messianic in focus?" or "Does the Old Testament contain specific, clear predictions of the promised Messiah?" One of the mottos of The Master's Seminary is "We preach Christ." Jesus Himself affirmed that He served as the consummation of God's intentions through the Old Testament (Luke 24:27, 44). So what is the controversy that this essay addresses?

On one hand, this essay will not address the issue of a Christocentric approach to the Old Testament.[1] Walter Kaiser expresses his concern with the Christocentric approach this way:

> We would express our concern over those who seem to rush to obtain an incorrect Christological re-interpretation or representation for every Old Testament text by incorrectly using a New Testament [sic] as the basis for re-establishing a new meaning for what it thought the Old Testament had originally meant to say.
>
> Each Old Testament text, however, must first be allowed to say what the author, who stood in the counsel of God, obtained, as we must remind ourselves over and over again, from the Lord who gave us his revelation, rather than our intrusively and arbitrarily projecting a "Jesus-only" message from every text in the earlier part of the canon. Not every Old Testament text is about Jesus! Some of those texts were meant to reprove, rebuke and to teach![2]

On the other hand, this essay focuses on how the Old Testament prepares the way for the birth, life, and ministry of Christ. It will not devote much space to the scholarly debate over this question. It will briefly summarize that debate, but focus on the big picture of how the Old Testament lays the groundwork for a

---

[1] That approach involves a backward look at the Old Testament and affirms that every Old Testament passage has a fundamentally important Christological truth that must receive prominence in any teaching or preaching if that teaching or preaching is to have eternal value. A classic example often cited as an example of this approach involves the conflict between David and Goliath. Christocentric proponents argue that this passage primarily points to Christ dying on the cross for our sins. I don't embrace the Christocentric approach to Scripture and have grave concerns about it. However, this essay will not address that concern.

[2] Walter C. Kaiser Jr., "The Hasel-Kaiser and Evangelical Discussions on the Search for a Center or Mitte to Biblical Theology," *Journal of the Adventist Society* 26, no. 2 (2015): 48.

growing understanding of the Promised Messiah.[3] My hope is that we will better appreciate the way the Old Testament superbly and helpfully prepares the way for the coming of Jesus, the promised Messiah.

First, let us summarize two interpretive extremes to avoid and then three other approaches to understanding Messianic passages.

Interpretive Extremes to Avoid

While various scholars have provided examples of extreme approaches to understanding the Messiah in the Old Testament, here are two notable ones.

First, greatly minimizing or even rejecting the idea that the Old Testament explicitly promises a coming Messiah.[4] For example, Tremper Longman writes, "It is impossible to establish that any passage in its original literary and historical context must or even should be understood as portending a future Messianic figure."[5] Klyne Snodgrass adds that the "early church applied such texts to Jesus because of their conviction about his identity. The conviction about his identity did not derive from the Old Testament. They found Jesus and then saw how the Scriptures fit with him." He goes on to say that it would be better to view Jesus as the *climax* rather than the *fulfillment* of the Scriptures.[6]

Larry Hurtado suggests that out of the postexilic biblical hope for a renewed Davidic monarchy, Jews began to look for "a future agent ('messiah') to be sent by God, usually to restore Israel's independence and righteousness." This expectation did not derive from the predictions of the Hebrew Bible but rather grew out of the hopes of the post-biblical Hellenistic age. He maintains that "recent research suggests, however, that ancient Jewish eschatological expectations of deliverance and sanctification of the elect did not always include the explicit or prominent anticipation of a 'messiah.'"[7]

Finding predictive Messianic statements or Christological connections in many passages that God intended (at least initially) to address people and circumstances in the

---

[3] Although scores of books, essays, and articles have been written concerning the Messiah, here are just a few suggestions: Walter C. Kaiser, Jr. *The Messiah in the Old Testament* (Grand Rapids: Zondervan, 1995); Michael Rydelnik, *The Messianic Hope: Is the Hebrew Bible Really Messianic?* NAC Studies in Bible & Theology (Nashville: Broadman and Holman, 2010); William Varner, *The Messiah: Revealed, Rejected, Received* (Bloomington, IN: AuthorHouse, 2004); Christopher J. H. Wright, *Knowing Jesus Through the Old Testament* (Downers Grove, IL: InterVarsity, 1995).

[4] The below summary of these three scholars draws on Michael Rydelnik's helpful observation in his volume, Rydelnik, *The Messianic Hope: Is the Hebrew Bible Really Messianic?*, 4.

[5] Tremper Longman III, "The Messiah: Explorations in the Law and Writings," in *The Messiah in the Old and New Testaments*, ed. S. E. Porter (Grand Rapids: Eerdmans, 2007), 13.

[6] K. Snodgrass, "The Use of the Old Testament in the New," in *The Right Doctrine from the Wrong Texts?*, ed. G. K. Beale (Grand Rapids: Baker, 1994), 39, 41.

[7] Larry Hurtado, "Christ," in *Dictionary of Jesus and the Gospels*, eds. Joel B. Green, Scot McKnight, and I. Howard Marshall (Downers Grove, IL: InterVarsity, 1992), 107.

near context of those passages. This does not just involve interpretive abuses of a Christocentric approach to the Old Testament. There are plenty of examples of writers arguing that the details of tabernacle construction find fulfillment in Christ (e.g., A. W. Pink).[8] An older view of typology—in which all kinds are a type of some aspect of Christ's life and work—is often part of this problem. Various passages in the historical books referring to the "anointed" one refer to the Davidic king or kings in Israel's history. The way we interpret these, and some psalms or some prophetic passages, could provide examples of this approach.

Eventually Messianic

Besides these two extremes, some scholars see most "Messianic" passages as only "eventually Messianic."[9] This is a huge point of the debate, which we can only summarize here. In a relatively recent volume focusing on the Messiah, for example, the authors affirm that the Old Testament contributes to the development of the Messianic concept or theology. However, they argue that the vast majority of the passages that have traditionally been called Messianic are not direct predictions of the promised Messiah, nor were they meant by the original writer to be Messianic in significance. They reach this set of conclusions by means of: (1) "Non-Revelatory Readings of Human Interpreters" in Second Temple Literature; (2) "Some Eschatological Messianic Reflections"; and (3) "Revelatory Readings" in the New Testament. In light of those interpretive guidelines, the "eventually Messianic passages" present an "Already/Not Yet Christological Reading."[10]

Directly Messianic

Many conservative scholars identify many passages as *directly Messianic* in their original setting, having somewhat incidental relevance to the immediate context. We are most familiar with this view, of which the work by Walter Kaiser and Michael Rydelnik are good representatives.[11]

---

[8] A. W. Pink, *Gleanings in Exodus* (Chicago: Moody Press, 1962), 131–35, 180–230, provides examples of this extreme.

[9] Herbert W. Bateman IV, Darrell L. Bock, Gordon H. Johnston, *Jesus the Messiah: Tracing the Promises, Expectations, and Coming of Israel's King* (Grand Rapids: Kregel, 2012), 21, 25, 32. They would also use the expression "ultimately messianic," affirming that "not all prophecy is exclusively pointing to Jesus, just ultimately" (Herbert W. Bateman IV, "Jesus the Messiah," *Mishkan* 70 [2012], 41).

[10] Bateman, Bock, Johnston, *Jesus the Messiah*, 31. These passages culminate with Messianic significance even if that significance was not present in the original setting of the passage.

[11] W. Kaiser, *The Messiah in the Old Testament*; M. Rydelnik, *The Messianic Hope*.

Directly and Indirectly Messianic

Many Old Testament passages build toward a clear understanding of the Messiah. According to this view, not all traditional "Messianic" passages are "directly Messianic." Some of those passages have *initial primary reference* to the immediate context, but still contribute to the growing understanding of the coming Messiah. Other passages provide a less direct presentation of concepts that later are understood as relating to the Messiah in a more detailed way (e.g., Gen. 3:15; Isa. 7:14).

Let's consider the first Old Testament passage that begins the introduction of the promised Messiah.

God's Creation Mandate (Gen. 1:26–27)

In Genesis 1:26, God affirms, "Let Us make man *in Our image, according to Our likeness*" (emphasis added). This statement is better translated, "Let Us make man *as* Our image, *according to* Our likeness." The second expression, "according to Our likeness," serves as a statement of essence. The Lord is affirming that there is a certain degree of likeness between God and humanity. Our personhood, our rational thought processes, and our capacity to have fellowship with God set us apart from the animal world.

The first expression, "as Our image," presents a statement of function. God created man to function as the image or image-bearer of God. The statement that the godhead created mankind "as Our image, according to Our likeness" delineates man's function (what he is to do) and not merely his essence (what he is like). Human life is to reflect God's nature and person.

In the rest of 1:26, God delineates a key part of that "image-bearing" function: "and let them have dominion over" all creation (KJV). The Lord declares that He created mankind as God's image *in order to represent Him as the sovereign ruler* over all areas of creation. From the moment of God's creation of man, God intended that human beings function as His representatives on earth. Each person was to be emblematic of God's sovereignty and manifest His character in their dealings with all of God's creation.

God's Solution to the Fall (Gen. 3:15)

After God spoke the universe into existence and created Adam and Eve, He gave the first couple instructions for their life in the Garden of Eden. In Genesis 3, Satan tempted Eve, and then both Adam and Eve chose to sin against God. Consequently, God pronounced judgment on everyone involved, starting with the serpent (Satan). This might seem like a totally bad news situation. However, amid God's pronouncement of judgment we find good news:

> I will put hostility between you [Satan/serpent] and the
> woman,
> and between *your* seed [Satan/serpent] and *her* seed [woman's].
> *He* [the seed of the woman] will strike *your head* [Satan],
> and *you* [Satan] will strike *his heel* [the seed of woman] (3:15;
> emphasis added).

A central idea here is that a promised one ("He") will come as God's resolution to the sin introduced through the fall. This prediction—though much more ambiguous than several other "Messianic predictions"—points to an important reality that finds its fulfillment in the redemptive death of Christ.

As the Lord unfolds His intentions for the world in the Old Testament books, He keeps adding to what this person, the "He," would be like. It is as if the Lord, through various passages, is weaving a tapestry or painting a portrait depicting the promised one who will resolve humanity's sin problem.

The Abrahamic Covenant: The Beginning of Israel's Story (Gen. 12:1–3)

After Genesis 1–11 depicts God's intentions for and dealings with humanity—as broad as the entire world—He narrows His focus on Abraham and his descendants as the means by which He will accomplish His plans for the world. In 12:1–3, God promises to show Abraham a land that will become his, to make him into a great nation, and that He will bless all the peoples on earth through him and his descendants. Indeed, the descendants of Abraham will be a conduit of blessing for all nations, a vehicle for the revelation of God's Word and a people from whom the promised Messiah (the "He" of Gen. 3:15) would come.

The Blessing of Jacob: A Scepter for Judah (Gen. 49:10)

After establishing the covenant with Abraham, God reaffirmed it with Abraham, Isaac, and Jacob. He was narrowing further His focus and the unveiling of His plan to bring Himself glory on earth.

Eventually, Jacob and all his descendants moved from Canaan to Egypt. After living there for some time, Jacob neared his time of death. He blessed his son Judah, saying, "The *scepter* will not depart from Judah or the *staff* from between his feet until He whose right it is comes and the *obedience* of the peoples *belongs* to Him" (Gen 49:10; emphasis added). The term *scepter* can literally refer to a rod or staff symbolizing a king's authority. The prophet Amos also refers to the kings of Syria and the Philistines as ones who hold a scepter (Amos 1:5, 8). But more importantly, Psalm 45:6 states, "Your *throne*, God, is forever and ever; the *scepter* of Your kingdom is a *scepter* of justice" (emphasis added). Clearly, use of "scepter" signifies ruling.

The first two lines of Jacob's blessing on Judah refer to the rod that marks off a person as a ruler. The final line of this blessing refers to the people who will submit to this future ruler's authority. So in Jacob's blessing on the tribe of Judah, which describes the destiny of the tribe, Jacob talks about ruling and obedience.

Moving forward a few centuries, after the death of Jacob and then Joseph, a major transition in Egypt took place, and the Egyptians enslaved the Hebrews. God eventually raised up Moses to deliver the Hebrews from bondage. After they arrived at Mount Sinai, Yahweh established the Mosaic covenant with His covenant people, which involved giving them the Mosaic Law. Let's see how the Mosaic Law contributes to the developing Old Testament portrait of the promised Messiah.

The Giving of the Mosaic Law

While much could be written on the Mosaic Law, I will summarize four categories of evidence of it that relate to the promised Messiah. First, the sacrificial system, part of the *vertical dimension* of the Mosaic Law, introduces several important concepts: the problem of sin; death, involving the shedding of blood, which was required for forgiveness; and faith that God would forgive.

Second, the tabernacle—constructed according to God's instructions—served as the nexus between God and His covenant people. It was the means by which God dwelled in their midst. This concrete reality, which existed for hundreds of years for the nation of Israel, conceptually prepared the way for God's people to understand the future reality of God's dwelling in their midst in two ways: the God-man, the Messiah, living in their midst, and the Holy Spirit dwelling in them as believers.

Third, the demands of the *horizontal dimension* of the Mosaic Law involved those laws that would impact the way God wanted His covenant people to treat others—both fellow Israelites and surrounding Gentiles. Israelite obedience to these horizontally focused laws would have highlighted two key sets of concepts that would put Yahweh on display to each other as well as to Gentiles around them: justice/equity and kindness/compassion.

Fourth, it is essential to consider God's purpose in giving the Mosaic Law to His covenant people, Israel. Obviously, Yahweh gave the Mosaic Law to Israel to reveal truths that prepared the way for the coming of the Messiah and His provision of salvation. Beyond that, according to Exodus 19:4–6 and Deuteronomy 26:16–19, God gave the Law to Israel to provide them a concrete understanding of how they could live in a way that would put God's surpassing character on display before each other and the Gentiles around them. (We will return to that concept later.)

Let's again move forward a few centuries. The Israelites have become a nation in charge of much of the land promised them. They have a king who rules over them under God's authority. During the reign of their second king (David), the first king of God's choosing, the Lord provides another piece to the puzzle of God's plan.

Promise of a Future Davidic Ruler (2 Sam. 7)

For the sake of space, I will focus on verses 11, 12, and 16, starting with 11: "ever since the day I ordered judges to be over My people Israel. I will give you rest from all your enemies. The LORD declares to you: The LORD Himself will make a house for you." What does God promise here? He will give His people rest from all their enemies and will establish a dynasty ("house") of kings through David. Verse 12 reads: "When your time comes and you rest with your fathers, I will raise up after you your descendant, who will come from your body, and I will establish his kingdom." God promises to provide an heir who will continue ruling over Israel under God's authority. Finally, verse 16 concludes: "Your house and kingdom will endure before Me forever, and your throne will be established forever." God declares that the Davidic kingdom will never end. What is clear at this point? *God will place Davidic rulers over Israel into the far future.*

So what have we seen thus far concerning the Messianic tapestry God is weaving? The "He" promised in Genesis 3:15 as God's resolution to the sin problem will come through Abraham's descendants, Judah, and David—a ruler over a kingdom!

From the time of David on, various Israelites (psalmists) wrote expressions of their walk with the Lord. They described their love for the Lord and His Word; praised God for His greatness, majesty, and countless deeds on their behalf; and even lamented painful circumstances through which they walked. As men who were carried along by the Holy Spirit, and who had been listening to Scripture recorded before their time, these psalmists wrote about God's future plan for the world He created. Several psalms contribute to the Old Testament's preparation for the coming of the Promised One.

The Psalter: A Hymnic Presentation of the Coming Messiah

An important starting point for understanding how the Psalms contribute to our understanding of the promised Messiah is to grasp its big-picture message.

Robert Chisholm provides a helpful summary of the theological message of the Psalter: "As the Creator of all things, God exercises sovereign authority over the natural order, the nations, and Israel, His unique people. In His role as universal King, God assures order and justice in the world and among His people, often by exhibiting His power as an invincible warrior. The proper response to this sovereign King is trust and praise."[12]

Another way of saying this is that as vassals of the Great King, the psalmists *praise* Yahweh for who He is and what He does; they *long and pray* for the comprehensive establishment of His sovereign rule over the earth *through His Davidic anointed one* (trusting Yahweh to bring it to pass); and they *lament* its present incompleteness. In light of this basic thesis, there are three primary elements or categories to consider in a synthesis of the theology of the Psalms: Yahweh, the Great King (the suzerain), mankind (His vassals), and the relationship between the two (Yahweh's rule).

God as Creator, Redeemer, and King

Out of the many themes found in the Psalter, God's identity and activity on behalf of His people relates especially to the development of the Messiah concept. The psalmists give careful attention to God's character and activity, who He is and what He does.

Who He is. The Psalms provide a vivid and amazing overview of God's attributes, which include, but are not limited to: His sovereignty (47, 93, 96–99), holiness (29:2; 71:22; 89:35; 96:9; 103:1; 111:9), immutability (90:2–6; 102:25–27), omnipresence and omniscience (139), eternality (90:2–6), steadfast love (חֶסֶד, [*hesed*]; 25:10; 62:12; 136, which emphasizes God's faithfulness to His covenant), righteousness and justice (33:5; 37:28; 145:17), and love (אָהֵב; [*'āhēb*]; 47:4; 78:68; 87:2).

What He does. In addition to being Creator,[13] Redeemer,[14] and Judge,[15] Yahweh is also All-Controlling. The Historical Psalms (68, 78, 105–6, 135, and

---

[12] Robert B. Chisholm Jr., "A Theology of the Psalms," in *A Biblical Theology of the Old Testament*, ed. R. Zuck (Chicago: Moody Press, 1991), 258.

[13] Yahweh created the universe and all that it contains (33:15; 74:16; 95:5; 96:5; 100:3; 104:19; 136:4–9). This creation is not only the product of His decree and power, but also a revelatory vehicle of His character (19:1–4). It is by virtue of His creation that Yahweh stands as the absolute Sovereign over everything outside of Himself (33). The creative activity of Yahweh also sets Him on a different plane than impotent idols (74:12–17; 86:8; 95:3; 96:4–5; 135:5).

[14] Yahweh's role as the Savior represents a key theological element both outside of (Ex. 3:8–10; Isa. 43:1–3; Jer. 14:8) and within the Psalter (7:10; 18; 19:14). The thanksgiving and praise proclaimed and the petitions and laments uttered most often revolve around the appreciated or anticipated redemptive activity of God.

[15] Because Yahweh is both King and God, He is also Judge. His function in this capacity has two sides. On the one hand, He vindicates and delivers the faithful and, on the other hand, he punishes the wicked (35:24–26; 48:5–11; 50:6; 89:17).

136) depict clearly His involvement in history as the Planner and Executor of all events. The most common figure used to express His sovereignty is *kingship*— His intention to rule over all creation and its inhabitants.

God's sovereign rule is the point of contact between Himself as the great King and His subjects. The Psalter presents at least two aspects of his rule. First, in the earthly focal point of His rule, the Psalter affirms that God has planned that the earthly administrative center of His rule would be in Zion (i.e., Jerusalem). Many passages celebrate Jerusalem as the city of God, the religious and civic center of the theocracy. God dwells in Zion (84:2; 76:1–3). From there, He controls all other nations (46:4–8; 48:5–9; 76:4–11; 2:1–6), and in Zion He will be exalted over all the earth (46:9–11; 48:11–14; 87:5–6). The pilgrim songs (102–34) celebrate Jerusalem as the center of the theocracy and focus on the festivals established by Yahweh.

Second, the Psalter delineates the chosen Administrator of His rule—the Anointed One. To further develop this, consider two foundational issues. First, we must consider God's expectations for current Davidic rulers versus God's promise of a coming Davidic King. Consider the following concepts and the below illustration that attempts to visualize the main ideas.

God ordained that His anointed Servant, the Davidic Ruler/King, should conduct the earthly administration of His theocracy. The Royal Psalms (2, 20–21, 45, 72, 89, 101, 110, 144) present the historical Davidic king(s) in the foreground. The king served both as the representative of the people as well as the

GOD'S PROMISE OF A DAVIDIC RULER:
"straight on" view

GOD'S PROMISE OF A DAVIDIC RULER:
"side" view

GOD'S EXPECTATION AND PROMISE TO THE HUMAN OT DAVIDIC RULER

GOD'S EXPECTATION AND PROMISE TO THE PROMISED ULTIMATE DAVIDIC RULER—MESSIAH

A given psalm can provide divine parameters for the reign of the Davidic king. Some of these expectations are never met by that total human and historical king.

Besides that psalm or those psalms that only refer to the promised Messiah, various elements from several "royal" psalms find their fulfillment in the future coming and reign of the promised ideal Davidic ruler, the Messiah.

administrative representative of God (see Ps. 72). The assertions made concerning the king in some of these psalms immediately apply to him, but also look forward to the future and final king, Yahweh's anointed Son, the promised Messiah.

The fact that merely human Davidic kings did not measure up to the clear expectations of a Royal Psalm increased expectation for the Messiah.

The second foundational issue asks, "How do different psalms point forward to the promised ideal Davidic ruler, the Messiah?" Put another way, "What psalms can be called "Messianic"? The Royal Psalms repeatedly refer to an anointed ruler, from the line of David, who will rule over His kingdom with justice and compassion. These psalms focus on the king of Israel and depict Him as God's representative, through whom God rules over His chosen people. These psalms not only refer to the king, but also present him as the "anointed one." Consequently, several Royal Psalms are also regarded as "Messianic Psalms." Different Royal Psalms describe His divine placement on the throne (2), the affliction He would experience (16, 22), and the incomparable nature of His reign (72).

From our perspective in history, it is obvious who brings all this to fulfillment—Jesus the Christ/Messiah. The debated issue revolves around the question of primary focus. Do these psalms focus on their present and near future (history) or the distant future (eschatology)? Further, what are some potential categories[16] for these psalms? There are potentially three categories of psalms that relate to the Messiah: (1) exclusively or primarily Messianic (Ps. 110), (2) typologically Messianic (Ps. 22), and (3) indirectly Messianic (Ps. 72). For the sake of space, we will look at the last two types.

Typologically Messianic (Ps. 22)

Some take Psalm 22 as exclusively Messianic. However, because many of the psalms are rooted in God's revelation of His intentions for human kingship under His rule, they have some relevance to their immediate context. Regardless, the nonfulfillment of those messianic expectations gave rise to an anticipation of the ultimate fulfillment, Jesus Christ.

In Psalm 22, the psalmist's intense suffering foreshadowed Christ's suffering. The terms used by the psalmist to describe the intensity of his own suffering provide a pattern that the gospel writers utilize. According to Allen Ross:

---

[16] Delitzsch proposed five types of Messianic psalms: purely prophetic (only 110), eschatological (96–99), typological-prophetic (22), indirectly Messianic (2, 45, 72), and typically Messianic (34:20; 109:8) (Franz Delitzsch, "Psalms," in *Commentary on the Old Testament* [Reprint; Grand Rapids: Eerdmans, 1976], 1:66–71.

Christians cannot read this psalm without remembering how
Jesus appropriated it to his own sufferings on the cross, and
so the passage must be read on both levels to gain all that the
Spirit of God intended when he spoke through the psalmist.
It has to be read first in the suffering psalmist's experience
as an urgent prayer to be delivered from enemies who were
methodically putting him to death; then it may be read on the
higher level to see how the psalm was applied to the greater
sufferings of Jesus. That the words of the psalm find their
greatest meaning in the suffering of Jesus in no way minimizes
the suffering of the psalmist or the thanksgiving and praise
that resulted from his being delivered from death. In both set-
tings the suffering in the psalm describes a death by execution
at the hands of taunting enemies—its seriousness cannot be
minimized. In both cases the lament is intensified because
God seems not to hear the cry of the sufferer, but is apparently
laying him in the grave.[17]

Ross recognizes that some regard the psalm as direct prophecy—its meaning
fits only the Messianic fulfillment. Ross, however, contends that although this
psalm includes some predictive or anticipatory elements, it is not direct prophecy or clearly Messianic—it never refers directly to the future anointed king. He
writes further,

By all assessments the psalmist was describing a time when
his enemies attempted to put him to death, a time of intense
sufferings that left him almost dead; but the LORD did
eventually hear his prayer and deliver him so that he was able
to praise the LORD in the congregation. Whether it should
be called prophetic or Messianic may be debated, but what is
certain is that Jesus appropriated this psalm to himself in his
greatest sufferings, and thereafter the evangelists and apostles
saw the connections between the psalm and his passion. We
are safe in calling it typological; the psalmist may not have
known how the psalm would be fulfilled, but God did. Since
typology does not nullify the original intent and meaning of

---

[17] Allen P. Ross, *A Commentary on Psalms 1–89*, Kregel Exegetical Library (Grand Rapids: Kregel, 2011–2013), 1:526.

a passage, we are also free to use this psalm as an inspiration for our perseverance in praying even when God seems not to be there.[18]

The below comparison delineates the clear connection between Psalm 22 and the experience of Jesus, the Messiah.

PS. 22	KIND OF REFERENCE	MATT., JOHN, HEB.
22:1	Direct quotation	Matt. 27:46; Mark 15:34
22:7	Indirect allusion	Mark 15:29
22:8	Indirect allusion	Matt. 27:43
22:15	Indirect allusion	John 19:28
22:16	Indirect allusion	John 20:25
22:18	Direct quotation	John 19:24
22:22	Direct quotation	Heb. 2:12

Indirectly Messianic (Ps. 72; cf. Isa. 11:1–5; 60–62)

As Zimmerli affirmed, "The king of Israel makes the dominion of Yahweh visible on earth."[19] The king epitomizes God's reign. As the king goes, so goes the nation. In the *more immediate realm*, these psalms present God's intentions for all the descendants of David who would rule over Yahweh's servant nation. In *the ultimate sense*, they serve "as a witness to the Messianic hope which looked for the consummation of God's kingship through his Anointed One."[20]

These psalms set a high standard for every Davidic descendant who would become king. They envision an "ideal Davidic ruler." In addition to focusing on different key periods of a king's reign, they place great emphasis on this king's unflinching commitment to ruling over His subjects with justice and compassion. This presentation of what the king would/should be like created a problem. Consider Psalm 72:1–14:

> God, give Your justice to the king
> and Your righteousness to the king's son.

---

[18] Ross, *Psalms, 1–89*, 1:527–28.
[19] Walther Zimmerli, *Old Testament Theology in Outline*, trans. David E. Green (Atlanta: John Knox, 1978), 92.
[20] Brevard S. Childs, *Introduction to the Old Testament as Scripture* (Philadelphia: Fortress, 1979), 517.

He will judge Your people with righteousness
and Your afflicted ones with justice.
May the mountains bring prosperity to the people
and the hills, righteousness.
May he vindicate the afflicted among the people,
help the poor,
and crush the oppressor.

May he continue while the sun endures
and as long as the moon, throughout all generations.
May he be like rain that falls on the cut grass,
like spring showers that water the earth.
May the righteous flourish in his days
and prosperity abound
until the moon is no more.

May he rule from sea to sea
and from the Euphrates
to the ends of the earth.
May desert tribes kneel before him
and his enemies lick the dust.
May the kings of Tarshish
and the coasts and islands bring tribute,
the kings of Sheba and Seba offer gifts.
Let all kings bow down to him,
all nations serve him.

For he will rescue the poor who cry out
and the afflicted who have no helper.
He will have pity on the poor and helpless
and save the lives of the poor.
He will redeem them from oppression and violence,
for their lives are precious in his sight.

Consider this psalm's description of the character, extent, and length of this king's reign. The language is clearly idealistic! Who could measure up to this?

The truth is no Davidic descendant measured up to this divine standard. This "nonfulfillment" in the reigns of all the Davidic kings who ruled over Israel in the Old Testament created an expectation of some future king who might rule in this manner. So while these psalms initially refer to the human Davidic rulers who would rule over the nation of Israel, they pave the way for a Messianic expectation. Their anticipation of an ideal Davidic king finds fulfillment in Jesus (see below figure). As Ross points out, the Messiah "will be the ideal king, what the world has been looking for; and his kingdom will be one of righteousness, peace and prosperity, the likes of which have never been seen on earth."[21]

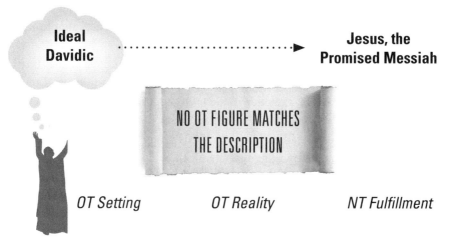

We have seen that Psalm 22 provides the agonizing tone and gripping words that Jesus used to express the depth of His own suffering. Psalm 72 presents what God expected would be the result of any Davidic king who lived according to His expectations—genuine inside-out loyalty to Yahweh. These and other psalms provide an important part of the tapestry that God is weaving into the biblical presentation of the Messiah—a tapestry that finds its culmination in the birth, life, ministry, death, burial, and resurrection of Jesus.

Isaiah: A Huge Step Forward

As part of being one of the "mountain peaks" of the Old Testament, the book of Isaiah provides a huge step forward in the Old Testament's putting together the concept of a coming Messiah. Leading up to the book of Isaiah, numerous passages developed the concept of an anticipated ideal Davidic ruler. The "He" of Genesis 3:15 would come through Abraham's descendants (Gen. 12:3), specifically Judah (Gen. 49:10), then through David (2 Sam. 7:11–16). That person would be a ruler over a kingdom! In the book of Isaiah, we find increasing clarity about this promised one.

---

[21] Ross, *Psalms 1–89*, 533.

Isaiah 1–39

Especially in chapters 7–11, the Lord demonstrates how His kingdom is enduring in contrast to the frail human kingdoms of the world. On one hand, He points to human kingdoms that will not endure. Judah's weak kingdom will be dominated by the powerful Assyrian Empire. But even that empire will be held accountable by Yahweh and judged for their arrogance. Unlike those brittle kingdoms, God's kingdom will last forever. As part of that presentation, Isaiah points to building blocks for that reality. He unveils some amazing aspects about that promised kingdom and Ruler.

9:6–7: He is born, and will serve as a ruler, Mighty God, everlasting Father. Isaiah writes that "a child will be born for us, a son will be given to us, and the government will be on His shoulders" (v. 6). Of the four names for this child mentioned, these two would prove to be somewhat shocking for an Israelite: Mighty God, and Eternal Father. How could this promised ruler receive these names? Isaiah continues by writing that there will be no end to the increase of His government, which will be characterized by justice (v. 7).

11:1–9: He comes from the line of David, will be anointed by the Holy Spirit, will rule with justice, and will establish peace. Isaiah returns to this promised anointed one in chapter 11. He will be a descendant of Jesse, enabled by the Holy Spirit (which refers to theocratic anointing), will rule with genuine justice and will punish the wicked. Verses 6–9 present the classic picture of peace in every realm of life. At this time, God's knowledge will fill the entire earth (envisioning the millennium—the rule of this promised one for a thousand years).

Isaiah 35: He inaugurates the future age of blessing. Isaiah 34–35 present a striking contrast between a productive region turned into a barren desert (ch. 34) and an inhospitable desert converted into a fruitful garden (ch. 35). Chapter 34 delineates death, destruction, and the wrath of God, focusing on the destruction of the nations who oppose God and on the avenging of God's people. Chapter 35 stresses health, restoration, and the glory of God—blessings of salvation to be enjoyed by the Lord's redeemed. John Oswalt says, "To align oneself with the nations of the earth is to choose a desert; to trust in God is to choose a garden."[22]

Notice the progression of thought in chapter 35:

- Barren lands will be changed into lands of beauty and abundance (vv. 1–2)
- The weak and fearful will be strengthened and encouraged by the Lord's intervention on their behalf (vv. 3–4)

---

[22] John N. Oswalt, *The Book of Isaiah, Chapters 1–39*, New International Commentary on the Old Testament (Grand Rapids: Eerdmans, 1986), 607.

- Afflicted people will be healed and, as said above, the dry land will become a well-watered region (vv. 5–7)
- The way to Jerusalem will have no obstacles or predatory beasts to hamper the spiritual pilgrims on their journey to Zion (vv. 8–10)

More specifically, Isaiah employs four word pictures to depict the glories and blessings of this future time of salvation (vv. 5–6). They look forward to the time of future blessing, that time when the anointed one would rule over them. In that regard, consider the correlation between those statements in Isaiah 35 and statements in the Gospels that describe the ministry of Jesus, the promised Messiah:

> Then the eyes of the blind will be opened [Matt. 9:27–30; 12:22; 20:30–34; John 9:6–7],
> and the ears of the deaf unstopped [Matt. 11:5; Luke 7:22].
> Then the lame will leap like a deer [Matt. 15:30–31; 21:14],
> and the tongue of the mute will sing for joy [Mark 7:32–37; 9:25].

The central point of this comparison demonstrates that the Messiah's ministry in His first coming provides an intentional connection between His activity and that expected by the Anointed One who will bring to pass the future Messianic Age. That descriptive resonation provided part of the divine credentials for Jesus during His earthly ministry—He was the Promised One who would provide resolution to humankind's sin problem and serve as the ruler of a future kingdom that would encompass the entire earth.

Isaiah 40–66

Isaiah 42:2–4: He will epitomize justice and compassion, as called for in the Mosaic Law. A key figure introduced by the prophet Isaiah in the last half of the book is the Suffering Servant. Scholars have long debated his identity, but I heartily embrace the conviction that this servant figure anticipates the promised Messiah, Jesus Christ. Keep in mind that the Mosaic covenant provides part of the theological backdrop for the ideal Davidic ruler already presented in 2 Samuel 7—He would rule with justice and equity as well as kindness and compassion. In language that reflects that found in the Royal Psalms, Isaiah 42:2–4 presents this servant as humble (v. 2) and one who demonstrates kindness for the broken in His world (42:3). One of His ultimate objectives is to teach truth and establish justice throughout the earth (42:4).

Isaiah 49:6, 8: He will bring light to Israel and the world. Isaiah's presentation of the servant figure totally agrees with numerous prophets who describe a future day when the nation would repent and embrace by faith the Messiah they had rejected, and that this promised one would regather those believing Israelites and restore them to the land of promise. The servant would raise up and restore God's chosen people, providing salvation (light) that will extend to the entire world (49:6). Rather than abandoning His chosen people, the servant will restore them to the land promised them by Yahweh (49:8).

Isaiah 53:5–6: He will die for the sins of His people. Isaiah 53 describes the most amazing yet most humbling reality—the Servant dying on behalf of the sins of humanity, in their place, for their benefit, as the sinless one. Remember when the Lord promises a "He" in Genesis 3 who will bring resolution to the sin problem occasioned by Adam and Eve's sin? Isaiah 53 connects this promised ruler, the Suffering Servant, to the resolution of humanity's sin problem.

The Place of Christ's Birth (Micah 5:2)

The context of Micah sheds important light on the significance of 5:2. Micah 3 focuses on the destruction that the Lord planned to bring upon His chosen nation, which had consistently participated in covenant treachery. This judgment is well-deserved. Since they refused to live in accordance with His demands, He would evict them from the land of promise. A foreign invader would defeat God's people and send them into exile. Micah 4–5 gives most of its attention to the restoration that the Lord will provide to Israel after they experience this judgment.

In chapter 4, the prophet goes back and forth between the ideas of judgment and restoration. There is a reason for this close connection of these two themes. Think about the big picture in Micah's message here. First, because of who He is, God must judge sin—in this case, sin from which His chosen people would not turn away. Once He judges Israel, God will not restore a hard-hearted nation to a place of blessing. No, this promised judgment will be God's tool to convict them of their sins and to lead them to repentance of their rebellion. The close connection between this promised judgment and the predicted restoration was meant to teach His people (and us) another very important truth.

Second, without God's intervention, His people have no hope for deliverance! How does Micah say God will make this happen? Micah 5:1 depicts Israel as one besieged by their enemies. Notice how the verse ends (5:1c): "They are striking the judge of Israel on the cheek with a rod." The word *rod* here is the word *scepter* we mentioned earlier. Do you see the horrific situation in which Israel finds itself? Instead of Israel's ruler holding or wielding the scepter, Israel's enemies are pictured as taking that scepter and striking Israel's ruler with it on the cheek.

For Israel, this describes an *upside-down* world. Instead of being a nation on top of the world, they are humiliated by their enemies. The rod that was a symbol for the authority of the king became the instrument of humiliation and defeat.

Does God intend that this is the end of the story for Israel? Do the curtains close on Israel's destiny with the scene presented in Micah 5:1? Praise God this is not the end of the story. In 5:2, we read: "Bethlehem Ephrathah, you are small among the clans of Judah; One will come from you to be ruler over Israel for Me. His origin is from antiquity, from eternity." The Lord announces that from Bethlehem—in the region of Ephrath/Ephrathah—will come a person who will rule over Israel as God's representative. Of the many things that deserve attention in this verse, let us consider three important truths.

First, why from Bethlehem? The name of the tribe in which Bethlehem was located was Judah. We learned in other passages that the scepter will not depart from Judah. Who else was born there? David, king of Israel. In 2 Samuel 7, God promised there would always be a descendant of David ruling over Israel. From the New Testament, we know that Micah 5:2 looks forward to Jesus' birth at Bethlehem.

Second, what is the primary point, in this context, of the statement "His origin is from antiquity, from eternity"? On one hand, the Bible clearly describes Jesus as fully God. Consequently, He is eternal. The language of Micah 5:2 does not contradict that truth. In order to fully understand this passage however, let us turn to Amos 9:11. In Amos 9:11–15, the prophet Amos relates to us God's intention to restore the Davidic kingdom. Verse 11 states Yahweh's intentions: "In that day I will restore the fallen booth of David: I will repair its gaps, restore its ruins, and rebuild it *as in the days of old*" (emphasis added). What God will do in the future is connected to what He established through King David. The very same expression that occurs in Amos 9:11 occurs here in Micah 5:2. While I certainly am not trying to undermine the eternality of Jesus—a clearly biblical truth—I think Micah is working hard to get his audience to think back to the time of David. He wants them to connect the dots. He wants them to see that what God promises to do in Micah is in concert with many of the passages we have looked at above. This is not a prediction that is distinct from numerous other prophecies. No, what Micah declares in this verse is part of a long line of declarations, part of this building crescendo.

Third, what is this promised one going to do? He will rule over God's creation, including Israel. He does not just come to be a sweet, cuddly baby, as fun as they are. No, this promised One will one day rule over all of creation on behalf of His Father.

Conclusion

This essay has sought to walk through a set of Old Testament passages and reach a conclusion that is not surprising. The Old Testament intentionally and effectively prepared for the coming of the promised Messiah. The Old Testament's "construction" of that individual's character and divinely intended roles reminds us as Christ followers that God will bring His plan for His creation to pass, in accordance with the way He presented that plan in numerous Old Testament passages.

Why did God orchestrate the coming of His beloved Son through these varied Old Testament passages?

- To demonstrate His intention and plan to provide salvation for sinful humanity (Matt. 1:21).
- To demonstrate His total sovereignty and the *precise way His fulfillment matched His predictions* (e.g., Bethlehem, child).
- To enable people to recognize Jesus as the long-promised Messiah. Isaiah 35 gave them a measuring rod to identify the Messiah—the anointed one. Through the miracles of Jesus, He clearly made evident His absolute supremacy over disease, death, and creation—God in human flesh.
- To reveal God's glory to the world, to put God on display (Gen. 1:26–27; Ex. 19:5–6; cf. John 14:9–11).
- To reveal who and how He will extend His rule over creation (Gen. 1:26–27; cf. Phil. 2:9–11)

PART 4

THE WITNESS

TO CHRIST

18

BEGINNING WITH MOSES: THE OT WITNESS TO THE SUFFERING MESSIAH

LUKE 24:27

Iosif J. Zhakevich

A messiah who died was not the type of messiah that the first-century Jewish community expected. When Jesus said to His disciples that He would suffer and die, Peter adamantly rejected this notion and exclaimed, "Far be it from you, Lord! This shall never happen to you" (Matt. 16:22). Later, when Jesus did in fact die, two of His followers traveling to Emmaus betrayed their perspective that Jesus failed to be the Messiah when He died. The men stated, "Our chief priests and rulers delivered [Jesus] up to be condemned to death, and crucified him. But we had hoped that he was the one to redeem Israel" (Luke 24:19–21).[1]

This sentiment, in fact, appears to have been common in the Jewish community at that time. In Acts 5:35–39, a prominent Jewish leader named Gamaliel articulated the notion that a so-called messiah who dies in fact proves to be a failed messiah:

> Men of Israel, take care what you are about to do with these men. For before these days Theudas rose up, claiming to be

---

[1] Peter Lewis, *The Glory of Christ* (Chicago: Moody, 1997), 171–72.

somebody, and a number of men, about four hundred, joined him. He was killed, and all who followed him were dispersed and came to nothing. After him Judas the Galilean rose up in the days of the census and drew away some of the people after him. He too perished, and all who followed him were scattered. So in the present case I tell you, keep away from these men and let them alone, for if this plan or this undertaking is of man, it will fail; but if it is of God, you will not be able to overthrow them. You might even be found opposing God!

Gamaliel's point is clear: if the so-called messiah dies, and if God does not intervene on His behalf, then He is a failed messiah.[2]

This raises the question: How is the death of Jesus different from the death of every other supposed messiah who died? How is it that every supposed messiah who died proved to be a failed messiah, while Jesus, who also died, proved to be the true Messiah?

According to the Old Testament and the New Testament, the death of the true Messiah is unlike any other death in the history of humanity. The death of the Messiah is unique in three respects. First, the *revelation* of the Messiah's death in the Scriptures makes it unique from the deaths of others. Second, the *purpose* of the Messiah's death is unique. Third, the *glory* of the Messiah's death is distinct. A proper understanding of these three aspects of the Messiah's death ought to prompt us to worship the Messiah for His death.

The Revelation of the Messiah's Death

From the very beginning, the Scriptures reveal that the death of the Messiah was part of the plan of restoration decreed by God.

Genesis 3:15

Arguably the first messianic prophecy recorded in the Scriptures, Genesis 3:15 reveals that the offspring who will reverse the ramifications of the fall will suffer harm.[3] As God pronounces a curse on the serpent in 3:14–15 for deceiving Eve, God exclaims that a battle will take place between the serpent and an offspring of Eve. And God makes clear that while this offspring will ultimately be victorious, He will actually suffer harm in the event of this battle. God states: "I will put

---

[2] See Darrell L. Bock, *Acts*, Baker Exegetical Commentary of the New Testament (Grand Rapids: Baker Academic, 2007), 249–52.

[3] William Varner, *The Messiah: Revealed, Rejected, Received* (Bloomington, IL: AuthorHouse, 2004), 21.

enmity between you and the woman, and between your offspring and her offspring; *he shall bruise your head, and you shall bruise his heel*" (emphasis added).

While this prophecy is minimal in specifics, three observations of consequence can be discerned. First, the offspring will bear human nature: he shall be a descendant of the woman.[4] Second, the battle is one-on-one. It is between an offspring of the woman and the serpent himself. Revelation 12:9 (cf. 20:2) reveals that the serpent is the devil, and Hebrews 2:14–15 reveals that the individual who defeated the devil is the Messiah Jesus. Third, as already noted, while the offspring is ultimately victorious ("he shall bruise your head") the offspring still suffers harm ("you shall bruise his heel"). We may also note that God is eager to announce His plan of restoration, which involves the suffering of the offspring. Before God punishes Adam and Eve (3:22–24), or even pronounces such punishment (3:16–19), God already declares this plan of redemption (3:15). In short, though brief in nature, the prophecy reveals that the offspring will suffer.

Psalm 22

The suffering of the Messiah is made apparent more vividly in the extreme and superlative language that David employs to describe his personal anguish in Psalm 22. The question, however, is if Psalm 22 records the suffering of David, then how can this description of suffering also be attributed to the Messiah? The answer arguably lies in the concept that the Messiah is the greater David—that is, that the experiences of David foreshadow, to an extent, the experiences of the Messiah. In 2 Samuel 7:4–17, God promises David an offspring who will be a king like David, but who will be greater than David (vv. 12–13). And in Psalm 132:11, this promise is referred to as an oath that God swore to David. While the contexts of 2 Samuel 7 and Psalm 132:11 are no doubt about kingship, it is important to recognize that David's experience as king was also full of human suffering, even since the time of his anointing (see 1 Sam. 16–27). Consequently, if the greater David is to be like David, then He would be like David in His royal status and in His human experiences of suffering (see Rom. 1:1–4).[5]

In fact, Peter seems to presuppose this very perspective about such a correlation between the experiences of David and the greater David when he preaches about the death and resurrection of Jesus in Acts 2:30–31. Peter exclaims,

---

[4] Whether this verse implies a divine offspring, see Varner, *The Messiah*, 22. Whether this verse implies a virgin birth, for one view, see Varner, *The Messiah*, 22, and, for a contrasting view, see Michael Rydelnik, *The Messianic Hope: Is the Hebrew Bible Really Messianic?* (Nashville, TN: B & H, 2010), 135, n. 19.
[5] Lewis, *The Glory of Christ*, 176–177.

> Being therefore a prophet, and knowing that God had sworn
> with an oath to him that he would set one of his descendants
> on his throne, he foresaw and spoke about the resurrection of
> the Christ, that he was not abandoned to Hades, nor did his
> flesh see corruption.

In this message on the death and the resurrection of the Messiah, Peter appeals to two passages—one that speaks of God's promise to David of a royal offspring (Ps. 132:11; cf. 2 Sam. 7) and one that speaks of the death and resurrection of David's offspring (Ps. 16:10), as Peter explains it. In referencing these two passages together, Peter argues that God's promise of a royal offspring to David guaranteed that this offspring would triumph over all the suffering and death that He would endure. Peter's perspective, therefore, seems to have been that the Messiah would be the greater David with respect to both aspects of David's life—his royalty and suffering. And, significantly, Peter suggests that this is precisely how David understood his relationship to the greater David: David was confident that the greater David would overcome all suffering and death (Acts 2:31), because David knew that God made a promise of a royal offspring to him (Acts 2:30; see 2 Sam. 7:19, 21, 25–29). As regards Psalm 22, then, we may conclude that because the greater David would be like David both in his royalty and in his suffering, David's expression of anguish in Psalm 22 may and, indeed, ought to be viewed as representative of the suffering of the greater David, that is the Messiah, as well.[6]

Further, close analysis of David's outcry in Psalm 22 indicates that even if David genuinely felt that he was suffering to the greatest degree possible, the fact is that there was still greater suffering that was conceivable and that would correspond more appropriately to the superlative language of anguish in this Psalm, which David as a human could not in fact endure. The Psalm begins with the exclamation: "My God, my God, why have you forsaken me?" (v. 1) To experience the sense that you are forsaken by God is indeed a severe trial. But even if David genuinely felt that he was forsaken by God, this sense of forsakenness by God is far more severe when the sin of the entire world is placed on your shoulders; when in the eyes of God, you become sin itself; and when in this condition, you appeal to God, but God seems not to answer (see Matt. 27:46; Mark 15:34; 2 Cor. 5:21). Thus, when *Jesus* cries out with the same words on the cross, these words correspond to the intensity of His distress much more precisely than to the suffering of David.[7]

---

[6] Cf. Walter C. Kaiser, *The Messiah in the Old Testament* (Grand Rapids: Zondervan Publishing, 1995), 113 and 118.
[7] Ibid., 118.

This manner of suffering manifests itself even further throughout the remainder of the psalm. In verse 6, David bemoans, "I am a worm and not a man, scorned by mankind and despised by the people. All who see me mock me; they make mouths at me; they wag their heads." In verse 16, he utters, "Dogs encompass me; a company of evildoers encircles me; they have pierced my hands and feet," or as the Masoretic text states, "like a lion [they are at] my hands and my feet."[8] In verse 17, David continues, "I can count all my bones—they stare and gloat over me; they divide my garments among them, and for my clothing they cast lots." In short, the image portrayed is that of violence and a threat of death. And as David suffered in this way, so would the greater David, the Messiah, but to a greater degree. In other words, even if David was surrounded by wicked men, even if he was treated violently, and even if he felt that his life was being threatened, these words are more precisely realized when you are hanging on a cross, when your hands and your feet are pierced, when people are staring at you and mocking you, and when people are dividing your clothing (see Matt. 27:33–44). Accordingly, when John describes the crucifixion of Jesus, he refers to Psalm 22: "This was to fulfill the Scripture which says, 'They divided my garments among them, and for my clothing they cast lots'" (John 19:24). Richard Belcher expresses this idea clearly when he states, "David's suffering was real, but Christ's suffering was so much greater in being crucified and in bearing God's wrath for the sins of his people."[9] While this psalm no doubt describes the suffering of David, because David is a figure of the greater David, and because this language is so extreme, this psalm also serves to reveal the greater suffering of the greater David, the Messiah.

Isaiah 53

The revelation of the Messiah's suffering is further developed in Isaiah 53, with additional depictions of violence, an explicit mention of death, and the identification of the agent behind the suffering of the Messiah. Speaking of the suffering servant, Isaiah writes in 53:3, "He was despised and rejected by men; a man of sorrows, and acquainted with grief; and as one from whom men hide their faces." As in Psalm 22, the individual here is persecuted by human beings. In 53:7, Isaiah describes this oppression even more vividly: "He was oppressed, and he was afflicted, yet he opened not his mouth; like a lamb that is led to the slaughter

---

[8] For a brief discussion of the text-critical issue, see Peter C. Craigie, *Psalms 1–50*, 2nd ed., Word Biblical Commentary 19 (Nashville, TN: Nelson Reference & Electronic, 2004), 196, n. 17; Gerald H. Wilson, *Psalms Volume 1*, The NIV Application Commentary (Grand Rapids, MI: Zondervan, 2002), 417.
[9] Richard P. Belcher, *Prophet, Priest, and King: The Roles of Christ in the Bible and Our Roles Today* (Phillipsburg, NJ: P & R, 2016), 154.

and like a sheep that before its shearers is silent, so he opened not his mouth." In verses 8–9, Isaiah brings the audience to the scene of the servant's death and states: "By oppression and judgment he was taken away; and as for his generation, who considered that he was cut off out of the land of the living, stricken for the transgression of my people? And they made his grave with the wicked and with a rich man in his death." In other words, hatred is expressed in violence, and this violence ultimately produces death. The enemies that merely threatened the life of the sufferer in Psalm 22 actually murdered the individual in Isaiah 53.

But then the passage takes a sudden and a surprising turn as Isaiah reveals who ultimately orchestrated the suffering and death of the Messiah. In 53:10, Isaiah declares, "Yet it was the will of the LORD to crush him; he has put him to grief." Without any equivocation, Isaiah announces that God not only was pleased with this plan but also designed this plan.[10] Isaiah asserts a marvelous proposition that God, who does not delight in the death of anyone, delighted in a plan that put the Messiah to death (see Ezek. 18:32). According to this passage, the Messiah suffered and died because this was the preordained plan of God that pleased God.

Zechariah 12

The prophet Zechariah delivers yet another unfathomable revelation as he unveils the identity of the Messiah. In Zechariah 12:10, as Yahweh declares that the people of Israel will one day repent, He explains, "I will pour out on the house of David and the inhabitants of Jerusalem a spirit of grace and pleas for mercy, so that, when they look on me, on him whom they have pierced, they shall mourn for him, as one mourns for an only child, and weep bitterly over him, as one weeps over a firstborn." Yahweh is speaking and He states that the people of Israel will look *on Yahweh, whom they pierced.* This passage asserts that the Messiah who will die is God Himself.

But how could God be pierced? Is not death the fate of the human? Indeed, this points to the complex nature of the Messiah. Genesis 3:15 revealed that the Messiah is human; Zechariah 12:10 reveals that the Messiah is God. The Messiah is, in fact, both man and God (see Isa. 9:6; Jer. 23:5–6; Mic. 5:2).[11] Because of His complex nature, therefore, the Messiah, who is the God-man, can endure death. For this to take place, God would need to assume human form, live on this earth, and ultimately be crucified and die in His human flesh (John 1:14,

---

[10] Robert B. Chisholm Jr., "Forgiveness and Salvation in Isaiah 53," in *The Gospel According to Isaiah 53: Encountering the Suffering Servant in Jewish and Christian Theology,* eds., Darrell L. Bock and Mitch Glaser (Grand Rapids, MI: Kregel Academic, 2012), 192.

[11] Varner, *The Messiah,* 22.

18; Col. 1:15–20). Accordingly, John recalls the prophecy of Zechariah in his crucifixion narrative and applies this text to Jesus, stating, "And again another Scripture says, 'They will look on him whom they have pierced'" (John 19:37; cf. Rev. 1:7). God was pierced when Christ was crucified.

As these passages show, the death of the Messiah was a plan designed by God from the very beginning (see also Acts 2:23; 13:27–29; 1 Peter 1:20–21). The Messiah's death was not an expression of failure. Nor was it the manifestation of weakness. Rather, it was the fulfillment of God's plan. According to the Scriptures, the Messiah had to die. In fact, whoever denies the fact that the Messiah had to die is more aligned with the mind of Satan than with the mind of God. When Jesus told His disciples that He would suffer and die, and when Peter then responded to Him, "Far be it from you, Lord! This shall never happen to you," Jesus said to Peter: "Get behind me, Satan!" Why did Jesus utter such a harsh rebuke? Because it was the plan of God for the Messiah to die, and to reject this plan would be to reject the plan of God.

So we return to our original questions: How is the death of our Messiah not failure? How is the death of the Messiah different from every other death? The death of the true Messiah is not failure because His death was part of the decreed plan of God. In fact, if Jesus had not died, *then* He would have failed to be the true Messiah because He would not have fulfilled God's plan as revealed in the Scriptures.

The Purpose of the Messiah's Death

The death of the Messiah distinguishes itself also because of its purpose—the forgiveness of sin. The death of the Messiah served a purpose that no other death has ever served and that no other death could ever serve. In Mark 10:45, Jesus, the Messiah Himself, states, "Even the Son of Man came not to be served but to serve, and to give his life as a ransom for many" (cf. Matt. 20:28; 26:28; Luke 24:45–47; Heb. 9:26–28; 1 Peter 1:18–19). The purpose of the Messiah's death is to achieve the forgiveness of sin.

Implications of Death

No other death, however, is able to accomplish this, for death marks the end of all manner of one's activity. When God pronounced the consequences of Adam's disobedience in Genesis 3:19, He explained, "By the sweat of your face you shall eat bread, till you return to the ground, for out of it you were taken; for you are dust, and to dust you shall return." Adam's death, in other words, marked the end of his productivity. Solomon poignantly exclaimed in Ecclesiastes 9:5–6, "For the living know that they will die, but the dead know nothing ... and forever they have no more share in all that is done under the sun." And in 9:10: "Whatever your hand finds to do, do it with your might, for there is no work or thought or knowledge or wisdom in Sheol, to which you are going" (cf. 2:18; 5:13–17; 8:8). With death ends the human capability for any form of activity. Hebrews 9:26–28 affirms that such is the fate of man and articulates the contrast between the Messiah's death and the death of every other human being, stating, "But as it is, [Jesus] has appeared once for all at the end of the ages to put away sin by the sacrifice of himself. And just as it is appointed for man to die once, and after that comes judgment, so Christ, having been offered once to bear the sins of many, will appear a second time, not to deal with sin but to save those who are eagerly waiting for him." While the death of every human being results in judgment by God, the death of the Messiah results in the forgiveness of sins.

Death in Isaiah 53

This is precisely what the Scriptures prophesied concerning the Messiah's death.[12]

Isaiah explicitly articulates, "Surely he has borne our griefs and carried our sorrows. . . . he was pierced for our transgressions, he was crushed for our iniquities; upon him was the chastisement that brought us peace, and with his wounds we are healed. All we like sheep have gone astray; we have turned—every one—to his own way; and the LORD has laid on him the iniquity of us all" (53:4–6). In verse 12, he reiterates, "He poured out his soul to death and was numbered with the transgressors; yet he bore the sin of many, and makes intercession for the transgressors." This is the very function that Jesus attributed to Himself in Mark 10:45—that He came to give His life a ransom for many. On one hand, Jesus affirmed the words of Isaiah—that the Messiah was supposed to die and to bear the sins of many. On the other, He explicated the meaning of Isaiah's prophecy in that He applied the role of this substitute to Himself.[13]

The Sacrificial System

This function of the death of the Messiah is also foreshadowed in the sacrificial system of ancient Israel. God established a detailed system of sacrifices for the Israelites within which much blood was shed on account of the sins of the Israelites (see Lev. 1–10; 16–17).[14] Leviticus 17:11 describes the function of the shed blood in sacrifices: "For the life of the flesh is in the blood, and I have given it for

---

[12] Chisholm, "Forgiveness and Salvation in Isaiah 53," 191–210.
[13] Lewis, The Glory of Christ, 172–73.
[14] Ibid., 281–89.

you on the altar to make atonement for your souls, for it is the blood that makes atonement by the life" (cf. Gen. 9:4; Deut. 12:23).[15] Hebrews 9:22 reiterates this principle, stating: "Indeed, under the law almost everything is purified with blood, and without the shedding of blood there is no forgiveness of sins." Yet Hebrews 10:1–4 makes clear that these sacrifices were actually a foreshadow of the final sacrifice and that they could not in fact achieve ultimate atonement: "For since the law has but a shadow of the good things to come instead of the true form of these realities, it can never, by the same sacrifices that are continually offered every year, make perfect those who draw near. . . . For it is impossible for the blood of bulls and goats to take away sins" (cf. Heb. 10:1–18; 13:11–12).[16] These sacrifices, therefore, anticipated the ultimate sacrifice who would in fact take away the sins of mankind.

The High Priest

Additionally, this function of the death of the Messiah to achieve atonement is also foreshadowed in the life and death of the high priest in the Scriptures. Hebrews 9:24–28 draws a parallel between the function of the Israelite high priest and Jesus, the ultimate high priest, contending that as the Israelite high priest offered sacrifices, so Jesus offered Himself as the ultimate sacrifice. Verse 26 states, "[Jesus] has appeared once for all at the end of the ages to put away sin by the sacrifice of himself" (cf. 9:11–12). In other words, the sacrifices that the high priest offered, as recorded in the Old Testament, anticipated the ultimate sacrifice that the high priest *par excellence* would offer in His own death.

Moreover, Numbers 35 illustrates specifically how the death of the high priest served as a shadow of the Messiah's death and of the ultimate forgiveness of sin. The text discusses the penalty for intentional and unintentional killing. In the case of intentional killing, the law demands that the murderer be put to death (vv. 16–21). But in the case of unintentional killing, the law allows the manslayer to flee to a city of refuge to preserve his life (vv. 9–15, 22–28). A remarkable nuance within this law, however, is that the manslayer is released of his constriction to the city of refuge at the death of the high priest. Verse 28 explains, "[The manslayer] must remain in his city of refuge *until the death of the high priest, but after the death of the high priest* the manslayer may return to the land of his possession" (cf. v. 25; emphasis added). The death of the high priest, in other words, rendered the manslayer free of his penalty of confinement. In this way, the death

---

[15] Mark F. Rooker, *Leviticus*, vol. 3A, The New American Commentary (Nashville: Broadman & Holman, 2000), 237.

[16] Thomas R. Schreiner, *Commentary on Hebrews*, Biblical Theology for Christian Proclamation, eds. T. Desmond Alexander, Andreas J. Köstenberger, and Thomas R. Schreiner (Nashville, TN: B&H, 2015), 288–93.

of the high priest served as yet another foreshadow of the death of the Messiah and of its function to achieve absolution.[17]

As these passages demonstrate, the purpose of the death of the Messiah was to accomplish redemption, and the Scriptures testify to this both in explicit prophecy and in the customs of the sacrificial system. This function of the death of the Messiah, in effect, distinguishes the Messiah's death from every other death in human history. Consequently, the death of the Messiah proves not to be failure for the Messiah, but, to the contrary, to be a unique accomplishment of the forgiveness of sin.

The Glory of the Messiah's Death

Finally, the death of the Messiah distinguishes itself because of its glory—that in His death, the Messiah conquered death and saw glorious resurrection. When Jesus rose from the dead, He demonstrated that He overpowered Satan, overpowered the potency of death, and attained triumph. Whereas death marks defeat in every other case, it marked the path to glory for the Messiah. This is precisely what Jesus articulated to the two men on the road to Emmaus: "Was it not necessary that the Christ should suffer these things and enter into his glory?" (Luke 24:26; cf. Acts 17:2–3; Phil. 2:5–11; 1 Peter 1:21; Heb. 2:9) And, again, this is exactly what the Scriptures revealed—that the Messiah would rise from the dead.

Psalm 22

While Psalm 22 foreshadows the suffering of the Messiah, it also foreshadows His glory by describing the deliverance that follows His suffering. Whereas in 22:1, the sufferer cries out, "My God, my God, why have you forsaken me?" in 22:24, the psalmist states, "He has not hidden his face from [the afflicted], but has heard, when he cried to him" (cf. Isa. 53:3). Whereas in 22:2, the sufferer states, "O my God, I cry by day, but *you do not answer*" (NASB; emphasis added), in 22:21, he declares, "*You have answered me* from the horns of the wild oxen" (emphasis added; ESV renders it: "You have rescued me"; cf. Isa. 53:10–12; Heb. 5:7). Whereas in 22:6, the sufferer groans, "I am a worm and not a man, scorned by mankind and *despised by the people*" (emphasis added), in 22:24, he announces, "*For he has not despised* or abhorred the affliction of the afflicted" (emphasis added; cf. Isa. 53:3). In other words, the sufferer experiences a reversal in his circumstances. While initially it seemed that God would not deliver the sufferer, ultimately it is made clear that God does deliver him.

---

[17] Michael L. Brown, *The Real Kosher Jesus: Revealing the Mysteries of the Hidden Messiah* (Lake Mary, FL: Front Line, 2012), 156–57.

The result of this deliverance, moreover, is the vast worship of God. In verses 22–23, David exclaims, "I will tell of your name to my brothers; in the midst of the congregation I will praise you: You who fear the LORD, praise him! All you offspring of Jacob, glorify him, and stand in awe of him, all you offspring of Israel!" This response of widespread praise and recognition of God is then developed in verses 25–31. Verse 27 states, "All the ends of the earth shall remember and turn to the LORD, and all the families of the nations shall worship before you."

Referring to this worship of God, Hebrews 2:12 cites Psalm 22:22 and applies the words to Jesus Himself: "I [Jesus] will tell of your name to my brothers; in the midst of the congregation I will sing your praise." As Thomas R. Schreiner explains, "[Jesus] praises God with his brothers and sisters whom he has ransomed from Satan's power."[18]

In other words, the real but temporary suffering in Psalm 22 ultimately turns into deliverance for the sufferer and the glory of God. Thus, the psalm prefigures both the suffering *and* deliverance of the Messiah, the greater David.

Psalm 16

A similar image of deliverance—indeed, of resurrection—is articulated in Psalm 16. The overall message of this psalm is that God is David's place of refuge and source of good, delight, counsel, security, and life. And within this expression of absolute dependence on God, David exclaims the declaration about death and resurrection: "For you [God] will not abandon my soul to Sheol, or let your holy one see corruption" (v. 10).[19] While the verse imagines death and the grave, the actual point of the verse is that death and the grave will not hold the victim captive. In fact, the language here resembles that of Psalm 22:1; but the claim of Psalm 16 is the exact reversal of Psalm 22. In 22:1, David cries, "My God, my God, why have you forsaken me?" But in 16:10, he declares, "For you [God] will not abandon my soul to Sheol." If the sufferer is to see death and the grave, he will not remain in that state forever. Rather, he will rise from the grave and from death.

Yet whose soul will God not forsake? And who will not see the pit? This matter is not easy to resolve.[20] Is David referring to himself with the hope that God will ultimately raise him from the dead? Or is he referring to the greater David, meaning that if the Messiah dies, then God will raise Him from the dead? The immediate context of the Psalm appears to be referring to David. But again,

---

[18] Schreiner, *Commentary on Hebrews*, 101.
[19] See Eugene H. Merrill, "שְׁאוֹל New International Dictionary of Old Testament Theology and Exegesis*, vol. 4 (Grand Rapids: Zondervan, 1997), 6–7; Merrill, "שַׁחַת," in ibid., 93–94.
[20] See Kaiser, *The Messiah in the Old Testament*, 118–22.

David understood that he would produce an offspring who would be the greater David, and he understood that his life prefigured the life of this greater David (see 2 Sam. 7; Ps. 132:11–12). Accordingly, while this psalm does refer to David to a degree, David arguably penned these words with the view that they would ultimately refer to and represent the greater David more precisely. Analyzing this passage, Kaiser writes, "The Messiah will come out of the grave/Sheol. How, when, and under what circumstances, the text does not elaborate. It is enough for David to realize that one of his relatives, who will live forever, will triumph over death."[21] In other words, when David articulated these words, David wrote in the light of his personal circumstances, but with the understanding that his circumstances foreshadowed the life of the Messiah.

In his sermon in Acts 2, Peter declares that this psalm ultimately refers to the Messiah (cf. 13:26–39). After referencing Psalm 16:8–11, Peter explains,

> Brothers, I may say to you with confidence about the patriarch David that he both died and was buried, and his tomb is with us to this day. Being therefore a prophet, and knowing that God had sworn with an oath to him that he would set one of his descendants on his throne, he foresaw and spoke about the resurrection of the Christ, that he was not abandoned to Hades, nor did his flesh see corruption. This Jesus God raised up, and of that we all are witnesses. (vv. 29–32)

Peter makes clear that Psalm 16:10 did not apply in its fullest extent to the life of David, but that the ultimate referent of Psalm 16:10 is the offspring of David, namely, Jesus. Thus, while Psalm 16:10 envisions David and the greater David in a context of death, the psalm in fact sees beyond this death in regard to the greater David and proclaims that the greater David will rise from the dead.

Isaiah 53

Isaiah also reveals the fact that life follows the death of the suffering servant by, in effect, referring to the servant's resurrection. After the greater part of Isaiah 53 describes the suffering and death of the righteous servant—culminating with the statement that God was pleased with and even orchestrated the servant's death—the prophecy proceeds with a series of statements that declare God's deliverance of the servant. In the second portion of 53:10, Isaiah declares, "When his soul makes an offering for guilt, he shall see his offspring; he shall prolong

---

[21] Kaiser, *The Messiah in the Old Testament*, 122.

his days; the will of the LORD shall prosper in his hand." However, one cannot produce offspring if he is dead. Nor can one prolong his days if he is not alive. The meaning here is clear, then: these statements presuppose life. Further, in 53:12, God declares, "Therefore I will divide him a portion with the many, and he shall divide the spoil with the strong, because he poured out his soul to death and was numbered with the transgressors." Yet one cannot divide any spoil if he is defeated. Therefore, these lines assume that the servant will triumph and see life after His death. These statements presuppose resurrection. Thus, while the servant suffered and died, He also conquered death and saw life after death.

This indeed is the glory of the Messiah's death—that in His death, He conquered death. Hebrews 2:14–15 captures the Messiah's triumph well: "Since therefore the children share in flesh and blood, he himself likewise partook of the same things, that through death he might destroy the one who has the power of death, that is, the devil, and deliver all those who through fear of death were subject to lifelong slavery." Thus, the death of the Messiah fulfills the promise announced in Genesis 3:15—that an offspring of Eve will defeat the serpent.

To help understand how the Messiah overcame death and the agent of death, Jesus provides a parable in Luke 11:14–22. After Jesus had cast out a demon from a man, Jesus' opponents accused Jesus of casting out demons by the power of Beelzebul rather than by the power of God. In response to these accusations, Jesus said, "When a strong man, fully armed, guards his own palace, his goods are safe; but when one stronger than he attacks him and overcomes him, he takes away his armor in which he trusted and divides his spoil." Jesus states here that He is the stronger one. This is the very language that Isaiah employs in 53:12 to describe the ultimate triumph of the suffering servant: "Therefore I will divide him a portion with the many, and he shall divide the spoil with the strong." As Jesus tells this parable—possibly alluding to Isaiah 53:12—He applies the characterization of the strong to Himself. He is the strong one. He is the triumphant one. He is the champion.

Every other death is a testimony of defeat. Yet the death of the Messiah is a testimony of total triumph. Thus Paul exclaims in 1 Corinthians 15:54–55, "Death is swallowed up in victory. O death, where is your victory? O death, where is your sting?" (cf. Isa. 25:8; Hos. 13:14; Acts 2:24; Rev. 20:14; 21:4)

Conclusion

How is it that every supposed messiah who died proved to be a failed messiah, while Jesus, who also died, proved to be the true Messiah? Because His death was unique. It was revealed in the Scriptures, it served the purpose of atonement, and it resulted in a glorious resurrection. Consequently, the death of Jesus the Messiah is not an event that begs an apology. The death of the Messiah is rather an event that ought to prompt us to worship God. Indeed, the death of the Messiah will be an event of eternal worship for all the saints in heaven, who will forever cry out, "Worthy is the Lamb who was slain" (Rev. 5:12).

19

JESUS IS BETTER: THE FINAL WORD

HEBREWS 1:1-3

Austin Duncan

recently had an impromptu elders meeting on my porch, but not with the faithful men that I have the privilege of serving alongside at Grace Church. It was with two baby-faced, tie-clad young men from Utah. These two self-identified elders approached me, wanting to talk about Jesus. They weren't the kind of elders that you'd find in my church, ones who lead and feed the flock of God. They were Mormon missionaries, and that October afternoon, I was their mission. When they began asking the familiar questions about "The Great Apostasy" and the prophetic Word of God, I went to a part of the Bible I hadn't used in an apologetic encounter like this before. I went to the book of Hebrews.

For the previous two years, I had been teaching through the book of Hebrews in the college ministry at my church and exhorting students from the greater Los Angeles area to persevere in Christ, because Christ, our High Priest, is better. Better than their previous way of life, better than the lure of sin's pleasure, better than anything this world could ever offer them. Better.

As we walked through the text, the glories of Christ the Son shone out of every chapter, exalting Him over angels, over Moses, over the Levitical priesthood, over all. Hebrews demonstrates that in every way and from every angle, Jesus is the perfect fulfillment of everything the Old Testament prefigures, and is the only sure hope for beleaguered believers in need of persevering strength.

So when two starched white shirts showed up on my porch that day, I invited them to look upon the Jesus from the book of Hebrews, summed up in the introductory verses of the epistle. This Jesus looks different from the fair-haired demigod of polytheistic Mormonism and has little in common with many modern conceptions of the Nazarene prophet. This Jesus is God of very God, the better Adam, the Son of a virgin, the sinless substitute, and the risen King. And in the beginning of the book of Hebrews, He is described as God's final word. But it's not just Latter-Day Saints who need to encounter the Jesus of the epistle to the Hebrews. This epistle was written to convince persecuted believers on the brink of recapitulation and apostasy that endurance and faithfulness is not an option but a necessity, and that the enduring Christian pilgrimage needs to be sustained by fixing our eyes on God's Son.

That's what I hoped to show my Mormon visitors and a room full of collegians and my own heart—that Jesus is the full and final revelation of God. The opening lines of the letter to the Hebrews demonstrate that in Jesus we find God's final statement about Himself. The text then extols the unequalled greatness of His final word. Hebrews 1:1–3 shows us that Jesus is God's final revelation, and Jesus as God's messenger has a supremacy that is unequalled. It is this vision of Jesus that can sustain our faith.

The Final Revelation

More than any book in the Bible, the epistle to the Hebrews compellingly presents Jesus as the definitive revelation of God to man. The author of Hebrews makes that clear in his introduction. He begins his sermonic letter in soaring, lofty, and sonorous words: "Long ago, at many times and in many ways, God spoke to our fathers by the prophets" (v. 1). For the original recipients of this letter, years had passed without a word from God for the Jewish people. This silence was deafening because they had been the recipients of God's ongoing revelation for millennia. The Old Testament is the story of thousands of years of God speaking through priests, prophets, a burning bush, a donkey, dreams, visions, the Urim and the Thummim, sages, and singers. After a long period of silence between the Testaments, something different and remarkable happened. In former times, God spoke through servants. Now God has spoken through His Son. A footnote in the New English Translation Bible explains the phraseology of verse 1 like this:

> The Greek puts an emphasis on the quality of God's final
> revelation. As such, it is more than an indefinite notion ("a
> son") though less than a definite one ("the son"), for this
> final revelation is not just through any son of God, nor is the
> emphasis specifically on the person himself. Rather, the focus

here is on the nature of the vehicle of God's revelation: He is no mere spokesman (or prophet) for God, nor is he merely a heavenly messenger (or angel); instead, this final revelation comes through one who is intimately acquainted with the heavenly Father in a way that only a family member could be.

Jesus is the vehicle of God's fullest communication of Himself, the one who is the closest to God and who displays the reality of who God is. If anyone heeds the words of Hebrews 1, they will not seek some secondary spiritual experience, another baptism, another snap, crackle, and pop of a higher spiritual afflatus because they would be aware that Jesus is the final word. He is the one through whom God has spoken fully and finally, no longer "prophet-wise" but "Son-wise," and He is the exact representation of His being.

In the fullness of time, God spoke in a way that He had never done before and will never again. This Word is full and He's final and He's enough to sustain His people to finish the Christian race. F. F. Bruce says, "Had God remained silent, enshrouded in thick darkness, the plight of mankind would have been desperate indeed, but now he has spoken in his revealing, redeeming, and life-giving word. And in his light, we see light."[1] God's revelation of Himself in Jesus is a mercy that has the power to sustain our faith.

This is not to say that God's former revelation was faulty or unclear. In Jesus, the shadow has been replaced by substance. The incomplete has been finished. The promise has been replaced by fulfillment, and God's spokesmen are no longer mere men speaking on behalf of God. Now, God will speak through His own Son. And it all hangs on those two little words: "has spoken." That verb "has spoken" appears sixteen times in the book of Hebrews. It has a synonym that is usually translated with the word *spoken* that occurs thirty-one times, and it is that initial affirmation that is basic to the whole argument of this epistle. It is crucial that we see Jesus as the pinnacle of God's self-disclosure. The incarnation is a merciful forthtelling of God to us.

Have you felt the force of God's self-revelation in Jesus? Consider that God spoke through Adam, Abraham, Jacob, Moses, Elijah, Ezekiel, Isaiah, Amos, Haggai, history and narrative, wisdom and poetry, law and prophecy, romantic stories like Song of Songs and Ruth, battle scenes on the plains of Moab, oracles of Haggai, and confounding monodramas of Ezekiel. He spoke in nature and He spoke in inspired words. His revelation was good and clear and merciful, given in bits and pieces. God spoke to a small nation of chosen people and to the pagan

---

[1] F. F. Bruce, *The Epistle to the Hebrews*, NICNT (Grand Rapids: Wm. B. Eerdmans Publishing Co., 1990), 45.

society of Nineveh. God spoke and spoke and spoke. Often, generations would pass without a word from God, and then a prophet would rise up and the people would finally hear from God. Sometimes in a booming voice, and sometimes in whispers, yet always through a mediator, prophet, or priest. But now, says the author of Hebrews, in these last days, we have the final word from God, and it did not come through a spokesman. It has arrived incarnate in His own Son.

Tom Schreiner summarizes the nature of Jesus as God's final revelation thus: "God has spoken in His Son. . . . The revelation in the former era was diverse and partial, but the revelation in the Son is unitary and definitive. The final revelation has come in the last days for God has spoken His last and best word. No further word is to be expected, for the last word focuses on the life, death, and resurrection of the Son. . . . Believers await the return of the Son (9:28), but they don't expect a further word from God. No more clarification is needed. The significance of what the Son accomplished has been revealed once for all."[2]

Why would we look anywhere else for a sustaining vision for our faith? Why do we beg to hear a mystical word from God? Why do so many Christians close their Bibles and ask God to speak to them? In an age of cults offering "Another Testament about Jesus Christ" and even Bible-believing Christians seeking out esoteric spiritual experiences to get them further along in their faith, Hebrews 1 simply shows us that God *has* spoken, fully, finally, and persuasively for the satisfaction of our eternal souls in Jesus, His final word.

If you want to know God, then you must meet Jesus. If you want to hear from God, then you must listen to Jesus. If you wonder what God is like, then simply open your Bible and take in the glory of God, the Word of God, beholding the treasure that is the disclosure of God in Jesus, His Son. When you stop seeking a new word from God and realize that God has given us His final word in Jesus, you see, in a phrase, His unequalled greatness.

The Supreme Revelation

Having shown his readers the momentous nature of God's self-revelation in Jesus, the pastor writing to the persecuted Hebrews tells them why this Jesus is worthy of their attention. In staccato phrases, he presents a vision for sustaining faith that is driven by his description of Jesus' unequalled greatness. A brief look at these phrases can help us see the glory of Jesus, a glory intended to sustain our own faith.

---

[2] Thomas R. Schreiner, *Commentary on Hebrews* (Nashville: B&H Publishing Group, 2015), 54.

Heir, Creator, and Sustainer

According to LegalZoom.com, fifty-five percent of Americans do not have a will or other estate plan in place. Few seem to want to make final arrangements. Those who do put their affairs in order understand the importance of leaving a legacy and caring for their loved ones when they are gone.

When God calls Jesus His heir, He does not anticipate His own demise. Instead, He uses the ancient concept of inheritance to demonstrate that everything that belongs to God belongs to Jesus. "Heir of all things" is a title of dignity. This has been the promise of God all the way back in Psalm 2:6–7: "'As for me, I have set my King on Zion, my holy hill.' I will tell of the decree: The LORD said to me, 'You are my Son; today I have begotten you. Ask of me, and I will make the nations your heritage, and the ends of the earth your possession.'" The heirship of Christ reminds us that all that belongs to God will finally and eternally be given to His Son.

A rich man may leave His possessions to many sons and daughters or donate to many worthy organizations, but God will give "all things" to His Son. Everything will someday belong to Jesus. The solar system, massive stars, every planet, the vast oceans, continents, forests and jungles, every creature within, every stream and river, massive sequoias and tiny mold spores, Bengal tigers and single cell organisms, and every single person. You and me. All are under the rightful ownership of a sovereign God and all will be given to His worthy Son (Heb. 2:5–9).

Stunningly, Romans 8:16–17 says that Christians will be "fellow heirs with Christ." Our final destiny and possession is linked inextricably to God's promise that all He possesses and has authority over will be fully and finally in the possession of His Son. And through faith, we will share in Jesus' heirship. The future belongs to Jesus and, therefore, to those who belong to Jesus. What a breathtaking truth! What a word to huddled and persecuted believers who were imprisoned and joyfully accepted the confiscation of their property (Heb. 10:34)! And what a word to materialists who need to learn to let go of our greedy grasp on our stuff and anticipate an eternal inheritance that can never perish, spoil, or fade (1 Peter 1:4)!

To further demonstrate the excellency of God's final word, the author asserts that Jesus is the one "through whom also He made the world" (Heb. 1:2 NASB). Now portraying the Son as co-Creator of the universe, the preacher to the Hebrews pulls back the curtain on the first chapter of the Bible to show that Jesus was active in creating. Through Christ, God made all things. This demonstrates the preexistence, power, and deity of the Son. God made the ages, space and time, and all created things in this universe through His Son: "All things were made through him, and without him was not any thing made that was made" (John 1:3). Colossians 1:16 combines the concept of Jesus as heir and Creator with these words: "For by him all things were created, in heaven and on earth, visible and invisible, whether thrones or dominions or rulers or authorities—all things were created through him and for him." The final revelation from God is also the one who made heaven and earth. Jesus is your Creator. He made you. This is proof of His knowledge of you and His love for you.

If Owner and Creator were not enough, reaching down to verse three, Jesus is also described as the one "who upholds all things by the word of his power" (Heb. 1:3 NASB). The concept behind this phrase is that of sustainer. The basic meaning is about upholding, and carrying all that He created in an ongoing manner to its proper goal. Jesus did not cease His involvement with creation after speaking it into existence. Nor did He walk away from creation after the fall of man. Jesus has maintained His providential control and sustenance of all things for all time. Unlike the god of the deists, He remains engaged in His creation. As Bruce explains, "He upholds the universe not like Atlas supporting a dead weight on his shoulders, but as one who carries all things forward on their appointed course."[3] How does He do it? "By the word of His power" or "by His powerful word." He does it omnipotently and effortlessly, with a word.

In 2005, a team of Princeton astrophysicists made headlines when they calculated the radius of the observable universe as 45.7 billion light-years. Their estimate was three times larger than the prior estimate! This area includes billions of galaxies and hundreds of billions of stars. What their research did not observe is that every single corner of that large chunk of real estate was created by Jesus, is upheld by the word of Jesus' power, and will belong to Jesus by throne rights and heirship for all eternity. Not a small oversight. Jesus' greatness is seen clearly in His work as heir, creator, and sustainer.

Radiance, Replica, and Conqueror

Jesus is the "radiance of God's glory" (1:3 NIV). The Greek word translated "radiance" appears only here in the Bible, though it is used in other ancient Greek literature. It's a word that means "effulgence" or "a reflection." These two concepts come together in this way: one is like a mirror and one is like the sun. One shines and one reflects. Both of those words describe how Jesus is the visible manifestation of the glory of God. Jesus shares the same divine nature as the Father, yet He is distinct from the Father in His person. At the same time, Jesus is the effulgence of God's glory because He radiates the Father's nature to His

---

[3] Bruce, *Hebrews*, 49.

creation. They are distinct in their personages, yet one in their essence. As the Nicene Creed states, Jesus is: "light from light."

How do you describe the united three persons of the Godhead? The doctrine of the Trinity stretches the bounds of our imaginations and reminds us that Jesus is both the radiance of God's glory and God of very God. It ought not to be easy to wrap your mind around an infinite being. Christ existed before He was a baby in a manger. He was pre-incarnate and He shared in eternity past, the divine glory, because Jesus is God. In Jesus' incarnation, He revealed that divine glory because He embodied God's essential glory. So when Jesus said, "If you have seen me, you've seen the Father," He's saying exactly what the author to the Hebrews writes. He is the radiance of the glory of God.

This reference to glory would bring to the original recipients' minds all their history, as a people, with the glory of God—from Moses's encounter with God's glory in a bush that burned to a pillar of fire that was a visible manifestation of the glory of God that led the Israelites out of Egypt. The Old Testament is all about the awesome glory of God.

In the tabernacle that God commanded Moses to build, behind the curtain, shrouded in smoke and thick darkness, God's glory surrounded a box called the ark of the covenant. Some translations call it a mercy seat, a reminder to the people of the necessity of a blood sacrifice even in this most holy place. Maybe you remember seeing it in the movie *Raiders of the Lost Ark*. That divine piece of furniture is just a box, but it's a box that kills 55,000 people in the first five chapters of Samuel. This is a sacred manifestation of God's visible glory, and it's just a box.

What the author of Hebrews is saying, then, is that all of that glory, coming and leaving Ezekiel's temple vision, attending the visions and preaching of the prophets, accompanying the people in their wanderings, and sitting in the heart of the tabernacle was only a prelude of the greater glory of God that would be seen incomparably in Jesus. He is the radiance of the glory of God. That's why John 1:14 says, "And the Word became flesh and dwelt among us." That word "dwelt" means "tabernacled." The Word, Jesus Christ, became flesh, incarnate, as a baby, lived as a boy, grew to be a man, and lived a perfect sinless life. And John describes that as God tabernacling among us.

God set up residence among us in Jesus, purposefully using a word that would remind us that He came to manifest the glory of God among us. He came as the one who would die in our place, the one that could suffer as an adequate sacrifice, the one who is fully God and fully man. He tabernacled among us. John continues, "And we saw his glory, glory as of the only begotten from the Father, full of grace and truth" (John 1:14 NASB). This is the effulgence. This is the visible glory of God in the face of Jesus. This is the radiance of the glory of God.

The author of Hebrews also extols the greatness of Jesus as the "exact representation of [God's] being (1:3 NIV). " The ESV says "the exact imprint of his nature." The word translated "imprint" describes an impress, a reproduction, or a representation. This concept would have been familiar to all the original listeners. The coins they carried in their pockets were cast in a die, a mold that pressed coins from hot metal, giving each coin the same face. Even in the United States today, coins are still cast in an official way with a particular stamp. The idea is that the die that stamps the coin and impresses the image into the coin is the same image of the coin itself. Likewise, the author says that Jesus is precisely like God, exactly in God's image.

Another similar analogy that the original audience would have associated with the phrase "exact representation" is the signet ring. Rather than signing a document of significance, hot wax would be pressed into by an official ring, leaving a particular match of the ring in the wax. It would be an impression, a reproduction, a representation. This is the illustration that God employs through the author of Hebrews to describe Jesus as a direct parallel with God. Jesus is an exact representation of God's being. If you have seen Jesus, you have seen God.

While Jesus and the Father are distinct persons, they share the same divine nature. All that the Father is in His nature, the Son is as well. We never think in terms of greater and lesser when it comes to Jesus and His Father, though we will employ terms of incarnate submission in their role and relationship, but never of greater and lesser. Gregory of Nyssa got after people when they would use that kind of language in Hebrews 1. He would essentially tell them, "Don't measure things that are unmeasurable because all the fullness of Deity is in him."[4]

Jesus Christ, Son of God, is not like the Jesus of the Jehovah's Witnesses or the Mormons. He is not the most important angel or the chief being or the greatest of all created beings. Jesus Christ is God of very God. The Son is the exact impression of God's nature. The Son represents the nature and character of the one true God. He reveals who God is. Jesus shares with the Father the being, nature, and essence of God. That's why John 1:1 says that Jesus is the Word of God. Jesus expresses to human beings in Himself who God is (John 1:18). He is the image of the invisible God (Col. 1:15). He is in the form of God (Phil. 2:6). Jesus, unlike the prophets of old, is not merely representing God as a spokesman or as one who carries God's message. He is God Himself.

Hebrews 1:3 concludes by introducing concepts that the author will detail in the chapters that follow. Compressed into this verse is an outline of the rest of

---

[4] *Gregory of Nyssa*: Contra Eunomium *III. An English Translation with Commentary and Supporting Studies, Proceedings of the 12th International Colloquium on Gregory of Nyssa (Leuven, 14-17 September 2010)*, Johan Leemans and Matthieu Cassin, eds. (Leiden, Netherlands: Brill, 2014), 52.

the epistle. Christ is presented as a purifying priest and an enthroned king. That is to say, Jesus is the conquering King who will fully and finally eliminate the problem of our sin. "When He had made purification of sins, He sat down at the right hand of the Majesty on high." He defeats sin and every enemy and sits on the throne to prove that through the cross and the resurrection He has won.

The Bible teaches that without the shedding of blood, there is no remission of sins (Heb. 9:22). There is no forgiveness of sins apart from a blood sacrifice. The author of Hebrews will go on to describe to us what these Hebrew Christians already understood: animal sacrifice was the prerequisite for their worship. Over and over again animals were slaughtered as blood sacrifices for the sins of the nation of Israel. The Bible says that the wages of sin is death. So year after year, morning and night, the livestock would come. At feast time, they would even kill half a million lambs.

The author of Hebrews wants us to see not only Jesus' superiority in His glorious upholding of the universe by the word of His power, but also His glory in His humiliation and death. He came into this world to die. He was struck. He was murdered. He was crucified. He was sacrificed on a Roman cross, all according to the plan of God. But His death was a victory. In His death, He made purification for sins. This is His high priestly work, as the author of Hebrews will describe for us in chapters 8–10. He will tell us why His priesthood is a better and more lasting priesthood. His sacrificial, substitutionary death would lead to His exaltation. We have a High Priest who sat down at the right hand of the throne of the Majesty in heaven. As He was dying on the cross, Jesus spoke about the perfection of His sacrifice. He said, "It is finished" (John 19:30). He is the perfect High Priest, the one who atones for sin and who does it lastingly, once for all.

Even in his introduction, the author of Hebrews indicates the amazing truth that Jesus has conquered death and sin. That Jesus "sat down" is no small matter. The priests did many things in their temple work. They sacrificed animals. They lit the lamp stands. They cared for the temple and oversaw worship. But one thing they never did in that place of sacrifice was to take a seat. There are no chairs in the holy of holies. That's because their work was never finished. But Jesus' atoning work was once for all. It is finished. "When Christ had offered for all time a single sacrifice for sins, he sat down at the right hand of God" (Heb. 10:12).

The author of Hebrews goes on to describe Jesus' enthronement, saying, "He sat down at the right hand of the Majesty on high" (1:3). The use of the word "Majesty" stands in for the name of God. The atonement is complete. God is satisfied. Jesus' work is permanently finished. He has received His rightful and royal supremacy. Jesus takes the place of honor, authority, and power. This is the significance and the relationship between Jesus' sacrifice and Jesus' enthronement. Jesus' place at the right hand of the Father declares God's approval of His Son's perfect sacrifice.

The focus of this phrase is rightfully given to the Son. God bestows this status at His right hand to His Son because of His high priestly sacrifice. He exalts this Son as the conquering King. And that's why He's superior to the angels. That's why He's been given a name superior to every earthly name.

None of us could see the glory of God or behold the magnificence of His Majesty apart from divine intervention. Our response, then, is to live for this supreme Son. We must never pass casually by the word "glory" in our Bibles. We eat and drink for His glory. We let our light shine before men so they can see our good deeds and give glory to the Father. We eagerly expect that now, as always, Christ might be magnified in our body, to His glory. Our lives are designed to bring glory to God through His radiant, atoning, conquering Son, Jesus Christ.

The Final Word

The author of Hebrews extols Christ, the final revelation and the perfect sacrifice provided by God. There's no other way for people to persevere in their faith than by an encounter with the only hope for all, Jesus Christ. In these opening words of the letter to the Hebrews, God says that although He has spoken through prophets and prophecy, he no longer speaks that way. He has spoken in these last days through His Son. That Jesus is the Son of God is our confession.

If we would heed the words of Hebrews, we would not seek some secondary spiritual experience, another book about Jesus, another snap-crackle-pop, or a higher spiritual level because we would be aware that Jesus is the final word. He is the one through whom God has spoken fully and finally, no longer "prophet-wise" but "son-wise." He is the exact representation of His being. In the fullness of time, we can enjoy the advantageous position of hearing God's final word. In Jesus, God has spoken in a way that He has never done before and will never again. He is full and final.

Michael Reaves sums up the supremacy of Jesus in this passage: "Here then is the revolution: for all our dreams, our dark and frightened imaginings of God, *there is no God in heaven who is unlike Jesus*. For he is God. . . . Let us be rid of that horrid sly idea that behind Jesus, the friend of sinners there's some more sinister being, one thinner on compassion and grace. There cannot be! Jesus is the Word. He is one with his Father. He is the radiance, the glow, the glory of his Father. . . . In Him, we see the true meaning of the love, the power, the wisdom, the justice and the majesty of God."[5]

---

[5] Michael Reeves, *Rejoicing in Christ* (Downers Grove, IL: InterVarsity Press, 2015), 14–15.

So, tell the Mormons at the door that Jesus is the final word. Tell the persecuted church that Jesus is the final word. Tell those tempted to return to their former manner of life that Jesus is the final word. Tell a lost and dying world that their sins can be forgiven by Jesus, the final word. Tell your weary heart, when perseverance seems too difficult, to fix your eyes on Jesus, the final word from God.

20

SALT AND LIGHT: THE BELIEVER'S WITNESS TO CHRIST IN AN UNGODLY SOCIETY

MATTHEW 5:14–16

Albert Mohler

When Christians feel unthreatened by the culture, they fail to think about the church's responsibility to the culture. Indeed, in the history of the church, the question of responsibility to the broader culture most often appears in the context of great controversy and crisis. The most prominent example of this is Augustine's work *The City of God*, which plumbs the depths of the church and culture in the midst of the collapse of the Roman Empire.

Christians in the West do not face the absolute collapse of all government and order. Believers certainly feel threatened, however, and at odds with the culture around them. The culture shift is not something that just happened in the last few years. This "moral revolution" has arisen in Western societies at least for the last 125 to 150 years. Thus, there should be little surprise that Christians have started asking questions like, "How is the church to engage the culture?"

The question of the relationship between the church and the culture confounds many, and dubious answers abound. Some suggest that Christians have zero responsibility to the culture. Others purport that culture bears little to no impact on the role of Christian ministry. The former of these perspectives fails to recognize the full implication of the Great Commission, while the latter holds a naïve belief on the reach and influence the culture can have on doctrine, theology, and Christian living.

Viewing culture as too important, however, raises a potentially greater danger to evangelicals in this generation. Evangelicals who see the culture as too important begin to adopt clever and sophisticated strategies aimed at erasing the clear distinction between the people of God and the people not of the kingdom. Yet this view is profoundly at odds with the teaching of Scripture and what Jesus taught His disciples in John 15.

Not *If* but *When* the World Hates You

In John 15:18, Jesus says, "If the world hates you . . ." The "if" can, if taken improperly, seize the reader and lead to a dangerous interpretation. It may cause the reader to think that there is a chance the hatred of the world may not come upon those who follow Christ. A close reading, however, of Jesus' words reveal that it is not so much a matter of *if*, but *when*:

> If the world hates you, know that it has hated me before it hated you. If you were of the world, the world would love you as its own; but because you are not of the world, but I chose you out of the world, therefore the world hates you. Remember the word that I said to you: "A servant is not greater than his master." If they persecuted me, they will also persecute you. If they kept my word, they will also keep yours. But all these things they will do to you on account of my name, because they do not know him who sent me. If I had not come and spoken to them, they would not have been guilty of sin, but now they have no excuse for their sin. Whoever hates me hates my Father also. If I had not done among them the works that no one else did, they would not be guilty of sin, but now they have seen and hated both me and my Father. But the word that is written in their Law must be fulfilled: "They hated me without a cause." (John 15:18–25)

As a Christian reading these words, tension should begin to rise. The Christian knows that they have been called by God to do good works (cf. Eph. 2:10). The kindness and love of Christian character should only stir up love and admiration, not hatred, for the broader culture. Christians, therefore, can feel that if they put on enough good works, love, and charity, the culture will adopt a friendly attitude towards the church. Christians feel a tension as they read John 15 because their works lead the broader culture to see the glory of God and desire Him rather than stir up hatred for God and His people.

The Bible seems to give warrant for the tension Christians feel as they read Jesus' words in John 15. For example, in Matthew 5:16, Jesus says, "Let your light shine before others, so that they may see your good works and give glory to your Father who is in heaven." And 1 Peter 2:12 adds: "Keep your conduct among the Gentiles honorable, so that when they speak against you as evildoers, they may see your good deeds and glorify God on the day of visitation." Thus, a biblical logic arises in these texts amounting to the idea that if Christians do good works, a light shines to the broader culture resulting in the glorifying of God.

The Scriptures, however, must be interpreted together. John 15 does not stand at odds with Matthew 5 or 1 Peter 2. In the latter texts, Christian obedience necessarily leads to good works that the culture will see and bring glory to God. When natural disasters like hurricanes occur, Christians lead the way in providing relief and care for those hurt and displaced. That shows the love of Christ to a dark world and gives glory to God. When Christians lead the charge against sex-trafficking and strive to help abused and subjected women, this culminates in a glorious display of beauty to the world and serves as an act of worship to God. The world, however, will not hate Christians for doing good deeds. We must, therefore, look at Christ's words in John 15 with great care if we are to understand how the hatred of the world comes upon followers of Christ.

To begin, have the conditions of the "if" clauses in John 15 been met? John 15 presents the reader with "if x, then y." Some may try to read that phrase and avoid "x" so that "y" does not happen. However, in John 15, Jesus makes it abundantly clear that every single condition necessary for the "if" to be fulfilled has occurred. Jesus addresses His disciples in a way that demonstrates all the conditions for the hatred of the world to come have been met. He says in verse 20, "Remember the word that I said to you: 'A servant is not greater than his master.' If they persecuted me, they will also persecute you." Christ was in fact persecuted and nailed to a cross. Persecution, therefore, comes to all those who seek to follow Jesus Christ. He continues, "If they kept my word, they will also keep yours." The world, however, already broke Jesus' words. Again, "If I had not come and spoken to them, they would not have been guilty of sin" (v. 22). Yet Jesus already came and preached the good news of the gospel.

The "if" clauses of John 15 lead us to conclude that all the conditions have been met in Jesus Christ, even before He spoke these words to His disciples. The coming of the cross looms over this discourse in John 15. Christians, therefore, must understand that the "ifs" of John 15 are in fact reality. They are fulfilled.

Jesus' ministry met the conditions that make clear Jesus' words, "But all these things they will do to you" (v. 21). Therefore, Christians must see John 15 and know that the question is not if persecution will come, but when.

How Did We Get Here?

A full range of emotions should set in as the Christian realizes the reality of Jesus' words in John 15. No doubt, fear and anxiety can seep into our minds as we understand that faith in Christ necessarily leads to persecution from the world. In grappling with this reality, perhaps we need to ask, "How exactly did we find ourselves in this predicament?" The Christian might be tempted to think that a life of persecution denotes a failure of the divine Messianic strategy or a mere plot of Satan himself. Both of these hypotheses, however, fail to understand the context of John 15 and the mysterious beauty of what Christ teaches us as He Himself was about to head to the cross.

Chosen by God Himself

In John 15:16, immediately before Jesus tells His disciples of the coming persecution they will face, He says, "You did not chose me, but I chose you." Christians must know that persecution and suffering in the Christian life do not come as lapses in God's strategy. Nor does persecution come because God cannot protect His Bride from the attacks of Satan. Jesus reveals that His people endure persecution because of divine sovereignty. You were chosen by God's good pleasure and love.

Indeed, Christians find themselves in a life of persecution and suffering because they were chosen by God out of the world. John 15 reveals that Christians live as vines, abiding in the very person of Christ for strength and nourishment. Christians find themselves at odds with the world because they have been called out of the world and now live as ones who belong to the King of kings and Lord of lords. Christians abide in a new Master and live for a new kingdom. Christians face a hostile world because they belong to the Father, and the world hates the Father.

Therefore, whatever Christians face in this life, they face by the sovereign plan of the triune God. Through this truth comes Christians' hope and strength. We can hope because Christ has gone before us and, as He tells His disciples in John 16, has overcome the world before us! The Christian also finds strength from this glorious truth. If persecution comes as a sovereign plan of God, then we know God supplies His people with the necessary resources to endure and bring glory to His name. Christians hope and survive all that the world and Satan throw their way because they abide in the very person of Jesus Christ.

Thus, Christians find themselves in their current predicament because God chose them out of the world by His good pleasure for His glory. Though persecution comes, Jesus comforts believers with the vivid imagery of abiding in Him. Though hatred and even death await the people of Christ, Jesus shows that His people live *in* His very person. Their lives *are* hidden with Christ in God (Col. 3:3). Christians, therefore, dare not try to extricate themselves from this predicament. The thought that the church could somehow be sophisticated, smart, kind, or civil enough to assuage the hatred of the world is not only wrong thinking but blasphemous. Jesus said, "A servant is not greater than his master" (John 15:20). Jesus' very own people crucified Him and rejected Him. He was perfect in all His ways. It is, therefore, arrogance of the highest order to think that the world will treat us better than our perfect Savior.

Persecuted because of the Gospel

The culture rejects the gospel and persecutes its adherents because of the absolute scandal the gospel purports. The apostle Paul writes in 1 Corinthians 1:22–25,

> For Jews demand signs and Greeks seek wisdom, but we
> preach Christ crucified, a stumbling block to Jews and folly to
> Gentiles, but to those who are called, both Jews and Greeks,
> Christ the power of God and the wisdom of God. For the
> foolishness of God is wiser than men, and the weakness of
> God is stronger than men.

In this passage, Paul echoes Jesus' teaching in John 15. The message of the gospel offends the wisdom of worldly thinking. The culture trips over the gospel to their destruction because of its scandalous content. The Jews looked for a conquering king, not a murdered Messiah. The broader culture found the idea of a Father giving up His Son for the sins of mankind ridiculous. Yet Paul would not capitulate to the itching ears of his hearers, no matter the cost. He longed to proclaim Christ crucified, and only Christ crucified, for the gospel "is the power of God for salvation" (Rom. 1:16).

Christians must understand that it is the message of the gospel itself which elicits the response of persecution. Singer-songwriter Michael Gungor is a recent illustration of the offense of the gospel, even in "Christian" circles. He tweeted, "Questioning penal substitutionary atonement really brings out the 30-year-old white dudes on my feed. I would like to hear more artists who sing to God and fewer who include a father killing a son in that endeavor." For Gungor, the substitutionary atonement accomplished by Christ amounts to a horrific message of a father slaughtering his son. This type of message, in Gungor's mind, must end if the culture is to be reached for Christ. He goes on to say, "To see it as literal and out of context that God needed to be appeased with blood is not beautiful, it's horrific." Gungor is willing to stand with a gospel, but not *the* gospel. Gungor calls Christians to get away from substitutionary atonement because it is too crude to be respected.

The pagan culture believes they promote a message of tolerance. The culture believes that true morality does not impose belief systems on others. This emphasis on tolerance led to a radical shift in the ethics of American culture. America became intolerant of intolerance. The message of the gospel stands at odds with the new morality that abhors any claim to exclusivity. The world thinks it possesses the moral high ground to label anything it dislikes as intolerance.

The leading edge of the apologetic challenge in our generation is that the God of the Bible is an ogre. Gungor's sentiment abounds in the broader culture, revealing that the objection to the gospel is a moral one. The moral arguments against the gospel are not based in rationalism so much as in a great shift in morality. The culture feels hatred toward a God who would actually dare to be God. Hatred toward a God who actually is concerned first and foremost with His own glory. Hatred toward a God who doesn't offer multiple pathways for creative humanity to try to resolve their cognitive dissonance. That kind of God is hated. That kind of God who wills the death of His own Son on a cross and then vindicates His atoning work by raising Him from the dead. That kind of God is not admired in this society, morally as well as cognitively. Therefore, the entirety of Scripture is now held up as suspect.

Christians, as adherents to the Scriptures and believers in the infallibility of the God's Word, must understand the current trajectory of the culture. The accusations have come, and, no doubt, laws trying to stamp out the intolerable gospel of Jesus Christ will come. No doubt, Christians in America will face the threat of ostracization. Christians *must* understand this and be fully aware of the cultural landscape if they are to respond in a wise, godly fashion.

If the culture marches toward an increasing hatred of the message of the cross, how will Christians respond? Some abandon the gospel altogether. False teachers craft false gospels that promise our "best lives now." False teachers are raised up by the itching ears of the culture clamoring for messages of inclusion that promise social justice, happiness, wealth, and prosperity. As the moral revolution wars with the message of Jesus Christ, ministers of the gospel invariably capitulate on the central doctrines of the faith for the sake of relevance. Make no mistake, the desire for cultural relevance is nothing less than idolatry. The messages of these false teachers will lead, albeit in an inoffensive way, countless souls to eternal perdition. Capitulating on the central truths of the gospel will only play into the hands of Satan himself, who longs to devour as many souls as he can.

Christian, do not forfeit the message of the gospel. Only the people of Jesus Christ possess the words of truth. The culture may be offended by the message of the gospel. Well, let the culture be offended! No doubt, however, as offense comes, salvation will come too. The message of the gospel must necessarily wound if it is to bring healing. The gospel does offend. It reveals our sin and the depth of our depravity. It manifests in the darkest terms the end that we deserve as rebellious people. The gospel displays the glory and holiness of an infinite God who burns with wrath against our sin. Furthermore, the gospel reveals that we cannot save ourselves. This is offensive! Yet it is the same gospel that brings healing and hope as it gloriously tells of the God who sent His Son to die in our place. If the church abandons the gospel, it abandons the only hope for salvation.

Yes, the world may hate you. For carrying this message, countless have died, giving their lives for the sake of the gospel. Their lives, however, live as fragrant offerings, used by God to draw many to Himself. Christian, realize that suffering is coming and it is promised to you. Our enemy abhors the message you carry and will do anything to silence you. We, however, *cannot be silent*. Though suffering may come as a result of proclaming the truth, the glorifying of our God comes, too, as the lost are found. It is only through the gospel, not cultural relativism, that sinners will be won for Christ. Press on, then, for the prize of the upward call of God in Christ (Phil. 3:14). Hold fast to the words of life (Phil. 2:16). Proclaim the excellencies of Christ (1 Peter 2:9). Guard the good deposit entrusted to you (2 Tim. 1:14).

Why Persecution?

Jesus teaches His followers the inevitability of suffering and persecution in the Christian life. The reason for this hatred stems from the message of the gospel itself. The culture questions the morality of a gospel articulating that all must have faith in a murdered Savior, hung on a cross by the will of His Father. Blood is needed for forgiveness of sins. This entire notion enrages the culture and wars with their fallen morality. This leads to persecution of God's people.

This hard truth can lead a Christian to ask, "Why?" When approaching the Scriptures, it can feel impertinent to ask "Why?" of certain commands. When God commands something, a proper response should not be to get His reason for the command. We simply obey because of who He is as God. John 15, however, displays the mercy and grace of God by answering the question "Why?" for us. Jesus says:

> But when the Helper comes, whom I will send to you from the Father, the Spirit of truth, who proceeds from the Father, he will bear witness about me. And you also will bear witness, because you have been with me from the beginning. (vv. 26–27)

Jesus tells His disciples that all their suffering, all their persecution, the need for the Helper to come and be with them, is for witnessing. The root of the word for *witness* is *martyr*. The word *martyr* conjures up images of saints in the history of the church burned at the stake, fed to lions, beheaded, and subjected to countless other torturous acts. Those images, however, seem far removed from our civilized day. To preach "Be a martyr for Christ" in the comforts of our Western society feels safer than what Christians had to endure in previous ages or in other places. However, Jesus never promised that His disciples would die safely and sweetly in their beds. He never promised us a tranquil life.

We have been lulled into a false complacency by the pervasive reality of nominal and cultural Christianity. Christians have allowed the culture around us to create something of a safe zone, lulling us into longing for the respect and adoration of the masses. We believe that the title "Christian" should endow us with privileges and rights from a pagan world hostile to God and the gospel of Jesus Christ. If a church claiming the name of Jesus Christ exists in harmony with a culture that rages against the reign of God, then it is no church of Jesus. A church at peace with the culture, rather, has capitulated to the influences of the world around them for the sake of relevance and peace. This is not what Christ called His disciples and His bride to do when He commissioned them as His witnesses.

Christians must recognize that the saints' witness and martyrdom verifies and amplifies the gospel of Jesus Christ. The persecution of believers powerfully magnifies the worthiness and glory of God. The persecution of God's people is the vindication of the Son of God. *This is not a losing strategy.* This is the Father vindicating the Son and the Son vindicating His own. Therefore, when the apostles were persecuted, they could cry out with joy and rejoice that they had been "counted worthy to suffer dishonor for the Name" (Acts 5:41). The suffering of God's people, in a peculiar way, brings glory and honor and praise to His name. Your suffering for the gospel displays powerfully the worthiness of the triune God.

But Take Heart—He Has Overcome the World

The scandalous nature of the gospel and the promise of persecution might cause some to become depressed or discouraged. Jesus' words in John 15 appear to be the worst rallying cry of any leader. Jesus promises that the world will hate you. Does this foster depression? If the suffering that Christians will face brings depression in the people of God, then they have failed to understand the glory of Christ, the beauty of the cross, and the power of an empty tomb.

Though Christ promises His disciples suffering in John 15, He promises them something glorious in 16:32–33:

> Behold, the hour is coming, indeed it has come, when you will be scattered, each to his own home, and will leave me alone. Yet I am not alone, for the Father is with me. I have said these things to you, that in me you may have peace. In the world you will have tribulation. But take heart; I have overcome the world.

If depression fills us by the promise of suffering and the warnings that Christ issued for all who follow Him, then we trust not in Christ and the fact that He has overcome the world.

"In this world, you will have trouble. Fear not, take heart, I've overcome the world." Do you believe that? If Christ has overcome the world, and we know He has, then we can face whatever may come. If Christ has overcome the world, then we can leave everything to Him. If Christ has overcome the world, then no sermon that is truly faithful and is genuinely biblical will ever go without an increase, because the Word of God never returns without accomplishing what God sent it out to do. If He has overcome the world, then we can die with confidence and joy—whether in our beds or in the marketplace or in jail or anywhere it may happen—because we are safe in Him.

Christian, know that Jesus Christ has overcome the world. Without knowing His conquering power over Satan, sin, and death, little reason remains to endure persecution. Through Christ's victory, however, Christians can and must preach the gospel. We can engage the culture and stand firm upon the solid rock of God's Word because Christ reigns supreme over the creation, has secured the victory, and is coming again.

John 15 provides a clear instruction on the manner of the church's engagement and responsibility to the culture. Jesus teaches us that even with the promise of persecution, the gospel must be proclaimed. Indeed, it is through the proclamation of the gospel that persecution will come. This remains the duty of all disciples of Jesus Christ and it is a duty of the highest delight. Christians proclaim a message none other than that which exalts the excellencies of Jesus Christ. Though the gospel spurs persecution, it also brings salvation to the lost. Though we will meet hostility orchestrated by Satan himself, we go forward in the resurrection power of our risen, conquering Savior.

21

COUNTED WORTHY: SUFFERING FOR CHRIST IN A WORLD THAT HATES HIM

ACTS 5:41

Paul Washer

this chapter, I want to explore Acts 5:27–42, and other related passages in Acts, focusing on four things: (1) how apostles were persecuted, (2) the cause of their persecution, (3) what was *not* the cause of their persecution (which is crucial to understand), and (4) how they were able to respond with joy and endurance amidst their persecution to the end of knowing how we can do the same.

How the Apostles Were Persecuted

Once, I was being interviewed on a radio program in Detroit, and the interviewer said to me, "Mr. Washer, there are a lot of people who do not like you. How do you handle persecution?" I thought, *When was the last time I was beaten forty times? When was the last time all my possessions were taken from me? When was the last time I was thrown down and kicked until my ribs broke?* I said, "Sir, I'm not persecuted."

It's amazing how in America, we take the word *persecuted* and redefine it to mean that someone looked at us harshly. That is not what happened in Acts. Luke tells us that the apostles were flogged (Acts 5:40). The Greek word translated "flogged" (*deró*) means "to scourge, to thrash, to beat." It also can mean "to flay open" or in regard to skinning something. What these men suffered was incredibly severe.

Flogging comes out of Deuteronomy 25:3, where we read of a punishment consisting of forty lashes. By the first century, Jewish tradition had come to practice what is known as forty minus one lashes. Scholars debate why this came about. Many think that when Jewish officials were giving the lashes, they weren't certain of their count in some instances. So, in order to prevent miscounting, they figured, "Let's do thirty-nine, because it's better to err on the side of mercy than to err on the side of severity." In this beating, the person's back was the target, but often the punisher did not have good aim. So it was not only the back left open and bleeding. Sometimes, the shoulders, neck, face, lower back, legs, and even the stomach were also struck. This was not a minor beating. It was not just getting in a fight and getting beat up. The person flogged was flayed open, so to speak. And the pain would last more than just a day or week. So we need to be careful when we talk about how we are being "persecuted" in the world today, because we need to find our definition of persecution from the New Testament.

All that we—at least most of us in America—suffer today is not quite the same. However, there is something that we have in common with these early Christians. They were not only beaten and flogged, but also shamed. Shame is something we experience today, even in our culture. The Greek word for *to honor* means "to esteem, to value" and when the negative particle is added to the beginning of the word, it means "to not value, to not esteem them, to not honor." I am describing not only what happened to the apostles, but also what happens to the average preacher today in America. Whether it comes through personal interactions or the media, it is shame. The word can also mean "to render infamous, to despise, to dishonor, to treat with great contempt." When the world's own suffers for the world's cause, the world will greatly honor them. However, when the Christian suffers for Christ's cause, the world will never advertise the suffering in a way that will make others think that the Christian is suffering for an honorable reason.

When a Christian is persecuted, he or she is often persecuted as an enemy of God. For example, Christians are shamed as enemies of God. Look at what Jesus said in John 16:2, "They will make you outcasts from the synagogue, but an hour is coming for everyone who kills you to think that he is offering service to God." One of the most comforting truths in the midst of persecution is that Jesus told us it would come. When it happens, we shouldn't be thinking that, somehow, the sovereignty of God has fallen apart. Christ told us it would be this way. If there were no persecution, that would bring doubt upon His word because He promised persecution.

I believe we are headed for a time like this in the West. In the West, we are re-defining Christianity as love without truth. Too often, when a Christian speaks gospel truth in love, he is automatically somewhat cast out of Christianity. He is not really labeled a Christian. He is not suffering as a Christian. He is suffering as some right-wing, radical bigot or some unstable person with mental prob-lems. And things will get worse. We are going to suffer not as Christians, but perhaps as enemies of God.

Christians are also shamed enemies of the state. Acts 17:7 shows us that Christians were accused of acting contrary to the decrees of Caesar because they claimed there was another king, Jesus. Now, this is in itself a distortion. It is a false accusation. Nonetheless, it is an accusation being railed against Christians. This is very important because of all the political activity going on in our society today. Christianity is not advanced by Christians fighting against the govern-ment. In fact, we are commanded to pray "for kings and all who are in authority" (1 Tim. 2:2). In Romans 13:1, Paul says that we are to be in subjection to the governing authorities. The kingdom to which we belong is somewhat unseen. It is a spiritual kingdom. It is not advanced by physical, carnal means. It is ad-vanced by the preaching of the gospel and by prayer. That being the case, I want you to realize that whenever God is removed from a society or culture, some-thing must take His place. What often takes the place of God in a godless culture is the state. The state, in time, begins to demand worship and obedience so that it can rule over even conscience and religion. It begins to make demands and prohibitions that contradict Scripture. In such times, we must preach the gospel. We must pray. And we must realize that we will seek to live in harmony with all people, a time may come when we will suffer for siding with the gospel. It is not an exaggeration to say that such a time may be on the horizon.

Christians are also shamed as ignorant, mentally unstable, self-righteous, intol-erant bigots. We hear that kind of language all the time, but it's not unusual. Acts 26:24 recounts, "While Paul was saying this in his defense, Festus said in a loud voice, 'Paul, you are out of your mind! Your great learning is driving you mad.'" Here we see one of the greatest tools of the world, one of the greatest tools of Satan, and one of the greatest weapons used against Christianity. Do you know what it is? It's a logical fallacy, *argumentum ad hominem*. Such a strategy disre-gards what is being said and does not deal with the merit or the virtue of the argument set forth but rather simply attacks the person giving their case.

The world is utterly convinced of its own mythology. What mythology? The world says there may very well be a God, but that God has not spoken. The world says that because if God has not spoken, then there is no truth. If there is no truth, then there is no wrong. If there is no wrong, then we are free from God and righteousness. We can do anything and everything we want, either privately or corporately, without any affliction of conscience. The world is having a party. Everyone is singing, dancing, and saying, "I'm okay. You're okay." But then the Christian shows up and says, "None of you are okay." And how does the world respond? They will not sit down and have a discussion with the physician. They simply silence the Christian, and shame him—*argumentum ad hominem*. They say, "You arrogant imbeciles think you alone have the truth. You're ridiculous. You don't belong here." People said of Paul, "Away with such a fellow from the earth, for he should not be allowed to live!" (Acts 22:22). Why should he not be allowed to live? Because he loved the truth and preached the truth and the world hates the truth.

Years ago, I was debating epistemology with a Spanish man, and we went on for several hours. I found out his favorite philosopher was an influential Spanish philosopher named Miguel de Unamuno. Unamuno said, "La vida es sueño," life is dream, and that the most noble thing a man could ever do is be a seeker of the truth and that the most arrogant or stupid thing he could ever say is that he found it. I looked at my Spaniard friend and I said, "I finally figured you out. Now I know where you're going with this." I said, "You want to be a seeker of the truth because there is nobility in being able to say you are a seeker of the truth. But you do not want to find the truth because the moment you find it, you have to submit to it, and you don't want to do that." That is how the world operates today.

The Reason for Persecution

What was the reason the early church was persecuted? The answer is simple: Christ. And the same is true today. Why does Christ bring persecution? Well, the world hates Christ. The world hates the biblical Christ but loves the Christ of the liberal—a man who is not *the* Savior but a savior and a teacher who loves everyone without judgment and truth.

Whenever we lower who Christ is, it does not impress the world. That just gives them more grounds to laugh. And then the liberal loves his Christ, because He is nothing more than an idol, a figment of man's imagination. Man simply creates Christ in his own image, and then he worships the image he has made. Make no mistake: if you preach the biblical Christ, there will be persecution. There will be persecution not only outside the doors of the church, but even inside the church, because so much of the world is in the church and because preachers are not preaching truth.

Christ Himself said, "The world cannot hate you but it hates Me because I testify of it, that its deeds are evil" (John 7:7). Why does the world hate Him? In John

3:19, Jesus says, "This is the judgment, that the Light has come into the world, and men loved the darkness rather than the Light, for their deeds were evil."

I grew up on a farm, a ranch. I loved fishing as a boy, but to fish, you need worms and bugs and all sorts of creepy-crawly things. So you find rocks and logs, and you turn them over. Light enters into the darkness, and all those worms and bugs run because they hate the light. Why do men hate Christ? Because He is good. Why would anyone hate a good Christ? Because they are evil. Why do men hate Christ? Because He is love. Why would anyone hate a loving Christ? Because they are loveless.

Everyone will talk about love, but when you teach in the name of Christ, "Sir, you cannot divorce your wife for a prettier woman because you need to love," that is when the world rebels. The world hates Christ and His teaching, and if you and I preach Christ, the world will hate us. We do not need to try to make ourselves hateful. If we are like Christ, we *will* be hated. Jesus said, "If the world hates you, you know that it has hated Me before it hated you" (John 15:18). Jesus was giving His disciples not only an explanation for why they would be hated, but also comfort. Jesus essentially said, "This is not something unusual that will happen to you. Your identification with Me, the Light, will bring hostility from the darkness."

I remember when I was a young Christian, preachers would say, "If we were just more like Jesus, then there would be revival. People would be converted. Amen." That is not true. If we were more like Jesus, there would be a lot more of us nailed to crosses.

The world's heart must be regenerated through a supernatural work of God's Spirit. That is why, as preachers and pastors, you should never think you are going to be able to achieve something by your own actions, your own cleverness, or some church-growth strategy. The kingdom advances only through a supernatural work of God when men submit themselves to the Word of God, preach the Word of God, and live lives of intercessory prayer. The world is going to hate us, but let us make sure they hate us because we're good and Christlike. As Peter states, "Make sure that none of you suffers as a murderer, or thief, or evildoer, or a troublesome meddler; but if anyone suffers as a Christian, he is not to be ashamed, but is to glorify God in this name" (1 Peter 4:15–16).

The world persecuted the apostles not only because they were identified with Christ, but also because they were preaching Christ. We see in texts like Acts 5:20 that they preached the full gospel. In America, we have taken the glorious gospel of our Lord and Savior Jesus Christ and reduced it down to four spiritual laws, five things God wants you to know, or how to live your best life now. But the gospel is none of that.

When you preach the gospel, start with the character of God and then move to the character and work of man. Bring in the Law and commands in Scripture. Show people that they are condemned, and work in such a way that they cannot escape the verdict. Then turn the page, so to speak, and speak of our glorious Savior. Tell them who He is—that He is not just a man, not just a teacher—but God in flesh. Speak of what He did—that He did not just give us a new way to live or a new morality. He redeemed us. That is the heart of Christianity. We are not primarily a religion of morality, even though we have morality. We are a religion of redemption, and we preach redemption—not redemption in the church, but redemption in Christ and Christ alone.

We rightly speak of His death. Yet we should speak much more of His resurrection and exaltation. Speak the full gospel, pleading with men to turn from their sins and return to God by faith in the person and work of His Son. And when they say they have returned to Him, we teach them from Scripture what biblical assurance truly is and we fill their mind with gospel warnings so they do not turn away from the truth they have received.

So what was so offensive to the world in the first century? First, the apostles preached repentance. They preached warnings of judgment. In Acts 2:22–23, Peter says, "Men of Israel, listen to these words: Jesus the Nazarene, a man attested to you by God with miracles and wonders and signs which God performed through Him in your midst, just as you yourselves know—this *Man*, delivered over by the predetermined plan and foreknowledge of God, you nailed to a cross by the hands of godless men and put *Him* to death" (emphasis added).

I was told in preaching class never to use the word *you* but instead *we*. But we should use the word *you*. I use *you* because I am preaching, and you are not. You would be the one I'm pointing to. Not only that, I do not want you comfortable. Even sinners gather great power when they mass together, don't they? That is why you have all these support groups supporting each other in their sin, each one affirming the other, so their conscience dies. I want the spotlight to be on you alone, seated there by yourself with no help, no comfort. "You," Peter said, "crucified Him. You're guilty." Of course, we must say such direct words in love. But even if we speak truth in love, the world will say we are loveless. After Peter told them what they had done, he said, "Now when they heard *this*, they were pierced to the heart, and said to Peter and the rest of the apostles, 'Brethren, what shall we do?' Peter *said* to them, 'Repent, and each of you be baptized in the name of Jesus Christ for the forgiveness of your sins; and you will receive the gift of the Holy Spirit'" (Acts 2:37–38). Here, he is teaching us something important: if you truly believe, you will publically identify with this Christ that almost everybody else hates.

Acts 3:13–14 reports something similar: "The God of Abraham, Isaac and Jacob, the God of our fathers, has glorified his servant Jesus, the one whom you delivered and disowned in the presence of Pilate, when he had decided to release Him. But you disowned the Holy and Righteous One and asked for a murderer to be granted to you." Then verse 19: "Therefore repent and return, so that your sins may be wiped away, in order that times of refreshing may come from the presence of the Lord." That is preaching! Why? Because it deals with the sin of men, repentance, and then such joy and fullness. It offers grace and salvation.

And then in verse 22, Peter reminds them what Moses said: "The Lord God will raise up for you a prophet like me from your brethren; to Him you shall give heed to everything He says to you. And it will be that every soul that does not heed that prophet shall be utterly destroyed from among the people." When was the last time you told people, "If you do not repent and you remain in this hardness of heart, you will be destroyed"? Our society is too psychologically fractured to hear this kind of language. But it's this kind of language that is effective.

In Acts 4:8–11, we read that Peter said, "Rulers and elders of the people, if we are on trial today for a benefit done to a sick man, as to how this man has been made well, let it be known to all of you and to all the people of Israel, that by the name of Jesus Christ the Nazarene, whom you crucified, whom God raised from the dead—by this name this man stands before you in good health. He is the stone which was rejected by you, the builders, but which became the chief corner stone." Peter basically said, "The reason we are on trial is Jesus." When people scream all sorts of reasons why we should be outcast or locked away, let it be that we've given them only one reason, and that is our sincere devotion to Jesus Christ, not a political meddler or an antagonist.

Next in Acts 5:28, the leaders said, "We gave you strict orders not to continue teaching in this name, and yet you have filled Jerusalem with your teaching and intend to bring this man's blood upon us." Notice two things here. First, the apostles were pointing out that there is guilt. They're saying like Nathan to David, "You're the man. You're responsible." They are bringing the blood of Jesus upon their hearers because they want to truly bring the blood of this Man upon them. They want them to be washed in the blood of this Man and realize that this death that so pricks the conscience of sinners and makes them angry is the very death that can save them. Second, they spread this name throughout all Jerusalem. Of course, not everyone has the same calling, but sometimes we take all these passages that have to do with the power and the importance of preaching, and it seems as though they only apply to a pulpit ministry. These men were not standing behind a pulpit expounding Scripture. They were in the streets expounding Scripture. This doesn't mean everyone has to be a street preacher, but we are not children of the Reformation if we believe "Build it, and they will come." Jesus said, "Go out into the highways and along the hedges" (Luke 14:23). If you love the Reformers and think they just sat in robes in beautiful old stone chapels and just wrote books and treatises, then you have the wrong idea about them. They were men who got out of those stone buildings and preached the gospel everywhere, and because of it, they suffered.

Those of us who preach the gospel in the pulpit need to get out more. We need to proclaim the gospel of Jesus Christ to the masses. Why is it that so many people who do not have very good theology are constantly in the streets, and those who have really good theology are constantly in the library and the pulpit? Let us do both! Let us learn to reach out! Again, I am not suggesting you have to be a street preacher, but I am saying there are opportunities when you walk out of the confines of the church building or study. There are lost people waiting for you.

The apostles not only preached a message that incriminated men; they preached the exclusivity of Christ. This is what really makes the world angry. Acts 4:12 says, "And there is salvation in no one else; for there is no other name under heaven that has been given among men by which we must be saved." If you want to avoid persecution, you don't have to attack Scripture or even orthodox Christology. You can even teach justification by faith and you don't say certain books of the Bible aren't canonical. If you want to avoid persecution in this world, all you have to do is change the definite article in Acts 4:12 to an indefinite article. You can go on a television show tomorrow and say, "Christ is wonderful. Christ is the Son of God. Christ is so special to me. Christ saved me. Christ is my way." But you cannot say He is *the* way. The world will let you say Christ is a Savior, but not *the* Savior. That's how it was in the Roman Empire during the second and third centuries. Rome was polytheist, and you could worship as many gods as you wanted. So the reason early Christians were persecuted as "atheists" is they preached the exclusivity of Christ.

In evangelicalism today, it seems that almost everyone holds to the fact that Jesus is the only mediator between God and man. But not everyone holds to that truth, and it seems to be becoming less prominent in American churches. People are afraid of saying Jesus is the only way. We have to fight for this truth in our churches. Churches in Europe are fighting for it, and it's a serious battle.

Consider also the statement often supposedly made by Francis of Assisi: "Preach the gospel always, use words when necessary." I understand what is trying to be communicated, but the statement is dangerous and wrong. There is no way to preach the gospel with your life. You can *affirm* the gospel with your life, but you cannot *preach* the gospel with your life. You can preach the gospel only by opening up your mouth and speaking the Word of God.

Another reason the apostles were persecuted is that they obeyed God rather than men. Paul wrote in 2 Timothy 3:12, "Indeed all who desire to live godly in Christ Jesus will be persecuted." If the world has shown us anything recently, it is that it does not tolerate anyone who disagrees with it, even in the smallest way. You don't have to walk around rebuking the world in order to be persecuted. All you have to do is live a godly life. If you live a godly life, say godly things, and make godly choices, the world will persecute you. Pastors are sometimes very cloistered. We get up in the morning and study our Bibles. We go to the church, we talk to other elders and people in the church, Christians come visit us, we go visit other Christians, and then we preach. We are protected. It is easy for us to forget that many Christians are not protected when they go to work. They bow their head in prayer before eating lunch, not even saying anything out loud, and their coworkers attack them. Or consider that most Christians are surrounded by such ungodliness, that it is a real battle to remain faithful. Never forget that a pastor's life is easier, not harder than the people they're pastoring.

The apostles were also persecuted because they were filled with the Holy Spirit. Consider Galatians 5:17: "For the flesh sets its desire against the Spirit, and the Spirit against the flesh; for these are in opposition to one another." In this context, Paul is talking about the internal struggle in the life of the Christian. But the principle hearkens all the way back to Genesis 3:15. There is this great battle going on in the cosmos between God and evil, between God and Satan. The world and the devil oppose the Spirit of God and whoever is filled with the Spirit of God.

Also, the devil and the world do not act nicely when their people become Christ followers. When I was young, I sat under the preaching of Leonard Raven-hill. He would say things like, "Are you making such a dent in the kingdom of Satan that your name is known in hell?" If you are a believer, then your name is known in heaven, and it is loved. But as a minister, is your name known in hell? Is it hated there? Are you having an impact? When I say "impact," I'm not asking whether your church is big. I don't care to know if you are a conference speaker. Rather, have you set yourself to know, obey, and preach the Word of God? When you know, obey, and preach God's Word, you get a target on your head, because the world and the devil don't want you to be fruitful and effective.

Not the Reason for Persecution

So what did not cause persecution against the apostles? They were not persecuted for deviant behavior. I counseled a man for a while, and one day he came into my office with his head hanging low. I asked, "What's wrong?" He said, "I'm being so persecuted at work for being a Christian." I responded, "I know you really well. You're not being persecuted for being a Christian. You're being persecuted because you're the laziest human being I've ever met." Let us not be persecuted for deviant behavior. Nor let us be persecuted for unchristian behavior. In Acts, when church leaders saw deviant, unchristian behavior in the church, they dealt with it.

They also were not persecuted for conjuring absurd ideas. One reason I love reading through the book of Acts is it's filled with the Old Testament, with the Scriptures the early church had. Now, the apostles were inspired, and they left us the New Testament. When they made their defense and proclamation of the gospel, they quoted Scripture. Everything they said was drawn out of Scripture, affirmed by Scripture, and conformed to Scripture. So they weren't persecuted for some deviant, silly interpretation.

Nor were they persecuted for religious fanaticism. The problems we see in the church in Corinth are non-existent in the book of Acts. Even when we get to Acts 2 and see the extraordinary outpouring of the Spirit and the disciples speaking in tongues, it is in accordance with the Scriptures. It is tongues, real languages with real phonetic value through which biblical truth could be communicated. This was miraculous and it was validated by Scripture. So there was no religious fanaticism like we see so often today.

Finally, they were not persecuted for their political stance. They were not attacking the government. People today are asking, "What are we going to do now to change the leadership?" But the Leadership hasn't changed. Read Psalms 2. Instead of putting our hope in political parties, we must put our hope in the resurrected glorified Christ. And in the early church, there was no political activism. Rather, there was preaching and prayer. Before the Sanhedrin, what did Peter do? He preached. Before Agrippa, what did Paul do? He preached. Before Festus, what did he do? He preached. And when Paul had an opportunity to appear before Caesar's tribunal, what did he do? He preached. In 1 Timothy 2:1–2, we read, "First of all, then, I urge that entreaties and prayers, petitions and thanksgivings, be made on behalf of all men, for kings and all who are in authority, so that we may lead a tranquil and quiet life in all godliness and dignity." I believe that when Paul wrote this, he had Jeremiah in the back of his mind. Jeremiah told the people that they were going to be exiled. But the false prophets said they wouldn't be exiled. And when the people were exiled, the false prophets told them not to build houses because they would soon return home. However, God, through Jeremiah, said something completely different: "Seek the welfare of the city where I have sent you into exile, and pray to the Lord on its behalf; for in its welfare you will have welfare" (Jer. 29:7). We're not going to change the world by activism. We are going to change the world by our preaching, by our character, and by the way we treat even our enemies.

Scripture says *you* are the salt of the earth, and that if the salt has lost its saltiness, then it is thrown out. This text basically means that a true disciple of Christ has certain characteristics. If you take those characteristics away, you no longer have a disciple. If you take those characteristics away and replace them even with other good things, you no longer have a disciple who can change the world. If you want to change the world, you need to be a disciple with the characteristics of a disciple. What are the characteristics of a disciple? The Beatitudes tells us: poor in spirit, merciful, broken, righteous, and so on.

Pray and preach the gospel. That's what we are called to do.

The Response to Persecution

Now, how did the apostles respond to persecution? They responded by rejoicing. They were living out the Beatitudes. "Blessed are you when people insult you and persecute you, and falsely say all kinds of evil against you because of Me" (Matt. 5:11). They were also living out James's admonition to rejoice in trials (James 1:2). Now how can we do that? We can rejoice in the midst of suffering—not because of the suffering, but because of four things.

First, when we suffer, it puts us in great company. We are in the same company with the prophets and with the Lord Jesus Himself. Second, it brings eternal reward. Some people think that talk about eternal reward suggests our motives aren't right or that it promotes works-righteousness. Jesus talked about eternal rewards, and we should have that concept in our mind. Rewards should not be *the* motivation, but it should be a motivation, because the Lord Jesus Christ has promised reward: "Blessed are you when people insult you and persecute you, and falsely say all kinds of evil against you because of Me. Rejoice and be glad, for your reward in heaven is great" (Matt. 5:11–12). Your reward is truly great. Persecution results not only in greater reward in heaven but also in greater holiness on earth.

Third, suffering conforms us to Christ. Sometimes when we're struggling and in the midst of a great battle—maybe a trial, maybe people attacking us, maybe a sickness—we cry out, "Lord, why are you allowing this to happen?" John Newton wrote a beautiful hymn in which he communicates how he prayed that God would make him holier and draw him nearer to Himself. He expected that in one night of prayer, God would just visit him. Instead, God opened up the gates of hell. He was tormented and he went through terrible trials. And in the hymn, Newton cries out, "God, why?" and God responds, "This is what you asked me for."[1]

---

[1] John Newton, "I Asked the Lord that I Might Grow" (1779), *Sovereign Grace Music*, https://sovereigngrace music.bandcamp.com/track/i-asked-the-lord-that-i-might-grow (I have modernized the wording).

In the midst of a trial, when you want to give up so the trial will end, ask yourself what you ultimately want. Do you want what God wants? Do you want an easy life? Or do you want to be conformed to Christ?

Fourth, persecution advances the church. History proves this. In some places in the Middle East, for example, the church—the persecuted church—is growing faster than any other place in the world. Persecution never hurts the church. Rather, the prosperity gospel hurts the church.

When Acts says that the apostles went away rejoicing, it uses the present tense participle. Their rejoicing wasn't just some flamboyant moment of religious zeal. They were rejoicing deeply. We see that in Acts 5:42: "and every day, in the temple and from house to house, they kept right on teaching and preaching Jesus as the Christ." They kept teaching and preaching, and that is what you and I have got to do. Don't get sidetracked by sin. Don't get sidetracked by gimmicks. And don't get sidetracked by the fact that maybe in your neighborhood or your city, somebody did something else, and their church just grew magnificently. If it wasn't according to the Word of God, ignore it. Put your head down and keep on preaching and praying.

But what enabled the apostles to meet persecution head-on with rejoicing and endurance? The very things they continued to do were not so different from the things that gave them such confidence and perseverance in the first place. First, God, Christ, heaven, and heaven's reward were greater in reality to these men than any shame or praise or reward that the world could give. When I read the Puritans and the Reformers, I find the same sort of perspective. If we want to face persecution head-on like these men, we must saturate our lives in the Word of God. In no other way will what is unseen become a greater reality to us than what is seen.

We must tarry with Christ in prayer. I have found that my flesh hates studying the Word of God, but it hates prayer even more. Even the great expositor Martin Lloyd-Jones said at the end of his life that he wished that he had given more time to prayer. In Romans 2:7, Paul writes, "To those who by perseverance in doing good seek for glory and honor and immortality, eternal life." This seems so Spartan, doesn't it? Yet that is what we are called to, to be men who are on guard, standing firm in the faith.

Yet how do we move from fear to confidence, from vacillation to perseverance? How did Peter undergo such a transformation? After all, he denied Christ before a servant girl, and then after the day of Pentecost, he defied an entire nation. What was the difference? The life and the power of the Holy Spirit. Only when the Spirit transforms us, gives us a hunger for God's Word, and leads us into unceasing prayer will the unseen become more real to us than that which is seen, and the heavenly reward greater than anything this world could ever offer. Only then will we persevere in the face of persecution.

Consider Hebrews 11, where we read that faith in the unseen enabled some to endure mocking, scourging, and imprisonment. They were stoned, they were cut in two, they were put to death with a sword, they went about in sheepskin and goatskin, being tested and afflicted with ill treatment. They were men of whom the world was not worthy, wandering in deserts and mountains and caves and holes in the ground. And all these have gained approval through their faith. Hebrews 11:40 says that God has promised something better for us. We need a new reality, to see what is ultimately real. We need to stop living in shadowland. Stop looking at this world, and look at God in Scripture. In doing so, you will be able to meet persecution head on like our forefathers did.

22

AROUND THE THRONE: THE HEAVENLY WITNESS OF THE REDEEMED TO THE WORK OF THE LAMB

REVELATION 4–5

Conrad Mbewe

The church on earth is a persecuted and suffering church. It may experience seasons of rest, but the hatred of sinners against the church's Head, the Lord Jesus Christ, soon issues into a new wave of persecution and suffering. God's people during such seasons need a word of encouragement from God Himself. Both the Old and the New Testaments are full of such encouragements. I want us to see how the apostle John encourages us in Revelation 4, where he provides a vision of the crucified, risen, and exalted Christ to encourage the persecuted people of God in his own day.

These were difficult times for the church. It was as though evil was about to triumph. We, too, are going through incredibly difficult times as the church. The form of difficulty may differ between the church in America and Africa, or Asia and Europe. Yet the sense that evil may be triumphing is felt by us all. We, too, need a fresh vision of the crucified, risen, and exalted Christ so we may be encouraged.

That is precisely what we long for each time we go to church. We plead words similar to that in Doug Plank's and Bob Kauflin's song, asking for God to show us Christ and to reveal His glory.[1]

The apostle John was probably the last surviving apostle at the time of writing this book. The friends and colleagues that he had labored with in the church probably either died from natural causes or had been martyred. History suggests that most of them were martyred. The book of Revelation was written in a time when the church was persecuted and most of its leaders were dead.

John took refuge on the island called Patmos. There the Spirit of God ministered to him by revealing the things of Jesus to him. "In the Spirit," he saw the risen Lord and received letters for seven churches in Asia (chaps. 2–3). They were letters showing that even though the church was being persecuted, Jesus still expected them to live in faithfulness, holiness, and love toward Him. After recording the last of these letters, John gives us the vision we are interested in for our present purposes.

John begins, "After this I looked, and behold, a door standing open in heaven! And the first voice, which I had heard speaking to me like a trumpet, said, 'Come up here, and I will show you what must take place after this.' At once I was in the Spirit, and behold, a throne stood in heaven, with one seated on the throne" (Rev. 4:1–2). This must have been quite a moving moment. He peeped into heaven itself. The only other person that we know of who had done this was the apostle Paul, who said he was forbidden to speak of what he saw there (2 Cor. 12:1–4). It must have been, for him, an overwhelming experience.

In Revelation 4, John not only saw what was happening in heaven but also was commanded to write what he saw. That's why we have this record. Granted, the book of Revelation is full of symbolism, and there is much in this chapter that we must process with that reality in mind. The symbolism enabled John to capture and convey something of the atmosphere that he witnessed when he was given a peep into heaven. John desperately needed to see this because he needed encouragement. The church also needed encouragement and would get it once John shared what he had been uniquely privileged to see. We, too, need to see something of what John saw. As we unpack and meditate upon this chapter, may it put steel into our beings!

---

[1] Doug Plank and Bob Kauflin, "Show Us Christ" (Sovereign Grace Worship [ASCAP]/Sovereign Grace Praise [BMI], 2011).

Heaven's Throne Room

What did John see that we, too, are invited to participate in? John saw that no matter what is happening here on earth, God is still on the throne. You cannot miss this. As you make your way through this chapter, the word *throne* leaps from the sacred pages over and again:

> And he who sat there had the appearance of jasper and carnelian, and around the ***throne*** was a rainbow that had the appearance of an emerald. Around the ***throne*** were twenty-four ***thrones***, and seated on the ***thrones*** were twenty-four elders, clothed in white garments, with golden crowns on their heads. From the ***throne*** came flashes of lightning, and rumblings and peals of thunder, and before the ***throne*** were burning seven torches of fire, which are the seven spirits of God, and before the ***throne*** there was as it were a sea of glass, like crystal.

> And around the ***throne***, on each side of the ***throne***, are four living creatures, full of eyes in front and behind: the first living creature like a lion, the second living creature like an ox, the third living creature with the face of a man, and the fourth living creature like an eagle in flight. And the four living creatures, each of them with six wings, are full of eyes all around and within, and day and night they never cease to say,

> > "Holy, holy, holy, is the Lord God Almighty, who was and is and is to come!"

> And whenever the living creatures give glory and honor and thanks to him who is seated on the ***throne***, who lives forever and ever, the twenty-four elders fall down before him who is seated on the ***throne*** and worship him who lives forever and ever. They cast their crowns before the ***throne***, saying,

> > "Worthy are you, our Lord and God,
> > to receive glory and honor and power,
> > for you created all things,
> > and by your will they existed and were created."
> > (vv. 3–11; emphasis added)

What a sight! John, who was acquainted with seeing only the dirt and garbage of life on earth, had been given a view of the indescribable glory of the throne room of heaven. The word *throne* is used twelve times in this chapter alone, and we find it five times in chapter 5. The sight of that throne and Him who was seated on it must have overwhelmed John. Indeed, as Thomas Binney wrote in his hymn in 1826,

> Eternal light! Eternal light!
> How pure the soul must be
> When, placed within Thy searching sight,
> It shrinks not, but with calm delight
> Can live and look on Thee
>
> The spirits that surround Thy throne
> May bear the burning bliss;
> But that is surely theirs alone,
> Since they have never, never known
> A fallen world like this
>
> O how shall I, whose native sphere
> Is dark, whose mind is dim
> Before the Ineffable appear,
> And on my naked spirit bear
> The uncreated beam?[2]

It was that "uncreated beam" that John saw. It was an indescribable glory emanating from the throne itself. Sadly, in today's political dispensation, we have lost something of the majesty that surrounds a throne. It is a picture that perhaps a previous generation would have appreciated when reigning kings were really kings and reigning queens were really queens.

In Africa, we still have something of that earthly power and glory because authority is still vested in an individual. Therefore, you sense it when you visit a village headman or a chief. Yet you sense it even more if you ever have the opportunity to visit a paramount chief. You may not have the glitter and the splendor, but you sense an atmosphere that is truly overwhelming. To reach the throne of the paramount chief, you have to get past rows of headmen that surround the throne

---

[2] Thomas Binney, "Eternal Light! Eternal Light!" (1826), Hymnary.org, https://hymnary.org/text/eternal_light_eternal_light.

and then past the rows of individual chiefs in their regalia. Then you go past the elders, whom we call *indunas*. Finally, deep within that dimly lit room, you find the paramount chief himself. You would have already been warned that you dare not look him in the face. You keep your eyes on the ground or, at the most, close to his feet. To look him in the eyes, once upon a time, was to invite death.

An African throne room is nothing compared to the infinite glory, splendor, and majesty that John saw. That was why the most he could do was provide comparisons. He said, "He who sat there had the appearance of jasper and carnelian, and around the throne was a rainbow that had the appearance of an emerald" (4:3). He spoke of twenty-four thrones around this preeminent throne. On those thrones sat twenty-four elders in dazzling white garments and with sparkling golden crowns on their heads. From that exalted throne came flashes of lightning and rumblings and peals of thunder.

Can you sense something of what John experienced? Most of us can't. Our presidents these days try to behave like guys you play around with. Not so with John. He beheld the throne room of the entire universe.

The message that John was getting out of all this is fairly clear. He was realizing perhaps more than ever before that whatever confusion was taking place on earth, someone was still ruling—God! We need to recapture something of this experience ourselves by reading passages like this. The God who is the eternal being, who knows neither beginning nor end, the ever-living One, Father, Son, the Holy Spirit, who existed before Genesis 1, was in a fellowship of mutual satisfaction with absolutely no need of anything outside Himself. He created everything that exists by His own will and for His own glory. He *rules* the universe.

In making the universe, He did not leave it in automatic motion. He controls all things. That is what a throne room is all about. It is the control center of an entire kingdom. That was what John was seeing here. He was seeing the One who not only knew all things but who created all things, including the very individuals that were wreaking havoc in and on the church. The God who was on the throne was unperturbed by all this because He ruled and controlled all things.

Notice that the twenty-four elders were sitting on thrones and wearing crowns as evidence that they were ruling at the next level. Notice that at the center of the throne room they bowed down and worshiped Him who sat on the throne. They also cast their crowns at His feet (4:10). That was meant to signify that the one being spoken of here is the paramount of all paramount chiefs, to use an African expression. He is the King of all kings, the Chief of all chiefs, and the President of all presidents.

This must have been a great encouragement to John as he realized that the one who is the monarch is not biting His nails, wondering what was going to happen to His chosen people. He is still in absolute sovereign control of all things and still being worshiped in heaven. We need to see that in view of the confusion all around us today. Our omnipotent God still reigns!

So when the church gathers to worship God, we engage in the most important activity of all creation. We join our voices to worship Him who is Lord of all.

Our Discouragements on Earth

The current impediments in the church on earth cause righteous souls to experience momentary anxiety. We see this happening to John at the beginning of chapter 5.

John was still "in the Spirit" when he wrote, "Then I saw in the right hand of him who was seated on the throne a scroll written within and on the back, sealed with seven seals. And I saw a mighty angel proclaiming with a loud voice, 'Who is worthy to open the scroll and break its seals?' And no one in heaven or on earth or under the earth was able to open the scroll or to look into it, and I began to weep loudly because no one was found worthy to open the scroll or to look into it'" (Rev. 5:1–4).

John wrote here that he was anxious for the welfare of the church. He shed tears. He broke down and wept loudly. It was a real wail because the One seated on the throne had this scroll in His hands that no one could open. What was this scroll? Commentators have wrestled to understand it and have come up with various suggestions, some of which are more praiseworthy than others. It is important for us to admit that the Bible itself does not tell us what the scroll was—whether here or in any other passage. At least two aspects about the scroll are clear.

First, it pertained to what was going to happen after this. It was about the future. This is evident from the sequel. In chapter 6, the Lamb began to open the seven seals on the scroll, and what we see there is an unfolding of history. As each seal is opened, ramifications take place on the earth: A rider goes forth to conquer the earth; people begin to slay one another; national economies tumble; people die from famine, pestilence, and wild beasts; martyrs cry out for vengeance; and the final day of judgment arrives.

Second, whoever holds the scrolls determined the point in time when these events would take place. We see this clearly in chapter 6. It was only when the Lamb opens a seal that the respective events happen. Here is an example: "When he opened the fourth seal, I heard the voice of the fourth living creature say, 'Come!' And I looked, and behold, a pale horse! And its rider's name was Death, and Hades followed him. And they were given authority over a fourth of the earth, to kill with sword and with famine and with pestilence and by wild beasts of the earth" (Rev. 6:7–8). The one holding the scroll determines what would happen and when, between now and the final judgment. John was very concerned about this because he was anxious for the future of the church. As one of the very last initial leaders of the church, he was longing to see a better day and age for the church in the years that lay ahead.

It is nearly two thousand years since the book of Revelation was written, and the church has spread across the world. It is the largest religion. That's why we fail to appreciate John's anxiety, which caused him to weep loudly when he feared no one was worthy to open the scrolls (5:4). Imagine your country is in a state of war. Or remember World War II. Imagine that Adolf Hitler's armies have invaded your land. Each morning, when you turn on your radio or television, one anxious question floods your mind: Who is winning this war? You read of various places that have been bombed, of ships that have been sunk, and of soldiers that have been killed. You are anxious about the future of your nation. Will you survive the war on the victor's side? That was the state of mind and heart the apostle John had when he wrote this book. He wrote earlier, "I, John, your brother and partner in the tribulation and the kingdom and the patient endurance that are in Jesus, was on the island called Patmos on account of the word of God and the testimony of Jesus" (1:9). It was a time of tribulation and patient endurance on account of the gospel.

The external circumstances were bad enough. Additionally, the internal state of many of the churches was a cause of concern, as is evinced in the letters to the seven churches (chaps. 2–3). The church in Ephesus had backslidden from its first love. In the church in Pergamum, where Antipas had been martyred, people were ascribing to the wrong teachings. In the church in Thyatira, a woman was leading many individuals to be sexually immoral. The church in Sardis had a reputation of being alive, but it was in fact dead. The church in Philadelphia had little power. The church in Laodicea was neither hot nor cold, and instead was "wretched, pitiable, poor, blind, and naked" (3:17). No wonder John was anxious about the future of the church.

In his first epistle, John wrote, "Children, it is the last hour, and as you have heard that antichrist is coming, so now many antichrists have come. Therefore we know that it is the last hour. They went out from us, but they were not of us; for if they had been of us, they would have continued with us. But they went out, that it might become plain that they all are not of us" (2:18–19). Individuals in the church were imbibing heresy and many of them were abandoning the church.

John was now in the Spirit in heaven itself. He knew that the scroll in the hand of Him who sat on the throne had something to do with the future. He heard the challenge that went out for someone to come forward and open the scroll by breaking its seals. As no one was coming forward, he wept loudly. His heart was broken.

Revelation 4 and 5 should not be taken as mere theory. Otherwise we miss an all-important issue. If you are a pastor or church leader, do the high levels of backsliding taking place in the pews and pulpits of the land not bother you? Do you not have sleepless nights sometimes as a result? Do you not ask God, "O Lord, where is all this going? Where are the voices faithfully sounding out the glorious message of the cross?" Do you not sometimes feel like Elijah before God, saying, "Oh, Lord, am I the only one left?" That was what John was going through. If we are truly godly in our souls and know something of spending time in the Word and in prayer, there ought to be times when our pillows are wet with tears because of this sad reality.

The Lamb's Victory in Heaven

John's longing was answered by the triumph of the crucified, risen, and exalted Christ. What John saw in the remainder of Revelation 5 spoke eloquently to him that the church's future was bright, despite its present setbacks. This is because the triumph of the church is tied up with Christ's triumph secured by His atoning work. This is captured for us as John's attention is drawn to the Lion of the tribe of Judah:

> And one of the elders said to me, "Weep no more; behold, the Lion of the tribe of Judah, the Root of David, has conquered, so that he can open the scroll and its seven seals." And between the throne and the four living creatures and among the elders I saw a Lamb standing, as though it had been slain, with seven horns and with seven eyes, which are the seven spirits of God sent out into all the earth. (5:5–6)

The language in this passage is incredibly deliberate. John was asked to look at the Lion of the tribe of Judah. When he looked, he saw a Lamb in a bad state—looking as if it had been slain. Also, notice the use of the number seven, which in this book stands for completeness. There are seven horns, seven eyes, and seven spirits. The Lamb is omnipotent and omniscient. He is omnipresent through His Spirit.

The Lamb did what no one else could do. "And he went and took the scroll from the right hand of him who was seated on the throne. And when he had taken the scroll, the four living creatures and the twenty-four elders fell down before the Lamb, each holding a harp, and golden bowls full of incense, which are the prayers of the saints" (5:7–8). The historic nature of this moment is hard to fully capture. The history of the universe hangs on it as much as it hangs on the moment when Jesus was crucified. This is the moment that all anxious souls waited to see. The response of the four living creatures and the twenty-four elders is the equivalent of a full stadium that erupts in joy and excitement when a much-awaited goal is finally scored and the trophy is lifted. Yet even that pales into utter insignificance when compared to what took place when Jesus went forward to receive the scroll from Him who sat on the throne. You might as well compare an anthill to Mount Everest.

In 2017, the Zambian national soccer team won the Africa Cup—to the amazement of the entire continent. I missed the game because I went to bed early. However, when the final whistle was blown and our team won, I could not sleep. In one moment, the whole nation burst forth in shouts and songs to the sound of loud drums. Car horns could be heard everywhere. It was incredible. When the team captain was handed the trophy, the noise was deafening. I thought the nation had gone mad. Again, that was nothing compared to the moment captured John in this passage.

One hymn-writer captures it so well:

> Look ye saints the sight is glorious
> See the Man of Sorrows now
> From the fight returned victorious
> Every knee to him shall bow
> Crown him, crown him!
> Crowns become the victor's brow.
>
> Hark, those bursts of acclamation
> Hark, those loud triumphant chords!
> Jesus takes the highest station;
> O what joy the sight affords!
> Crown him! Crown him!
> King of kings, and Lord of lords![3]

---

[3] Thomas Kelly, "Look, ye saints; the sight is glorious" (1809), Hymnary.org, https://hymnary.org/text/look_ye_saints_the_sight_is_glorious.

The four living creatures and the twenty-four elders bowed to the Lamb. They are the closest to the throne. And from that epicenter, the adulation goes outward like a mighty wave until it engulfs the whole universe.

First, you have the four living creatures and the elders. "And they sang a new song, saying, 'Worthy are you to take the scroll and to open its seals, for you were slain, and by your blood, you ransomed people for God for every tribe and language and people and nation, and you have made them a kingdom and priests to our God, and they shall reign on the earth'" (5:9–10). Then we have the next ring around the throne, comprised of millions of angels. John records, "Then I looked, and I heard around the throne and the living creatures and the elders the voice of many angels, numbering myriads of myriads and thousands of thousands, saying with a loud voice, 'Worthy is the Lamb who was slain, to receive power and wealth and wisdom and might and honor and glory and blessing'" (5:11–12). Finally, the wave reaches the outer ring, and John records, "And I heard every creature in heaven and on earth and under the earth and in the sea, and all that is in them, saying 'To him who sits on the throne and to the Lamb be blessing and honor and glory and might forever and ever!'" (5:13).

John ends by going back into the throne room and to the first circle of thrones around the throne of God to see their reaction to all this. He says, "And the four living creatures said, 'Amen!' and the elders fell down and worshiped" (5:14). What a sight! Jesus was being acknowledged as victor because He was slain (5:6, 9, 12). Calvary was not a mere product of the miscarriage of justice. It was not an afterthought in the mind of God. Jesus was the Lamb of God that was slain from before the foundation of the earth. In the eternal counsel, God the Father and God the Son had entered into a pact of redemption. In that pact, the Son was to undergo humiliation by taking on Himself the form of man and suffer until finally He would hang on a cross to bear the full penalty for our sin.

In undertaking this, the Son of God carried a heavy weight on His heart. Nothing shows this more than what Jesus went through in the garden of Gethsemane on the eve of His crucifixion. The shadow of Calvary fell upon His soul and He recognized that in a few moments He would bear upon Himself the guilt and the punishment we deserved. He knew that He was about to drink in hell on our behalf. He paused and prayed, "Father, if it be possible, let this cup pass from me; nevertheless, not as I will, but as you will" (Matt. 26:39). He knew He was about to suffer the consequences of our sins. The righteous God, whose throne must remain righteous and holy, had come up with this plan.

There was no other way that sinners would be allowed into His eternal presence. Jesus paid the price. He ransomed us. He purchased our souls with His own blood. When He said, "It is finished," it was done, and He died. The Father had promised an elect people for His Son. He had promised a throne from which He was going to rule to bring in His elect people. He was to be on the driving seat of history. This is what the apostle John was given an opportunity to witness. To John, this was a most glorious sight. He was realizing afresh that in the midst of all the confusion, the backsliding, and the persecution that was taking place, evil was not going to triumph. The Son of God was reigning over all. John had the opportunity to see this, and it was a real game-changer, as we say. From this point onward, it is simply one seal after another being broken by the Lamb. He is in charge.

Conclusion

Redemption is not primarily about us, and our frail attempts to better our lot. It is about God, and His plan and power, as these two chapters in Revelation eloquently show. Jesus was slain, and by His blood He ransomed a people for God. Therein lies the future of the church. It is in the finished work of Christ on Calvary. This is why we must preach Christ.

We must preach the preexistent, the humiliated, and the exalted Christ. Christians need to hear about and feast on Him so their souls may overflow with Him. Are we doing that? Too many pulpits are full of nothing but motivational speaking. Sermons consist of little more than stories of individuals that are larger than life, told to inspire those who are giving up. The stories are meant to encourage us to pursue the success that others have pursued and achieved. But what are those individuals compared to the King of kings and Lord of lords? Jesus Christ is the truly victorious one. And through His victory we, too, are victors.

We need to center our thoughts on Him who is the Alpha and the Omega, the beginning and the end, and the firstborn from among the dead. We need to read passages like this and feel as though we have been caught up in the third heaven, seeing what John saw—the Lamb who was slain, taking the scroll and taking charge of history. It would make a great difference in our lives as we face a world that hates us and the truth of God. Yes, it would make a great difference as we lie on our deathbeds awaiting entrance into the glory. We would walk through the valley of the shadow of death with a defiant peace. May God help us to see, as John saw, the triumph that lies ahead. We are on the winning team!

23

DO YOU LOVE ME?: THE ESSENTIAL RESPONSE TO THE HIGH KING OF HEAVEN

JOHN 21

John MacArthur

Two key verses at the end of John 20 spell out the apostle's purpose for writing the fourth gospel: "Many other signs Jesus also performed in the presence of the disciples, which are not written in this book; but these have been written so that you may believe that Jesus is the Christ, the Son of God; and that believing you may have life in His name" (John 20:30–31). Thus, John acknowledges that his gospel is an abridged account. He is giving his readers a condensed summary of evidence showing the deity and messianic credentials of Jesus Christ. This is truth meant to lead readers to believe so they might have eternal life. He could have said much more. Indeed, in the book's final verse, John will say, "There are also many other things which Jesus did, which if they were written in detail, I suppose that even the world itself would not contain the books that would be written" (21:25).

But that purpose statement at the end of chapter 20 is the climactic pinnacle of John's Gospel, the *Höhepunkt*, as the Germans would say. In fact, that verse would make a fine ending to the gospel of John. But John doesn't quit there. He adds chapter 21 as a kind of epilogue. Upon first reading, that whole final chapter seems completely anticlimactic. For one, it's a jarring change in tone. Chapter

20 focuses on the glorious revelation of the risen Christ and ends with that clear statement of John's purpose. Then without any warning whatsoever, chapter 21 takes us to Galilee, where the disciples are about to go fishing—fruitlessly. "That night they caught nothing" (v. 3). The shift to chapter 21 is like being dropped off a cliff and landing with a thud. It's a crashing descent.

In fact, the contrast is such a jolt that some have suggested John didn't even write that final chapter. To make it worse, we run smack into Peter again. *What a pain! Can't we just end with Christ? Do we have to go right back to Peter? Why not let the book of Acts show us Christ's Ascension? And then on the day of Pentecost, we can meet up with Peter again when he's at his boldest and most triumphant. Why this scene in John 21?*

Called by Christ

There's an answer to those questions. It's because, with all the glory that has come through to the end of chapter 20, eventually, that glory ends up "in earthen vessels" (2 Cor. 4:7)—literally, clay pots. John 21 is for us. This part of the story needed to be told.

Luke, of course, followed his gospel with the book of Acts. In Acts 1:1, he wrote, "The first account I composed, Theophilus, about all that Jesus *began* to do and teach." Christ's finished work launched the beginning of the gospel era. When our Lord ascended and the Spirit came, the work was handed over to clay pots—weak, ugly, breakable, marred, and replaceable.

These eleven disciples might have seemed too weak and inadequate for the task. But Christ did not leave them ill-equipped. He told them, "I will ask the Father, and He will give you another Helper, that He may be with you forever; that is the Spirit of truth, whom the world cannot receive, because it does not see Him or know Him, but you know Him because He abides with you and will be in you" (John 14:16–17). Furthermore, He told them, "You will receive power when the Holy Spirit has come upon you; and you shall be My witnesses" (Acts 1:8). So in the words of the apostle Paul, "[It is] not that we are adequate in ourselves to consider anything as coming from ourselves, but *our adequacy is from God*" (2 Cor. 3:5; emphasis added).

James and John could even say with Peter, "We were with Him on the holy mountain" (2 Peter 1:18). Peter was speaking, of course, about the Mount of Transfiguration, where those three disciples were eyewitnesses when the physical spectacle of Christ's divine glory was put on full display.

We, too, have seen God's glory revealed in Christ, though in a different sense. "For God, who said, 'Light shall shine out of darkness,' is the One who has shone in our hearts to give the Light of the knowledge of the glory of God in the face of Christ" (2 Cor. 4:6). Now it is our duty to guard what has been entrusted to us (1 Tim. 6:20; 2 Tim. 1:14), and to pass it on to the next generation (2 Tim. 2:2). We are to carry the glorious gospel forward, even in our frailty and weakness.

Peter faltered often enough and blundered badly enough that some might argue that he should have lost his ordination papers. If he had presented his testimony as an application to any of today's finest evangelical seminaries, he likely would have been rejected. The interview notes in the margin of his application form might read, "He occasionally speaks for the devil. He occasionally pulls Jesus aside and tells Him what to do. When it gets tough, he repeatedly denies that he ever knows the Lord and then swears." His was not a stellar resumé.

The first three verses of John 21 are instantly anticlimactic:

> After these things Jesus manifested Himself again to the disciples at the Sea of Tiberias, and He manifested Himself in this way. Simon Peter, and Thomas called Didymus, and Nathanael of Cana in Galilee, and the sons of Zebedee, and two others of His disciples were together. Simon Peter said to them, "I am going fishing." They said to him, "We will also come with you." They went out and got into the boat; and that night they caught nothing.

This group of disciples probably included all the ones who were in the fishing business before Jesus called them. That includes the three most prominent disciples from Jesus' closest inner circle—Peter and the sons of Zebedee (James and John)—and probably Andrew (Peter's brother) as well. Galilee was their home and fishing was their business before they were called as disciples.

When Peter announced that he was going fishing, what he had in mind was not a night of recreation. This was not about grabbing a rod and a hook on a sunny day and enjoying a relaxing pastime. Matthew 28:16 indicates that Jesus had told them to go to a specific mountain in Galilee. That was the designated place where they were to wait for Him. Furthermore, fishing is what Peter had forsaken in order to follow Christ (Luke 5:11). But in a predictable, impulsive, disappointing move, Peter—still feeling the sting of shame and defeat from his denial of Christ—decided to go back to his former career. He was a leader, so like ducklings, all the rest of the fishermen went after him.

"I am going fishing." There's a note of finality in that statement. Again, he was not looking for one night's diversion. He was talking about going back to his old way of earning a living. Verse 3 says, "They went out and got into the boat." Not *a* boat;

not a hired or borrowed boat. They were back in the area where they once lived and worked, and this was not a recreational boat. It was a commercial fishing vessel (most likely either Peter's or one of Zebedee's), big enough for this entire crew.

Besides, they took nets, and you don't use nets for recreational fishing. In verse 7, it says, Peter "was stripped for work," wearing the type of loincloth that was standard workwear for commercial fishermen. Verse 8 says they were fishing "about one hundred yards away" from the shore with a drag-net. That is a method commercial fishermen used to bring in the biggest haul possible. They were clearly going back to their old occupation.

Why did Peter do this? Why was he going back to fishing? Was that what he was resigned to do for the rest of his life? Hadn't he already seen the risen Christ?

Yes, of course. But now, after his notorious failure, perhaps for the first time ever, he had absolutely no confidence in himself. He was a proven failure. And it wasn't a one-time failure. His faith and faithfulness *often* seemed to waver. One minute he could be serving the Lord, and the next minute, speaking for the devil. He could say, "I will lay down my life for You" (John 13:37), and then when all he had to do was confess Christ, he would deny Him repeatedly to irrelevant people in the dark. He had overestimated his own wisdom and strength. The pompous way he had bragged about his willingness to die with Christ now hung over his head like a banner of shame. He had underestimated the power of temptation. He openly declared that he could handle any severe threat and never waver in his loyalty to Jesus. Such brash, boasting self-confidence had led him to blatant betrayal.

On the night he denied Christ, he really didn't seem much different from Judas. Now, full of self-doubt, he was weighed down by a crushing sense of overwhelming weakness. The history of his failure had demolished his own trust in himself. Feeling his inadequacy, he must have thought, *I can't do ministry for Christ anymore, but I can fish.* And since he was the leader of the group, when he announced he was going back to fishing, the other disciples followed him.

"But when the day was now breaking, Jesus stood on the beach; yet the disciples did not know that it was Jesus. So Jesus said to them, 'Children, you do not have any fish, do you?'" (John 21:4–5).

That is irritating, even if it's Jesus.

"They answered Him, 'No'" (v. 5).

It wasn't the first time this had happened. Luke 5 describes a similar incident at the beginning of Jesus' ministry. On that occasion—one of Peter's earliest encounters with Christ—when Peter realized who he was dealing with, he said, "Go away from me Lord, for I am a sinful man!" (Luke 5:8). Now here he was again, the same sinful man in the presence of the same Son of God, and when the Lord said, "You do not have any fish, do you?", He was in effect saying, "You can't fish any more. I control the fish. You can't catch fish. I called you to catch men."

This was no coincidence. It was a deliberate reminder to them about the call of Christ on their lives. "And He said to them, 'Cast the net on the right-hand side of the boat and you will find a catch.' So they cast, and then they were not able to haul it in because of the great number of fish" (John 21:6). They had fished all night and found no fish in the area. When the Lord said to them, "Try the right side of the boat," a fisherman's instinct would be to think, *What? Is he crazy? It's the same lake and the same location whether we fish from the right of the boat or the left.* But He spoke with such authority that they did what He said, even though at this point they didn't seem fully aware that it was Jesus.

They cast the net from the right side of the boat. He had said, "You will find a catch." So they cast, and the haul of fish was so great that all of them combined had trouble bringing it in. "Therefore that disciple whom Jesus loved [namely John] said to Peter, 'It is the Lord'" (v. 7).

That is the final miracle in the gospel of John. "So when Simon Peter heard that it was the Lord, he put his outer garment on (for he was stripped for work), and threw himself into the sea" (v. 7).

This is quintessential Peter—totally out of control and impulsive. He doesn't help the guys who are trying to haul in this massive amount of fish; he just dives in and swims to Jesus. "The other disciples came in the little boat, for they were not far from the land, but about one hundred yards away, dragging the net full of fish" (v. 8). There were so many fish they couldn't get the catch into the boat. They were pulling with all their might to get the fish to the shore.

"So when they got out on the land, they saw a charcoal fire already laid and fish placed on it, and bread" (v. 9). Breakfast was ready. Jesus, of course, had the power to make breakfast merely by saying the word *breakfast.*

But He said, "Bring some of the fish which you have now caught" (v. 10). He evidently wanted to put some of the freshly caught fish on the grill, adding to what He had already prepared.

At that point Peter, who had jumped from the boat and swam ashore, took charge—as was his habit. He "went up and drew the net to land, full of large fish, a hundred and fifty-three; and although there were so many, the net was not torn" (v. 11). The exact count was given, not round numbers. That is John's way of emphasizing that this is an eyewitness account. It also underscores the miraculous nature of the catch. These were not small fish, and such a large haul would normally be enough to strain the limits of the net.

The lesson of the miracle was clear: The Lord is in control of the fish, so Peter and crew could not go back to the fishing business. Christ had called them to fish for men.

Restored by Christ

The disciples, feeling defeated and ashamed, could not assume their standing with Jesus was unchanged since that terrible night when Judas betrayed Him, Peter denied Him, and the others "all left Him and fled" (Mark 14:50). So Jesus does something amazing. He undertakes to restore them—Peter in particular.

> Jesus said to them, "Come and have breakfast." None of the
> disciples ventured to question Him, "Who are You?" knowing
> that it was the Lord. Jesus came and took the bread and gave
> it to them, and the fish likewise. This is now the third time
> that Jesus was manifested to the disciples, after He was raised
> from the dead. (John 21:12–14)

I don't know what the conversation was like, but it must have been intense. There must have been some apologies—for the overconfidence that made them boast of their willingness to die with Him (Mark 14:31), for the cowardice that caused them to scatter, for their failure to wait for Him in Galilee as instructed, and for whatever weakness of character made them fail so frequently.

But Christ was there to restore them. They might have expected Him to give them final termination notices and move on in search of replacement disciples. They had been with Him for three years. They had witnessed His miracles. Twice before this they were eyewitnesses to the resurrection. He had given them clear instructions. But they still went back to fishing?

If it surprises you that the Lord would restore these reluctant, weak disciples, just remember that clay pots are all He has to work with. Like Isaiah, any of them could truthfully say, "I am a man of unclean lips, and I live among a people of unclean lips" (Isa. 6:5).

Here we see how Jesus disciples His disciples. This is how He restores a disobedient disciple. This is how He does biblical counseling. This is how He shepherds wayward sheep. This is how He leads them to sanctification and obedience. This is how He recovers the usefulness of someone who has failed.

We might expect Him to use a long and complex process requiring extended counseling sessions replete with homework and a regimen of scheduled follow-ups. The complexity of some of today's counseling and discipleship programs seems endless. I've read countless books describing puzzling paradigms of sanctification.

For years as a young man, I thought of sanctification in passive terms: "Surrender." "Yield everything to God." "Rest in faith." "Let go and let God." A gospel song that gained popularity in the late nineteenth century says it like this:

> "Doing" is a deadly thing—
> "Doing" ends in death.
> Cast your deadly doing down—
> Down at Jesus' feet;
> Stand in Him, in Him alone,
> Gloriously complete.[1]

I'd been exposed to a deeper-life doctrine that encouraged total passivity in the quest for sanctification. I was waiting for something to happen to me. I don't think I fully understood the means of sanctification even when I was called to be the pastor of Grace Community Church in 1969.

It was 2 Corinthians 3:18 that began to open my understanding of sanctification: "Beholding . . . the glory of the Lord, [we] are being transformed into the same image from glory to glory." That's not passive; it's aggressively active. I began to realize that my sanctification was dependent not on creating a vacuum for the Holy Spirit to fill, but on the relentless pursuit of the knowledge of the glory of Christ. I realized a good way to do that would be to dig into the Gospels. So for the next eight or nine years, I preached through Matthew. For many years after that, I taught our people from Mark, Luke, and John. I went through Hebrews and Revelation. Then I preached through a few of those books a second time. All I wanted to do was gaze at the glory of Christ. And when I had preached through the entire New Testament, I did a series on finding Christ in the Old Testament. I just couldn't let go of Christ.

This was by far the most important truth I ever learned about holiness and Christian growth: Our sanctification is directly related to our pursuit of the knowledge of Christ in all His glory. It's not passive. "Let the word of Christ richly dwell within you" (Col. 3:16).

When I got to the end of John's gospel and studied this passage, I was amazed at the simplicity of what our Lord said to recover and restore the most critical disciple of the bunch for the early church. It was not complex. In fact, it's shocking for its simplicity. Nevertheless, what Jesus said to Peter certainly did not foster passivity. He asked Peter one question three times: "Do you love me?"

All the preaching I had ever heard was focused on the need to believe in Christ, serve Him, witness for Him, and obey Him. I don't think I had ever been challenged

---

[1] James Proctor, "It Is Finished," Hymnary.org, https://hymnary.org/text/nothing_either_great_or_small_nothing_si.

to think very deeply about loving Him. But, after all, this is the first and Great Commandment: "You shall love the Lord your God with all your heart, and with all your soul, and with all your mind, and with all your strength" (Mark 12:30). Christ "is the radiance of [God's] glory and the exact representation of His nature" (Heb. 1:3). "In Him all the fullness of Deity dwells in bodily form" (Col. 2:9). That makes love for Christ essential if we are to fulfill the greatest of all commandments.

What does God want from me on behalf of Christ? He wants me to love Him with all my heart, soul, mind, and strength. That's the sum and substance of the Christian life. First Corinthians 16:22 says, "If anyone does not love the Lord, he is to be accursed." Love for Christ is the defining feature of saving faith. Paul describes Christians as "those who love our Lord Jesus Christ with incorruptible love" (Eph. 6:24). The driving force in all our sanctification and the motive for all our service is this simple: "Do you love Me?"

Look at the conversation:

> So when they had finished breakfast, Jesus said to Simon Peter, "Simon, son of John, do you love Me more than these?"
>
> He said to Him, "Yes, Lord; You know that I love You."
>
> He said to him, "Tend My lambs." He said to him again a second time, "Simon, son of John, do you love Me?"
>
> He said to Him, "Yes, Lord; You know that I love You."
>
> He said to him, "Shepherd My sheep."
>
> He said to him the third time, "Simon, son of John, do you love Me?"
>
> Peter was grieved because He said to him the third time, "Do you love Me?" And he said to Him, "Lord, You know all things; You know that I love You."
>
> Jesus said to him, "Tend My sheep. (John 21:15–17)

Jesus typically called Peter by his old name, Simon, when he was acting like his old self. The first question, "Do you love Me more than these?" is believed by some commentators to mean, "Do you love Me more than the other disciples love Me?"—because Peter had boasted that if all the others defected, he would remain faithful. But they *all* had abandoned Christ on the night of His arrest. *All* of them also went back to fishing, rather than wait where Jesus said. They were equally disobedient.

So the true meaning of the question seems to be, "Is your love for me deeper than your attachment to your fishing gear—these boats, nets, corks, weights, anchors, and trappings of your former life? Didn't you once forsake these things to follow me?" (Matt. 4:20). Have you left your first love? (cf. Rev. 2:4). He was subtly reminding Peter of the call to discipleship: "If anyone wishes to come after Me, he must deny himself, and take up his cross daily and follow Me" (Luke 9:23). The word for "love" in that question is the Greek verb *agapaō,* the highest, noblest love of the will.

Peter was well aware of one of Jesus' most famous sayings: "He who loves father or mother more than Me is not worthy of Me; and he who loves son or daughter more than Me is not worthy of Me. And he who does not take his cross and follow after Me is not worthy of Me. He who has found his life will lose it, and he who has lost his life for My sake will find it" (Matthew 10:37–39). As John Calvin once said, "No man . . . will steadily persevere in the discharge of [ministry], unless love for Christ shall reign in his heart."[2]

Peter must have been deeply sorrowful. He affirmed his love for Christ, but he used a different verb for "love": *phileo*—a word that speaks of warm affection and brotherly love. Peter's arrogance was broken; he was exposed; he was too ashamed to claim he had the highest, noblest love of the will. He would have been a fool to make that boast again. So he used a diminished verb—as if to say, "Lord, you know that I have much affection for you."

It was a sad admission, with a doleful appeal to Christ's omniscience. He *couldn't* say, "Lord, you've seen my life and behavior. Isn't it obvious that I love you?"

But Christ did not contradict Peter's claim. He simply replied, "Tend My lambs." Peter may have been braced for a rebuke or even expulsion from the group. Instead, Jesus' response was a great moment of blessing and relief, because it was a subtle indication that Peter was right about at least one thing—namely, that the Lord knew Peter truly loved Him. He still wanted Peter to serve Him.

I'm glad the Lord knows the things I desperately want Him to know. I take great comfort in that. I'm okay if He knows things about me that I really wouldn't want Him to know, because it means He also knows I do love Him, even when that's not obvious. I don't love Him as I should, and my love isn't everything it should be. But it's real.

That's what Peter was saying.

This is Peter's ordination. Despite Peter's impulsive disobedience, Jesus put him right back in the ministry: "Tend My lambs."

Don't neglect to notice that pronoun here. It's vital for anyone in ministry to remember that the people we shepherd are not *our* flock. They are Christ's, and He has put them in our care, even though our love for Him falls far short of what

---

[2] John Calvin, *Commentary on the Gospel of John,* 2 vols., trans. William Pringle (Edinburgh: Calvin Translation Society, 1847), 2:288.

it should be. Indeed, Peter is being restored to ministry despite the fact that his love for Christ isn't even obvious to anyone except the Lord in His omniscience. And Jesus simply tells him, "Tend My lambs"—*My little ones, young, tender, weak, vulnerable, prone to wander, prone to stray. I'm putting them in your hands.*

It brings to mind John 17, where our Lord, at the end of His earthly ministry, as He anticipates the cross and later His ascension, hands the care of His people over to His Father: "Holy Father, keep them in Your name.... While I was with them, I was keeping them in Your name which You have given Me; and I guarded them.... I do not ask You to take them out of the world, but to keep them from the evil one" (John 17:11–15). When He couldn't care for them personally, He put them in His Father's hands, where no one could ever snatch them away.

Here's the wonder of wonders: He also turned them over to Peter.

The second time Jesus asked the question ("Simon, son of John, do you love Me?"), Jesus again used the word *agapaō*.

Peter again replied, "Yes, Lord; You know that I [*phileo*] You" (John 21:16). "Shepherd my sheep."

Then Christ asked a third time, but this time He used the diminished term: "Simon, son of John, do you [*phileo*] Me?" *Do you even have strong affection for me?*

That stung. It probed into Peter's heart. Our Lord was doing a spiritual biopsy, cutting into Peter's soul. "Peter was grieved [*lupeō*] because He said to him the third time, 'Do you love Me?'" The word speaks of deep sorrow, sadness, heaviness of soul. It hurt not merely because Jesus asked a third time. After all, Peter had denied the Lord three times. It was fitting for him to have three opportunities to declare his love. Moreover, Pater had denied Christ while standing before a charcoal fire (John 18:18); Jesus had recreated even that detail (John 21:9). But what pierced Peter's heart most, I'm sure, is that the third time Jesus interrogated him, He questioned even the diminished love Peter hoped he could credibly profess.

Again, Peter calls on Jesus' omniscience: "Lord, You know all things; You know that I [*phileo*] You."

"Tend my sheep."

Again, this is reminiscent of Isaiah 6. Isaiah sees the glory of God and says, "Woe is me, for I am ruined! Because I am a man of unclean lips, And I live among a people of unclean lips" (v. 5). He's feeling not merely inadequate, but utterly doomed.

But then he hears the voice of the Lord, saying, "Whom shall I send, and who will go for Us?" (v. 8). Isaiah was the only earthly being there. There wasn't a plethora of options.

When the prophet answers, "Here am I. Send me," I don't imagine that he said it boldly. He was still conscious of his own filthy mouth. I think he volunteered timidly: Lord? *I'm here. You could send me.*

And the Lord said, "Go." *You're my man.* We are all just clay pots, with flaws and failures and the imperfection of our love for Him. But in His omniscience, He knows whether our love is real—despite its wavering inconsistency.

I now realize that in my younger years I didn't really understand that cultivating my love for Christ must take priority over doing things for Him. True service for Christ is not a work done for merit; it is simply the natural fruit of loving Him. Sanctifying love naturally fosters serving love.

For those who think, *I'm a weak person struggling, failing, with a lack of self-confidence, unclean lips, a sense of my own utter inadequacy and wretchedness,* Jesus has a question: Do you love Me?

Love for Christ has a cost. Jesus told Peter, "'Truly, truly, I say to you, when you were younger, you used to gird yourself and walk wherever you wished; but when you grow old, you will stretch out your hands and someone else will gird you, and bring you where you do not wish to go.' Now this He said, signifying by what kind of death he would glorify God. And when He had spoken this, He said to him, 'Follow Me!'" (John 21:18–19).

Twenty-five times in the gospel of John, we read the words "Truly, truly, I say to you." It signifies that something very important is about to be said. This is a verbal call to attention.

The phrase "you will stretch out your hands" is a euphemism for crucifixion. That's why John says it signifies the means by which Peter would die. The earliest church historians record that Peter was crucified. One second-century source says that at his own request he was put on the cross upside down, because he considered himself unworthy to die as Christ had died.

Jesus had told them repeatedly, "If anyone wishes to come after Me, he must deny himself, and take up his cross and follow Me" (Matt. 16:24). Peter was a living illustration of that. In effect, Jesus was saying, *Welcome back into ministry. You'll be a martyr. (Remember when I told you if the world hated Me, it will hate you, too?)*

Why would Jesus tell him that? Was He trying to deepen this heartbroken disciple's discouragement? Did He want Peter to live his life thinking any day could be the day of his crucifixion?

Actually, I think it was the best news Peter ever heard. What it told Peter was that the next time he faced death for Christ, he would not deny Him. Peter lived the rest of his life in the triumph of that promise. It steeled him for the future.

Up to this point, Peter had no history of faithfulness. In the face of danger, he was a disaster. After this, from the day of Pentecost until the day of his crucifixion, he was a new man—bold, dynamic, a little bit humble, a little less impetuous—

but steadfast in the faith and unwavering in his love for Christ to the very end.

"Do you love Me?" *Do you love Me enough to deny yourself?* Real love demands a sacrifice. "Greater love has no one than this, that one lay down his life for his friends" (John 15:13). Peter ultimately proved himself a true friend to Jesus.

Real love also demands obedience. Jesus said, "If you love Me, you will keep My commandments" (John 14:15). Here he tells Peter, "Follow me" (John 21:19). Notice: those are the three components of Matthew 16:24—deny yourself; take up your cross; follow Christ. That is what it means to be a disciple.

Peter learned the lesson. At the height of his apostolic career, Peter addressed his fellow under-shepherds:

> I exhort the elders among you, as your fellow elder and witness of the sufferings of Christ, and a partaker also of the glory that is to be revealed, *shepherd the flock of God among you,* exercising oversight not under compulsion, but voluntarily, according to the will of God; and not for sordid gain, but with eagerness; nor yet as lording it over those allotted to your charge, but proving to be examples to the flock. And when the Chief Shepherd appears, you will receive the unfading crown of glory. (1 Peter 5:1–4; emphasis added)

He was repeating the commission Jesus had three times given to him. Peter went from being an unstable disciple who needed to be discipled to becoming our inspired teacher, instructing us *how* to shepherd the flock of God.

And as Peter says elsewhere, "Though you have not seen Him, you love Him" (1 Peter 1:8).